THE APPRENTICE'S SORCERER

Studies in Critical Social Sciences Book Series

Haymarket Books is proud to be working with Brill Academic Publishers (http://www.brill.nl) to republish the Studies in Critical Social Sciences book series, edited by David Fasenfest, in paperback editions. Other titles in this series include:

Crisis, Politics and Critical Sociology
edited by Graham Cassano and Richard A. Dello Buono

Dialectic of Solidarity: Labor, Antisemitism, and the Frankfurt School
Mark P. Worrell

The Destiny of Modern Societies: The Calvinist Predestination of a New Society
Milan Zafirovski

Engaging Social Justice: Critical Studies of 21st Century Social Transformation
edited by David Fasenfest

The Future of Religion: Toward a Reconciled Society
edited by Michael R. Ott

Globalization and the Environment
edited by Andrew Jorgenson and Edward Kick

Hybrid Identities: Theoretical and Empirical Examinations
edited by Keri E. Iyall Smith and Patricia Leavy

Imperialism, Neoliberalism and Social Struggles in Latin America
edited by Richard A. Dello Buono and José Bell Lara

Liberal Modernity and Its Adversaries: Freedom, Liberalism
and Anti-Liberalism in the Twenty-First Century
Milan Zafirovski

Marx, Critical Theory, and Religion: A Critique of Rational Choice
edited by Warren S. Goldstein

Marx's Scientific Dialectics: A Methodological Treatise for a New Century
Paul Paolucci

Profitable Ideas: The Ideology of the Individual in Capitalist Development
Michael O'Flynn

Race and Ethnicity: Across Time, Space, and Discipline
Rodney D. Coates

Transforming Globalization: Challenges and Opportunities in the Post 9/11 Era
edited by Bruce Podobnik and Thomas Reifer

Western Europe, Eastern Europe and World Development 13th-18th Centuries
edited by Jean Batou and Henryk Szlajfer

THE APPRENTICE'S SORCERER

LIBERAL TRADITION AND FASCISM

BY ISHAY LANDA

Haymarket Books
Chicago, Illinois

First published in 2010 by Brill Academic Publishers, The Netherlands
© 2010 Koninklijke Brill NV, Leiden, The Netherlands

Published in paperback in 2012 by
Haymarket Books
P.O. Box 180165
Chicago, IL 60618
773-583-7884
www.haymarketbooks.org

ISBN: 978-1-60846-202-5

Trade distribution:
In the US, through Consortium Book Sales, www.cbsd.com
In the UK, Turnaround Publisher Services, www.turnaround-psl.com
In Australia, Palgrave Macmillan, www.palgravemacmillan.com.au
In all other countries, Publishers Group Worldwide, www.pgw.com

Cover design by Ragina Johnson.

This book was published with the generous support of Lannan Foundation and
the Wallace Global Fund.

Printed in the United States.

Library of Congress Cataloging-in-Publication Data is available.

Und nun komm, du alter Besen!	Come on now, old broom, get dressed,
Nimm die schlechten Lumpenhüllen	these old rags will do just fine!
Bist schon lange Knecht gewesen:	You're a slave in any case,
nun erfülle meinen Willen!	and today you will be mine!
Auf zwei Beinen stehe,	May you have two legs,
oben sei der Kopf,	and a head on top,
eile nun, und gehe	take the bucket, quick
mit dem Wassertopf!	hurry, do not stop!
Walle, walle,	Go, I say,
manche Strecke,	Go on your way,
dass zum Zwecke	do not tarry,
Wasser fliesse,	water carry,
und mit reichem, vollem Schwalle	let it flow abundantly,
zu dem Bade sich ergiesse....	and prepare a bath for me....
Stehe! Stehe!	Stop! Stand still!
Denn wir haben	Heed my will!
deiner Gaben	I've enough
Vollgemessen!	of the stuff!
Ach, ich merk' es! Wehe! Wehe!	I've forgotten—woe is me!
Hab' ich doch das Wortvergessen!	what the magic word may be.
Ach, das Wort, worauf am Ende	Oh, the word to change him back
er das wird, was er gewesen!	into what he was before!
Ach, er läuft und bringt behende!	Oh, he runs, and keeps on going!
Wärst du doch der alte Besen!	Wish you'd be a broom once more!
Immer neue Güsse	He keeps bringing water
bringt er schnell herein,	quickly as can be,
Ach, und hundert Flüsse	and a hundred rivers
stürzen auf mich ein!	he pours down on me!
...Nass und nässer	...Wet and wetter
wird's im Saal und auf den Stufen,	get the stairs, the rooms, the hall!
Welch entsetzliches Gewässer!	What a deluge! What a flood!
Herr und Meister, hör' mich rufen!	Lord and master, hear my call!
Ach, da kommt der Meister!	Ah, here comes the master!
Herr, die Not ist groß!	I have need of Thee!
Die ich rief, die Geister,	from the spirits that I called
wird' ich nun nicht los.	Sir, deliver me!
,In die Ecke	'Back now, broom,
Besen, Besen!	into the closet!
Seids gewesen,	Be thou as thou
denn als Geister	wert before!
ruft euch nur zu seinem Zwecke	Until I, the real master
erst hervor der alte Meister!'	call thee forth to serve once more!'

From Johann Wolfgang Goethe, *Der Zauberlehrling/ The Sorcerer's Apprentice.*[1]

---

[1] I am grateful to Brigitte S. Dubiel, for kindly permitting me to quote from her poetic translation.

CONTENTS

Epilogue
Sub-Man, Underman, *Untermensch*:

ACKNOWLEDGMENTS

I am grateful to the David-Herzog-Fund, of the Karl Franzens University of Graz, Austria, for giving me a research grant, and to the Minerva Fellowship (Munich, Germany) for the indispensable scholarship, named after Gerhard Martin Julius Schmidt, without which this book would not have been completed.

I would like to thank David Fasenfest, for his interest in this project and help in getting it published, and Lesley Kenny, for her incisive reading of the manuscript and for numerous helpful suggestions.

I am happy to acknowledge my substantial debt, personal as well as intellectual, to Bernhard H. F. Taureck. I have greatly benefited from his advice and friendship. Also, for their steadfast encouragement, varied and munificent assistance, and invigorating thoughts, I warmly thank Bertell and Paule Ollman.

My love and gratitude to Maria, my wife, for her enduring inspiration, and for—gently and resolutely—providing the granite-like foundation sustaining all my work; and to Judith, our daughter, for the infecting joy she takes in life and gives so liberally—as distinguished from *neo-liberally*.

Very special thanks to Luis, my father, for invaluable help and guidance. If I have sometimes been the willful apprentice, he has been the wise, but never severe, magician. To him, this book is also dedicated.

Ishay Landa
Vienna
Spring 2009

"WHAT DO WORDS MATTER?" PRELIMINARY REFLECTIONS ON FASCISM, SOCIALISM, LIBERALISM AND SEMANTICS

It is strange that, before addressing the question of what fascism actually was, we must first grapple with semantics, since some of the most important questions pertaining to the nature of fascism involve the way certain words were, and still are, used. This is an even greater necessity if we bear in mind that the mainstream of today's historiography insists that to understand fascism we must take fascists *at their word*. According to a notion that has increasingly gained in currency over the last 20 years, fascist ideology should no longer be dismissed as a mere hodgepodge of half-baked and obscure ideas, nor as a cynical, propagandistic smokescreen used to facilitate the implementation of actual, and quite different, political intentions. Initially resonant in its demand that we "take fascism seriously" and place fascist ideology at the heart of the discussion, Zeev Sternhell's approach has now become something of a hegemonic paradigm,[1] so much so that leading historians, acknowledging Sternhell's influence, have spoken of a "new consensus" in the research of fascism, that assigns decisive importance to ideology (Griffin 1998: 15). Thus, according to Eatwell (1996: 313), "fascism is best defined as an ideology."

This approach is promoted as a long due corrective to the scholarly tradition of *not taking* fascists at their word, of insisting upon disbelieving fascist avowals and searching for the motives and interests such rhetoric conceals. The main fault of this tradition, according to proponents of the "new consensus," has been the materialistic reduction of fascist ideas to their supposed class kernel. This method is now criticized as a problematic tendency to search for an external explanation of fascism, which might expose a *hidden* rationale behind fascist regimes. Such skepticism, we are told, has blocked the possibility of

---

[1] Sternhell's main writings on fascist ideology are *Neither Right nor Left* (1986) and *The Birth of Fascist Ideology* (1994). But even before Sternhell, Eugen Weber (1964: 3) has made similar claims: "my objectivity," he argued, "consists of taking Fascists and National Socialists at their word, whenever possible."

understanding fascism on its own terms: "by centering on 'social base' and 'objective functions,' most class theorists obviously ignore fascists' own beliefs. They view fascism 'from outside,' from a perspective that made little sense to fascists, who rebutted class theories as they did all 'materialism'" (Mann 2004: 21).[2] With this recognition of its proper role, ideology advances to the forefront, after years of relegation to being a mere handmaid of politics and, still more so, of economics. Unshackled from the rigid preconceptions of class analysis, historiography can now address the fascist epoch with much subtler tools. The picture of fascism yielded by such a new approach is commended as being richer, more complex and, obviously, much more in accord with historical reality, than the simplistic views inherited from the past.[3]

Within this theoretical framework, the words "socialism" and "liberalism" become crucial in grasping the fascist phenomenon, just as they lose their initial, though deceptive, clarity and become very tricky to manage and make sense of. Such ambiguity notwithstanding, there can be little doubt concerning the identity of the "losers" and the "winners" emerging under this new light. Whatever the merits of the new "idealistic" historiography, it is clear that under the terms it dictates, "liberalism" fares better than it did under the old, "materialistic" ones, whereas "socialism" fares incomparably worse (under the assumption, that is, that ideological proximity to fascism is not to be considered a good thing). We are dealing here with a theory that "takes fascists at their word." Did not fascists regularly proclaim themselves socialists,

---

[2] Another case in point would be Boaz Neumann's assertion that, if we are truly to understand Nazism, we must enter the Nazi mindset, adopt its particular point-of-view, and discard the old pattern of social critique which insists on seeing Nazism as an *epi*phenomenon, as a by-product of something else (Neumann 2002). Finally, I quote George Mosse who, in 1996, could affirm that the "study of fascism is slowly emerging from the period when this movement was almost solely discussed from the point of view of socialist theory, anti-fascism, or parliamentary government—measured by the standard of other ideologies—to a time when we can take the measure of fascism on its own terms, investigating its self-representation, and attempt to grasp it from the inside out" (Mosse 1996: 245).

[3] The claim to an abiding consensus made by this school of thought, however, is exaggerated (and not without a measure of intellectual bullying). Though such views are prevalent enough, there are a number of well-argued and innovative studies that take such theories to task on key issues. Amongst these can be counted the incisive critiques by Donny Gluckstein (1999)—re-emphasizing the importance of class to the understanding of National Socialism, Dave Renton (1999)—challenging the primacy of ideology and directing attention to the objective social function of fascist movements, and Mark Neocleous (1997)—an alternative view on the nature of fascist ideology, insisting on its counter-revolutionary dimension.

to the point of seeing fit to add this adjective to the title of the most significant fascist movement of all, the German one? Conversely, fascists were far less prone to associate themselves with liberalism, and certainly no fascist party ever included the adjective "liberal" in its title. As a consequence of this new stress on the primacy of ideology, the central claim made by these theorists is the demand that we cease to conceive of fascism as an essentially rightist political movement, and acknowledge: a) the critical importance of radical, even socialist ideas in shaping fascist ideology, and b) the sincere ambition on the part of fascists to provide a "third way" between capitalism and communism, a distinct mode of political action that declines to be subsumed under the binary categories of the radical left/the conservative right, and whose main purpose is to transcend class strife and bring about social harmony. Certain variants of this theory go even further; as a result of this theoretical re-appreciation of fascism, it has been relocated ever more to the left where, if not submerging outright into socialism, it becomes a kind of antagonistic-kindred spirit, in many ways an analogous political force. In the words of the German philosopher Peter Sloterdijk (2000: 21), Nazism was "a quasi socialism from the right." This definition shows how "socialism" loses its habitual fixity and begins to wander across our political map, since it is implied that it can be practiced not only by the left, but also by the right.

In pointing out an elective affinity between socialism and fascism, and for all its claim to break with the doctrines and preconceptions of the past and offer a fundamentally new interpretation, the "new consensus" in fact ties into existing traditions, offering a somewhat different variation on a familiar theme. There have always been, of course, currents in historiography and in political science, that have insisted on such affinities and expounded on them in detail. The general argument, though expressed in different hues and emphases, goes somewhat as follows: fascism emerges as a violent reaction to liberal-democratic 19th century politics, to individualistic society and to the economic foundation of both: capitalism. This liberal compound found staunch and fanatical enemies on both the left and the right poles of the political spectrum, seeking to put a violent end to liberalism and capitalism in order to pave the way for their eschatological projects: the classless society, in the leftist variety, and the harmonious corporatist state or *Volksgemeinschaft*, in the rightist one. While superficially deadly hostile to each other, a second examination reveals the ultimate affinity between both anti-liberal projects, their common denominator being precisely their joint enmity to what Karl Popper famously called "the open society." Thus, historian Eugen Weber stated in 1970 at an international conference in Moscow that, "fascism and communism were not antithetical but *frères ennemis*" (Boyd 1999: 1284).

A similar conception was also the gist of the interpretation of fascism as a manifestation of "totalitarianism," going back to the works of such philosophers and political scientists as Hannah Arendt (1960), Jacob Talmon (1952), Raymond Aron (1965), and Carl Friedrich and Zbigniew Brzezinski (1956), that purports to reveal, beneath the surface, many common features and a "dialectical relationship of fascism and communism" (Furet and Nolte 2004: 31). Both political movements, for example, aimed at a revolution, being contemptuous of the weakly politics of constant compromises involved in parliamentary rule, and strove for a unified, totalitarian denouement of the liberal, open dilemma. These revolutionary solutions were carried out with recourse to ruthless, terrorist means, discarding all rules of consensual politics, and ultimately relying on complete suppression of political dissent, finding its epitomic expression in the Nazi concentration camps and the Stalinist Gulags. Ernst Nolte's claim from the mid 1980s, that Auschwitz was a reaction to the Gulag was perhaps scandalous but scarcely new: as early as 1951, Ludwig von Mises made precisely such claims and, if anything, with far greater exclamation:

> When the Soviet policies of mass extermination of all dissenters and of ruthless violence removed the inhibitions against wholesale murder, which still troubled some of the Germans, nothing could any longer stop the advance of Nazism. The Nazis were quick to adopt the Soviet methods. They imported from Russia: the one-party system...the concentration camps;...the methods of propaganda;...and many other things besides. There were nowhere more docile disciples of Lenin, Trotsky, and Stalin than the Nazis were (Mises 1951: 580).

Mises also anticipated the later claim that fascists need to be taken at their word, particularly when they spoke of socialism: "The philosophy of the Nazis, the *German National Socialist Labour Party*, is the purest and most consistent manifestation of the anti-capitalistic and socialistic spirit of our age" (578). The language of the Austrian liberal is perhaps extreme and the formulation flagrant, but the basic idea seems fairly consensual: while proposing somewhat different solutions to social discord, both the left and the right sought to replace individualism with a form of collectivism. Hence, a number of historians, ever since Talmon, attest to the common root of both fascism and communism in the "totalitarian democratic" thought of Jean-Jacques Rousseau. This idea was reiterated, for example, in one of George Mosse's latest publications (1989: 20). "The French Revolution," the celebrated cultural historian maintained, "stood at the beginning of a democratization of politics which climaxed in twentieth-century fascism."

In recent years, even such differences between right- and left-wing brands of "totalitarianism" that were formerly acknowledged, if only to be, as it were, theoretically transcended, have been questioned. In fact, in the light of much of this literature, one begins to wonder whether there was ever such a thing as *right-wing* totalitarianism at all. An exemplary case is Sternhell's theories of fascism in Italy and France which was, as the title of a central book suggested, "*ni droite, ni gauche.*" The title might lead one to surmise that fascism, thus rendered, consisted of a distinct amalgam of radical and conservative elements, hence a phenomenon "neither right nor left." But Sternhell's argument is different. The book's title is a misnomer inasmuch as what is actually maintained is that fascist ideology was predominantly the product of socialistic thought, whereas traditional right-wing motifs, by comparison, played an infinitely smaller role: "it should be pointed out that in France the sources of the fascist movement, as well as its leaders, were to be found as much on the left as on the right of the political spectrum, and often more to the left than to the right. To be sure, this was also the case elsewhere in Europe" (Sternhell 1986: 14). In Sternhell's voluminous book, the emphasis was almost exclusively on the socialist origins of fascism:

> The socialist left was not the only group to provide members for fascist or quasi-fascist formations...However, it was the revision of Marxism that constituted the most significant ideological aspect of fascism. In many respects, the history of fascism can be described as a continuous attempt to revise Marxism and create a national form of socialism (19–20).

Fascism, according to such an influential reading, is thus not a blend of right and left but *primarily* a product of leftism, a ramification of socialism, "a socialism for the entire nation," as the title of one chapter of *Neither Right nor Left* has it, albeit eventually transmuted into a new and autonomous political stream (here Sternhell would of course disagree with Mises, for whom fascism was simply the extension par excellence of socialism in its classical, "pure" form).

To the same extent that socialism becomes implicated in fascism, liberalism, in most mainstream accounts, is construed as the ultimate antithesis of fascism. For between the "brotherly enemies," prospering and coming to power on the grounds of war and economic crisis, was caught, as if by the claws of a scorpion, the common enemy: liberalism and its attendant democracy, which for half a decade at least seemed to be everywhere on the defensive. Hence the familiar explanation of fascism as the "defeat of liberalism."[4] Fritz Stern, in a seminal study on the origins of Nazi ideology, characteristically argued that at its very heart were opposition to the bourgeoisie and to capitalism, combined with an attempt to forge a new socialism:

> The National Socialist ideology, in motive, form, and content, resembles the Germanic ideology. Their negative views were indistinguishable. For both, liberalism was the chief enemy, an alien and corrosive force... Both were embittered critics of the bourgeois way of life, of the spirit of capitalism, and Moeller anticipated the National Socialist belief in Germanic socialism (Stern 1961: 295).

This common discourse in contemporary writing usually points out with satisfaction the final triumph of liberalism, following the cataclysmic failures firstly of world fascism at the end of the Second World War, and little more than four decades later, the anticlimactic implosion of the leftist variant, in Eastern Europe. With the consoling simplicity of a fairy tale ending, the forces of light emerge all the more resplendent, after their successful enduring of darkness.

This quick survey of previous traditions helps us to appreciate how the attempt of the "new consensus" to question the rightist genealogy of fascism is not so much the break with the past it claims to be, as it is a vindication of the theories of numerous previous authors. Attacked and dismissed are in truth only those past interpretations that emphasized the class nature of fascism, its allegiance and subservience to a capitalist and bourgeois agenda. By contrast, when it comes to those previous interpretations that emphasized the left-wing roots of fascism, what one finds is a marked, if usually tacit, continuity.

In what follows, I wish to tell a different story. I will, for the most part, not dispute the *idealistic* separation of fascism and liberalism. Fascists usually spoke ill of liberalism and rejected this concept decisively, sometimes with vehemence. We shall see that there were significant exceptions to this stance. Yet I will not make these exceptions

---

[4] For a short and representative formulation of this idea, see Furet and Nolte (2004: 32–34).

the center of my analysis. Rather, I will dispute the consequences regularly drawn from this fact, two such consequences above all: a) that the habitual fascist rejection of liberalism implied an approximation, however "dialectical" to socialism and b) that it implied a rejection of capitalism and the bourgeois socioeconomic order. As far as *that* problem is concerned, of mapping fascism with relation to socialism and to capitalism, the word "liberalism" offers little help. For what does it mean that one is "anti-liberal"? One can, of course, embrace anti-liberalism from an anti-capitalist and anti-bourgeois position, whereby liberalism means roughly the same as the ideology and practice of capitalism. But, and this is often ignored, one can be anti-liberal from a markedly *pro*-capitalist and *pro*-bourgeois position, whereby liberalism means an ideology and practice that burdens capitalism and stands in its way. So words, in and of themselves, do not mean much, and taking the "fascists at their word" means even less unless we are willing to interrogate what words concretely denote, to ask what forces, institutions, and projects, whether political, social or economic, are attacked or promoted when certain words are uttered. But this approach necessitates a methodology that is not idealistic but historical, one that inquires into how concepts have been used concretely in history and to what end, rather than assuming their a-historical, platonic fixity.

Among those who struggled to invest socialism with a new meaning, one amenable to fascist and conservative purposes, was Oswald Spengler, notably in his post-First-World-War treatise *Prussianism and Socialism*, which found significant resonance among German right-wing circles. Spengler, idealistically and technically, was thus by his own avowal a socialist, like so many other fascists who adopted the term socialism and affixed it with some qualifying adjective, be it "Prussian," "German," "new," "national," "real" or any other. Yet I will argue that Spengler, like most pro-fascists, did not approach words and concepts with reverent awe. They signified for him not sacred ideals but profane tools. Below, I will inspect the exact nature of Spengler's "socialism," and in doing so I will, to some extent, have recourse to materialist de-construction, now so out of fashion. But at this introductory stage let us only register the fact that Spengler himself found his own use of the word "socialism" disconcerting and felt that explanations were in order. Thus, in his later book, *Jahre der Entscheidung*, published in 1933, reflecting on his prior use of the term "socialism," Spengler wrote:

> The colored man sees through the white man when he speaks of 'human-ity' and of eternal peace. He smells the incompetence and the lack of willingness to defend oneself. Here a great education is necessary, which I have called Prussian and which for all I care might be called 'socialis-tic'—what do words matter! [was kommt auf Worte an!] (Spengler 1980: 210; my translation).[5]

The methodological question arises: how can we take someone like Spengler "at his word," when he tells us that words, precisely, scarcely matter? But words, of course, *do* matter, particularly for an intellectual like Spengler, someone who produces nothing but words. And we shall see that Spengler chose the term socialism not quite as casually as he later implied. Nor was Spengler the only German on the right to express such semantic qualms. Adolf Hitler was similarly irritated by the habit of taking some words literally. Of the many words in the German lan-guage, he, too, made this point with reference to the exact same word as Spengler, as the following dialogue with Otto Strasser shows:

> 'If you wish to preserve the capitalist regime, Herr Hitler, you have no right to talk of Socialism. For our supporters are Socialists, and your programme demands the socialization of private enterprise.'
> 'That word "socialism" is the trouble,' said Hitler (Strasser 1940: 112).

As these examples demonstrate, we cannot simply take fascists at their word when they themselves found words, especially "socialism," evasive and irksome. The historian, particularly one who claims to adopt the fascists' own perspective, is not allowed to *un*-problematize words and concepts which the fascists themselves expressly regarded as problemati-cal. And socialism is not the only word which must be put in historical context. Fascist avowals concerning "liberalism" ought to be approached with similar caution. Indeed, fascists themselves were not unaware of the tensions, difficulties and ambiguities presented by the semantic field in that direction, too. For example, in September 1921, the highly-placed Italian fascist Massimo Rocca, formerly a revolutionary syndicalist, published a short essay entitled "A Neo-Liberalism?" in which he argued, among other things, that "the disastrous experience of politi-cal democracy, socialistic and leaning towards socialism [socialistoide], had amply rehabilitated the liberal conception," and that a movement that "would rebel against the collectivist mania…would end up being

---

[5] Throughout the book, unless otherwise indicated, all translations of non-English titles are my own.

a liberal neo-conservatism from the right" (Rocca 2004: 90). Sensing, however, that such argument would surprise some of his fellow fascists, Rocca then added: "The conclusions we have reached might astonish the young, in particular, *who are afraid of old words*, like some of the old are afraid of new ones. But there is nothing dishonorable in connecting the noble exuberance of so many young people to what had been the old Right, creator of the political and economical unity of Italy" (91; italics added). Yet it is not quite clear, in that formulation, what precisely the author suspected would be found "astonishing" about his conclusions: is it the suggestion that fascist politics should, in practice, renew the tradition of the *Destra storica*, or rather the fact that to this politics would be affixed that "old" and "frightening" *word*—"liberalism"? Did he, in other words, feel that the political content of his views would be alarming, or rather his chosen terminology, his readiness to call such politics by its proper name?

Be that as it may, it is clear that Rocca's rhetoric is not that of the run-of-the-mill fascist. As already mentioned, fascists typically refrained from affiliating themselves with liberalism. Yet fascist rhetoric notwithstanding, I will claim that fascism was not an outsider to the liberal, "open society," but in fact an *intimate insider* to that society, which was not particularly open, either. Far from being the antithesis of fascism, its absolute Other, the liberal order significantly contributed to fascism, informing many of its far reaching manifestations. I will attempt to make the case that most of the pernicious and extremist aspects of fascism, aspects usually seen as attacking liberalism— repudiation of democracy; dictatorship; assault on rationalism and scientific objectivity; propaganda; chauvinistic nationalism; imperialist and racial war—are historically unthinkable outside of the liberal framework. Fascism was an organic product of developments *largely* (that is to say: not *entirely*) from within liberal society and ideology. It was an extreme attempt at solving the crisis of liberalism, breaking out of its aporia, and saving the bourgeoisie from itself.

I am aware of the fact that this claim of a liberal-fascist affinity, of an ideological, social and historical nature, will startle some readers. It is understood that many liberals will find it objectionable, if not outright offensive. This indignation is to be expected, although, as I shall shortly explain, it would in many cases be unwarranted by my precise argument, which does not advance a sweeping criticism of liberalism. More problematic for my argument, seems to be the fact that remarkably few *non*-liberal critics, either from the right or from the left, have so far undertaken a sustained scrutiny of the liberal tradition in the context of studying fascism, or thought it worthwhile to investigate classical liberal texts in search of the roots of fascist ideology. It is partially as a result of such surprising omission that the pervasive narrative construing fascism and liberalism as antithetical has attained something of a hegemonic status. What—on the assumption that my theory is not completely off the mark—can possibly explain such lingering neglect? But let us address right- and left-wing critics separately.

If truth be told, certain conservative critics of liberalism did occasionally emphasize, and with evident relish, the liberal responsibility for fascism. Leo Strauss, for example, one of the most important conservative voices in post-Second-World-War USA, regarded the rise of Nazism as a direct outcome of the leveling down brought about by liberalism, its indiscriminate dismissal of traditional values, its boundless permissiveness, and, most insidious of all, its blind faith in popular education and in mass democracy. The political science advocating liberal democracy, he wrote, "by teaching the equality of all values, by denying that there are things which are intrinsically high and others which are intrinsically low as well as by denying that there is an essential difference between men and brutes,... unwittingly contributes to the victory of the gutter" (Strauss 1968: 222). By eliminating "the tutelage of the princes" and handing power over to the people, liberalism neglected to consider the following dilemma: "will the people come into full possession of its freedom before it has become enlightened, and if so, what will it do with its freedom and even with the imperfect enlightenment which it will already have received?" (21). For Strauss, working with a classical conception of mass irrationality, and with the still fresh lessons of fascism in mind (the text is from 1962), the answer is simple: at worst, the semi-enlightened people will abuse its freedoms to crown Hitlers. In England, during roughly the same time, the maverick conservative thinker Michael Oakeshott went even further: for him, German fascism did not simply exploit the opening first created by liberalism; it was itself, its anti-liberal rhetoric notwithstanding, an emanation of liberalism: "The so-called 'liberal' beliefs which [Nazism] rejected are precisely those which conflict with *the characteristic liberal project* of a science of politics, and are, indeed, *not liberal at all*, but of a far more ancient lineage in European politics" (Oakeshott 1993: 102; italics added). Liberalism was construed as a form of planned economy and administered society, a pernicious manifestation of modern "rationalism," onto which was readily grafted the Nazi mode of collectivism. Yet such critiques, far from helping the present study, obstruct it; for in reality they are coded liberalisms. Strauss, as a matter of fact, said so in almost as many words, indicating that his conservative position is in truth a vindication of genuine, ancient liberalism—stringent, secretive, elitist—as distinguished from the lax, egalitarian, and massified liberalism of modernity. "The conservatism of our age," he affirmed, "is identical with what originally was liberalism" (Strauss 1968: ix). And Oakeshott's socioeconomic postulates, conservative avowals aside, could scarcely have been more (neo)-liberal: small government, opposition to the Welfare State, maximum of individual initiative, and a recommendation to junk all "the claptrap about 'capitalism' that has for so long disfigured political discussion" (Oakeshott 1993: 113). It is obviously not with such theories that the liberal legacy can truly be challenged.

So, what about left-wing critics (which, counting the left-liberals out, essentially means those theorists focusing on class)? It may be tempting to put this oversight—namely, the usual failure to juxtapose fascist texts with liberal ones—down to their tendency to dismiss ideology as a mere part of "the superstructure," and rather go for the jugular, namely for the analysis of socioeconomic factors and processes. So, while quite a lot has been written about the relationship between fascism and *capitalism*, a mode of production, much less has been concerned with *liberalism*, a political ideology. Although there may be some truth in that explanation, it hardly provides a satisfactory answer. It is clearly incorrect to imagine that the traditional "materialistic" or "class" interpretation of fascism, even in its most classical form, was simply indifferent to fascist ideology or failed to engage with it seriously. Numerous class theorists in fact dedicated significant attention to such ideology, sometimes making it their major concern. The notion that the Marxist approach to fascism, for example, could be given short shrift by a reference to the Third-International view of fascism, without bothering to consider the precise position of a Gramsci, a Bordiga, a Lukács, a Zetkin, a Trotsky or a Benjamin, to name just a few such theorists, is convenient but obviously insufficient.[6]

---

[6] Such notion is certainly quite widespread. Writing in 1986 in critique of trends then dominant in Western-German historiography—and one might add that things have not drastically changed since then even though West Germany as such no longer exists—Geoff Eley (himself providing a highly sophisticated mode of "class analysis")

Be that as it may, there is in my view a far more important reason that liberalism has so far gotten off the hook largely unscathed. This has to do not with the putative blind spots of class analysis, but rather with the grey zones of liberalism itself, its deceptive boundaries and its inherent incongruities. Consider the ambiguity of the term "liberalism" itself: most critics of capitalism understand liberalism in such a way as to make them reluctant to engage with it critically. Take the American context: for many Marxists, liberalism, while clearly regarded as different from (as well as inferior to) their own position, is surely the next best thing? It is associated with a defense of democracy, welfarism, civil rights and liberties, opposition to military adventurism, and so forth. It seems, indeed *is*, preposterous to look for fascist affinities in that direction. And even in Europe, say England, such a notion would seem farfetched to say the least: were not "liberals" the closest political and social allies of socialists? Just think of the long-standing Lib-Lab alliance, against the forces of "reaction" and "privilege." Hence the thorny issue of liberalism is recurrently, and more often than not silently, bypassed. While such a procedure may appear somewhat justifiable on political grounds, it is disastrous for an historian because it obscures the crucial historical contradictions of liberalism. As well, it makes us forget that many modern day "liberals" are in fact not only different but in some respects *opposed* to "liberalism" as it was first conceived and practiced, and that, conversely, many modern day conservatives are in fact classical liberals, a fact in which they sometimes expressly take pride.

I therefore cannot emphasize enough the need to conceive of liberalism not as a timeless *given* but as an historical *process*. If we compare the ideas of a fascist at the heyday of his movement to the thought of a classical liberal, we will notice, of course, many important differences. And fascism did indeed subvert and eradicate many of the ideals and institutions central to classical liberalism: parliamentary rule, commitment to law and order, freedom of conscience and expression,

---

thus felt obliged to add: "It should be noted that this approach to the analysis of fascism is advanced as an explicit alternative to Marxist approaches, which for this purpose are reduced by these authors polemically and rather simplistically to a set of orthodox variations on themes bequeathed by the Comintern, in a way which ignores the contribution of (amongst others) Poulantzas, the Gramsci reception and Tim Mason" (Eley 1986: 258).

and so on and so forth. Yet liberalism, from the point of view guiding this study, is a complex of concepts and institutions developed at a specific historical period to answer concrete needs; and hence we should allow for the possibility of changes in liberalism if changing circumstances and altered needs are to be met and fulfilled. I contend that fascism became feasible because of the profound difficulties of liberalism in its classical form to cope with the challenge represented by that many-sided phenomenon to which we now refer as "mass society." Liberalism, like the sorcerer's apprentice in the famous poem/story, called into existence forces, immensely useful at first, but which it subsequently could not control, those unruly, and uncannily multiplying mops, the modern workers, which refused to accept their role as mere tools in the production process and were gaining lives and wills of their own. So the liberal apprentice *conjures a sorcerer*, too, in order to re-establish order, re-transform the animated brooms into plain wood. Fascism, in spite of words and gestures, came not really to do battle with liberalism, but primarily as an ally, albeit a bullying, patronizing one, offering much needed succor. And it offered its services at a price. The price was for liberalism to change, to modify its behavior, even to *change its name* (and indeed sometimes to call itself "socialism"). While liberalism, for its part, in some exemplary cases, thought the price worth paying, thought the transformation worth going through, not least because fascism signified a project of supposed restoring to health and "restructuring," to use a trendy term, with which liberalism itself had a lot to do in devising and developing. In order to salvage the vessel of capitalism, economic liberals were quite often ready and willing to throw overboard the excess baggage of liberal political institutions and ideals. This is what I refer to as the momentous "liberal split," whereby economic liberalism and political liberalism began drifting apart to the point of finding themselves on opposite sides of the socioeconomic divide. Let us again listen to Rocca (2004: 89):

> [I]f it is true that a part of Italian liberalism had degenerated while courting democracy, which in turn had courted socialism, it is not less true that for a long time nationalists and liberals of the right had found themselves in agreement even with regards to spiritual positions. If presently the vaster and healthier segment of fascism continues the ideal position of original nationalism, and if it does not degenerate, its programme and its practice will be a continuation... of the old programme of right-wing liberalism, at least in its economical part, whereas in politics it will be more patriotic and conservative.

My concern in this study is therefore almost exclusively with those liberals who have landed on the economic side of the split, not with their namesakes who have landed on the political side. If we would like to think of these two legacies with concrete names in mind, we might, for example, say that we are not interested here in the liberal disciples of a Charles James Fox, the Whig who warmly endorsed the French Revolution and became the people's tribune under George III, but with the legacy of his long-time friend and colleague, Edmund Burke, a Whig of a different sort, who was, of course, an implacable foe of French radicalism as well as a devout champion of the free market.[7] Fox and Burke split politically and personally over such differences. Burke sided with the King and with Pitt the Younger, and eventually gained recognition as a founding father of modern conservatism, and Fox became increasingly a fringe figure in the politics of Georgian England, although he had a strong influence on the subsequent development of British liberalism. This mention of Burke should again remind us that much of what we take to be "conservative" is in fact, in its original impulse, *liberal*. As born out by Strauss and Oakeshott (and I will throughout this study address a number of analogous cases): scratch the modern conservative and a liberal appears. It is by no means fortuitous, that the revival of classical liberal economics known as "neo-liberalism" was brought about by British and American nominally *conservative* political forces (in England, by the Conservative Party and in the US by the Republicans, most outspoken opponents of "liberalism"). This is a telling historical irony, which is one of the remarkable results of the liberal split. One of the main aims of this study, indeed, is to disperse this terminological confusion, by treating political categories historically, not idealistically. It is very difficult to call things by their name, if we don't know what their name in fact designates, and words, in the case of "liberalism," can mean at least two things. Again we see how words matter, and how, in addition, they can confuse, put us off the track or set us on the wrong one.

To always bear the liberal split in mind, to remember that there are two main liberal traditions informing the politics of the modern world, is to realize that the argument advanced in this book, far from

---

[7] Between Burke and Adam Smith there was mutual admiration, and a paradigmatic modern free marketer such as F. A. Hayek often harked back to Burke, whom he regarded an estimable specimen of the "old Whig."

representing a comprehensive "indictment" of liberalism, is in fact an intervention on behalf of its *political* ramification, against the direct or indirect libel of its critics: more or less direct in the case of the Strausses and Oakeshotts, and more or less indirect in the case of those numerous writers who, under pretense of defending liberalism from democratic and socialistic excess, in fact strike at the very heart of the liberal political tradition. When Mosse argued that fascism signified the apex of "a democratization of politics" ushered in by the French Revolution, did he not indirectly condemn the English Whig, Fox, an unwavering defender of that Revolution? And when Arendt (1960: 316), in her analysis of the preconditions of totalitarian rule, under-lined "the affinity between democracy and dictatorship, between mob rule and tyranny," did she not obliquely criticize that most central plank of the liberal *political* project, that of generalizing democracy? And when Mises, like countless other economic liberals, argued that Nazism was merely a logical extension of socialism on account of its putative attempt to direct economic life, did he not in a roundabout way chastise the whole of political liberalism, inasmuch as it rests on the assumption that democratic rule takes precedence over the free market? It is a telling fact that under such economic-liberal terms the bogey word "collectivism" by no means circumscribe only Bolsheviks or Maoists, but rather regularly expands to encompass *all* forms and sub-forms of social democracy, although conducted in strict adher-ence to liberal-political norms, from so-called Austro-Marxism,[8] to the policies of the Weimar Republic,[9] to Roosevelt's New Deal.[10]

So, upon closer inspection, it is not really a question of whether liberalism is to be rebuked or commended. Rather, when fine-tuning our position, the fundamental question we are confronted with is the following: was fascism the outcome of *political liberalism*, understood

---

[8] Which Mises, the Austrian, detested.

[9] In *The Road to Serfdom*, Hayek (2007: 81) affirmed that Hitler's allegedly limit-less hatred of liberalism "had little occasion to show itself in practice, merely because, by the time Hitler came to power, liberalism was to all intents and purposes dead in Germany." To find those blamable for this death, indeed the murderers of liberalism, the author didn't bother to round up the usual suspects, say, Prussianism, authoritari-anism, conservatism, Bismarckism. He rather summarily arrested, tried and convicted the guilty party, curtly proclaiming: "And it was socialism that had killed it."

[10] Ritually denigrated by free marketers as a sinister if natural collusion of socialist and fascist practices. For a recent example of such interpretation, see Schivelbusch (2006).

in its broadest sense, or of *economic liberalism*, also in its widest possible application? In other words, was fascism the product of a democratic excess entailed by political liberalism, or was it rather, in its mainspring, the result of the protracted struggle *against* democracy, the attempt to limit, control, even eliminate it? If indeed the latter was the case, then the question needs to be asked: was this anti-democratic struggle substantially informed by an economically liberal concern to protect and expand the capitalist system?

Methodologically, to the "new consensus" stress on the ideological, I will raise two main objections: first, while I fully recognize that ideology is important, I will argue that *ideological reduction* might be just as restrictive as any other forms of analytical reductionism. If "taking ideology seriously" means to compute fascist ideology as one component in a broader theoretical construction, interacting with social, political and economic factors, then such recommendation is well taken.[11] All too often, however, such a legitimate claim for consideration of ideology becomes a form of turning the fascist world-view into some *causa prima*, a self-propelling force operating in a historical vacuum. Ideological analysis thus runs the danger of becoming not a means to enrich our historical perspective but a way to elude vital questions concerning the socioeconomic and political functions of fascism. My own ideological analysis, tying into existing traditions, will by contrast strive to evade the pitfall of idealism, of what one scholar appositely called "the prison of ideas" (Renton 1999: 18).

Yet, in dealing with this historiographic approach, I do not intend merely to reproduce the old, "materialistic" arguments it claims to have superseded. Rather than doing that, I will pick up the gauntlet it throws down, that of "taking fascist ideology seriously." The focus of my research is, for the most part, on ideology, on what liberals and fascists said and wrote. I do not try to disprove the hegemonic reading by appealing primarily to "external," non-ideological evidence, such as statistics, or socioeconomic analysis. Such aspects inform the discussion whenever necessary, but the focus is on texts, and on the ideas and arguments found in them, and these are taken seriously. I hope to show that the "new consensus" is vulnerable precisely where it imagines itself the strongest, namely when it engages in ideology.

---

[11] Again, with the caveat that the tradition of Marxist historiography is not thereby polemically simplified.

By making fascist and liberal ideas the focal point of my own inquiry, I will query some of the premises of this ideological analysis. For example, these authors frequently argue against the claim that fascism was devised to crush mass egalitarian movements; this is dismissed as economic reductionism, a view of fascism from outside. According to representatives of the narrative, fascist ideologists were sincerely pursuing the transcendence of class struggle. Yet do we, in fact, need to step outside fascist ideology and introduce an external yardstick in order to confirm the cynicism and the elitism inherent in fascism? In describing fascist ideology as one of social reconciliation, do we not underestimate the elitist currents of such ideology, its belief, for instance, in the necessary chasm between the elite and the masses? Do not interpretations that emphasize "sincerity" overlook the importance of a properly "Machiavellian" and "Nietzschean" side to fascism, one of manipulation and suggestion, that many of its ideologists did not hesitate to brandish? From a sheer practical perspective, one of the great political advantages of fascism, noted by numerous observers, lay precisely in its disregard for ideological coherence and its emphasis on achieving results, a trait sometimes referred to as "pragmatism," which found expression in uninhibited use of demagoguery. Hence a blatant paradox in the argument that fascists need to be "taken at their word," as if there was one "Word" which could be "taken," rather than many different words, and as if these words were in turn not frequently used in willful deception. Those who wish to comprehend fascist ideology would do well to reckon with the fact that lies, myth-mongering and demagoguery were built into it. This means that anybody who treats fascists as sincere immediately fails, whatever else he or she might be doing, to "take them *seriously.*"

Fascists, especially Nazis, said about themselves that they were "socialists" of sorts, a superior type; perhaps in some cases they even *fancied* themselves as such, though this subjective aspect is more difficult to determine. Yet fascists also said different things, uttered quite different words, which confronts the historian with difficult choices as to *when* precisely to take them at their word and when *not* to. When can we believe fascists and when are they merely courting votes, seeking to expand their "mass basis"? Historians of the "new consensus" (understood in its broadest sense) have not been very consistent when going about this task. Whenever the fascists say things that do not sit well with the theory, the tendency it to silently revert to the old and bad habits of "suspicion." Sternhell, for example, writes that "fascist activism, which adorns itself with elitism, supports a strong political rule, free from the chains of democracy" (1988a: 11). Elitism, thus, is taken as a superficial aspect of fascism, a mere "adornment." But the fascists themselves took their elitism quite seriously, at least they never implied that it was a mere façade. It might be argued that the very opposite is true: that fascist activism adorned itself *with populism*, elitism being its essential truth, tactically kept somewhat concealed (thus, Hitler is radically contemptuous of the masses in his written texts and in his private conversations, not so in his public speeches, where he effuses love of the *Volk* and of ordinary Germans). But since the historian is intent on showing that fascism was not the rightist politics it is thought to be, populism is deemed sincere and substantial, elitism superficial and subsidiary. Michael Mann (2004: 1), for his part, argued against a view of fascists "from outside" and began his discussion stressing the need for "taking fascists seriously." This he indeed does, as long as fascists express their heartfelt wish to find a third way between capitalism and socialism and declare their desire to transcend class, etc.[12] Yet presently, when confronted with their visceral aversion to communism—not to be entirely overlooked, certainly—suspicion creeps right back in, and the fascists are *no longer* taken at their word:

> Did Hitler believe more in the 'Bolshevik threat' or in its electoral utility? Mussolini only pretended to believe in a 'communist threat'...Metaxas used the 'communist threat' as a pretext for his coup in Greece. But the Greek communist party was small and split, and the British embassy reported home that Metaxas's claim was a smokescreen for a coup that in reality was the result of faction fighting on the right (Mann 2004: 61).

The old school-of-suspicion is back with a vengeance! Notice the language: "in reality" and "smokescreen." The "Bolshevik threat," likewise, is enclosed in quotation marks; the fascists, Mann is confident, did not mean this particular word, it was a mere "pretext." If the British embassy so reported, then its view of the fascists' hidden motives surely ought to be trusted. Yet is this report in any way less a view of fascism "from outside" than that, say, of the Soviet embassy, with its discredited, Comintern notions? The real point is not whether or not

---

[12] Which accords with Mann's general, "Sternhellian" interpretation. Mann cites (2) Sternhell's emphasis on the coherence and solidity of fascist ideology approvingly, thus incorporating it into the methodological foundation of his own analysis.

to take fascists at their word, but *when* to do so, and *when not to*. Yet these are largely *ideological* choices, a fact which lends an altogether new and unintended meaning to the "primacy-of-ideology" claim of the "new consensus."

I choose in what follows to call attention to that which fascism owes to economic liberalism, as an ideological expression of capitalism. I do so in the belief that such a reminder is greatly needed today, when anti-fascism is widely used as a pretext to battle democracy, particularly social democracy, and to cement capitalism, in a way which would probably have pleased a Mises. And I do so in the conviction that the debt of fascism to liberalism is indeed a considerable one. At the same time, I wish to clarify that my historical reconstruction does not simply equate liberalism—not even economic one—with fascism, nor do I assume that fascism derived its worldview strictly from liberal sources, however historically transmuted. In its attempt to form a broad social coalition, often described as the fascist "mass-basis," fascism was willing to employ the most eclectically incongruent ideological arguments, as long as they appeared useful in appealing to a given constituency. Among these sources were included ideological motifs from the 19th century stock of anti-liberalism, and an appeal to sentiments, to cultural traditions, beliefs, desires, phobias and prejudices, as well as interests, which to a greater or lesser extent were antagonistic to the capitalist socioeconomic order (even if such motifs and sentiments, as often observed, were usually more "petty-bourgeois" than working-class). Nor were these elements, once incorporated into the—rather loose—body of fascist ideology, bereft of practical implications. Yet economic liberalism, I claim, was much closer to the core of the fascist experiment than anti-economic-liberalism, and the anti-liberal aspects were ultimately functional in drawing support and in weakening resistance to an agenda which was aggressively capitalistic. Over the years, liberal and conservative interpreters have strayed far and wide in their search for "the roots of fascism," examining at one point or another the ideas of a Rousseau, a Herder, a Fichte, a Hegel or even a Luther, among others; they should instead have looked under their very noses, and examined the liberal tradition in its *longue durée*, from its very beginnings in the political thought of John Locke, to discover the immanent contradictions and the deep-seated determinants which, if not necessitating fascism, at least rendered it possible. But this is an argument which I must now begin to unfold.

CHAPTER ONE

THE LIBERAL SPLIT: DIVORCING THE ECONOMIC FROM THE POLITICAL

Liberalism and Democracy in the Longue Durée

An indispensable historical precondition for fascism[1] was the inherent tension between the political dimension of the liberal order and its economic one. Liberalism was the socioeconomic doctrine with which the ascending European bourgeoisie of the late 18th and early 19th century challenged the nobility.[2] It began optimistically, a "progressive" movement which demanded political "freedoms," such as constitutional and representative government which, in turn, were seen as undergirding a market society emancipated from antiquated burdens of feudal and absolutist protectionism, mercantilism, etc. But in the course of the 19th century it became clear that the demand for popular representation is a political weapon that cuts both ways: wielded by the bourgeoisie in the name of the people against the aristocracy, it was effective in bringing about and consolidating bourgeois society. But once "the people" wished to dispense with their bourgeois proxies and speak and act for themselves, demanding, as a necessary first step, that the suffrage be universally extended, popular representation threatened to encroach upon bourgeois prerogatives and interests. After wresting the economy from the nobility, the bourgeoisie now had to defend it from "the masses." Pessimism and disillusion increasingly set in among bourgeois ranks, initially so buoyant. The future of "civilization," now seemed uncertain and beset with dangers.

---

[1] "Precondition" in the sense of those long-term, structural determinants "which create a potentially explosive situation," which Lawrence Stone (2002: 8) conceptualized in his *The Causes of the English Revolution*, as distinguished from the medium-term "precipitants" and the short-term "triggers." Stone, in turn, was elaborating on the familiar tripartite scheme of the *Annales* school of social history, distinguishing correspondingly between "structure," "conjuncture" and "events." In the case of fascism, the latter two categories would include such more immediate developments as the First World War and the world economic crisis, as well as still more specific, local developments and the contingent contribution of concrete personalities.

[2] In England, as is well known, the process took place significantly earlier, throughout the turbulent 17th century, culminating in "The Glorious Revolution."

The more "the masses" rose, the more bourgeois ideologues brooded over "decline" and "degeneration": cultural, economic, political, and racial. Capitalism, fundamentally, was seen to be at odds with democracy; the *economic liberal sphere* was seen to be at variance with the expansionary dynamics of *political liberalism*.

Putting Property under Locke *and Key*

Historically, liberals were never particularly keen about democracy. From the start, the notion of representative government, to which most liberals were willing to subscribe, meant a limited suffrage, which would yield results favorable to the propertied classes.[3] For a constitutive liberal such as John Locke, democracy was not yet a problem, since the bulk of the working people were not yet politically articulate or, rather, no *longer* so, after the diverse radical movements of the English revolution had been subdued;[4] he thus took it for granted that "the rule of the majority," which he espoused, would entail little more than the rule of the propertied. A postulate which an eminent historian of early modern England summarized as follows:

> ...Locke argued...that the executive may forfeit its rights if it endangers the stability of property, maintenance of which is the reason for the existence of the state.... Locke talked ambiguously of government deriving from and being responsible to 'the people,' but it was perfectly clear that by 'the people' he meant the propertied class. Their control of society had been established against monarchical absolutism [and] against the lower orders by the defeat of the radicals during the interregnum...(Hill 2006: 295–6).

Only the members of the propertied class were thus truly *of* civil society—entitled to and capable of politically managing it—rather than simply being *in* it: subjected to its authority, laws and discipline but deprived of active political rights.[5] Wage laborers, the huge majority

---

[3] As one scholar affirmed, modern liberals "were from the outset extremely suspicious of all forms of popular government (throughout the nineteenth century, and later, they upheld and defended limited suffrage)" (Bobbio 2005: 31). Geoff Eley, similarly, questioned the often drawn correlation between liberalism and democracy, "given the consistent attachment of nineteenth-century liberals to restricted and exclusivist systems of political representation" (Blackbourn and Eley 2005: 80).

[4] For two excellent historical studies sympathetic to these movements' cause see the classical account by Hill (1972) and the more recent one by Holstun (2000).

[5] My discussion of Locke's understanding of property follows in particular C. B. Macpherson's seminal account (1964). A good survey of the different criticisms

of the English people who lived from hand to mouth, "alienating" in market transactions their only property, their ability to work, were considered not "rational" enough to exercise political rights, not having at their disposal the leisure time necessary to consider matters exceeding their daily struggle to subsist (and this quite apart from the idle poor, who were considered morally depraved and hence excluded as a matter of course from political management). It must be borne in mind that the whole purpose of the liberal civil society from a Lockean point of view was to shore up nascent capitalist property and production. The political aspect of liberalism, namely parliamentary and constitutional rule, far from being an autonomous sphere alongside the economic one, was entirely a function of capitalism, conceived at all times as fully subservient to it. Civil society was essentially a mechanism for guaranteeing that capitalism would function smoothly, and for imposing on individual capitalists an indispensable modicum of class cohesion and concerted action—for example agreeing on taxation so as to allow the state to finance its role as defender of property—without which the system would have been untenable.[6] But taxation emanating from the *outside* of capitalism, independent of the initiatives of property owners and contrary to their wishes, was anathematized. "Locke's primary and overriding interest," as underlined by Peter Laslett (1988: 107), "was in taxation, arbitrary taxation and its iniquities." Under such terms, there can be no question whatsoever of the political domain making independent demands on the economy, of a "social" or "moral" nature. Any such demands, unless agreed upon by "the majority" of the propertied and hence as serving their class interest, would simply mean an act of spoliation. Property and capitalist production were not, Locke insisted, a political arrangement, which could thus be potentially subject to political modification. Rather, they were inscribed in natural law, and hence *preceded* the political.[7] The very purpose of political civil society, a point which could not be emphasized enough, was to outlaw and exclude any such possibility, turn it into a logical absurdity and a moral outrage:

Macpherson's theory was subjected to, as well as a generally persuasive defense of his position, is provided by Townshend (2000).

[6] Cf. Macpherson (1964: 253).

[7] Cf. Macpherson (1964: 218). Or consider Leo Strauss' (1953: 235; emphases added) understanding of Locke's position: "Yet, while civil society is the creator of civil property, it is *not* its master: civil society must respect civil property; civil society has...*no other function* but to serve its own creation."

> The *Supream Power cannot take* from any Man any part of his *Property* without his own consent. For the preservation of Property being the end of Government, and that for which Men enter into Society, it necessarily supposes and requires, that the People should *have Property*, without which they must be suppos'd to lose that by entring into Society, which was the end for which they entered into it, too gross an absurdity for any Man to own.... Hence it is a mistake to think, that the Supream or *Legislative Power* of any Commonwealth, can do what it will, and dispose of the Estates of the Subject *arbitrarily*, or take any part of them at pleasure (Locke 1988: 360–1; emphases in the original).

By natural right, politics thus dutifully ends where property begins and, if the government mistakes its place, the propertied are entitled to avail themselves of force against the unlawful law. As Domenico Losurdo (1988: 249) observes, with regards to Locke's position: "Even if mediated by the legislative power, the intrusion of those without property in the sphere of property is always an act of caprice and of plunder, an act of violence, and therefore an act which may be legitimately countered by the violence of the victim." Parliamentarism and the rule of law were thus from the very beginning not the liberal end itself, to be defined, say, in terms of guaranteeing political pluralism; rather, they were mere means to an end, that of protecting capitalism. And means are by their very nature not absolute; they might change along with changing circumstances. That is why Locke himself, far from absolutizing parliament, at different times could and did envisage alternative political models. As C. B. Macpherson observed (1964: 261), Locke "was consistent throughout in wanting a civil authority which could secure the basic institutions of a class society. In 1660 this required the recall of the Stuarts and the doctrine of the magistrate's absolute and arbitrary power in things indifferent; in 1689 it required the dismissal of the Stuarts and the doctrine of the *Second Treatise*." Liberal *doctrines* are thus amenable to change, as long as *class society* persists.[8] Rather than being limited by a political framework, liberal capitalism was in fact equipped with a built-in option to bail out of constitutionalism and revert to the rule of force, upon seeing its economic interests imperiled.

---

[8] Let us also not forget that Locke's formidable antecedent, Thomas Hobbes, developed a theory of absolute sovereignty upon postulates of ultraist individualism and the *Bellum omnium contra omnes*; which refutes the notion that capitalism by nature implies a "pluralistic," to say nothing of a democratic, political model.

We are accustomed to think of the liberal tradition—to the extent that we perceive it through its own, largely hegemonic, historiographic and theoretical prism—in terms of a radical *opening out* of political horizons, an extension of liberties, an underpinning of "toleration" and pluralism, a curtailment of diverse oppressions and absolutisms; but this is to lose sight of the irreducible moment of political *enclosing* that liberalism contained. For the founders of the liberal order were interested not only in outlining all that which politics should do, but also, and at least as keenly, in rigorously defining what it *shouldn't.* And if this prohibitive demarcation was initially meant to deter the monarch from trespassing on property boundaries, there is no reason to think that the interference of a democratic sovereign would have been any less resisted. Instead, there is every reason to take Locke literally, when he insists on putting property beyond the reach of "the Supream or legislative Power of *any* Commonwealth." James Tully (1991: 621–23) construes Locke as "subversively populist," a "revolutionary" who "repudiates…500 years of elite political holism and reconceptualises the origins of political power in a radically populist way." One might almost get the impression that he is talking about one of the Levellers or the Diggers. Yet Locke was hardly a populist, still less a subversive one. It is a tad difficult, to start with, to reconcile populism with one who was "receiving annually the near astronomical remuneration of around £1,500 for his services to Government," and who did "not hesitate to praise the prospect of the poor earning 'a penny per diem'…, i.e., a sum approximately 1,000 times lower than his own income" (Mészáros 2006: 41). Still less can one discern an ardent populist commitment in someone endorsing child labor starting with the age of three and who, for all his "toleration" in matters religious wished to criminalize beggars and vagabonds, advocating penal severity exceeding that of the absolutist monarchs. As István Mészáros points out:

> …while the brutal laws of Henry VIII. and Edward VI.…wanted to slice off only 'half the ear' of the second offenders, [Locke] suggests an improvement on such laws by solemnly recommending the loss of both ears, to be administered already to first offenders. These are his words: 'That whoever shall counterfeit a pass shall lose his ears for the forgery the first time that he is found guilty thereof, and the second time that he shall be transported to the plantations…, as in case of felony' (41).[9]

---

[9] The quotation from Locke is from Fox Bourne (1876, vol. 2: 378).

Some might object that such postures, while compromising the view of Locke as a personal or a practical populist, do not affect the larger claim that he was a *theoretical* subversive populist, who sanctioned the right of the people to rise in revolt against the king. Yet this is to ignore the extent to which Locke's justification of revolt[10] was not meant to ground popular sovereignty, but rather to appeal to it in order to underscore the unassailability of property. Tully himself, strangely enough, seems to acknowledge this fact, while remaining oblivious to its implications. Characterizing Locke's position he writes that, "once government has determined a system of 'property'...a transgression of these rights constitutes a violation of natural law and hence a ground for legitimate revolt, just as in the state of nature" (Tully 1991: 629). Yet precisely from this correct observation follows the realization that what stood at the heart of Locke's system was not populism but property rights, and terms such as "revolutionary" or "subversive" are here singularly misleading.[11] To be sure, as long as the "legitimate revolt" is conducted against the monarch and in defence of property, one may with greater or lesser justification speak of a "revolution." But what if the transgressing sovereign happens precisely to be "the people," and it is they who, collectively, make a *radical* and *subversive* claim, legal or revolutionary, on property? In that case, the term that suggests itself to describe Locke's legitimate revolt would more appropriately be "*counter*-revolution." But Locke did not believe that the political order ushered in on behalf of "the people" would ever be questioned by them. Nor was there any intention on his part to permit them to voice their opinion in the matter or, indeed, to *form* one in the first place. Knowledge and reasoning, essential and laudable though they certainly are, were conceived of as luxuries, the preserve of the elite, "proper only for a few, who had much leisure, improved understandings, and were used to abstract reasonings." Such things were not meant for the vast majority:

---

[10] A justification which, in any case, was not made public until after the revolt had been already successful. As Peter Linebaugh reminds us (2006: 48), Locke "waited prudently until 1690 to publish [his] *An Essay Concerning Human Understanding* and *Two Treatises of Civil Government*—because after that date James II had been deposed by Parliament, and William of Orange, a Protestant, had become King." Locke might thus be described more correctly as a revolutionary *post-festum*.

[11] For a succinct critique of Tully's reading of Locke as a proto-welfarist see Cohen (1995: 188–194).

> And you may as soon hope to have all the day-labourers and tradesmen, the spinsters and dairy-maids, perfect mathematicians, as to have them perfect in ethics this way. Hearing plain commands, is the sure and only course to bring them to obedience and practice. The greatest part cannot know, and therefore they must believe (Locke 1824: 146).

Believe and *obey*. Two tenets which came, after all, more than two centuries later, to pertain to "the most well-known of Fascist slogans: *Credere Obbedire Combattere* (Believe, Obey, Fight)" (Payne 1996: 215). And it should not be imagined that the third and most sinister part of this tripartite motto—*Combattere*—was a perverse fascist addition. Rather, the liberal order was founded on a class-based allocation of freedoms and of unfreedoms, of elite liberties and of mass duties, the latter certainly including the duty of fighting.[12] Christopher Hill powerfully summarized the all-encompassing distributive inequality of this order at its very inception:

> The struggle for freedom, then, in the seventeenth century, was a more complex story than the books sometimes suggest. The men of property won freedom—freedom from arbitrary taxation and arbitrary arrest, freedom from religious persecution, freedom to control the destinies of their country through their elected representatives, freedom to buy and sell. They also won freedom to evict copyholders and cottages, to tyrannise over their villages, to hire unprotected labour in the open market. The 'unfree' had always been press-ganged into army or navy whenever their betters decided to have a war. But regular conscription dates from Anne's reign. The act of 1708 made it clear that only those with "no lawful calling or employment"—and no parliamentary vote—were to be conscripted. Through Justices of the Peace, employers used the threat of call-up against recalcitrant workers. The smaller men failed in all spheres to get their freedom recognised, failed to win either the vote or economic security (Hill 2006: 308).

Thereafter, in England, for more than a hundred years, the "small men" who formed the bigger part of the people, *believed* (at least usually feigned to), *obeyed* (with sporadic interruptions, to be sure, when fierce riots erupted and other forms of popular defiance became evident)[13] and *fought* (quite frequently, as it turns out: "between 1689

---

[12] Locke himself, as Leo Strauss (1953: 232) pointed out, "asserts more emphatically than did Hobbes the individual's duty of military service."

[13] Such resistance, however, was more properly that of "the mob," the *mobile vulgus*, erratic, unpredictable, resembling more a series of conflagrations than the permanent, organized and comprehensive political challenge presented by the modern "masses,"

and 1815 Britain was under military arms... roughly one year in every two" [Hay and Rogers 1997: 152]).[14] They were, at any rate, largely excluded from politics as liberally circumscribed: at the end of the 18th century and start of the 19th, Britain's affairs were thus directed, Hay and Rogers further inform us, by "a Parliament stupendously over-representative of the very wealthiest Englishmen," a Parliament which was busily liberalizing the economy in conformity with free-market notions, getting rid of the last remnants of the traditional, "moral economy" (113). Capitalist property was from the beginning the liberal *sine qua non*, and politics—whether tyrannical, monarchical, aristocratic, or democratic—was regarded as legitimate to the extent that it respects and protects the economic core, and illegitimate to the extent that it turns against it. Writing some two hundred years after Locke and in direct polemics against democracy, the English liberal Henry Maine (1909: 49–50) makes it unmistakably clear that capitalists had not shaken off the economic yoke of absolute monarchs, only to be taxed by the people: "it makes not the smallest difference to the motives of the thrifty and industrious part of mankind whether their fiscal oppressor be an Eastern despot, or a feudal baron, or a democratic legislature, and whether they are taxed for the benefit of a Corporation called Society, or for the advantage of an individual styled King or Lord." For Maine, capital formation—"the resuscitation of wealth in ever-increasing quantities"—depends upon "the strenuous and never-ending struggle for existence, the beneficent private war which makes one man strive to climb on the shoulders of another and remain there through the law of the survival of the fittest" (50). Uncurbed democracy defies not just capitalism but science itself. "The prejudices of the people," he maintains, "are far stronger than those of the privileged classes; they are far more vulgar; and they are far more dangerous, because they are apt to run counter to scientific conclusions" (67–68). And among such scientific facts the most crucial concerns the need for capitalist competition of the most ruthless kind:

> The central seat in all Political Economy was from the first occupied by the theory of Population. This theory has now been generalised by Mr. Darwin and his followers, and, stated as the principle of the survival of

---

which later supplanted the mob in upper class' rhetoric. For this discursive shift from "mob" to "mass" and its social background see Williams (1983: 193).

[14] The book provides an excellent and comprehensive survey of English society and politics in the 18th century.

the fittest, it has become the central truth of all biological science. Yet it is evidently disliked by the multitude, and thrust into the background by those whom the multitude permits to lead it (39).

Since any attempt to gainsay scientific capitalism would be catastrophic, "popular government," if it is at all to be tolerated, must emulate the model developed in the United States (as putatively opposed to dangerous tendencies in contemporary England), where democracy is strictly *political* and leaves *the economy* wholly to itself:

> The Government of the United States,…rests on universal suffrage, but then it is only *a political government*. It is a government under which coercive restraint, *except in politics*, is reduced to a minimum. There has hardly ever before been a community in which the weak have been pushed so pitilessly to the wall, in which those who have succeeded have so uniformly been the strong, and in which in so short a time there has arisen so great an inequality of private fortune and domestic luxury.… It all reposes on the *sacredness of contract* and the *stability of private property*, the first the implement, and the last the reward, of success in the universal competition (51; italics added).

From Locke to Maine, these postulates, and these alone, remain the basis upon which a democracy can legitimately operate. We can therefore say that along with *political absolutism*, liberalism strove to dispose of the *absoluteness of politics*.[15] Its narrow definition of the role of politics as guardian of bourgeois economic interests, installed a kind of time bomb at the very heart of the liberal order. But as long as the political enfranchisement of the masses was either inconceivable or a mere potential threat, liberalism could function more or less according to the original recipe, notwithstanding the disagreeable, and ever

---

[15] Its own, contrasting propensity to absolutize property was not lost upon contemporaries, such as the observant Hobbes (1990: 4), who, precisely from a more traditionalistic-aristocratic vantage point, often expressed his distaste at miserliness of the supporters of Parliament:

> King, they thought, was but a title of the highest honour, which gentleman, knight, baron, earl, duke, were but steps to ascend to, with the help of riches; they had no rule of equity, but precedents and custom; and he was thought wisest and fittest to be chosen for a Parliament that was most averse to the granting of subsidies or other public payments.

The socioeconomic mindset of embryonic liberals, it appears, was indeed very similar to that of their modern-day, neo-liberal, descendents. Elsewhere, Hobbes poked bitter fun at the way the members of parliament had branded as monarchical "oppression" even the lightest and most requisite of taxations: "by one of their members that had been taxed but 20s. (mark the oppression; a Parliament-man of 500l. a year, land-taxed at 20s.!) they were forced to bring it to a trial" (37).

louder, ticking in the background. It is only at a later stage, particularly in the course of the 19th century, that politics began to defy economic liberalism, in the process unveiling the anti-democratic implications of the liberal order and, sometimes, triggering its dictatorial potentialities.[16]

From Constant to Donoso Cortés

Unsurprisingly, therefore, we find that 19th century liberal writers of different nationalities, faced with an increasingly articulate and organized working class demanding political representation, were spending much effort not so much in promoting popular democracy or advancing reasons to extend it, but in warning against the dangers it allegedly entails. Henry Maine was by no means alone. "In all countries," wrote J. S. Mill (1862: 133), "there is a majority of poor, a minority who, in contradistinction, may be called rich.... [I]s there not a considerable danger lest they [the poor majority] should throw upon the possessors of what is called realized property, and upon the larger incomes, an unfair share, or even the whole, of the burden of taxation...?" And Benjamin Constant, one of the foremost French liberal thinkers of the 19th century, was even more explicit about the need to defend property from any democratic intervention by the majority, thus distinguishing in his *Principles of Politics Applicable to All Representative Governments*, between legitimate, *economic* freedom and illegitimate, *political* freedom:

> Notice that the necessary aim of those without property is to obtain some: all the means which you grant them are sure to be used for this purpose. If, to the freedom to use their talents and industry, which you owe them, you add political rights, which you do not owe them, these rights, in the

---

[16] Hay and Rogers (1997: 186–7) outline the move from the "mob politics" characteristic of the 18th century to the "mass platform" of the 19th: "The meetings themselves were remarkably orderly, revealing not only the degree to which the emergent working class had given up mob politics, but the depth of popular self-activity and organization.... The mass platform represented the people assembled; it signified the advance in popular political organization." In the aftermath of the wars against Napoleonic France, the liberal order in England faced a grave social and political test: "Two nations faced one another...and the divide between them was immense. What the post-war crisis revealed most clearly was that the ruling class was losing the capacity to govern" (208).

hands of the greatest number, will inevitably serve to encroach upon property.... In all those countries which have representative assemblies it is essential that those assemblies, whatever their further organization, should be formed by property holders.... A nation always expects that men grouped together will be guided by their own interests. It is certain that the love of order, justice and conservation will enjoy a majority among property holders (Constant 1988: 215–216).

While it is difficult to disagree with Constant that love of order and conservation, during his time as well as ours, are indeed sentiments close to the heart of property holders, his notion of "justice" was somewhat idiosyncratic (though not in a personal, as in a collective, class sense). It asserted, for example, that political rights be denied to those who work, while being the exclusive privilege of those who do not:

Those who are kept by poverty in eternal dependence, and who are condemned by it to daily labour, are neither more knowledgeable than children about public affairs, nor more interested than foreigners in national prosperity...I do not wish in any way to wrong the labouring class. As a class it is by no means less patriotic than the others.... Yet the patriotism which gives one the courage to die for one's country is quite different, I believe, from the patriotism which enables one to fully understand its interests. There must be a further condition [for voting]...This condition is the leisure indispensable for the acquisition of understanding and soundness of judgement. Property alone makes men capable of exercising political rights (214).

Constant's early (1815) endorsement of liberalism and representative government were already founded on the insurmountable difference between the elite and the masses, the former being free to vote, the latter free to work (as well as die for their country). It is not surprising that the concern of such exemplary liberal writers as Constant, Mill or Tocqueville, was primarily to defend *minorities* against the "tyranny of the *majority*," the quintessential majority being the poor, the quintessential minority being the well off.

About a century later, a leading fascist intellectual and politician, Alfredo Rocco, came remarkably close to replicating Constant's arguments regarding democracy. More remarkably still, he did so in the very attempt to prove, of all things, that fascism not only had a distinct political doctrine, but one which signified a clean break with the *liberal tradition of the 18th and 19th centuries*. Against the supposedly democratic concept of liberalism, which places sovereignty in the hands of the masses, Rocco thus proudly advocated the following, strikingly original, fascist conception:

> Fascism wishes that government will be in the hands of men capable
> of rising above the consideration of their own interests and realize the
> interests of the social collective...Fascism does not only reject the dogma
> of popular sovereignty and substitutes for it that of the sovereignty of
> the state; it maintains in addition that the least able interpreter of the
> interests of society is precisely the popular mass, since the ability to rise
> above the consideration of one's own interest and consider the great
> historical interests of society, is an extremely rare gift and the privilege
> of few (Rocco 2004: 239).

Also like Constant, Rocco took care to clarify that his political elitism was not the product of any general low regard for the common
people. He, too, was willing to acknowledge the patriotic instinct of
the masses, manifesting itself in times of exceptional national need—
and given that the text was written in 1925, it is legitimate to assume
that he had the mass sacrifice of the Great War eminently in mind. But
such patriotism was clearly not to be regarded as politically viable in
normal times: "among nations of long history and great traditions," he
affirmed, "an instinct concerning the necessities of the stock is formed
even among the more humble social strata, which manifests itself with
an almost infallible certainty in the great hours of history. Allowing
this instinct to assert itself is just as wise as entrusting to the more elect
spirits the normal management of public affairs" (239–40). In short,
both Constant and Rocco share an appreciation of the multitude's
"courage to die for one's country," while denying its wisdom when it
comes to voting. Rocco, to be sure, made a great deal of the claim that,
even when fascism and liberalism act superficially in a similar way, an
examination of their underlying *motivations* reveals the radical difference between them: fascism, namely, always acts with a view to state
and to national interest, whereas liberalism is solely concerned with
the private well-being of individuals. He could make such argument,
of course, because it was—and still is—supported by a widespread,
common-sense notion about classical liberal priorities, which is nonetheless profoundly inadequate, misrepresenting as it does the actual
position of many, perhaps most, classical liberals. I will return to
deal with these important issues separately in the last chapters; in the
meantime, it should suffice to note that our present liberal interlocutor under discussion, Constant, was by no means concerned only with
"individuals." For him, just as for Rocco, the interests of the "public,"
"the nation," and "the country" were at stake.

Already at this stage in our discussion, it is possible to appreciate
how the anti-democratic spirit of the fascists was not simply a rebel-

lion against or repudiation of liberal values. Fascism did not have to "defeat liberalism" on that ground, as much as it needed to meet it half way. Against the widespread notion that a modern, capitalist, industrial and liberal nation would be naturally inclined towards a democratic political structure, it should be recalled that democracy can often complicate things for the capitalist order, by imposing on it political, social and moral limits and inhibitions, while promoting a re-distribution of wealth through progressive taxation. While liberal historians of our time tend to overlook this simple fact and ascribe the anti-democratic thrust of fascism to the unwholesome sediments of "pre-industrial, pre-capitalist and pre-bourgeois traditions,"[17] 19th and early 20th century liberals throughout the Western world would not have needed any reminder of it. Extension of the suffrage to those without property thus regularly had to be carried through in the face of staunch liberal opposition. Sometimes, in fact, it required an unlikely alliance between the social forces that were more critical-antagonistic of bourgeois society, the lower classes and the conservative nobility. In the Austro-Hungarian Monarchy, for example, suffrage was gradually extended under the auspices of such noblemen as Taaffe (1882), Badeni (1896) and Beck (1906–07), and theoretically endorsed by such conservative social thinkers and politicians as Albert Schäffle and Karl von Vogelsang, whereas the liberal bourgeoisie resisted it. The *Neue Freie Presse*, the leading bourgeois-liberal organ in Austria, thus wrote in 1868 with regards to the demand for universal suffrage, that "As long as a liberal ministry is at the helm, as long as this *Bürgerminsiterium* is controlled by a parliament that comes from the bourgeois classes, as long as politically ripe men who are fervently devoted to the idea of liberty influence developments in Austria, the call in the desert of a politically uneducated mass will not find an echo" (as quoted in Rumpler 2005: 424). In his memoirs, the anti-liberal economist Schäffle, who vainly attempted to introduce universal suffrage in Austria during a short-term in office as minister of commerce (1871), recalled his exasperation at the anti-democratic policies of the liberals: "I openly set forth the pernicious and unnatural character of a parliamentary minority rule, which excludes entire nations and classes. This minority rule is in fact the rule of big business [Großkapital] supported by doctrinaire liberalism, a rule of money, to

---

[17] Jürgen Kocka, the German social historian, as quoted in Eley (1986: 258).

which liberal clerks, advocates, men of letters and professors apply the spiritual varnish" (as quoted in Rumpler 2005: 433–4).[18] It appears as if, at least as far as acceptance of democracy is concerned, anti-bourgeois attachment to pre-capitalist traditions could serve as an *encouragement*, rather than an impediment. Conversely, precisely those liberals committed to *laissez faire* were firmly opposed to the political enfranchisement of the masses. Once such opposition had been subdued and universal suffrage introduced, economic liberals habitually responded by insisting that capitalism should be placed beyond the reach of political intervention. Democracy was hence accepted, if indeed it was, solely to the extent that it did not meddle with capitalism, thus clearly placing political liberalism in a relation of subservience to economic liberalism. In the words of Ludwig von Mises, writing in 1922:

> Grave injury has been done to the concept of democracy by those who, exaggerating the natural law notion of sovereignty, conceived it as limitless rule of the *volonté générale*.... It is a small confusion of ideas, but a confusion with profound consequences, when [the legislator] takes his *formal freedom* to be a *material one* and believes himself to be above *the natural conditions of social life*. The conflicts which arise out of this misconception show that only within the framework of Liberalism does democracy *fulfill a social function*. Democracy without liberalism is a *hollow form* (Mises 1951: 76; emphases added).

The economy is equated with "the natural conditions of social life," and becomes a forbidden territory for democracy. Notice the way that the liberal critic of democracy does not openly state such opposition; rather, he fumbles with a democratic cloak. For even as Mises denudes democracy of all power vis-à-vis capitalism, he affects to defend from a "great injury," not capitalism, but "the concept of democracy." Clearly aware of the fact that words matter, the liberal author is at pains to call anti-democracy, precisely, democracy. Democracy, for its own good, must explicitly remain *formal*, renounce all "*material* freedom." But

---

[18] See also Wadl (1987: 53–56, 152–3). On the strong misgivings about popular democracy on the part of contemporary German liberals see, for example, Sheehan (1978: 154–7, 222) and Langewiesche (1995: 14–15, 201–2). With regards to British liberalism, we may recall John Vincent's following summary of the attitudes of Gladstonian liberals: "The Liberals, flatly, were not democrats, their Reform Bill of 1866 was an exclusion Bill, and when they adopted democracy after 1867 for political purposes, they knew neither its feelings nor its justifications" (Vincent 1966: xxxv; see also: 251–3).

this must strike some readers as a rather bitter remedy. So the final couple of sentences attempt to sweeten the pill with a rhetorical sleight-of-hand: the purely formal democracy actually favored by Mises, one which accepts its natural limits and refrains from doing anything in the economic domain, is said to be material, to "fulfill a social function" (whatever one thinks about such political recipe, it is clear that it makes it extremely easy for democracy to be useful). That democracy, by contrast, which bypasses economic liberalism and assumes a "material freedom," actively intervening in the economy, is not so much misguided or harmful, as much as it is a mere "hollow form." How a mere empty procedure might possibly have the power to contravene "the natural conditions of social life," must remain a mystery.

If among the abiding lessons learned from the fascist experience we ought to count the general recognition of the democratic tenet, this was a lesson taken not simply in vindication of the liberal-bourgeois tradition, but also against it. In fact, even after the experience of fascism, many liberals—particularly economic ones—persisted in opposing the democratic principle and proposing limits to its rule. Writing in the immediate aftermath of the Second World War, Wilhelm Röpke (1946: 188) echoed the standard liberal positions of the 19th century when he wrote about the need to "work against the honestly undeniable dangers of general franchise and permit a true government by responsible people." In the same spirit, Friedrich August von Hayek, the emblematic figure of 20th-century economic liberalism, reiterated the old point that "liberalism is incompatible with unlimited democracy," which he also characterized as "totalitarian democracy" and "the dictatorship of plebiscites" (as quoted in Kühnl 1999: 119). To his credit, Hayek at least dispenses here with the tortuous double-talk of Mises. He wishes, frankly enough, to limit democracy, not, like Mises, to fill it with real content. But Mises' full-blown democracy, of course, is the exact same thing as Hayek's shriveled one.

Yet, even though liberalism and democracy cohabited uncomfortably from the beginning, it is still meaningful to distinguish an optimistic liberal phase, in which a reasonable agreement between the partners of capitalism and democracy still seemed possible, from a pessimistic liberal phase, in which the relationship became ever more turbulent. The watershed between the two phases was marked by the revolutions of 1848, in the course of which the bourgeoisie and the proletariat of different European countries, initially joined together in demands of greater political freedoms, drifted apart. The structural tensions between the "third" and the "fourth" class erupted into open, violent clashes, most famously during the June uprising of the Parisian workers, but in other European capitals as well, such as Vienna:

> The city's bourgeoisie, organized in the national guards, feared plunder- ing and marched against the workers. In the Prater-star it came to the so-called *Praterschlacht*, in which a great number of workers were killed or injured.
> The March revolutionary forces now split up definitively. The bour- geoisie was satisfied with the achievements and attempted to establish law and order, to defend against a proletarian revolution. The peasants, too, whose emancipation was settled, ceased from being carriers of the revolution. Only students and workers remained interested in the revo- lution and its further development (Vocelka 2004: 202).

Constant can again usefully illustrate this historical change. As we have seen, he was perfectly aware of the incompatibility of capitalism and universal suffrage, and yet, in a more confident mood, he could still at times sanguinely envision a harmonious social order, in which all classes of the population are embraced in liberal rupture, a *frater- nité* founded on *liberté*, while *égalité* has been successfully defused, universally taken out of the equation:

> [S]ee how our nation grows, with the first institution which restores to her the regular exercise of political liberty. See our countrymen of all classes, of all professions, emerge from the sphere of their usual labours and private industry, find themselves suddenly at the level of important functions which the constitution confers upon them, choose with dis- cernment, resist with energy, brave threats, nobly withstand seduction. See a pure, deep and sincere patriotism triumph in our towns, revive even our smallest villages, permeate our workshops... [T]hey, learned in the history of the evils they have suffered, and no less enlightened as to the remedies which these evils demand, take in with a glance the whole of France and, bestowing a national gratitude, repay with their suffrage, after thirty years, the fidelity to principles embodied in the most illustri- ous of the defenders of liberty (Constant 1988: 327).

Democracy? Yes indeed, but assuming that the people will "choose with discernment," namely for the preservation of the bourgeois order, and "nobly withstand seduction," obviously on the part of the social radicals. Oozing optimism, Constant was confident that the people would follow the defenders of liberty, among whom he clearly did not count a Saint-Just, a Marat or a Robespierre. This is liberalism before the split. Writing in 1819, in an age predating the full-fledged chal- lenge of the masses, Constant could be optimistic that they will be "enlightened" and "patriotic" enough to align themselves with the reason of an age of commerce, that they be integrated seamlessly into the bourgeois order of individual happiness, possessions, etc. Consider, too, the following, remarkable passage:

> While each people, in the past, formed an isolated family, the born enemy of other families, a mass of human beings now exists, that under different names and different forms of social organization are essentially homogenous in their nature. This mass is strong enough to have nothing to fear from barbarian hordes. It is sufficiently civilized to find war a burden.... War precedes commerce. War and commerce are only two different means of achieving the same end, that of getting what one wants.... War is all impulse, commerce, calculation. Hence it follows that an age must come in which commerce replaces war. We have reached this age (313).

It is striking that Constant, precisely from a liberal and individualistic point of view, should praise the commercial rationality of masses, indeed *the homogenous* masses, which for later liberals became the very anathema of liberty, both individual and commercial, and the subject of endless literature on the grey uniformity and the incurable irrationality of the multitudes. What is the source of this difference? Is Constant inherently more democratic and progressive than later liberals who betrayed his and other early liberals' commitment to "the people"? The answer, I suspect, is not to be found in Constant's superior morals or integrity. Rather, it lies in the difference in historical circumstances, reflecting an optimistic liberalism, or rather an oscillation between elated optimism and sober pessimism, which we have documented above. In the post-48 era, however, the balance tilted decisively towards the latter.

The bourgeois political revolution revealed itself as a centrifugal force whose waves refused to ebb according to bourgeois wishes. In order to defend the liberal socioeconomic order from democracy and/or revolution, the bourgeoisie was thus driven to demote—to a lesser or greater extent—political liberalism. Through the years, observers of all political persuasions recognized this basic scheme. On the Left, socialists and communists denounced the retreat from political liberalism, the bourgeois recoil from the consequences of their own revolution. This was most famously done by Karl Marx, with regards to shifting alliances of the French bourgeoisie in the course of the 1848 revolution, which ended—it is important to recall—by a Bonapartist dictatorship that many regard as a 19th century rehearsal for 20th century fascism. For Marx, this dictatorship was only superficially, and in the last instance, the result of the subversive activities of some external, anti-republican force, assaulting the political institutions of liberalism. Louis Bonaparte found the ground thoroughly prepared for him by the bourgeois liberals themselves who made a U-turn, once they realized that parliamentary rule, together with all other aspects of political liberalism, was now militating against their interests:

> The bourgeoisie had a true insight into the fact that all the weapons it had forged against feudalism turned their points against itself... If in every stirring of life in society it saw 'tranquillity' imperiled, how could it want to maintain at the head of society a *regime of unrest*, its own regime, the *parliamentary regime*...?... The parliamentary regime leaves everything to the decision of majorities; how shall the great majorities outside parliament not want to decide? (Marx 1963: 65–66).

Conservative critics of liberalism often saw the social and historical constellation eye to eye with Marx, but whereas he reproached the liberal bourgeois for betraying the revolution, they attacked them for allowing its forces to run riot in the first place. Writing in the 20th century, Eric Voegelin could thus define the dilemma of liberals, even as he asserted their blame:

> One can't get away from the revolution. Whoever participates in it for a time with the intention of retiring peacefully with a pension which calls itself liberalism will discover sooner or later that the revolutionary convulsion to destroy socially harmful, obsolete institutions is not a good investment for a pensioner.... The *political* aspect of liberalism is defined by the liberal opposition to certain abuses... [Liberals] oppose the old social order, that is, the privileged position of clergy and nobility. At this point can be seen the weakness of a political attitude which is tied to the situation;... In time when the rising working class becomes politically capable of directing it, the attack on privilege turns against the liberal bourgeoisie itself (Voegelin 1974: 512–14).

This analysis of the paradoxes of liberalism was by no means confined to the enemies of the liberal order, whether radicals or conservatives. Often enough, it came from liberals themselves. Consider the position of that eminent French liberal, Alexis de Tocqueville, a figure somewhere in between the past-oriented, aristocratic camp, and the modern, middle-class one. Writing on the eve of the 1848 revolutions, Tocqueville anxiously diagnosed the way the bourgeoisie, by destroying the aristocratic regime in order to establish their own reign—embodied in the figure of Louis-Philippe, the "Citizen King," and his July Monarchy—far from placing the rights of property once and for all on a firm footing, in fact for the first time in history made *property itself* questionable. By shortsightedly attacking all aristocratic social privileges, the supreme social privilege upon which their own rule rests, property, becomes susceptible to socialist and democratic attacks. The aristocratic order, too, according to Tocqueville's analysis, ultimately rested upon property. Yet a series of secondary issues of a legal and political character, extravagant in appearance yet not remotely as substantial, covered up this decisive question and drew attention *away from* it. Under bourgeois rule, by contrast, property becomes terrifyingly naked. This dangerous new state of things the author befittingly conveyed with recourse to graphic imagery of a logistic campaign, and of a civilization under siege:

> When the right to property was merely the basis of many other rights, it could be easily defended; or rather, it was not attacked: it was like the encircling wall of a society whose other rights were the advance defense posts; the shots did not reach it; there was not even the serious intention to reach it. But now that the right to property is the last remnant of a destroyed aristocratic world, and it alone still stands, an isolated privilege in a leveled society; when it no longer has the cover of other more doubtful and more hated rights, it is in great danger; it alone now has to face the direct and incessant impact of democratic opinions... Soon the political struggle will be between the Haves and the Have-nots; property will be the great battlefield.... Do you think it is by chance...that on every side we see strange doctrines appearing... which all deny the right of property...? who can fail to recognize in this the last symptom of the old democratic disease of the times, whose crisis is perhaps approaching? (Tocqueville 1997: 12–13).[19]

Dialectically, bourgeois rule signals the triumph of capitalism just as it harbours its moment of greatest peril. For all their materialism, the bourgeois are the first to make an issue of property; thus, in spite of themselves, they are weak, unreliable guardians of property. They imagine themselves well in charge, but they are more like the sorcerer's apprentice. Political liberalism, taken to its last, paradoxical conclusions, imperils property and with it, the future of a capitalist, bourgeois order.[20] Let us listen to the following justification of Louis Napoleon's coup d'état, by a foreign correspondent in Paris:

---

[19] Tocqueville quotes from his own speech in the French parliament, "De la classe moyenne et du peuple," written in October, 1847.

[20] It is illuminating to hear Marx, one of the most incisive critics of Tocqueville's bourgeois *parti de l'Ordre*, assessing the historical vulnerability of property in virtually interchangeable terms: "As long as the rule of the bourgeois class had not been organized completely, as long as it had not acquired its pure political expression, the antagonism of the other classes, likewise, could not appear in its pure form, and where

> Above all things, I have designed to prove to you that the French are by
> character unfit for a solely and predominantly parliamentary govern-
> ment; that so many and so great elements of convulsion exist here that it
> will be clearly necessary that a strong, vigorous, anti-barricade executive
> should, at whatever risk and cost, be established and maintained...—in
> a word, that riots and revolutions must if possible come to an end, and
> only such a degree of liberty and democracy be granted to the French
> nation as is consistent with the consolidated existence of the order and
> tranquillity which are equally essential to rational freedom and civilized
> society.

The correspondent in question was not some Russian, Austrian or
Prussian reporter, expressing the point of view of an authoritarian,
pre-industrial, pre-bourgeois regime; nor was he an archconserva-
tive opponent of liberalism. Rather, it is the young Walter Bagehot
(1891a: 429), very soon to become one of England's most influential
liberal voices on economic matters, and one of her foremost publicists,
the long-time editor of *The Economist*. In a series of reports to *The
Inquirer* published in January–February 1852, Bagehot defended all
aspects of the military dictatorship, from the repression of political
opponents to the elimination of the freedom of the press, marshalling justifications that a student of fascism would find quite familiar.
Political persecution was justified, notwithstanding minor reservations
about their extent, because "The Socialists who have been removed
from prison to the colony, it is agreed were 'pestilent fellows, perverting the nation'" (387). Those who loudly complained about the cruel-
ties of the measures taken did not see that such modus operandi was
not unlike the procedure by which Octavius and Mark Anthony "thoroughly purged old Rome of its turbulent and revolutionary elements"
(388). Whether or not Louis Napoleon can be considered a proto-
fascist leader, the terms in which Bagehot and other enthusiasts—one
of whom he approvingly quotes—hailed the ruler, certainly evoke the
adulation of the fascist leader as the steadfast, heroic man-of-action,
surrounded by an inexplicable charismatic aura, rising above the pettiness of small politics:

> Louis Napoleon is, as a pointed writer describes him: '...a superior
> man, but his superiority is of the sort that is hidden under a dubious
> exterior:...he thinks and does not discuss, he decides and does not

---

it did appear could not take the dangerous turn that transforms every struggle against
the state power into a struggle against capital" (Marx 1963: 66).

deliberate, he acts without agitation, he speaks and assigns no reason; his best friends are unacquainted with him, he obtains their confidence but never asks it' (382).

The press, for its part, must be strictly disciplined, given that "newspaper people are the only traders that thrive upon convulsion" (422). This last quotation exemplifies an important feature of Bagehot's apologia for dictatorship, namely the fact that at all times he wrote from the vantage point of commercial and economic interests, lending voice to the "commercial disquietude" of "the quiet classes," those who "mind their business and have a business to mind." This bourgeois material interest is the first priority, compared to which all political fancies must take second place:

> You will not be misled by any high-flown speculations about liberty or equality. You will, I imagine, concede to me that the first duty of a government is to insure the security of that industry which is the condition of social life and civilized cultivation...It is from this state of things, whether by fair means or foul, that Louis Napoleon has delivered France. The effect was magical:...Commerce instantly improved; New-Year's Day, when all the boulevards are one continued fair, has not (as I am told) been for some years so gay and splendid; people began to buy, and consequently to sell...(376).

Bagehot, commonly celebrated as an impassionate, detached and tolerant observer, did not here take particular care to disguise his predilection towards the bourgeoisie, nor did he restrain his sentimental empathy for their plight. Rhetorical manoeuvres helped him to make such partiality appear a self-evident choice. According to Bagehot, the socialist insurgents of June, led by "practical rascals and energetic murderers," were defied by "mostly solid shopkeepers, three parts ruined by the events of February," who

> ...fought, I will not say bravely or valiantly, but furiously, frantically, savagely, as one reads in old books that half-starved burgesses in beleaguered towns have sometimes fought for the food of their children. Let any skeptic hear of the atrocities of the friends of order and the atrocities of the advocates of disorder, and he will, I imagine, no longer be skeptical on two points: he will hope that if he ever have [sic] to fight, it will not be with a fanatic Socialist, nor against a demi-bankrupt fighting for 'his shop'...(412).

The historical appeal to the starving medieval burgesses creates in the reader the impression that the bourgeoisie were *hungry*, whereas the workers were merely blood*thirsty*. The actual situation is thereby ingeniously reversed in which the workers of Paris, left unemployed en masse after the closing of the National Workshops, were the ones actually fighting for their, and their children's, daily bread. The flash-back to the encircled burgs is also misleading in that in June 1848 the workers were those finding themselves in a "beleaguered town," under a state of siege, whereas the bourgeoisie was receiving vital enforce-ments of men and arms flowing to Paris from rural, conservative France. Tocqueville, himself no "skeptic" and wholeheartedly on the bourgeoisie's side against the workers, did not misrepresent, like the English liberal, the actual balance of forces:

> Down all the roads not held by the insurgents, thousands of men were pouring in from all parts of France to aid us. These men were drawn *without distinction from all classes of society* [this, to be sure, is not quite correct, as the following inventory makes clear. I.L.]; among them were great numbers of peasants, bourgeois, large landowners and nobles, all jumbled up together in the same ranks.... Thenceforth it was clear that we would win in the end for the insurgents had no fresh forces, and we the whole of France as reserves (Tocqueville 1997: 152–3; italics added).

Concluding his series of reports, Bagehot succinctly captured the conflict between political and economic liberalism and emphatically answered the question of which of the two is truly substantial:

> Mazzini sneers at the selfishness of shopkeepers: I am for the shopkeepers against him.... Legislative assemblies, leading articles, essay eloquence, such are good, very good; useful, very useful: yet they can be done with-out; we can want them. Not so with all things: the selling of figs, the cobbling of shoes, the manufacturing of nails, these are the essence of life... (1891a: 438–9).[21]

Capitalism, in other words, is vital, whereas democracy is "good, very good," but dispensable, all the more so if it turns against "the essence of life." Given the widening gulf between "shopkeepers" and "legisla-tive assemblies," liberals were forced to re-consider their old creeds, to

---

[21] In a 1865 supplement, Bagehot—indirectly—qualified his early enthusiasm about the Third Empire. He continued to acknowledge the "genius" of Bonaparte and his inestimable service to the cause of "free trade," yet he criticized the centralization and excessive reliance on the ruler, as well as the undue censorship of the press. Even then, however, it is instructive that he did not do so embracing a liberal defence of democracy. Quite the contrary, he assured *The Economist's* readers that "the French Empire is really the *best finished* democracy which the world has ever seen" (441). This was definitely not meant as a compliment.

modify their positions, at times even abandon them. We can illustrate this by referring to a 19th century conservative, Juan Donoso Cortés, who was to exert a great influence over a well-known 20th century fascist, Carl Schmitt. In his polemics against the liberal Weimar Republic, the German jurist often evoked with admiration the writings of the Spanish advocate of dictatorship. Yet it is important to bear in mind that Donoso was not always a conservative and vehement anti-liberal, in fact he started his career as a liberal politician, associated with the bourgeois and pro-capitalist *Partido Moderado*. It was only the reality of growing social conflict in France, which Donoso witnessed during his stay in that country in the early 1840s, and most forcefully the events of the 1848 revolutions, that led him to the same conclusion drawn by his contemporaries, Marx and Tocqueville, and by Voegelin more than a century later, that liberalism, namely, is not a good investment for a pensioner. The crucial fault of liberalism, according to Donoso, was that it inevitably heralds social revolution, which, once unleashed, it is completely incapable of thwarting. Liberalism began by putting into question the *political* order, and socialism radicalized it from there into a general questioning of the *socioeconomic* order:

> The liberal school takes it for granted that there is no other evil except that which resides in the *political institutions* that we have inherited from the past, and that supreme good consists in pulling such institutions down. The radical socialists [Los más de los socialistas] accept as an axiom that there is no other evil except that which resides in *society*, and that the great remedy is the complete transformation of the social institutions.... For both the ones and the others, supreme good thus consists in supreme transformation, which, according to the *liberal school*, should take place in the *political spheres*, and according to the *socialistic schools*, in the *social spheres* (Donoso Cortés 1851: 225–6; emphases added).

Liberal skepticism is subsequently, as well as consequentially, *turned against itself* by democratic socialism:

> Democratic socialism has reason on its side when it says to liberalism: 'what is this God which is presented for my adoration, and which must be less than yourself since it possesses no will and which is not even a person?...Everything makes me think that you have brought him into being in order that He will give you the legitimacy which you lack; your legitimacy and his existence are a fiction mounted on another fiction, a shadow upon a shadow. I have come to the world to disperse all shadows and end all fictions.... What is legitimacy and what is reason? And...how do you know that they reside in liberalism and not in social-

ism, in you and not in me, in the comfortable classes and not in the
people? I deny your legitimacy and you mine; you deny my reason and
I yours....' (202–203).

This is another classical articulation of the split between political and
economic liberalism. Political liberalism spills over into social radicalism, escapes from the control of "comfortable classes" and animates
"the people." To this original sin is added the fact that liberalism, having released the demons of the people, is pathetically helpless in containing them: "If in the great battle which keeps the world hanging
on a thread there were no combatants other than the socialists and
the liberals, the battle would not be long, nor would the identity of
the victor be in doubt" (207). Hence the need for another, stronger
power to intervene, that of the dictatorial, proto-fascist battalions of
Catholicism. Tellingly, for all its contempt for the weakly liberals, such
superior power intervenes ultimately *on their behalf*, to save them from
their own mischief. Even as he will severely scold him and show him
his proper place, the true sorcerer will come to deliver his apprentice
from the once enchanted, but now rebellious, mops.

Liberalism was caught between the monarch and the people, dictatorship and democracy, Catholicism and atheism, the elite and the mass,
"Christ" and "Barabbas," and could not choose between them (I return
to Donoso below, when discussing Carl Schmitt's position). Unlike
Constant, Donoso no longer placed any hopes in the people's ability
to choose wisely or resist temptation. The "barbaric masses," [bárbaras
muchedumbres] clearly follow the socialistic Barabbas. Donoso, at a
second remove, standing as it were behind Schmitt, can be seen as
one objective piece of evidence testifying to the liberal genealogy of
fascism, showing concretely how the anti-liberal impulse, even at its
most avid, not shy of espousing dictatorship, can spring from within
the liberal camp. Donoso's drastic transformation may have been an
extreme case, but in its basic, skeptic, post-48 realignment vis-à-vis the
tenets of political liberalism, it was by no means exceptional. He rather
embodied a sweeping move from an optimistic liberalism to a pessimistic one, one of whose variants, or at least derivatives, was fascism.

Pareto: on Foxes and Musso-Lions

The catholic dictatorship Donoso called for, however, was not yet,
of course, nor could have been, a fascist one, and might at most be

described as "proto-fascist." Moreover, since Donoso was not particularly interested in economic matters, his dictatorship was only implicitly capitalistic, concerned first and foremost with reinstating social hierarchy (to be sure, given the concrete socialist rebellion which such hierarchy was meant to put an end to, it would not make sense to doubt its fundamental affiliation with capitalism). Much more directly indicative of the liberal transmutation we are tracing is the figure of Vilfredo Pareto, the Italian sociologist. Pareto is traditionally considered one of the most important thinkers to have influenced Mussolini.[22] He is sometimes portrayed as an early liberal who turned his back on liberal principles.[23] This is misleading because Pareto only gave up on political liberalism, not on economic liberalism. Like Donoso, Pareto embodies in his person and ideological trajectory the evolution of an entire class. He began as optimistic liberal—believing that democracy would serve bourgeois interests and check state intervention in the free market by the obsolete and devious aristocracy. Yet the early advocacy of democracy in *Cours d'Economie Politique* (1896), was founded on the assumption that economic liberalism, which he endorsed as legitimate and useful, would not be hampered by political intervention, which he censured as an illegitimate and destructive means of class struggle, branded as "spoliation." Economically, he thus expounded the classical liberalism of a Smith or a Mandeville: "The class struggle at all times takes two forms. One is plainly and simply economic competition. When this competition is free, we find that it produces the maximum ophelimity [economic satisfaction. I.L]. Each class, like each individual, although looking exclusively to its own advantage, indirectly comes to be useful to the other classes" (Pareto 1966: 117). Yet to this benign mode of class struggle was contrasted a political, malignant one: "The other form taken by the class struggle is that whereby each class endeavors to get control of the government so as to make it an instrument for spoliation" (117). Befittingly, for an ideal political model he looked to the classical liberal economies of Switzerland and England, where wealth is allegedly earned "only by work, industry and trade," as compared to other countries, like Spain

---

[22] As early as 1935, Herman Finer (1935: 21) supplies the following lists' of Mussolinis "teachers": "Schopenhauer, Nietzsche, Blanqui, Georges Sorel, William James, Bergson, Vilfredo Pareto, and Machiavelli."

[23] Charles H. Powers (1984: 22), for example, described him as a "disaffected liberal."

and Italy, "in which wealth is, to a considerable degree, the fruit of fraud and political intrigue" (119). Like Constant during his sanguine moments, Pareto could envision a parliamentary system reasonable enough to acknowledge the iron laws of the economy, and hence adhere to free competition. Yet it was strictly on such sound economic foundations that political representation could be tolerated, since capitalism is based on nature itself. As implied in the following passage: "Above, far above, the prejudices and passions of men soar the laws of nature. Eternal and immutable, they are the expression of the creative power; they represent what is, what must be, what otherwise could not be" (122).

The naturalistic premises of Pareto's socioeconomic vision made reason, science and logic equivalent to, and dependent on, an unfettered capitalism. To amass political obstacles on its path amounted, in his eyes, to an act of blatant irrationality made in defiance of nature itself. And for all his confidence in the ultimate and general good bound up with market economy, Pareto minced no words about the fact that such an economy is as utterly ruthless and brutal as nature itself. Being rational thus meant accommodating oneself to such an order, accepting the desirability of the "struggle for life" and not shrinking from its atrocities. Anything other than that is a contemptible humanitarianism, which would ineluctably bring about exhaustion and degeneration:

> All species of living beings would degenerate without the operation of selection. The human race cannot escape this law. Humanitarians may be able to close their eyes to this truth, deliberately ignoring it, but this can in no way alter the facts. In every race reject-elements are produced which must be eliminated by selection. The grief and suffering caused by this are the price which has to be paid for the improvement of the race. This is one of the many cases in which the good of the individual is in opposition to the good of the species (159).

Soon enough, however, Pareto had to concede that human beings were unworthy of capitalistic logic and unwilling to pay it the "price which has to be paid." This disappointment with such human, all-too-human frailties, was the very motivation which made him plunge into a mammoth sociological effort to account for the way human social behavior is motivated centrally by sentiments, not logic, as expounded upon in his theory of residues and derivations. At the beginning, Pareto was more or less equally concerned in guaranteeing that the economy would not be plundered either from above, by the dominant classes, or from below, by the socialist masses. His support for parliamentary government was motivated precisely by the hope that it would help to balance out and neutralize such destructive forces. But the main challenge quickly became that of socialism, whose inherent scientific fallacies and biases he turned to analyze in *Les Systèmes Socialistes* of 1902. Significantly enough, at that time he was no longer a democrat.[24] Optimistic liberalism—which in Pareto, to be sure, was never quite as strong as in early 19th century liberals—fully gave way to pessimistic, embittered liberalism, once it became clear that the parliamentary system did not seamlessly prop up capitalism and in fact entails a new and even more pernicious form of statism, undertaken on behalf of the masses, a reality which became increasingly evident in turn-of-the-century Italy, where Marxism and trade unionism seemed to be growing by leaps and bounds. Pareto's verdict on political liberalism was thus unequivocal, encapsulating the split between politics and economics:

> The work of liberals in the first half of the nineteenth century paved the way for that era of demagogic oppression which is now dawning. Those who demanded the equality of all citizens before the law certainly did not envisage the privileges the masses now enjoy. The old special jurisdictions have been suppressed, but the same thing in a new form is being instituted: a system of arbitration which operates always in favor of the workers. Those who demanded the freedom to strike did not imagine that this freedom, for the strikers, would consist of beating up workers who want to continue working, and of burning down factories with impunity. Those who sought equal taxation to help the poor did not imagine that it would lead to progressive taxation at the expense of the rich, and to a system in which taxes are voted by those who do not pay them...(Pareto 1966: 157).

Faced by the ignominy of union's power and progressive taxation, perceived from the vantage point of an intransigent economic liberal, Pareto jettisoned his—never more than desultory—support for democracy and political liberalism. He now became a tireless voice denouncing the "decadence" of the bourgeois elite, and urging them to strike back, turn the political balance, and regain political power by eliminating popular democracy: "today we see that an element in the bourgeoisie is giving strong support to socialism, the leaders of which, moreover, are of bourgeois origins. Elites commonly end up by committing suicide... [F]orce is the foundation of all social organization. It is interesting

---

[24] Cf. Richard Bellamy's (2002: 237–9) short account of Pareto's intellectual and political trajectory.

to note that the antipathy of the contemporary bourgeoisie to force results in giving a free hand to violence" (157). Or, in a more graphic formulation: "When a living creature loses the sentiments which...are necessary to it in order to maintain the struggle for life, this is a certain sign of degeneration...The living creature which shrinks from giving blow for blow and from shedding its adversary's blood thereby puts itself at the mercy of its adversary. The sheep has always found a wolf to devour it" (135). Certainly, Pareto now assumed a cloak of impassioned scientific impartiality, stressing his mere concern for facts and elucidations, as opposed to the promotion of any policies or the passing of ethical judgments; yet his ferocious attacks on socialists and their fallacies, as well as the acerbic remarks on the weakly bourgeoisie who fails to combat them, ubiquitous throughout his writings, constantly gave the lie to such claim of scientific detachment. Whereas political liberalism was centered on the notion of representation, Pareto was a key thinker among those many who now discarded a priori the possibility of a real democracy and claimed that only elites ever rule: he is known as the introducer of the very term "elite" to the jargon of political science. This was meant to put an end to the democratic project not only politically and contextually, for certain periods and under specific conditions, but for all times and under all conceivable circumstances, by theoretically placing democracy in the realm of the impossible. Only elites can rule, Pareto insisted, yet, formulating the famous "circulation of elites" theory, he added that the elites perennially alternate between the politically liberal "foxes," sly, cunning, manipulative, governing by deals, alignments, combinations and compromises, and the conservative "lions," upright, steadfast, slow moving but hard hitting, ruling by force. Exasperated by the Giolittian elite of his time, which he regarded as the rule of the foxes brought to a height of deviousness, Pareto expected to see the vigorous lions attain power again. When Mussolini marched on Rome, the old Pareto is said to have risen "from a sick-bed and utter a triumphant 'I told you so!'" (quoted by Livingston 1935: xvii).[25]

Pareto insisted on the scientific impossibility of democracy, influencing a whole literature on the subject that directly informed fascism,

---

[25] Livingston was careful to add immediately the—unsupported—qualification that this was "the bitter exultance of the justified prophet, not the assertion, and by far, of a wish."

notably Robert Michels' theories, that linked the impossibility of genuine democracy with the impossibility of genuine socialism, formulating the "iron law of the oligarchy."[26] But the very need to formulate such inviolable political laws, already betrayed the political urgency underlying them, the fear of the very real and concrete political, economic and social gains made by the organized workers in Italy. The basic paradox of Pareto's thought could be summarized in the following question: if democracy is indeed immanently impossible, why struggle to abolish it? This inconsistency shot through Pareto's critique of democracy. And he himself indirectly conceded this by admitting that, fictitious and unfeasible though it may be, democracy can indeed provide the working class with a powerful and tangible means of promoting its interest as against those of the capitalists. As is clear from this complaint: "Tilling a field to produce corn is an arduous labor; lurking at the corner for a passer-by to rob is a dangerous venture. On the other hand, going along to the polling station to vote is a very easy business, and if by so doing one can procure food and shelter, then everybody—especially the unfit, the incompetent and the idle—will rush to do it" (Pareto 1966: 139). Foxes may hence be just as elitist as lions, but democracy is seen to put irresistible pressure on them to provide nourishment and abode to the non-elite at the expenses of the elite.[27] Hence the eager wait for an age of lions and Musso*lions*

---

[26] Pareto's theoretical elitism, to be sure, was firmly rooted in a tradition of anti-democratic thinking, which was to a large extent a liberal one. This can be demonstrated by the following quotation from Henry Maine's polemical book on democracy, published in 1885: "History is a sound aristocrat.... [T]he progress of mankind has hitherto been effected by the rise and fall of aristocracies, by the formation of one aristocracy within another, or by the succession of one aristocracy to another. There have been so-called democracies, which have rendered services beyond price to civilisation, but they were only peculiar forms of aristocracy" (Maine 1909: 42).

[27] A comparison with Maine's earlier position (1909: 29–30) is again illuminating, revealing the same kind of oscillation in the Englishman's critique of democracy: on the one hand, he reassures himself and his apprehensive, elitist readers, by an effort to cut democracy down to size. It does not, he insists, signify the real rule of the people but rather that of the professional "wire-puller." He approvingly quotes James Stephen to that effect: "In a pure democracy, the ruling men will be the Wire-pullers and their friends; but they will be no more on an equality with the people than soldiers or Ministers of State are on an equality with the subjects of a Monarchy.... [U]nder all circumstances the rank and file are directed by leaders of one kind or another who get the command of their collective force." On the other hand, though, Maine is anxious about the very real influence which the masses exercise from below. As is apparent from the following observation, the control of the elite over the rank and file is decidedly less firm than at first suggested: "The relation of political leaders to political followers seems to me to be undergoing a twofold change. The leaders

unshackled by the masses; hence the contempt at an elite that grows sentimental and refuses to use force.[28]

These motifs became a constant in Pareto's writings right up to the post-War Italian crisis of the so-called *biennio rosso*, the two years (1919–1920) preceding the rise of Italian fascism, which were marked by intense social agitation and trade union activism. The elites, allegedly aloof of genuine democracy and hermetically sheltered from its effects by the workings of a natural-cum-social law, were admitted to be fairly and squarely beaten by the masses, whom the very same law allegedly condemned to eternal servitude. *Trasformazione della Democrazia* (1921), one of the last texts published by Pareto during his lifetime, while adding little of novelty to his theories, nonetheless usefully sums up his thought and highlights its consequences, pointing directly towards fascism. To start with, it recapitulates Pareto's obituary to political liberalism, at the same time that it again manifests his abiding attachment to *laissez faire*, and his wistfulness for an age of innocence, before the fall of progressive taxation. In that vein, he proclaims the obsolescence of classical political liberalism:

> If we read John Stuart Mill's *Representative Government* and *Liberty*— books which at one time enjoyed an enormous reputation—we find ourselves breathing the intellectual atmosphere of a society which has no relation at all with contemporary English society, and which indeed now seems altogether unreal. Who bothers anymore about the 'balance of powers' in society, or about the 'just' balance between the 'rights' of

---

may be as able and eloquent as ever,…but they are manifestly listening nervously at one end of a speaking-tube which receives at its other end the suggestions of a lower intelligence. On the other hand, the followers, who are really the rulers, are manifestly becoming impatient of the hesitations of their nominal chiefs, and the wrangling of their representatives" (38).

[28] Interestingly, Pareto "lionized" the anti-democratic qualities of Mussolini as early as 1914, when the latter was still editor of the socialist organ *Avanti*:

The fight between the fox and the lion! The one side relies only upon cunning to win its battle; there is not a word that betrays the virile, courageous spirit of the man who has a faith. The other side shows the opposite traits. The government does not care to be known as the enemy of its enemies. The latter reply that they are, and will continue to be, its enemies and the enemies of every other government of the kind; and not to understand them is indeed to be deaf and blind. So it is that the men who write for the *Avanti* show that they have the qualities of virility and frankness, the qualities that assure victory in the end and which, after all, are beneficial to the nation as a whole. The fox may, by his cunning, escape for a certain length of time, but the day may come when the lion will reach him with a well-aimed cuff, and that will be the end of the argument (Pareto 1935, vol. IV: 1789–1790).

the state and the 'rights' of the individual? Is the highly revered *ethical state* still with us?...[T]he workers prefer the tangible benefits of higher wages, progressive taxation and greater leisure (Pareto 1966: 302).

That right behind the impartial social observer stands the disconsolate champion of *laissez faire*, who has remained as convinced as ever that capitalism is the only feasible economic order, is also obvious: "It may be 'just, laudable, desirable, morally necessary' that the workers should labor only a few hours each day and receive enormous salaries; but... is this in reality possible, that is, in terms of real, not merely nominal, wages? And what will be the consequence of this state of affairs?" (303). Likewise, the theorist who claimed to have proven that democracy is impossible, shows himself acutely aware of the shift in social power to the benefit of the masses at the expense of "the stupid bourgeoisie, degenerate like all decadent elites" (312). "Slowly but surely," he observes, "the use of force passes from the upper to the lower classes" (315). Or: "Since the force of the masses is now the stronger of the two forces in conflict in our society, the bourgeois state is lurching on its foundations and its power is disintegrating. Under demagogic plutocracy, plutocracy is weakening and democracy growing ever stronger"(323). Capitalism is everywhere on the receiving end:

> The old maxim, which lies at the heart of the parliamentary system, that taxes have to be subject to the approval of those who have to pay them, has now given way, implicitly or explicitly, to another maxim: taxes have to be approved and imposed by those who do not pay them. Once upon a time, it was the serfs who were mercilessly oppressed; now it is the well-to-do.... At one time, the emigration of serfs from their native manor was strictly forbidden; in our day there is a similar restriction on the free movement of 'capital' (312).

Constant's stern warnings from a century ago, about a condition where the property-less recklessly rule through parliament, had become a living reality. The bourgeoisie's day of reckoning had arrived. Its youthful sins of political liberalism return to haunt its old age, destroying the last remains of the liberal socioeconomic order. Clearly, therefore, we should not take Pareto's dismissal of democracy at face value. In that respect, I disagree with Richard Bellamy (2002: 238): "Reformist socialism, on this account, was simply an ideology or 'derivation' employed by the prevailing ruling class to maintain their power. Like democracy, with which it had an affinity, it was well suited to elites employing the consensual methods of the 'instinct of combinations,' giving their rule a veneer of popular legitimacy." This overlooks Pareto's angst vis-à-vis the real power of the lower classes and the gains they were attaining through, precisely, "reformist socialism." To argue that it was no more than a populist veneer skillfully employed by a confident "ruling class," agrees, perhaps, with the letter of Pareto's writings, but definitely not with their spirit. It is vital to understand that underpinning Pareto's theories was not a disenchantment with a *fictitious* democracy, but a mortal fear of a *functioning* one, busily catering to the masses. Pareto was an apprehensive elitist, not a crestfallen populist.

Unsurprisingly, therefore, behind the cynical resignation of an impartial scientist, lurked a political orator. The highly expressive depictions of the extraordinary heights to which the power of "the masses" has come, their boundless insolence and the near complete impunity they enjoy, compared with the utter meekness of the bourgeoisie, in their sheer repetition, cannot fail to arouse indignation on the reader's part. Upper-class attitudes are simply too stupid, too absurd, too suicidal, to be left at that, a mere object for sociological inquiry. In their accumulated effect, the observations read like a call-for-arms, goading the upper classes and summoning their flailing courage so that they finally unite, smash "the enemy" and restore class hierarchy:

> On the one side the trumpets are sounding and the troops moving to the assault; on the other, heads are bowed in submission... [T]he upper classes have become gutless and demoralized. They patiently endure every insult, threat and oppression; they are only too anxious to avoid irritating their enemies, kissing the hand that strikes them... Even when a strike is beaten they are too weak-kneed to follow up their victory... 'I will do the commons no wrong.' The upper classes have followed this advice throughout the nineteenth century and up to the present day.... In the past, the mass of the people was opposed, not so much to the principle of paying taxes as to the manner in which the principle was exercised. Today we find that it is the 'haves' who accept the principle of being squeezed...Never uniting to throw off the burden, each one of them strives to push it off on to the next man; by such internal discords they make themselves even weaker as a social group (Pareto 1966: 320–22).

Finally, one finds a nearly explicit endorsement of a reaction in the form of a military intervention to subdue the masses:

> The masses grasp intuitively that even extremists who want to go to lengths which, for the time being at least, the rest of them do not desire, are very useful as allies. Hence in all countries we find that there is general approval for the bolshevists. The 'haves' cannot find it in themselves to counter this by supporting the opposite extreme; the terror they feel

at the mere name of 'militarism' is positively comical. Cicero perfectly represents, in the terms of his own day, the attitude which is prevalent among our well-to-do middle class. He was utterly bemused by the double dilemma posed by the violence of the rabble and the might of the legions. Nobly, but vainly, he hoped for a government of the optimates based on the favor of the people (323).

The endorsement of right-wing extremism might hence be a less noble option than parliamentary rule, but an incomparably more effective one, to ensure the triumph of "the optimates" over "the rabble." Pareto's 1921 accusations of bourgeois meekness—if accusations they indeed were, rather than veiled provocations to take action—will prove soon enough to have been unfounded. The upper- and middle-classes were not nearly as muddled and selfishly atomized not to recognize where their interest as a "social group" lay; they will not long continue to "kiss the hand that strikes them" (the English word "strike" conveys here a very appropriate double meaning), nor will they "comically" recoil for long, from rallying behind the right-wing paramilitary forces, which will emphatically subdue the striking and striking masses.

It is important to note that Pareto's all-round theoretical defense of bourgeois dictatorship is grounded entirely on the premises of economic liberalism; the main challenge confronted is the political intervention in the economy, its restriction of the "free movement of capital," and its encroachment on private property via progressive taxation, Pareto's most resented enemy and favorite target. It is *not* the comprehensive revolutionary challenge of an altogether anti-liberal, "bolshevist" alternative, that will do away with liberalism *in toto*, both *economical* and *political*. Pareto is well aware of the fact that such an extreme option lacks the masses support. The threat of political liberalism, of mass democracy, is sufficient, for an economic liberal like Pareto, to justify the seizure of power by the despotic lion. Fascism is seen as a means to rescind all the social achievements of the working class since the expansion of the suffrage, the eight-hour work day, the right to unionize and strike, the gains in wages, and, last but not least, the possibility to impose progressive taxation. As Pareto puts it: "what is withheld from the taxman is withheld from the enemy" (323). In fact, to the extent that political liberalism does not interfere with the economy, and remains restricted to its original functions of guaranteeing diverse bourgeois liberties, Pareto can be said to have remained a political liberal even after his vehement rejection of democracy. Thus, in an essay published posthumously, *Pochi "punti" di un futuro ordinamento costituzionale* (*Some "Points" Concerning a Future Constitutional Order*), (Pareto 1974), while generally approving of fascist measures and alluding to Mussolini as a *"capitano geniale"* (a leader of genius), he asks him nonetheless to respect civil liberties, not to introduce corporatist economic measures, not to restrict freedom of expression, etc. Pareto thus wished for a conservative lion to face the workers, but for a liberal fox—or maybe even a rabbit?—to treat the bourgeoisie.

Engels and Gumplowicz Outlining the Overthrow from Above

The structural crisis of liberalism, its immense difficulties to accommodate mass democracy and its tendency to embrace a dictatorial option to escape from the menace of socialism, were thus recognized, by the end of the 19th century, by astute observers across the political spectrum. The problem, first clearly observed in 1848, was now visibly approaching a denouement. As the liberal apprentice was overwhelmed by the laboring mops, the fascist sorcerer was beginning to cast his shadow, though a flickering one, not yet betraying the precise features of its owner. On the left, writing in 1895, Friedrich Engels was remarkably anticipating dictatorship, as the response of the ruling classes to the fact that the liberal rule of law does not serve them any longer, and instead plays into the hands of their antagonists, the Social Democrats:

> The irony of world history turns everything upside down. We, the 'revolutionaries,' the 'overthrowers'—we are thriving far better on legal methods than on illegal methods and overthrow. *The parties of order*, as they call themselves, *are perishing under the legal conditions created by themselves*. They cry despairingly with Odilon Barrot: la *légalité nous tue*, legality is the death of us; whereas we, under this legality, get firm muscles and rosy cheeks and look like life eternal. And if *we* are not so crazy as to let ourselves be driven to street fighting in order to please them, then in the end there is nothing left for them to do but themselves break through this dire legality.... They can cope with the Social-Democratic overthrow, which just now is doing so well by keeping the law, only by *an overthrow on the part of the parties of Order*, an overthrow which cannot live without breaking the law. Mr. Roessler, the Prussian bureaucrat, and Mr. von Boguslawski, the Prussian general, have shown them the only way perhaps still possible of getting at the workers, who simply refuse to let themselves be lured into street fighting. Breach of the constitution, dictatorship, return to absolutism, *regis voluntas suprema lex*!

[The King's will is the supreme law!] (Engels 1895; Engels emphasizes the word 'we' and the French and Latin phrases. The other italics are mine.).

So an overthrow from above, an elimination of the rule of law not by its mortal enemies but by the very people who forged it, was not simply a product of the conditions created by the First World War and the ensuing crisis. Engels was putting his finger on the roots of the fascist "solution," as the "overthrow on the part of the parties of Order." To be sure, he did not and could not foresee the exact nature of this overthrow. Preceding the cataclysm of the Great War—which Engels, by the way, also saw coming as part of the escalating international imperialistic struggle[29]—and living under the Hohenzollern rule, he could not know that it would eventually be undertaken to make the Führer / Duce's "will the supreme law," not that of the King. But he could clearly perceive the structural basis for a future dictatorship, the junking of political liberalism precisely on the part of the self-proclaimed forces of law and order.

The lawmakers shall be the lawbreakers: such a realization was not reserved to the radical left. On the part of the conservative forces, we can bring in Ludwig Gumplowicz, the Austrian sociologist, and an important trailblazer of German Social Darwinism, who analyzed the basic constellation of social forces in terms strikingly similar to those of Engels. He, too, in 1885, realized that the triumph of the bourgeoisie over the aristocracy was to a certain extent pyrrhic, since it entailed the further challenge of the working-class, the "fourth estate," which then used the legal weapons of political liberalism against the bourgeoisie:

> The bourgeoisie in the struggle with the other property classes is *the first to appeal to universal human rights*, to freedom and equality.... And it succeeds *not without the support of the masses* whom it flatters...Its might like that of the higher class is now based on right, and though *for the moment* what it has won seems to be clear gain, *it has found the yoke of legal logic about its neck and must submit to its ideas*. For the lowest classes participation in the struggle was a profitable experience.... [I]n spite of exaggerations [the social demands of the masses] are logical consequences of principles which the ruling class asserted in its own interest and from which the middle class profited declaring them at the time

---

[29] Cf. his analysis of the European situation (Engels 1893).

to be universal. They cannot be *wholly eradicated*; they aid the struggle for the emancipation of the fourth class powerfully (Gumplowicz 1899: 149–150; emphases added).

Against this ensuing radicalism, Gumplowicz then adds, with an air of scientific finality, a dictatorship must inexorably ensue, which against the preponderance of "right" (i.e., of political liberalism and the rule of law), will re-assert the supremacy of "might":

> The false consequences must be corrected step by step back to the point where might of its 'own right' as spontaneous factor of public life undertakes the control of a society tired of revolution. This completes the period of evolution in the social struggle: from the freedom and equality of the anarchic horde through might and inequality, right and law to the freedom and equality of revolution and state-destroying anarchy; and from this *unbearable condition* to the *despotic might of reaction* and the beginning of a new period of evolution (149–50; emphases added).

"La *légalité nous tue*" and "the yoke of legal logic," were two ways of pointing at the same liberal impasse and disclosing the in-built necessity, on the part of the bourgeoisie, to brush aside such political obstacles and legal inhibitions, if social and economic privilege (Gumplowicz's "might") is to be preserved.[30]

Historians have often commented on the turn to "legal positivism" which characterized post-unification Germany, highlighting the way that legal issues were interpreted in an evermore rigid, narrow and formalistic form, disregarding the ethical and social dimensions of the law; yet this was usually construed as just another symptom of increasing German 'anti-liberalism.' Legalistic formalism supposedly reflected the way that authoritarian, feudal sections of German society, notably the Junkers, were able to impose their attitudes on a bourgeoisie which lacked the verve and the vision necessary to defend its emancipatory and liberal project, hence embarking on the road to fascism. Questioning the wisdom of this explanation, David Blackbourn incisively suggested to understand this development as emanating from the contradictions of bourgeois society itself, from the tensions

---

[30] Pareto, in his 1906 *Manuel d'Economie Politique*, admonishes the triumphant masses that the "democratic evolution" of the 19th century is bound, sooner or later, to be reversed. Against democracy, a reaction must come: "But history will not halt at the present stage of evolution. If life in the future is not to be wholly different in character than life in the past, the existing evolutionary process will be succeeded by a development in the contrary direction" (Pareto 1966: 154).

between the formal political equality promoted by liberalism and the substantive, economic inequality it presupposed. "Equality before the law and the sanctity of property rights," he pointed out, "stood in a potentially awkward relationship to each other.... Retreat into a narrow conception of the law was a response to the possibility that the law might become an arena invaded by social conflict" (Blackbourn and Eley 1984: 222–3). In other words, it was not so much the bourgeoisie which failed to defend the law, but rather the law which became a threat to the bourgeoisie. As a result of this quandary, bourgeois legal attitudes, according to Blackbourn, shifted "away from the idea of law as an offensive weapon against absolutist restrictions and corporate privilege, towards a more conservative view that what had to be inculcated was a 'sense of the law'. Law, in short, had started to become synonymous with order" (223). Yet, we may add, with Engels and Gumplowicz in mind, not even this transformation was sufficient to defuse the explosive, legal rise of the masses. The bourgeoisie was thus forced to move one step further away from its original embrace of legalism, into outright reaction, a breach of the law. This was a drama which unfolded in three main acts:

1) Law against order: the initial, *progressive* phase pitted the liberal law against the absolutist order.
2) Law and order: then came a *conservative* phase, where liberal law and the bourgeois order coincided—the phase of legal positivism.
3) Order against law: defensive positivism, in turn, would be superseded by an aggressively *reactionary* stage, in which the bourgeois order rebelled against the liberal law.

We shall have an opportunity below to discuss the position of a key defender and theorist of this third and last stage, the legal expert Carl Schmitt, justifying the Nazi dictatorship as a way of salvaging the state from parliamentary chaos.

To roughly the same extent that political liberalism was abandoned by economic liberals, tenets of political liberalism were embraced and defended by the sworn enemies of economic liberalism, the socialists. It would be difficult to think of a better example than Engels himself, who, in the same text, went as far as arguing against the possibility-desirability of a violent revolution. He deemed barricade fighting anachronistic, made impossible by the development of modern weaponry that provides the forces of order with hugely effective means of repression. Engels hence warned socialists against the folly of taking to the streets, since this would only provide the reactionaries with the best pretext for establishing a dictatorship and arresting *the democratic, and legal, rise* of socialism. The brooms are no longer violently revolutionary; they comfortably float and rise upon the tidal surges of political liberalism. Use of violence, instead, recommends itself to the liberal apprentice, who must break the legal spell of the masses, no matter what it takes. To such a task, however, only "the despotic might" of the sorcerer would be equal.

CHAPTER TWO

LIBERAL ECONOMICS, FASCIST POLITICS:
"A WONDERFUL WEDLOCK"

When dealing with their historical object of study, representations of fascism often employ a kind of Brechtian *Verfremdungseffekt* (usually rendered "distancing effect" in English), yet in the opposite sense to that meant by Brecht. The German dramatist, that is, aimed to cast everyday social reality under suspicion, to make us feel awkward and uncomfortable about what we usually take to be natural and unalterable conditions, therewith encouraging a critical appraisal of the present. By contrast, many a narrator of fascism describes the fascist *past* as bizarre, improbable, so utterly different from our own social and political reality, that we become, whether this is intended or not, comfortable, complacent and *un*critical about our *present*. Alastair Hamilton (1971: xv), for example, states that his choice to focus on intellectuals who were attracted to fascism was motivated by the wish "to examine, through them, some of those illusions which hung over Europe until the collapse of the Third Reich, some of those myths which now, less than thirty years after the war, seem so unreal, so absurd, so profoundly alien to us." Yet was fascism really so thoroughly alien to what we now consider socially, politically and economically normal? Does it indeed fly in the face of the presuppositions and norms of our own, post-fascist, Western order? With Pareto, I showed how support for fascism could have been compatible with tenets—"mythical" and "illusive" or not—that still sharply define our reality, such as "the free market economy," "the benefits of unbridled competition," etc. Today, if anything, such principles are even more strictly adhered to than during the early seventies of the former century, when Hamilton wrote his book. Yet I propose to have a look at one of the intellectuals discussed by Hamilton himself, Oswald Spengler, who played a somewhat similar role in ideologically preparing the ground for German fascism, as Pareto did within the Italian context. Revisiting his theories, where does Spengler stand in relation to our liberal society?

Spengler: The "Will to Property"

Spengler, no doubt, reveals himself an outspoken critic of liberalism, for example when he disparages (1980: 112) the "materialistic science which was founded around 1770 by A. Smith in the circle of Hartley, Priestley, Mandeville and Bentham, and which had the presumption to regard humans as accessories of the economic condition, and to 'explain' history with the notions of price, market and commodity." Such statements, combined with his effort to distill a new, improved, non-Marxist socialism, which he called "Prussian socialism," were seized upon by those attempting to construe German fascism as an attack on liberalism. For example, in his book *The Long Way to the West*, the German liberal historian H. A. Winkler traces the way Germany finally managed to join the capitalistic and liberal West in the latter half of the 20th century, following its calamitous detour from western paths during the 19th century, which culminated in National Socialism. Spengler is presented as a typical example of this anti-liberal German affliction, so arduously conquered; Winkler thus associates the philosopher and cultural critic with socialism, if a decidedly anti-Marxist one, peculiarly indifferent to the question of property (Winkler 2002: 464–5). He takes very seriously Spengler's endorsement of socialism, and paraphrases him to that effect: "The great world-issue... is the choice between the Prussian or the English idea, socialism or capitalism, state or parliament" (464). So Spengler, according to Winkler, was *a socialist*, albeit idiosyncratically, and a determined *opponent of capitalism*. And yet, epithets aside, what did Spengler's social and economic programme entail? How did he, a Prussian socialist and anti-capitalist, envision the ideal relationship between employers and workers? We already know that this socialism is not to be confused with Marxism and had no interest in transforming property relations. So what was it really after? In the great "world-issue" between socialism and capitalism, what concessions was it willing to make to the former, and what were its grievances with the latter?

Bearing in mind the widespread view of fascism as some third road between capitalism and communism, one might surmise that "Prussian socialism" designated some project of "mixed economy," a *völkisch*, authoritarian anticipation of post-War social-democracy, aiming to erect on the basis of capitalistic production and property relations a form of welfare state, guaranteeing fundamental work and living standards to the workers; Spengler's aim, putatively, was a kind of paternalistic socialism from above, which grants to the workers at least some of the benefits they might have attained by engaging themselves in class struggle, as they would have done in Marxist socialism. Yet Spengler's writings reveal him a most consistent and principled *opponent* of such a model. He endorsed a strict separation between the economic sphere and the political one, if by "politics" we understand any form of extra-economic intervention in the economy meant to favor the working-class, regardless of whether such intervention is a result of the workers' own initiative or is undertaken on their behalf from above. He states that "The labour leader won the War," which has led to a regrettable condition in which trade unions abuse their political power to inveigh against economic life:

> The governments, everywhere in the world, have since 1916 become more and more rapidly dependent on them and are obliged to obey their orders if they do not wish to be overthrown. These brutal interventions in the structure and meaning of economic life they must either accept or carry out themselves.... The natural centre of gravity of the economic body, the economic judgment of the real experts, was replaced by an artificial, non-expert, party-political one.... Have not the men with creative economic talents, those who sustain private economic enterprise, been sacrificed to this dictatorship...? (Spengler 1980: 145–6).

Notice that Spengler's vantage point is expressly that of "private economic enterprise" [*privaten Wirtschaftsstrebens*]. Vis-à-vis the workers, he is a classical economic liberal. To "intervene" in "the structure and meaning of economic life" is "brutal," and there is no suggestion that such measures would be any less violent or vicious if initiated by the state. Prussian socialism further rules out any form of unionized pressure on the economy, either through parliamentary action or through strikes, which are not to be tolerated. "The strike," Spengler maintains, "is the *unsocialistic* earmark of Marxism." Conveniently associating strikes with capitalistic mentality allows him to oppose them precisely from the standpoint of a devout socialist:

> It is the classical indication of [the strike's] origins in a businessman's philosophy to which Marx belonged by instinct and habit.... It was therefore an English attitude which, in our German Revolution [the Spartacist revolution], designed for the worker to exploit the rest of the people, by squeezing out of the least amount of work, as much money as possible...The *Prussian* conception...includes the *prohibition of the strike*, since it is an anti-state, private commercial [*händlerisch*] means (Spengler 1933d: 81–82).

Spengler vexes indignantly about the shortening of the working day, too. Not even this most basic of achievements on the part of traditional socialism can have a place within the scheme of its Prussian namesake. Spengler's socialistic ideal is, rather, from the 18th century, when "the working day amounted to more than twelve hours." Ever since that time, a harmful shortening of the natural length of the working day has been advancing, steadily curbing industrial output:

> From that time the trade unions of all countries undertook to exert increasing pressure to reduce the working day still more and to extend the rule to all wage-earners. Towards the end of the [19th] century the limit was nine hours, and at the end of the World War eight hours. Today, as we approach the middle of the 20th century, the forty-hour week is the minimum of the revolutionary demand. Since at the same time the ban on Sunday work is more strictly enforced, the individual worker delivers only half of the original, possible, and natural quantum of what he has to sell—namely, labour.... What profession would tolerate so slight an output? (Spengler 1980: 147–8).

In Spengler's Prussian utopia, the workers can hence look forward to working even on Sunday. It need hardly be said that progressive taxation and political pressure to increase wages are detestable in Spengler's eyes. He expends great energy in denouncing what he terms the current *Lohndiktatur* or *Lohnbolschewismus* ("wage-dictatorship" and "wage-bolshevism") of the trade unions; similarly, in a 1924 lecture dedicated to the issue of taxation, he excoriates the imposition of taxes on the rich, which has become nothing short of a "question of life and death" (Spengler 1933c: 299). He there equates the "West-European taxation policies" with "dry Bolshevism, which threatens to level down everything which protrudes above the masses" (309). In terms difficult to tell apart from those of a stringent economic liberal, he concludes this address by pressing to eliminate the political-democratic administration of taxation and—looking ahead to such organizations as *The World Trade Organization* or *The International Monetary Fund?*—to entrust all decisions on such matters to economic experts, a "world conference of insiders to the economic life." "The more 'just' a tax is," he avows, "the more unjust it is today. In the evaluation of such things the economy has the first word, not the jurist, the professional politician or the fiscal civil servant" (310).

Yet Spengler does not stop at that. Under his terms, not only are Marx, Bebel or Bernstein unacceptable, but the welfare policies of the great Prussian Prince Bismarck, whom Spengler greatly admires, are nonetheless equally to be excluded from Prussian Socialism. From an utmost Social Darwinist position, Spengler argues against any form of insurance, since "Every human being has, like every animal, to defend himself against the incalculable workings of destiny—or to submit to them. Each has his *own personal cares, full responsibility* for himself, and must inevitably make his own decisions in all dangers threatening himself and his aims." He who for whatever reason fails to cope with the trials and tribulations of existence must "bear the consequences and beg or go under in any other way he pleases. Such is life." Hence the decadence and "shrinking vitality" embodied in "the craving to insure oneself, against old age, accident, sickness, unemployment" (Spengler 1980: 151).

Spengler's socio-economic agenda constitutes a firm refutation of all the gains, big and small, that socialism in Germany and Europe obtained during the 19th century and the first decades of the 20th. No socialist, in the traditional sense, would see this agenda as anything but strictly antithetical to her own. For the worker, Prussian Socialism means working a whole lot, for the absolute minimum, but—and this is a vital aspect—being *happy* about it. Such socialism is not out to free the worker from the burden of hard work, but from the burden of *being ashamed* of hard work. For this is precisely what distinguishes the awesomely spiritual Prussian worker from the materialistically corrupt English one:

> Marx teaches therewith *contempt for work....* Work—hard, long, fatiguing—is a misfortune, effortless gain is a blessing.... [T]he manual labourer is in England more a slave than anywhere else. He is *morally* a slave; he feels that his occupation excludes him from having the title of a Gentleman.... This accounts for Marx's mental attitude, out of which arose his social critique and which had made him so disastrous for *genuine* socialism. He knew the nature of work only in its English version... The English lack the sense of the *dignity* of hard work.... Had Marx understood the sense of Prussian work, that of activity for its own sake, of service in the name of the collective [*Gesamtheit*], for 'all' and not for oneself, as a duty, which ennobles regardless of the *kind* of work, his Manifesto would probably never have been written (Spengler 1933d: 77–78).

"Prussian socialism" thus boils down to "English capitalism" shorn of worker's discontent. On this particular point, as on many others, Spengler echoed Friedrich Nietzsche (1997: 125), who likewise fantasized about a "happy slave": "poor, happy and a slave!—these things

can also go together and I can think of no better news I could give
to our factory slaves." With regard to the workers, Spengler's programme closely corresponded to a "Manchesterian" agenda, defending the primacy of the economy over politics and outlawing any social
regulation of the market. Hence the insufficiency—subtle but important—of those assessments which maintain that Spengler, though not
a Marxist socialist, still endorsed an idiosyncratic kind of socialism.
What such allegations obscure, even as they admit the unusual nature
of Spengler's "socialism," is the fact that behind it stood, precisely,
capitalism. As Spengler himself acknowledged in virtually as many
words: "Socialism, as I understand it, postulates a market economy
[*Privatwirtschaft*] with the old-Germanic delight it takes in power and
spoils" (Spengler 1933a: vii–viii).[1] Spengler abhorred all socialism and,
by contrast, wholeheartedly embraced, indeed celebrated, most tenets
of capitalism, such as competition and property accumulation:

> When the wealth that has accumulated among the ruling class is annihi-
> lated by the attacks of the mob, when it becomes suspicious and disdain-
> ful, a danger to the owners, then the Nordic will to acquire property, to
> power through property, ceases to create that wealth. The economic-
> spiritual ambition dies out. Competition no longer pays (Spengler 1980:
> 167–8).
>   [N]o race has such a strong instinct of possession as the Germanic,
> and that precisely because it has been the strongest-willed of all histori-
> cal races. Will-to-property is the Nordic sense of life. It rules and lends
> form to our entire history, from the conquering expeditions of semi-
> mythical kings down to the form of the family at the present day, which
> dies when the idea of property fades out. He who lacks the instinct for
> this, is not 'of race' (176).

He went still further to vindicate even the most extravagant socioeconomic inequalities. While protesting against the "luxury wages" politically extorted by the workers, Spengler makes the "genuine luxury" of
the rich equivalent with culture itself and as such indispensable:

> High culture is inseparably bound up with luxury and wealth.... And
> wealth, collected in few hands and among the ruling classes, is among
> other things the prerequisite for the education of generations of leading-
> minds through the model of a highly developed environment without

---

[1] The sentence quoted is from the introduction to this collection of writings, dated
October 1932.

which there is no healthy economic life and no development of political capacity (109).

Luxuries for the rich, asceticism for the poor; the injunction of any intervention in the market in the name of a healthy economy; the stress on the harm of strikes and the need to keep wages down; the belief in self-reliance, competition and individual enterprise: do such views sound absurd and alien to modern ears? Or is there rather, at least in that non-negligent respect of socioeconomic policies, an alarming continuity between such fascist absurdity and our own neo-liberal everyday? For if Spengler's views are "absurd," so is the entire modern economy. If Spengler provides a good idea of what fascist ideology was about, it seems that we need a counter *Verfremdungseffekt*, not a de-familiarization of fascism but precisely a familiarization of it, to do justice to the profound affinities it exhibits within our own social reality. Or is the fascist absurdity to be found not in its economics, but in the racist assumptions in which it was embedded, assumptions that have now become notorious? And yet Spengler, for one, when he speaks about the threat posed by the "colored races" to the whites, explains this in terms which, rhetorical excesses apart, would be quite familiar to modern ears:

> [I]ndustry...is now free to migrate, and it does so, indeed moving everywhere away from the domain of white trade-union dictatorships into countries with low wages. The dispersion of Western industry has been in full swing since 1900. The mills of India were established as branches of English factories, with the idea of getting 'nearer the consumer.' Such was the original intention, but the West-European luxury wages have produced a completely different result. In the United States industry has migrated more and more from Chicago and New York to the Negro areas in the South, and it will not halt at the Mexican frontier. There are growing industrial areas in China, Java, South Africa, South America. The flight of highly developed techniques to the colored areas continues, and the white luxury-wage is beginning to be rather theoretical, since the work by which it is earned is no longer needed (162–3).

Since "the colored" work for a small fee, industries reallocate to the colored (read: third world) countries, which means that white workers remain with no occupation or have to stomach drastic wage reductions. Again, nothing preposterous here, just neo-liberal commonplace in an age of full-blown globalization. This sounds like a standard complaint of many contemporary voices on the right, not least in Germany. Thus, for example, in an assiduously advertised television broadcast accompanied by a book, *The Case of Germany. Decline of a Superstar* (Steingart 2005), the steady devaluation of the German economy is blamed on years of deteriorating work ethic, employees' hedonism and inflated wages, that make the German economy powerless to compete with other national industries, where wages are low and the workers thrifty and tireless. Hence, in Spengler's spirit, Germany's decline (and, we may add, the decline of the west).

Given Spengler's intractable opposition to socialism and his profound convergence with economic liberalism, it is strange that he should resentfully gainsay such icons of capitalist doctrine as Adam Smith or speak about the "English idea" always with disdain. What is the source of such critique? It is twofold. To start with, in harmony with the pattern we have been tracing, Spengler's grievance with liberalism has to do with its *political and cultural superstructure*. Far from subservient to the demands of the "healthy economy," bourgeois rationalism, by turning its back on tradition and employing reason produces political economy which, in turn, culminates in ... socialism:

> This revolution does not commence with the materialistic Socialism of the 19th century, still less with the Bolshevism of 1917. It has been 'in permanence' ... since the middle of the 18th century. It was then that rational critique, proudly named the philosophy of Enlightenment, began to switch its object of destructive activity from the theological systems of Christianity ... to the facts of actuality, the state, society, and finally the evolved forms of economics. It commenced by emptying the concepts of nation, right, government, of their historical content, and interpreting the difference of rich and poor quite materialistically ... Here belongs 'political economy,' a materialistic science which was founded around 1770 by A. Smith in the circle of Hartley, Priestley, Mandeville and Bentham, and which had the presumption to regard humans as accessories of the economic condition, and to 'explain' history with the notions of price, market and commodity. From this derives the understanding of work not as the content of life and profession, but as the commodity in which the worker trades (Spengler 1980: 112–13).

Adam Smith is thus diagnosed as a founding father of communism, not of capitalism. And J. S. Mill and Herbert Spencer equally belong in that genealogy: "The English-liberal literature of Mill and Spencer ... supplies the 'world outlook' to the higher schools in India. The way from there to Marx the young reformers find by themselves" (199). The problem with the materialism of the liberals, a favorite target for fascists, has nothing to do with their decadent pursuit of luxuries or their insatiable greed—both of which, as we have just seen, Spengler gleefully justifies; he rather balks at its dispensing with age-old myths, the unveiling of the materialistic dynamic of market forces, and hence the exposure of such forces to a critique. Though using reason to support the market, the liberals endow the socialists with the analytical tools they need to *denounce* it. This rational impetus, coupled with the political reforms of liberalism, above all "universal suffrage," lead inexorably to socialism. The sequence could not be more clearly recorded: "This active liberalism progresses consequentially from Jacobinism to Bolshevism. This is no opposition between thought and will. It is the early and the late form, the beginning and the end of a unified movement" (115). Spengler deplores the way political liberalism did not beget or accommodate economic liberalism, but its very opposite, socialism and its derivations. The historic significance of the 1848 revolutions is likewise accredited: "It was only about 1840 that this 'social-political' tendency passes into an 'economic-political' one." Instead of undergirding capitalism, liberalism instigates an assault on its productive forces: "The scapegoats are now no longer the aristocrats, but the possessors, from peasant to entrepreneur" (115). Spengler scoffs at the idea that socialist upheaval, even at it most radical, is a force threatening the west from without. "Bolshevism," he affirms, "originated in Western Europe, and born indeed of consequential necessity as the last phase of the liberal democracy of 1770 and the last triumph of political rationalism" (120). Hence the logic of *attacking liberalism* from a *capitalist point of view*. To dissolve political liberalism would therefore mean, with an equal consequential necessity, the first step in arresting socialism and shielding capitalism. Therefore, whatever else Spengler attacks when he disparages the "English idea," it is decidedly *not* English capitalism, to be replaced by a "socialistic" Prussian idea, as liberal interpreters would have us believe. On the contrary, Spengler describes the way democratic pettiness had extinguished the formerly admirable English drive towards expansion and acquisition, whereas Germany, along with the USA, are declared the countries that have taken over the torch of capitalist imperialism:

> Galsworthy has portrayed the tragedy of this dying out with profound and painful insight in his Forsyte Saga. It signifies the economic triumph of the rentier-ideal over capitalist imperialism. One still possesses considerable fragments of former wealth, but the drive to fight for a new one is lacking. The methods of trade and commerce are falling slowly out of date, and the creative energy to reform them on American and German models is absent (84–85).

Quite like Donoso or Pareto before him, Spengler deplores the "blind-ness and cowardice of liberalism," the way it provides its butcher with the knife and then marches to the slaughterhouse:

> Facing the demagogic trend, liberalism is the form of suicide committed by our sick society. With this perspective it gives itself up. The merciless, embittered class war that is waged against it finds it ready to capitulate politically, after having helped spiritually to forge the enemy's weapons. Only the conservative element, weak as it was in the 19th century, can and will in the future, prevent the coming of this end (125).

What Spengler refers to as "conservatism" is thus simply a means to shelter liberal society from itself, rescue the economic order from the suicidal tendencies of its politically liberal "protectors." Like Donoso, Spengler palpably shows how "conservatism" and "anti-liberalism" are not necessarily motivated by opposition to capitalism or a longing for the socioeconomic order predating it, but can come precisely to succor the economic liberal order in its hour of greatest need. Con-servatives are thus willing to toss out the bathwater of political lib-eralism to save the baby of capitalism. This would challenge claims such as Michael Mann's (2004: 77), that "the lightning rod" of the fascist "crisis was not liberalism but conservatism." As Spengler's case illustrates, and we will have additional occasions to confirm this impression, the dividing lines between liberalism and conservatism are much vaguer than Mann allows for. Modern "conservatism," in many cases, was interested in conserving, precisely, capitalism, i.e., the liberal economic order, from democracy and socialism. In the words of the German-American conservative Leo Strauss (1968: ix), writ-ing in post-Second-World-War USA: "The conservatism of our age is identical with what originally was liberalism." Strauss, too, realized that there is a "liberalism" before and after the split, at least implicitly identifying his own position with classical liberalism, as opposed to the modern one: "Being liberal in the original sense is so little incompat-ible with being conservative that generally speaking it goes together with a conservative posture" (x).[2] To assume that conservatism had some strictly independent agenda, positing a pre-capitalist past, is questionable, though some such voices doubtlessly existed. Even more problematic is to ascribe to such harking back to the middle ages or the Roman Empire, the decisive role in motivating or directing fascist

---

[2] In the last chapter I return to examine Strauss' position more closely.

policies as opposed to such nostalgic gestures fulfilling a function that was primarily decorative and liturgical.

Spengler, however, and here we come to the second disagreement he had with liberalism, did not simply favor the economy over politics. Far from it. He was contemptuous of the liberal notion that the economy is a separate sphere that should be prioritized over politics and emphasized repeatedly that it is in fact politics that must come first. When speaking of politics, Spengler additionally specified that he does not have in mind the party politics of petty parliamentary rule, that, in his view, hardly counts as politics and is merely part of the democratic malaise. "Politics," for Spengler, means "grand politics," foreign policy, directing the affairs of the nation in the global struggle for supremacy. Into this overarching national goal, the economy must be integrated:

> For, as must be said again and again: the economy is no self-contained realm; it is indissolubly bound up with great politics; it is unthinkable without a strong foreign policy, and therefore, in the last resort, it is dependent upon the military strength of the country in which it lives or dies. But what is the sense of defending a fortress if the enemy is within it, if treason in the form of class war leaves it unclear whom and what one is really defending? (Spengler 1980: 170–1).

Spengler's view of the proper relationship of economics to politics can be illustrated with the following table:

small politics (socialism / democracy)	<	the economy (capitalism)	<	great politics (imperialism)

Juxtaposing the two elements of Spengler's worldview, a *market economy* geared towards *national greatness*, we get a political combination which should objectively be termed "national capitalism," or, maybe, "Prussian imperialism." Socialism in any meaningful sense just does not come into it at all. In fact, socialism is precisely that which is expurgated *at both levels*: at the economic sphere since it impedes growth, and at the "great" political sphere since it posits peaceful international coexistence, which would make impossible the Spenglerian endorsement of imperialism. Socialism is but the traitor that must be driven out of the fortress. We can now understand why Spengler himself, in his later years, explicitly took the air out of his former "socialism": "Here a great education is necessary, which I have called Prussian and which for all I care might be called 'socialistic'—what do words matter!" (210). But why did Spengler, being for all practical purposes a capitalist, use the term socialism in the first place? Why couldn't he have just brandished a project of "Prussian Imperialism," which would have represented his views infinitely better than the banner of "Prussian Socialism"? It is not difficult to guess the answer, unless one is straightjacketed by an approach that construes fascists as forthright. Capitalism had scarce little popular appeal after the First World War and amidst protracted world economic crisis. A much better prospect for supporters of capitalism lay in feigning to embrace socialism, so as to infiltrate it inside an ideological and political Trojan horse and defeat it from within. What might have been better, under such historical circumstances, than endorsing capitalism, without having to bear its unpopular reputation? This is the rationale behind *most* fascist flirtations with socialist slogans and gestures, their strange fascination with all kinds of socialisms and their abhorrence of all kinds of liberalisms, though some fascists were more sincere about it, and many adherents of fascism certainly have taken the bait to some degree or another. But we shall address this in greater detail when discussing the roots of fascist propaganda and the contradictions it entailed.

So, would it be right to say that Spengler—and by extension the fascists (Hitler's views on the relation of economics and politics will be examined in the next section)—were both liberal, with regards to the domestic economy, and anti-liberal, as far as the subordination of capitalism to imperialistic schemes is concerned? This would perhaps be true at a theoretical level, comparing fascism with liberalism on a strictly ideological plane and putting a nationalist treatise written by Spengler next to one written, say, by Adam Smith. Examined historically and practically, however, such theoretical distinctions lose much of their significance. For liberalism in practice was never simply the autonomy of the economy as secluded from the national and political context. This holds true even with regard to 19th century liberalism, putatively at its purest, preceding the compromises and contaminations of so-called "late," or "organized" or "monopoly" capitalism. Let us just think of J. S. Mill, an official of the British East India Company, to confirm the conjugation of liberalism with imperialism. Is 19th century English capitalism at all conceivable without the vital role of the state, for example in employing its military force in defense and promotion of Britain's foreign trade? Again, it suffices to think of Mill's support of military intervention to eliminate obstacles to English trade during The Second Opium War, which was granted precisely in the name of free trade: the Chinese opposition to the opium trade, he argued, restricts the freedom of the Chinese customer to choose what goods he would like to acquire:

> [T]here are questions relating to interference with trade, which are essentially questions of liberty; such as...the prohibition of the impor-tation of opium into China;...all cases, in short, where the object of the interference is to make it impossible or difficult to obtain a particular commodity. These interferences are objectionable, not as infringements on the liberty of the producer or seller, but on that of the buyer (Mill 1905: 180–1).[3]

This is a fine example of the way *laissez faire* combines forces with imperialism. And this does not change with 20th century capitalism, both before and *after* the fascist period. At the vanguard of the West-ern capitalist-liberal order, did US predominance rest on the primacy of the capitalist economy as divorced from foreign policy? Far from it. The American victors over fascism, in the aftermath of the Sec-ond World War, coined the term "the military-industrial complex" (president Eisenhower, 1961) to designate, precisely, the symbiosis of the economy with political and military aims.[4] So we see that fascism cannot claim the invention of either a path-breaking or a heretic amal-gam of national capitalism, compromising the purity of the market. Liberalism as such, in practice, always strove to combine the *primacy of the economy* vis-à-vis the working class, with the *primacy of the political*, with regard to the requirements of expansion and acquisition of new markets—if need be, with the aid of military force and at all events with political mediation, coordination, and regulation. So, in that regard, Italian and German fascism cannot be accused of distort-ing liberalism or, at least, of doing something from which classical liberal countries such as England or the USA refrained.

In general, one should be wary of any idealistic treatment of fascism and *laissez faire*. It has become commonplace among liberal and neo-liberal critics of fascism to present it as an economic system in which the state assumes large scale control over the market, and hence as

---

[3] For an excellent discussion of Mill's general commitment to imperialism see Sul-livan (1983).

[4] Eisenhower, be it noted, used this term critically, admonishing against such sym-biosis. But can it be doubted that such a warning has remained unheeded?

a form of socialism.[5] Equally, many contemporary admirers of Mussolini or Hitler hailed the corporatist organization as a superior solution to the social problem. This, they avowed, attests to fascism having superseded both capitalism and socialism. Both detractors and adherents conveniently registered the deviance from the doctrines of classical economy and refrained from putting the question historically and concretely, namely *on whose side* and *for whose benefit* did the fascists intervene in the economy? John Weiss' comment remains useful in contradicting such procedure:

> Although both regimes interfered with the economy and directed business policies to a great extent, this should not be taken as evidence for the 'mixed' or left-right character of Fascist and Nazi rule. On the contrary, as in Germany, controls were intended to make militarism a means for eventually resolving social and economic problems without recourse to liberal and radical domestic reforms. Hitler used tax relief policies, for example, to push production by heavy industry to a maximum…and companies were forced by controls to reinvest soaring profits in industrial expansion and government loans (Weiss 1967: 105).[6]

Thus, regarded historically, the market was intervened in *from the right*, to boost the socioeconomic and political interests of capitalism. This point was made with characteristic judiciousness by the great historian and anti-fascist political figure, Gaetano Salvemini, concerning Mussolini's dictatorship, which he knew and understood like few others. An acute observer of reality, free of dogmatism, he began by historicizing and contextualizing the lofty ideals of market purity, drawing attention to their concrete function in the profane here and now rather than focusing on their immaculate purity in an idealistic ever after. His lucid words deserve to be quoted at some length as an antidote to the (pseudo-)naïve Platonism of the neo-liberals:

> The policy of intervention in economic life is characteristic neither of free, nor of despotic, nor of oligarchical, nor of democratic governments. All governments in all periods have intervened, more or less thoroughly, in the economic life of their countries…Whether capitalists or proletarians, men are not favorable in an absolute sense either to *laissez-faire* or state intervention. They invoke such intervention when they expect

---

[5] Indeed for Mises, as we have seen, it represented socialism at its purest. Hayek, for his part, wrote of "The Socialist Roots of Nazism," in his *The Road to Serfdom*.

[6] In Weiss' discussion, it should be noted, the term "liberal" was used not to indicate liberal economics, but as broadly synonymous with radical, left-wing, social measures.

to profit by it, and they repulse it when they foresee no advantage or fear a positive injury from its action.... The world nowadays [Salvemini is writing in the 1930s] teems with people who have fits of enthusiasm whenever they hear of state intervention, planned economy, five-year plans, and the end of *laissez-faire*. They do not care to ask who are the social groups in whose interests the state, i.e., bureaucracy and the party in power, is to intervene and plan. It is for them a matter of indifference whether the *laissez-faire* of big business is limited in order to protect the little fellow and the worker, or the *laissez-faire* of the little fellow and the worker is sacrificed to the interests of big business.... Yet the first question which should be asked when invoking the end of *laissez-faire* is precisely this: in the interests of whom should such abolition take place? (Salvemini 1969: 379).

After solidly grounding and formulating the basic question, Salvemini proceeded to characterize Italian fascism as a limited planned economy deferential to capitalism and, going still further than Weiss, underlined the important fact that such economic intervention was scarcely different from that witnessed by other, western economies, whose capitalist pedigree is not doubted:

Italy has never seen anything similar to the type of planning exhibited by the government of Soviet Russia. When an important branch of the banking system, or a large-scale industry which could be confused with the 'higher interests of the nation,' has threatened to collapse, the government has stepped into the breach and prevented the breakdown by emergency measures.... *The policies of the Italian dictatorship during these years of world crisis has been no different in its aims, methods, and results from the policies of all the governments of the capitalistic countries.* The [Fascist] Charter of Labor says that private enterprise is responsible to the state. In actual fact, it is the state, i.e., the taxpayer, who has become responsible to private enterprise. As long as business was good, profit remained to private initiative. When the depression came, the government added the loss to the taxpayer's burden. Profit is private and individual. Loss is public and social.... The intervention of [Mussolini's] government has invariably favored big business (379–80; italics added).

In addressing economics under Mussolini, it is important to recall that for the not inconsiderable period between 1922 and 1925, that is, the first years of the regime, it in fact pursued strictly *laissez faire* lines; in these years, Alberto De Stefani, a member of the fascist squadristi from the very beginning and a convinced economic liberal, served as minister of finance. De Stefani "reduced controls over industry and cut expenditures and taxes...; telephone companies were restored to private control; the concessions given to electrical companies were

renewed; the state monopoly over life insurance companies was ended"
(De Grand 1982: 47). This was a period which one historian described
as "Liberal-Fascism," shaped according to the classic recipes of the
Manchester School.[7] Economic liberalism was inscribed into the programme of the PNF (National Fascist Party) in August 1922, gaining
the approval of liberal economists—including Luigi Einaudi—most of
whom at that time considered the fascist government "the best possible
solution" (De Grand 1982: 47). Having crushed the socialist workers
and peasants' movement in the cities and in the countryside, the fascists proceeded to liberalize the economy, becoming the "long-sought
instrument of bourgeois resurgence" (32). Salvemini, while dismissing
the notion that Mussolini was actually influenced by Pareto, affirmed
nonetheless that the Italian sociologist saw his project finally materi-
alizing. For Pareto merely gave voice to the aspirations of the middle
classes, who had been smarting under the advances of socialism for
a quarter of a century: "From 1921 onward Pareto saw in the Fascist
movement that ruthless bourgeois antisocialist onslaught whose advent
he had wished for twenty years before. It was not Pareto who taught
Mussolini. It was Mussolini who fulfilled Pareto's wishes" (Salvemini
1973: 89). And if this period of classical *laissez faire* eventually came
to an end and gave way to increasing state direction under the long
reign of the new financial administrator, Alberto Beneduce, this was
not because such liberal economics offended the ostensibly "collectivist" sensibilities of the fascists but because of internal contradictions
and pressures, not least on the part of industrialists themselves, who
preferred and demanded a more supportive state by their side (as well,
of course, as the subsequent impact of world depression). As the economic historian Marcello De Cecco intriguingly suggests, the move
from De Stefani's *laissez faire* to Beneduce's state dirigisme was hardly
one from capitalism to socialism; it was rather an internal capitalist
affair, the altered policies catering, precisely, to the interests of modern
big business at the expense of outmoded, small-scale production:

> In order to rise to power, [Mussolini] did not hesitate to play the role of
> the apostle of free enterprise, advocating the immediate dismantling of
> all forms of wartime planning of economic activities. He thus touched

---

[7] Franklin Hugh Adler in his entry on De Stefani (De Grazzia and Luzzatto 2005,
vol. I: 425). For Adler's in-depth analysis of "Liberal-Fascism," see his important study
(1995: 284–343).

the heart of the small-scale entrepreneurs who produced traditional labor-intensive industrial goods; but he would soon afterwards abandon them in favor of the large-scale industrial entrepreneurs who produced capital-intensive products and the great public managers (De Cecco 2002: 74).

Nor does there seem to have been any marked departure under fascism from the economic policies of the pre-fascist period, which were never, ever since the 19th century days of the "Historical Right" [*Destra storica*], ones of strict state neutrality in economic matters (64–67).

Was this perchance different in the case of German fascism? An emphasis on the economic liberalism of Spengler might be misleading, especially since he is today often remembered as a *critic* of National Socialism at least as much as its ideological precursor, one who distanced himself from the movement and its leader. So we now need to turn from a discussion of the precursors and fellow travelers of National Socialism to the Nazis themselves. I suggest doing so by addressing Hitler himself. After considering his economic views, we shall return to the question of Spengler's eventual dissatisfaction with Nazism, and examine its nature.

Hitler and Liberalism: a "Wonderful Harmony" of Politics and Economics

In representing Hitler's socioeconomic views, historians have often liberally resorted—pun intended—to the alienating strategy already described, that of making such views appear outlandish, radically different from what is today considered sound and normative. An important example of that tendency is supplied by Henry A. Turner, in his study of National Socialism and big business, first published in 1985. This has become a standard work, highly influential in its bid to dismantle the long-standing notion of a symbiosis between German fascism and capitalism. On the revisionist side at the time of publication, Turner's claims have now flown into the mainstream consensus, whose drift is quite clear: only incidental and superficial collusion— whether of a financial, political or ideological nature—is seen between capitalism and the rise of Nazism (and, indeed, of fascism in general). I therefore take Turner's argument as the main point of reference in confronting the predominant views on Nazi economy.

In his reconstruction of the relationship between Nazism and capitalism, Turner (1987: 70–71) ascribed Hitler an all-important role: "The Nazi party was at bottom a charismatic movement whose cohesion resulted from the loyalty of its members...to one man: Adolf Hitler.... He held the party together and determined its course...Any attempt to understand Nazi economic policies, or the absence thereof, must therefore turn on an analysis of Hitler's own attitude toward such matters." This statement is followed by a twelve-page discussion titled "Hitler's economics," which is supposed to get us right to the core of the Nazi attitude to economic matters. The discussion, however, is so structured, that it begins with a foregone conclusion, which is threefold: Hitler was 1) a dilettante in economic matters, putting forward peculiar, faulty and contradictory views. For example, Hitler's "ignorance of economics" (71) and his "contradiction-ridden thought" (73) are stressed. Turner asserts that "he never attained even a basic grasp of the formal discipline of economics.... [I]t is obvious that he knew virtually nothing about micro-economics and had no more grasp of macro-economics than could be gained by reading newspapers," while his economic doctrine "may best be described as a loose cluster of sometimes contradictory socio-economic attitudes" (71). 2) Hitler was generally disdainful of economic enterprise which he regarded a materialist, petty field of action, and considered politics and matters of state as the decisive issue. Hitler, Turner argues, "used the German economy...for his purposes rather than adjusting his purposes to economic constraints. This would prove a major factor in his ultimate failure. It demonstrated, however, that Hitler had meant what he said when he proclaimed that economics must play the role of the maidservant to politics" (81). Nazism is all about the primacy of politics, not economics. 3) Hitler's economic notions, hopelessly nebulous as they were, in any case crucially departed from Western, capitalist orthodoxy:

> [C]entral to his views on economic matters was another key element of his creed: Social Darwinism. By the time he entered politics he had accepted uncritically the collectivistic Austrian variant of that doctrine. Instead of seeing life primarily in terms of a competition for advantage and advancement among individuals, as did most English and American Social Darwinists, Hitler believed that for humans the crucial Darwinian struggle took place among nations (72).

The rest of the discussion proceeds to provide this threefold conclusion with supporting evidence. Yet it seems that the structure of the argument is not coincidental: for it turns out that much of the evidence Turner himself garners fails to support the conclusion, in fact raising serious objections to it. So it is all the more important that matters were settled in advance. Let us take as an example the above quoted claim that Hitler was not a Social Darwinist of a Western, individualistic mold, but rather of a collectivistic, central European one. Yet just a few pages further on it is in fact conceded that individualistic strife was quite important in Hitler's Social Darwinist outlook, which therefore "went beyond the collectivistic variant of that doctrine prevalent in central Europe" (76). Hitler, Turner thus affirms:

> ...accorded a place for struggle among individuals as well.... [H]e assumed that struggle among individuals within a nation took a mainly economic form. That assumption provided the basis for another, namely, that economic competition—or, as he sometimes characterized it, the 'play of free forces'—was essential for a nation's health. Only through competition could the 'aristocratic principle of nature' assert itself in the life of a nation, thus ensuring that the fittest persons, the 'superior individuals' (*Persönlichkeiten*), as he put it, would prevail (76).

The argument thus begins by emphatically driving a wedge between Hitler and Western Social Darwinism, only to quietly remove it, showing that he had in fact much in common with his English and American counterparts. On the one hand, Turner is too upright and meticulous a scholar to suppress or ignore the facts he encounters. On the other hand, committed as he is to disassociating capitalism from Nazism, he achieves this task by a particular structuring of the argument. In this fashion, it is not so much the facts presented that uphold the argument, but the formal way in which they are ordered, linked and signified.

So, did Hitler's views on economics really amount to little more than a paradoxical hodgepodge, a symptom of semi-education and dilettantism? And did he really perceive of the economy as subservient to political goals? We can approximate an answer by turning our attention to an important text, relatively short, a speech which Hitler delivered before the Industry-Club of Düsseldorf on January 27, 1932, almost exactly a year before he was appointed chancellor of Germany. I say the speech is important not because Hitler there expressed ideas elsewhere absent—in fact these, or very similar ideas, can be found throughout his writings, speeches and proclamations, as well as diverse second-hand recordings of his views—but because it provides a very succinct, concentrated and systematic treatment of the topic of economics, as well as a very useful exposition of the ideal relationship, as far as the future *Führer* was concerned, between the economic and the political domains.

As is to be expected, Hitler denounces the Weimar Republic to his audience and outlines his project of eliminating it and putting in its stead a dictatorial regime with himself at the top. Just as predictably, he expresses dissatisfaction about the way economic affairs are conducted in the Republic and proposes a drastic transformation. Yet what does he find reproachable about Weimar economics? Does he, as Turner's account would suggest, find it lamentable that the economy has gained the upper hand against politics? In fact, Hitler's attack on Weimar's institutions is based on the very contrary assumption that the Republic signifies the unlawful and pernicious political interference in the economy, indeed of a very particular mode of doing politics, i.e., democracy. Economic leadership under the present conditions is abducted from the hands of creative and able "personalities" and transferred into the hands of the incapable many. For "high culture," which embraces all fields of human activity, including the economic one, is naturally founded on individual achievement: "This entire cultural edifice is in its foundation and in its building-bricks nothing but the result of the creative achievement of the intelligence, the diligence, of individual people, in its greatest results the end-achievement of divinely-gifted geniuses" (Hitler, in Domarus 1973, vol. 1: 71). The problem begins when this natural ascendancy of the gifted few is checked, in times of decline, by the mediocre many: "It is hence...understandable that nations of illustrious pasts gradually begin to forfeit their position of leadership, once they succumb to unlimited, democratic mass rule; since the existing and potential top achievements of individuals in all fields are henceforth rendered ineffective because of their oppression by the great number" (72). This should sound familiar; for it is the standard economic liberal complaint against the smothering of individual enterprise by democratic, political liberalism; the tyranny of the sterile majority overriding the liberty of the inventive minority. It is highly interesting that, in justifying dictatorship, Hitler reveals himself an inversed Marxist: his starting point is not some political, ethical or cultural concept, which he then attempts to impose on the economy but, on the contrary, he proceeds from the base of capitalist economy to ask: what is the political superstructure that best accords with such base? In times of social and political upheaval, what political order can best guarantee the permanence of private property and the flourishing of individual enterprise, the *Leistungsprinzip* [the principle of achievement]? Hitler explains:

> It is therefore necessary to justify such traditional forms, which ought to be maintained in such a way that they will appear absolutely necessary, as logical and right. And here I must say: private property can only be justified morally and ethically, if I assume that human achievements are different. Only then can I ascertain: because human achievements are different, the products [*Ergebnisse*] of such achievements are different too. And since the products of human achievements are different, it is appropriate that the administration of these products will be accorded to people in roughly corresponding relation. It would be illogical to transfer the administration of a given product which is bound to the achievement of a given personality, to the hands of someone of inferior achievements, or to the hands of a collective, which, through the fact alone that they did not accomplish the achievement have shown that they are incapable of administrating it (72–73).

The inherent difference in economic achievement is thus the only coherent basis upon which political administration must be carried out. Capitalism cannot long survive if administration of property is hijacked from the producers—the gifted, individual capitalists—and transferred to the collective. Hitler now proceeds to provide a textbook formulation of the split between economic and political liberalism, the way democracy increasingly encroaches upon the economy, hence necessitating a decision, either in favour of democracy or in favour of capitalism:

> Acknowledging this, it would be madness to go on and say: on the economic domain there are inevitable disparities in merit, but not so on the political domain! It is absurd to construct life economically on the tenet of achievement, the value of personality, and so practically on the authority of the personality, but to deny the authority of the personality politically and to put in its place the law of the great number, of democracy. Therewith must slowly originate *a split* [*Zwiespalt*] between the economic and the political conceptions, which one will attempt to bridge by bringing the former into line with the latter. This has in fact already been attempted, since *this split* has not remained some empty, pale theory. The theory of the equality of merit [*Wert*], is by now not only political, but has already developed into an economic system.... Analogous to political democracy on the economic terrain is communism (73; emphases added).

Economy is thus the "maidservant" of politics *under democracy,* and Hitler's elimination of the Weimar Republic and the reinstatement of a strictly hierarchical rule is meant precisely to reverse this unwholesome tendency, to make *politics* toe the economic line.[8] Political liberalism splits apart from economic liberalism and effectively undermines it, since the logical economic upshot of democracy is not capitalism but its antithesis, communism. Hence the strange fact that Hitler's worldview dismisses political liberalism not as capitalistic, but as a milder manifestation of the Marxist syndrome. The *"bourgeois world,"* we are told in *Mein Kampf*, "worships a view of life which in general is distinguished from the Marxian view only by degrees or persons. The *bourgeois* world is Marxist, but it believes in the possibility of a domination of certain human groups (*bourgeoisie*), while Marxism itself plans to transmit the world systematically into the hands of Jewry" (Hitler 1941: 579). That liberalism, as far as Hitler was concerned, was but a form of Marxism, indulging the latter's basic vices—such as egalitarianism, compassion, and a reliance on the proletariat—is also evident from the following exchange with Otto Strasser, the leader of so-called leftist faction of the NSDAP:

> But your kind of socialism is nothing but Marxism. The mass of the working class want nothing but bread and games. They can never understand the meaning of an ideal and we cannot hope to win them over to one. What we have to do is to select from a new master class, men who will not allow themselves to be guided, like you, by the morality of pity. Those who rule must know they have the right to rule because they belong to a superior race... What you preach is liberalism, nothing but liberalism (Strasser 1940: 106–7–107).

These ideas form the core of Hitler's socioeconomic, as well as political, ideology. There is a fundamental opposition between capitalism and communism: both are not merely economic forms, but entail a political superstructure (as well as diverse cultural dimensions, which we cannot discuss here. In a nutshell: capitalism is synonymous with high culture, communism with mass culture-cum-*Kulturbolschewismus*). Communism goes along with democracy, capitalism with an authoritarian political system. To wish to maintain capitalism alongside democracy is a pernicious illusion. Hence the imperative to

---

[8] Consider also the following dialogue between Hitler and Otto Strasser, who advocated nationalization of industry. In response, Hitler is reported to have said: "Democracy has laid the world in ruins, and nevertheless you want to extend it to the economic sphere. It would be the end of German economy. You would wipe out all human progress, which has been achieved by the individual efforts of great scholars and great inventors" (in Strasser 1940: 110).

conduct the struggle against communism on the political arena, *not* because politics is more important than the economy (read: capitalism), but because the capitalist economy is impossible, at least in the long term, without the political elimination of democracy. When approaching Hitler's utterances one must be cautious not to eliminate their context, and rely on isolated sentences. Such would be easy to use to bolster the thesis of a "primacy of politics," as for example, when Hitler says, again in a speech before leading industrialists, but this time shortly after the *Machtübernahme*: "The political carrying out of the struggle is the primary decisive factor [*das primär Entscheidende*]" (in Kühnl 2000: 183). Yet the context of the speech makes it clear that this is not meant to put the economy in its proper, secondary place, but rather to ensure that it survives and prospers. Hitler again underlines the destructive rift between economic liberalism (private property, competition, individual achievement, etc.) and political liberalism (democracy): "Bismarck's word 'liberalism is the pacemaker of social-democracy' is now scientifically proven and substantiated.... It is impossible to sustain market-economy [*Privatwirtschaft*] in a period of democracy" (182). He then emphasizes the need to resolve this dilemma in favor of economic liberalism, by giving capitalism the fitting political expression:

> It is not a matter of fortune, that one man achieves more than another. In this fact is grounded the concept of private property, which gradually expanded into a general legal-concept and became a complex process of the economic life. The path, which we must tread, is clearly indicated. But it is not enough to say: we do not want communism in the economy. If we go further along the political way we have hitherto been treading, we go under. Economy and politics, this we have over the past years sufficiently experienced, do not let themselves be separated. *The political carrying out of the struggle is the primary decisive factor.* That is why, politically as well, clear conditions must be established (183; italics added).

We can appreciate how, for Hitler, politics was crucial, indeed "primary," if one wishes, *only* in the service of capitalism and given that capitalism is powerless to defend itself from democracy without political (fascist-authoritarian) propping.

Still, it must be questioned whether Hitler's views as expressed in speeches before industrialists, were much more than an opportunistic accommodation. Did he not tailor his statements to suit the expectations of the audience, in the process downgrading some "socialistic" aspects of his ideology? On that point, Turner is quite helpful, since he rightly dismisses the idea that Hitler was anything but sincere in rejecting socialism and in his devotion to private property:

> Observers have repeatedly alleged that Hitler abandoned the socialistic tenets of the NSDAP during his pursuit of power in order to placate big-business patrons. Yet an examination of his writings and utterances reveal that Hitler had nothing to abandon; he had never been a socialist, in the sense of favouring state ownership of the means of production. His commitment to economic competition and private property derived not from expediency but rather from his fanatically held Social Darwinist beliefs about the nature of mankind and human society (Turner 1987: 76).

This summary of Hitler's socioeconomic views is all the more important since it comes from one of the most influential scholars to have questioned the capitalistic affiliation of Nazism. So, Hitler's "loose cluster of contradictory socio-economic attitudes," as Turner put it, in fact rested, according to Turner's own analysis, on the firm bedrock of the "commitment," no less, to private property and competition, two tenets which happen, after all, to constitute the bedrock of capitalism, too. Hitler, consistently, is the *economic liberal*—understood not in terms of doctrinaire *laissez faire* but in terms of a defense of capitalism, which is by no means, of course, reducible to *laissez faire*— protesting against the insubordination of politics. As in the following passage from *Mein Kampf*:

> In the fields of thinking, of artistic creation, even of economy, this process of selection still takes place today, though especially in the latter it is exposed to a serious handicap.... Here in all cases the idea of the personality is still dominant...*Political life alone has today completely turned away from this most natural principle....* Marxism, indeed, presents itself as the perfection of the Jew's attempt at excluding the overwhelming importance of the personality in all domains of human life and of replacing it by the number of the masses. To this corresponds politically the parliamentary form of government...and economically the system of a labor union movement...In the same measure in which economy is deprived of the effect of the principle of personality and, instead, is exposed to the influences and effects of the masses, it is bound to lose efficiency, serving all and valuable for all, and will gradually fall into a definite regression (Hitler 1941: 666–7; italics added).

The bulk of Hitler's anti-liberalism is underpinned by the conviction that political liberalism is incompatible with capitalism. This is pertinent even with regards to what is probably the most notorious "anti-liberal" aspect of fascist ideology, its opposition to individualism. This is almost universally construed as a token of the fascist longing for an era of social harmony and cohesion preceding the rise of modern industrial society, when humans where engulfed in and guided by the organic collectivity of the *Gemeinschaft*, as opposed to the mechanical, atomized order of the modern, Western *Gesellschaft*. The collectivist past thus bitterly refuses to give way before the individualist present. It is undeniable that such motifs were indeed present in certain kinds of fascist or pre-fascist literature, and that they did constitute part of the appeal of fascism in the eyes of those many individuals dissatisfied and anxious about the uncertainties and dynamism of capitalism. This was especially true with regards to members of the middle classes and of the old *Mittelstand* who, particularly in times of crisis, feared sliding down to the ranks of the working class, and who were understandably susceptible to a vision of stable and hierarchic society, guaranteeing both their social status and their source of income (as opposed to a socialist, egalitarian society, which vouched only for a safe income, but at the expense of an elevated status). In short, according to such interpretations, fascist anti-individualism is a form of opposition to industrial, Western society, offering a collectivist refuge from the fluc-tuations of competition, even at the loss of individual liberties. Yet with a fascist as important as Hitler, we can see that anti-individualism could in fact represent a *defense* of the modern, industrialist order; drastic limitation of the rights and liberties of individuals could be motivated not by hostility to capitalism but by the reverse need *to deliver individuals to capitalism*, facilitate its workings:

> Work of culture is cooperation; yet cooperation requires organization. What would become of a factory which does not posses a tight organiza-tion, in which every worker comes to work when its suits him, and does only the work which entertains him.
> Without organization, without coercion, and so without individual sacrifices it would not function. Life is a continuous renunciation of individual liberty (Hitler in Picker 2003: 233).

Upon closer inspection, the warm haven of the medieval collective is nothing but the cold, modern factory. It is the immanent logic of capitalism that demands the subjugation of individuals. Or consider the following summary of Hitler's views:

> ...the mark of an especially high cultural level is not individual liberty, but the restriction of individual liberty through an organization encom-passing the greatest possible number of individuals of the same race.

> If one would grant people their individual liberty, they would behave like apes. No one would tolerate another man having more than he....
>
> [Hitler] could only smile about the never-ending chatter on the community, since the great windbags believe it is possible to talk community into being.... Only with the appearance of the gendarme did the entire society [Gesellschaft] weld together into a single great community [Gemeinschaft].
>
> For it is precisely through force alone which the community is created and preserved (Picker 2003: 301).

Left to their own devices, individuals will not strive to outdo each other and will not put up with differences of wealth; it is only the gendarme of (fascio-)capitalism who coerces them to be industrious and who clubs them into hierarchy. Individualism, one of the sacred tenets of liberalism, is thus sacrificed precisely since it is compatible with *egalitarianism*, not hierarchy and inequality, and therefore does not sit well with industrial growth. We will return to this point below, in Chapter 5, when addressing the paradoxes of liberalism.

Hitler's veneration of Wagner's music or of Emperor Barbarossa's heroics suggests a worldview steeped in the archaic and the mystic. And National Socialist culture in general is frequently represented in terms of the occult.[9] Again, a *Verfremdungseffekt* in operation. For behind the medieval paraphernalia, the actual political content was distinctly modern. Hitler did not wish to revive the closed caste society of the middle ages, but rather to construct society according to the paramount capitalistic-liberal tenet of equal opportunities, competition and individual merit. Like the great majority of his right-wing contemporaries, he endorsed *open* elitism, which admits into its ranks and promotes new talent from below.[10] Hitler's "aristocratic principle of nature" was thus in fact distinctly meritocratic, i.e., *bourgeois*. The whole system revolves—again, at least in theory—on "the principle of achievement." It refutes—theoretically at least—social privileges that do not reflect actual talent and achievement:

> Nepotism is the utmost conceivable form of protection: the protection of one's own I.
>
> Wherever it has become present in the life of the state—the monarchies are the best example thereof—weakness and decline have been

---

[9] Just one example out of a bulky literature: Goodrick-Clarke (2001).
[10] As lucidly analyzed in Struve (1973).

the consequences. With its appearance is suspended the *Leistungsprinzip* (Picker 2003: 237).

Notice the way, proper for a liberal economic discourse, in which productive meritocracy is contrasted with pernicious, stagnant *protectionism*. A major criticism levelled at the German upper classes is their snobbish complacency and unwillingness to recognize plebeian merit. This has led some historians to underline the "revolutionary" impact of National Socialism, its attack on the old elites.[11] Yet such infusion of new blood into the ruling elite was in truth regarded as a vital pre-condition in *preventing* social upheaval. Here, too, Hitler's position is quite typical of the elitism prevalent since the mid 19th century, evincing, for example, many parallels with that of Pareto, for whom the perennial decadence of elites was due to their ossification into a caste system, and their consequential inability to rob the lower classes of their best individuals. These men of talent thus become revolutionary tribunes, leaders of the new, upcoming elite. Hitler's following account of Social Darwinism operating *against* the docile elite might have been copied down from Pareto (without suggesting any influence; the ideological affinity is edifying in itself): "In the People's lower stratum life itself conducts a harsh selection, so that these social strata can be utterly ruthless when faced with a cowardly leadership. Only thus is it possible to explain the way that in 1918 the 'movement from below' swept off the ramshackle house of cards of the Monarchy" (Picker 2003: 261).[12] Nazi meritocracy, therefore, is decidedly anti-revolutionary. The following passage illustrates the way meritocracy was coupled with a zealous defense of the capitalist order:

National Socialism says: different occupations have nothing do to with bourgeois evaluation. That is its conciliatory aspect.... The child might

---

[11] E.g. Schoenbaum (1966).

[12] Pareto, for his part, contrasted the vigor of the lower-classes, hardened by natural selection, with the decadence of the squeamish rich:

The rich classes have few children and almost all of them survive; the poor classes have many children and lose a great number of those who are not particularly robust and well equipped for life.... The high-minded people who would persuade the rich classes in our societies to have many children,...are working without realizing it for the enfeeblement of the race, for its degeneracy. If the rich classes in our societies had many children, it is probable they would save almost all of them, even the sickliest and less gifted. This would increase further the degenerate elements in the upper classes and delay the emergence of the elite coming from the lower classes (Pareto 1966: 132–3).

posses the abilities, which the parents lack.... The strangling of permanent ascension must be prohibited.... He who turns against the social
order as such, I will ruthlessly shoot down. The social order which I build
is not subservient to the masses. On that point, one would run against
granite. Any attempt to violently unsettle this state will be drenched in
blood. But everything possible to promote decent people will be undertaken, from the standpoint of high accountability to the entire body of
the People (Picker 2003: 134–5).

Similarly, Hitler is almost invariably contemptuous of the bourgeoisie.
Yet this is the contempt of the exasperated insider, who feels that the
bourgeois, short sighted and cowardly, are digging their own grave:
"Cowardice, your name is the bourgeoisie" (258). The recurrent motif,
again as if echoing Pareto's elite theories, is the bourgeois helplessness before the forces of revolution, their sheep-like marching to the
slaughterhouse:

> Despite the fact that the Jewry, in England as well as the USA—through
> the politically decisive positions it had occupied in the press, film, radio
> and the economy; while in the USA, additionally, it has brought under
> its organized power the under-humans, above all the negroes—has put
> the rope around the neck of the bourgeoisie, these brave bourgeois shud-
> dered at the very thought of saying a single 'hard word' against the Jews
> (Picker: 258–9).

It is thus only consistent that Hitler should recommend himself to the
industrialists as the champion of the bourgeoisie:

> I know very well, gentlemen, that when National Socialists march through
> the streets and suddenly in the evening there is tumult and uproar, then
> the bourgeois draws back the curtain, looks out and says, 'Once again
> my night's rest is disturbed and I cannot sleep. Why must the Nazis
> always hassle and roam about at night?' Gentlemen, if everyone thought
> like that, then indeed no one's night's rest would be disturbed, but then
> the bourgeois today could not go into the street (in Domarus 1973,
> vol. I: 89).

Or, has he reportedly told the conservative journalist Richard Breiting
in 1931: "Communism...is the number one enemy of our organization and of the bourgeoisie. Only we are capable of saving the dying
bourgeoisie from this enemy" (Calic 1968: 63).

Certainly, the fascist clearing of political obstacles from the economy's path was not meant to serve as a prelude to an era of peaceful
trade and manufacture, as envisioned by an early liberal such as Constant. The latter, as we have seen, believed that civilized humanity was
now ready to switch from "impulse" to "calculation," having reached

an age "in which commerce replaces war" (1988: 313). The fascists clearly did not share such a vision. The elimination of "small politics" (democracy, socialism, social democracy), was part of a campaign to again make possible imperialistic expansion, the ushering in of "great politics," as the discussion of Spengler demonstrated. Yet this was not a violation or domestication of the economy, but a further implementation of economic logic. Imperialism, after all, is never simply about "political" goals but always a means to achieve, primarily, economic aims.[13] For that reason, when addressing the German industrialists, Hitler does not come dressed as a respectful businessman, carefully hiding his military uniform; he does not keep the next war secret, some nasty "political" surprise he has in store for his greedy and gullible "economic" audience, fixing its gaze on profits. He can afford to be quite upfront with them:

> It is impossible to have one part of the people supporting private property, while the other part denies it. Such a struggle tears the people apart.... In such struggles the people's power is consumed inwardly, so that consequentially it cannot act externally.... The question of the preparation [Herstellung] of the Wehrmacht will not be decided in Geneva but in Germany, if, through internal calm, we will obtain internal force. Internal calm, however, is unobtainable before Marxism is done away with (Kühnl 2000: 183–4).

Internal calm, the *Führer* makes quite clear, is the precondition for *external* mayhem. The whole point of eliminating small, democratic politics at home, is to be able to embark on great, imperialistic politics abroad. The military-industrial complex upon which Hitler's worldview rests, is spelled out:

> There is no thriving economy, which does not have at its front and at its back a thriving, powerful state to shield it, there was no Carthaginian economy without Carthaginian navy and no Carthaginian trade without a Carthaginian army. And naturally in modern times too, when the going get rough and the interests of the nations come to a collision, there can be no economy unless it has behind it the absolutely powerful and determined political will of the nation (Hitler, in Domarus 1974, vol. I: 80).

---

[13] A fact about which Constant, too, seemed to have little doubt: "War and commerce are only two different means of achieving the same end, that of getting what one wants" (1988: 313). And, be it noted, "what one wants," by hook (trade) or by crook (war), is riches, profit; otherwise, commerce alone would not suffice to get it.

Capitalism, in other words, is antithetical not only to democracy, but to pacifism as well: "The idea of pacifism in practical reality and translated into all domains, must gradually lead to a destruction of the competitive drive, of the ambition for special achievements of all kinds. I cannot say: politically, we will be pacifists, we will reject the notion that life must necessarily be preserved through struggle, but economically we will remain strong competitors" (74). Hitler does not impose willy-nilly some political aim on the maidservant of the German economy; he rather articulates the wish of significant sections of the German industry, which had been on their mind since the setback of the last war. Spengler's celebration of modern "Caesarism"—enthusiastically received by such eminent representatives of German industry and banking as Paul Reusch, Hjalmar Schacht, Wilhelm Cuno, Hugo Junker or Albert Vögler[14]—was a symbiosis of politics and economics; and so, too, was Hitler's ideal:

> I cannot understand at all the economically privileged master-position occupied by the white race in relation to the rest of the world, unless I see how it is in the tightest of manners connected with a political master-concept... [T]he white race was convinced of having the right to organize the rest of the world. It is a matter of complete indifference how this right outwardly disguised itself in every single case: in practice, it was the exercise of an extraordinarily brutal master-right.... A famous Englishman[15] once wrote that English politics was characterized by this *wonderful wedlock* [*Vermählung*] of *economic acquisitions* with consolidation of *political power*, and conversely the *expansion of political power* with *immediate economic appropriation*.... We stand today in front of a world condition which for the white race makes sense only when one acknowledges the indispensable wedlock of a master-spirit [*Herrensinn*] in political will with a master-spirit in economic activity, a wonderful harmony [*Übereinstimmung*] which left its mark on the whole of the last century... (Domarus 1974, vol. I: 75; emphases added).

At the foundation of Hitlerism was a fusion of economic and military might inspired by England, a point stated also in *Mein Kampf*:

> The talk of the 'peaceful economic conquest' of the world was certainly the greatest folly that was ever made the leading principle of a State policy.... Precisely in England one should have realized the striking refutation of this theory: no nation has more carefully prepared its economic

---

[14] On Spengler's personal and ideological ties to highly placed industrialists see Struve (1973: 235–9) and Petzold (1978: 181–5).

[15] This is likely an allusion to Cecil Rhodes, whom Hitler profoundly admired.

conquest with the sword with greater brutality and defended it later on more ruthlessly than the British. Is it not a characteristic of British statesmanship to draw economic conquests from political force and at once to mold every economic strengthening into political power?... England always possessed the armament that she needed. She always fought with the weapons that were required for success (Hitler 1941: 188–9).

If there was ever a choice to be made or a conflict to be settled between the English and the Prussian idea, it was certainly not on the agenda of Adolf Hitler.

Revisiting Turner's threefold analysis of Nazi economics (which he equates with that of Hitler), we see that:

1) Hitler, certainly, was not an academically trained economist, but neither were (or are) the huge majority of leading Western politicians. Were Margaret Thatcher or Ronald Reagan more proficient than Hitler in microeconomics or did they have a better grasp on macroeconomics? Far from having a merely fleeting or superficial concern in economics, Hitler often concerned himself with economic matters, which he approached quite seriously; far from being a "a loose cluster of attitudes," Hitler's economics presents a rather coherent worldview, one which did not strike German industrialists as a preposterous, dilettantish jumble, because it corresponded fairly closely with their own and with widespread contemporary views on the economy.[16] As a corrective to the belief that Hitler's economic notions were bizarre or amateurish, we might compare them to those entertained by Pareto, who was one of the celebrated economists of his time, and who shared many vital assumptions with Hitler, from the importance of competition and selection, up to the indispensable role of military force in buttressing socioeconomic prevalence. In fact, as the German economic historians Buchheim and Scherner (2006) have recently argued in an intriguing essay, Nazi economics would *still today* be considered in many

---

[16] Baron Kurt von Schröder, an important banker and, from 1932, a supporter of Hitler, though formerly a member of the liberal DVP, confirmed such pervasive concord in his testimony under oath at the Nuremberg Trials, where he stated, for example, the following:

It was generally known that one of most important points on Hitler's programme was the abrogation of the Treaty of Versailles and the re-establishment of a strong Germany, in both the military and the economic sense. It was clear that in a strong Germany the economy would thrive as well... Hitler's economic programme was generally known in the economic sector, and was welcomed by it (in Kühnl 2000: 160).

regards capitalistically normative, for example, in its emphasis on the value of private, as opposed to state, entrepreneurship and ownership: "Interestingly enough," they assert (409), this tenet "conforms well to modern economic reasoning." Nor, according to these researchers from Mannheim, was this an isolated facet. The Nazi administrative elite was in general committed to a liberal economic concept and procedure inherited from the Weimar Republic: "These decrees, originating in the Weimar Republic, were never repealed during the Third Reich and thus placed *the more liberally minded* bureaucracy of the Reich Ministry of Finance *in a strong position*" (407; italics added). The fact that this "Weimarian" aspect was not abolished, whereas so many other features of the Republic were violently done away with or trampled under foot was not coincidental, and did not stem, of course, from any excess of legalistic zeal on the part of the Nazis. Rather, it reflected the fundamental and genuine Nazi belief in the economic benefits of allowing business to remain in private hands: "one has to keep in mind that Nazi ideology held entrepreneurship in high regard. Private property was considered a precondition to developing the creativity of members of the German race in the best interest of the people." Furthermore, there was a conviction "even in the highest ranks of the Nazi elite that private property itself provided important incentives to achieve greater cost consciousness, efficiency gains, and technical progress" (408). Such conviction, finally and importantly, went all the way up the hierarchy, not stopping at Hitler himself:

> During the war Göring said it always was his aim to let private firms finance the aviation industry so that private initiative would be strengthened. Even Adolf Hitler frequently made clear his opposition in principle to any bureaucratic managing of the economy, because that, by preventing the natural selection process, would 'give a guarantee to the preservation of the weakest average [sic] and represent a burden to the higher ability, industry and value, thus being a cost to the general welfare' (409).

2) The economy was crucial in Hitler's worldview, *at least* as fundamental as politics, and to speak of the former being the latter's maidservant clearly misrepresents his own view, which always considered them irrevocably bound together. Nor was this conception of any originality. It was embedded in a tradition of European thought, attempting to steady the capitalist ship in the stormy waters of socialism and democracy. I offer just one example, that of the eminent

French scholar, and self-proclaimed liberal, Ernest Renan, who, some sixty years before the Nazis, advocated colonization as indispensable if France was to resolve its internal social conflict without sliding into socialism or revolution: "Colonisation on a grand scale is a political necessity of the first order. A nation which does not colonise will irrevocably succumb to socialism, to the war between the rich and the poor" (Renan 1875: 92). Military power forms an equally obligatory condition, both to bring property into being, and to furnish it thereafter with a permanent basis: "The economists are wrong in considering labour to be the origin of property. The origin of property is conquest, and the guarantee provided by the conqueror to the fruits of labour around him" (94). The entire enterprise, moreover, was based on a racial division of labour, between the warring, European master race, destined to rule, if "justly," and the non-European races, destined to do the dirty work, if contentedly:

> There is nothing shocking about the conquest of a country of an inferior race by a superior race...England practices this kind of colonisation in India, to the great advantage of India, of humanity in general, and to its own advantage.... *Regere imperio populos*, this is our vocation.... Nature has made a race of labourers, the Chinese race...; a race of tillers of the soil, the negro...; a race of masters and soldiers, the European race.... All our rebels are, more or less, soldiers given an unsuitable vocation, who are made for heroic life, but employed in a manner contrary to their race, which makes bad workers, and very good soldiers. The life which makes our workers revolt would render a Chinaman or a fellah—beings who are not in the least military—happy. That each should do what he was meant for, and all will be right (93–94).

3) As the example of Renan illustrates, Hitler's economics was compatible with, indeed unthinkable *without*, the Western tradition, of whose essence he saw himself an entrenched defender. In supporting the capitalist free play of forces, Hitler was very much a Westerner, and not some central-European anti liberal. While not as strict about *laissez faire* as a Hayek, he was more so than, say, an F. D. Roosevelt. Hitler's and Roosevelt's systems are sometimes mentioned as having in common a Keynesian basis, a system of state investment in the private economy. This is not altogether wrong, since both the "new deal" and the "Third Reich" indeed resulted from an acute crisis of *laissez faire* capitalism. Yet their solutions were importantly different: Roosevelt's statism aimed at introducing a measure of democratic regulation of the market, thus departing from economic liberalism. Hitler's statism,

by contrast, aimed at abolishing democratic intervention in the market, hence *defending* economic liberalism. To be sure, he aimed at channelling economic resources to an imperialistic campaign, which required statism. Yet this did not stem from a refutation of capitalism but from the assumption that capitalism and imperialist expansion are indissolubly interwoven. If anything, the American President comes closer to fit the bill of the anti-Western culprit, rebelling against the strictures of economic liberalism, than the German *Führer*.

Rather than seeing Hitler's system as a departure from the way of West, it makes more sense to conceive of Nazism as a fanatic, die-hard attempt to pursue the logic of Western 19th century capitalism to its utmost conclusion, to go all the way, rejecting the contemptuous compromises of the bourgeoisie with socialism. This, in fact, at times involved a conscious attempt to overcome, so to speak, the German *Sonderweg* and join the West. The British Empire was the model to be emulated, viewed expressly as superior to anachronistic German idiosyncrasies:

> Different nations [of the white race] secured this hegemonic position in different ways: in the most ingenious way England, which always opened up new markets and immediately fastened them politically...Other nations failed to reach this goal, because they squandered their spiritual energies on internal ideological—formerly religious—struggles.... At the time that Germany, for instance, came to establish colonies, the inner mental approach [*Gedankengang*], this utterly cold and sober English approach to colonial ventures, was partly already superseded by more or less romantic notions: to impart to the world German culture, to spread German civilization—things which were completely alien to the English at the time of colonialism (Hitler in Domarus 1973, vol. 1: 76).

The new German imperialism did not presume to invent anything or rebel against the Western guidelines, but rather to adjust to them, to mold itself after the Western example. The British Empire in India was the paradigm, repeatedly invoked by Hitler, and so was the Spanish colonization of Central America by Pizarro and Cortez and the white settlement in North America, "following just as little some democratically or internationally approved higher legal standards, but stemming from a feeling of having a right, which was rooted exclusively in the conviction about the superiority, and hence the right, of the white race" (75). And even some of the most horrendous aspects of this imperialism did not have to look for their models outside the Western orbit. The concentration camps, for instance: "Manual work," Hitler is reported to have told Richard Breiting (Calic 1968: 109), "never harmed anyone, we wish to lay down great work-camps for all sorts of parasites. The Spanish have began with it in Cuba, the English in South-Africa."

Was Hitler merely twisting the legacy of the West out of shape, grotesquely misinterpreting British Imperialism, in somewhat the same way that Mark David Chapman imagined that he was acting in agreement with the spirit of J. D. Salinger's *The Catcher in the Rye* when killing John Lennon? Perhaps. It is nonetheless a telling historical fact that Hitler's admiration of the British Empire did not go unreciprocated. Among the leading circles of the Empire, appreciation of Nazism went wide and deep. E. F. L. Wood, 1st Earl of Halifax, for example, one of the leading figures behind the British policy known as "appeasement," assured Hitler, in November 1937, that "he and other members of the British Government were fully aware that the Führer had not only achieved a great deal inside Germany herself, but that, by destroying Communism in his country, he had barred its road to Western Europe, and that Germany therefore could rightly be regarded as a bulwark of the West against Bolshevism" (Quigley 1981: 275–6). Indeed, Lord Halifax's words ought to be seen as representative of the current of opinion prevailing amongst the core, and largely secretive, circles directing the affairs of the British Empire, one of its most important being the so-called Milner Group and its organ *The Round Table* (first appearing in 1910).[17] The British policy towards Nazism—which, in view of the persistent efforts of the Chamberlain Group between 1933–1939 to set Nazi Germany on a course to a military collision with the USSR, might be better described as "incitement" rather than "appeasement"[18]—cannot be understood apart from a

---

[17] The best account of that group and its stealthy and unrelenting influence on British and world affairs remains that of Quigley (1981).

[18] Our habitual image of Chamberlain is that of a weary politician, well-intentioned but hopelessly naive and myopic, failing to appreciate the acute danger ahead. There is significant evidence to revise this common view; in truth, the politics adopted were not meant simply to keep Nazism at bay or to pacify it as much as possible, but to *endorse* Nazi *expansionism*, in the hope of putting pay to the Bolsheviks, as well as checking the advances of European mass democracy. In addition to Quigley's account just mentioned, there are two more classical studies that are greatly enlightening: Salvemini (1954) and Schuman (1942). The best re-statement and expansion of these themes is: Leibovitz (1993), subsequently published in a new, and more accessible version, Leibovitz and Finkel (1998). An alternative account by Preparata (2005) is informative and stimulating, but ultimately far less compelling.

context of profound ideological and practical affinity (which is *not* to say identity).

To examine the ideology of the British imperialists is to find in it many parallels to the basic tenets of fascist and Nazi ideology. Let us briefly indicate only the most outstanding of these points of contact. The British imperialists, to start with, were, at most, lukewarm about democracy: "To Milner, to Curtis, and apparently to most members of the Group, democracy was not an unmixed good, or even a good, and far inferior to rule by the best, or, as Curtis says, by those who 'have some intellectual capacity for judging the public interest, and, what is no less important, some moral capacity for treating it as paramount to their own'" (Quigley 1981: 134). Similarly, fascism is rightly associated with a view of the state as organic, a supra-individual unit, geared towards greater national goals, as opposed to the liberal view of the state as merely facilitating the competitive pursuit of individual well being at the expense of the whole. In 1929, Giovanni Gentile (2007: 54–55) wrote about "the Fascist ethical state" in explicit polemics against classical liberalism:

> Keep in mind: human life is sacred.... And still, the life of the citizen, when the laws of the Fatherland demand it, must be sacrificed.... An ethical State? Liberals will object.... They lapse into that materialism common to the century in which the doctrine of classical liberalism was formulated. Liberals contend that morality is the attribute of empirical individuals—who alone can possess will—the only personality in the proper sense of the term. The State is nothing other than the external limit on the behaviour of a free independent personality—to assure that the behaviour of one does no injury to others. This negative and empty concept of the State is absolutely rejected by Fascism... We believe that the State is the very personality of the individual divested of accidental differences, shorn of the abstract preoccupations of particular interests...

... etc., etc. This, no doubt, is quintessential fascism. Yet, in *The Round Table*, in an anonymous essay published in June 1913, bearing the telling title "The Ethics of Empire," we find a remarkably similar definition of "the function of the state" as "positive and ethical," which long precedes Gentile's text and indeed the very establishment of fascism:

> The State is not, as the Utilitarians used to think, merely an artificial aggregation of individuals who in order to secure protection for life and property frame a combination involving diminution of private liberty. Both common experience and philosophy teach that men are made what

they are through membership of the corporate life of the community. Their liberties, their rights, their personality have life and being only in the life and being of the State. The being of the State is to be sought... in the living spirit of patriotism that kindles men to jealousy for their country's honour and to sacrifice in their country's cause. The phrases 'national character,' 'national will,' and 'national personality' are no empty catchwords. Every one knows that *esprit de corps* is not a fiction but a reality; that the...co-operation of students or soldiers in a common endeavour, so far from restricting their scope for self development, endows each with capacities for action which could never be realized in a life of isolation. The individualist theory of the State, though moribund, persists with stubborn resistance. It is the last survivor in these days of the Utilitarian abstractions (anonymous 1912–1913: 497–8).

Could this anonymous text have been written by no other than Gentile, infiltrating the staff of the British Empire's organ? An absurd suggestion; yet it must be admitted that the author, whoever he was, was Gentile's kindred spirit. The ideas are eerily evocative of those put forward by the court ideologue of Italian fascism. H. A. Winkler, one of many German historians who hold to the notion that Germany, under Nazism, radically departed from the ways of the West, stated, as will be recalled, that, for Spengler, "the great world-issue was the choice between the Prussian or the English idea, socialism or capitalism, state or parliament," etc. Yet, if the notions expressed in *The Round Table* are anything to go by, "The English idea" was considerably closer to "the Prussian idea," than Winkler allows for. As if attesting to such international affinity, *The Round Table* even makes a token gesture towards the Prussian idea:

The conception of a *Realpolitik* uninspired by ideal motives betrays a childish ignorance of the realities of life. Modern Germany was not fashioned by blood and iron. It was the moral fibre of a great people that triumphed at Leuthen and Leipsic, at Königgrätz and Sedan. What counts in history is individual and racial character, and force of character is proportional to force of moral conviction. The only sure path for national statesmanship is that of a practical idealism which seeks something higher than mere expediency in the fulfillment of public duty and in the furtherance of the moral welfare of the community. 'Where there is no vision, the people perish' (498–9).

Spengler might have recognized many of his favourite ideals in the pages of *The Round Table*, from the abiding importance of imperialist possessions to the need for work and duty taking the place of mass enjoyments:

> Social reformers are prone to insist too strongly on an ideal of mate-
> rial comfort for the people. This prejudice is part of their inheritance
> from the school of Bentham. A life of satisfaction depends not on higher
> wages or lower prices or on leisure for recreation, but on work that calls
> into play the higher capacities of man's nature.... The cry of the masses
> should be not for wages or comforts or even liberty, but for opportuni-
> ties for enterprise and responsibility (495–6).

Conversely, the strategists of the British Empire would have found
little cause to disagree with the fascist socio-economic approach. We
already noticed the talk about "the *corporate* life of the community."
And this is no mere rhetorical resemblance. The policies of increased
state orchestration of the economy and the advocating of national protectionism, seen as typically fascist deviations from Western economic
orthodoxy, were already prefigured by the policy makers of the British Empire. This is evident in the following exposition of the Milner
Group's economics by the American historian Carroll Quigley:

> Milner wanted to isolate the British economy from the world economy
> by tariffs and other barriers and encourage the economic development of
> the United Kingdom by a system of government spending, self-regulated
> capital and labor, social welfare, etc. This program, which was based on
> 'monopoly capitalism' or even 'national socialism' rather than 'financial
> capitalism,'...was embraced by most of the Milner Group after Sep-
> tember 1931, when the ending of the gold standard in Britain proved
> once and for all that Brand's financial program of 1919 was a complete
> disaster and quite unworkable. As a result, in the years after 1931 the
> businessmen of the Milner Group embarked on a policy of government
> encouragement of self-regulated monopoly capitalism (Quigley 1981:
> 123).

Nor was this a rivulet on the margins of the British political landscape. On the contrary, it vitally flowed into the political main
stream: the "financial and economic policy followed by the British
government from 1919 to 1945 runs exactly parallel to the policy of
the Milner Group" (123). Which is to say, that from 1931 onwards,
British economic policy was one of "government encouragement of
self-regulated monopoly capitalism." In Germany, it is important
to realize, similar measures were introduced *before* the Nazis came
into power, as a response to the devastation wrought by the Depression. Economically, German fascism essentially took over from where
the leading economists of the Weimar Republic ended, a continuity
which is personified by the figure of Hjalmar Schacht, who served
as President of the *Reichsbank* both before and after the Nazis were

installed in power. Schacht's policies, in turn, were conducted under the auspices of the Governor of the Bank of England, Montagu Norman. As the economic historian Guido G. Preparata points out (2005: 194), "The financial shape of the 'new order' was delineated in the summer of 1931.... Tight exchange controls were introduced, along with the establishment of special banking consortia for rescuing the healthiest parts of the starved economy. State control over the economic apparatus was significantly extended. This would be the system that the Nazis would inherit." Even more strikingly, according to Buchheim and Scherner (2006), the economic measures undertaken by the Nazis during the war were in and of themselves quite in line with other war economies. The difference, they insist, was extra-economic, and involved, as a notable example, the ever-escalating racial discrimination against Jewish property owners. Their essay thus concludes with the following, strong finale:

> Economic reasoning is about institutions providing incentives to economic actors whose actions determine economic development. In that context the noneconomic characteristics of the actors such as nationality, race, beliefs, and so on are largely irrelevant. But that definitely was not the case with the Nazi economy.... Thus, the main difference between the Nazi war-related economy and Western war-related economies of the time can be detected only by an analysis *that transcends economics* (412; italics added).

To wit: in *strictly economic terms*, the Nazis were *commonplace*. Being economic historians, the authors seem unaware of the extent to which, in *extra* economic terms, too, the Nazis were not altogether heterodox, and that their biological racism was prefigured by others as well, *particularly* in the West, in France, the USA and England, even if they did bring such premises to chillingly unprecedented conclusions. To cite just one salient example, in a 1900 lecture, the English Eugenicist Karl Pearson, who was Francis Galton's favourite pupil and is now remembered mostly as a foundational figure in the academic application of statistics, laid out a basic programme for national regeneration of the British people, in fact race, which strikingly prefigures Nazism. The ideas expressed in this text are worth sampling, especially if we bear in mind that they precede the First World War, the Bolshevik Revolution, the world economic crisis, and the formation and then meteoric rise to power of European fascism. Pearson saw history as a ceaseless and inevitable racial struggle, and one, moreover, in which Aryan races have been particularly successful:

> History shows me one way, and one way only, in which a high state of
> civilization has been produced, namely, the struggle of race with race,
> and the survival of the physically and mentally fitter race. If you want
> to know whether the lower races of man can evolve a higher type, I fear
> the only course is to leave them to fight it out among themselves, and
> even then the struggle for existence between individual and individual,
> between tribe and tribe, may not be supported by that physical selection
> due to a particular climate on which probably so much of the Aryan's
> success depended (Pearson 1905: 21–22).

Racial war, Pearson asseverated, not infrequently results in the elimination of the loser, of the inferior race. He did not merely state this
as a fact, but actually endorsed racial extermination as preferable to
the option of superior and inferior races living side by side, even on
an exploitative basis, since that condition regretfully leads to miscegenation and deterioration of the "stock." Thus, the virtual elimination
of the American Indians, "painful and even terrible as it was in its
details" and in spite of the sentimental sympathy for the Red Indian's
plight, "generated by the novels of Cooper and the poems of Longfel-
low," is commended, since it "has given us a good far outbalancing its
immediate evil. In place of the red man, contributing practically nothing to the work and thought of the world, we have a great nation, mis-
tress of many arts, and able, with its youthful imagination and fresh,
untrammelled impulses, to contribute much to the common stock of
civilized man" (25). On the same page, and based on the same logic,
Pearson equally justifies the near elimination of the Australian aborigines, another "lower race unable to work to the full the land and its
resources." Racial war, and racial extermination, the most atrocious
aspects of Nazism, are scientifically sanctioned by this respectable British scientist at a time when Adolf Hitler was eleven years old.

We should thus be wary of attempts to de-familiarize or de-west-
ernize the geopolitics or the socioeconomics of fascism/Nazism. Their
absolute innovations, ideological as well as practical, were few; their
carry-overs were many. Fascism was a bad weed, no doubt, but one
that thrived in the hothouse of western imperialism.

Spengler and Hitler: the Bookworm Mistakes His Place

Adolf Hitler's views on the relation of economics and politics, were
very close to those of Oswald Spengler. Yet Spengler, as is well known,
distanced himself from Nazism, especially after the *Machtübernahme*.

His critique, more or less decoded, was publicly expressed above all in his book, *Jahre der Entscheidung* (Years of Decision), published in 1933. However, while Spengler *personally* rejected Nazism, it would be very difficult to unfold a coherent critique of Nazism on the basis of Spengler's *theories*. Spengler's critique thus appears strangely flawed in either of the two following senses: either his complaints against the Nazis seem simply "unjust," misrepresenting their policies and failing to acknowledge their "merit"; or, on those points in which the critique is justified, it has to fly in the face of *Spengler's* own theories. Let us look at Spengler's disagreement with National Socialism in power.

Spengler repeatedly rebukes Hitler for failing to subjugate internal matters to the requirements of foreign affairs. Nazism is so absorbed in resolving internal problems, engrossed in "small" politics, that it loses sight of the real task of conducting foreign, "great" politics. Germany is consequentially unprepared for the coming world war. In retrospect, such reminders about the inevitability of war and the need to prepare for it, create an almost comical effect, bearing in mind that they are addressed, of all people, to Hitler, as in the following examples: "The task is replete with enormous dangers, and it does not lie within Germany but outside, in the world of wars and catastrophes, where only great politics has the word" (Spengler 1980: 15), or:

> Germany is in danger. My fears for Germany have not grown lesser.... We may be standing already on the brink of a second world war with an unknown distribution of forces and means and aims which are not to be foreseen...We do not have time to limit ourselves to matters of inner-politics (18).

Hitler is not bellicose enough for Spengler's taste; he needs the guidance of the great history-expert [*Geschichtskenner*], in Spengler's thinly-veiled allusion to himself (14), to gain the insight that "Today, as when the Roman Empire was founded, the world is being remoulded from the foundations, not considering the wishes and desires of 'the majority' and not counting the victims which every such decision demands. But who understands this?" (34–35). Spengler asks: "Are we to be swallowed up by events, as dreamers, enthusiasts and squabblers, leaving behind us nothing to complete our history with certain grandeur? The throwing of the dice for world mastery has only just begun. It will be played to the end between strong people. Should not Germans be amongst them, too?" (90). A philosophical warmonger if ever there was one, Spengler should have had nothing with which to reproach the

Nazis. For surely, if those be the terms of the charge—of squeamishly counting the victims, of bowing to the peaceful wishes of the majority, of recoiling from waging war, and of failing to represent Germany among the warring nations—the Nazis have nothing to fear from the verdict of history. Spengler's critique proves, on that account, unwarranted.

Corresponding to what Spengler considers the Nazi's exasperating dearth of military spirit, is their excessive commitment to democracy. This, too, is a recurrent motif of Spengler's critique, which reveals itself as rooted in an utmost right-wing stance. The National Socialist party is in fact accused of being still a force on the *left* of the political map, simply because *it is* a party, because it partakes in the democratic courting of the masses:

> So what does 'Left' means?... 'Left' is party, that which believes in parties, for this is a liberal form of the fight against the higher society, of the class war since 1770, of the longing for majorities, for 'all' to be involved, for quantity instead of quality, for the herd instead of the master. But the genuine Caesarism of all closing cultures relies upon small, strong minorities.... 'Left' is the noisy agitation at street-corners and in public meetings, the art of whipping-up [*umwerfen*] the urban mass with strong words and mediocre arguments... 'Left' is the enthusiasm for the masses in the first place, as a foundation for one's own power... (175–6).

On the verge of expurgating the last remains of Weimar parliamentarianism, Hitler is reproached for being too much of a democrat, a charge which is not only perfectly unjust but also capricious coming from Spengler, who himself has "democratically" supported Hitler and his party by twice voting for him, as parliamentary democracy was still operating (as much as that was the case in the later years of the Weimar Republic). Spengler, like other self-styled "aristocrats," backed the regime as long as it was actively engaged in courting the masses. Paradoxically enough it is only *afterwards*, as Hitler *abolishes* democracy, that he gives him a wide berth. It seems as if the more Spenglerian Nazi practice objectively became, the more it lost favor in Spengler's eyes. The same paradox is thrown into vivid relief when we consider the way Spengler criticized modern parties, including fascist ones, for not properly eliminating the left, thus having it resurface in the form of the party's own left wing:

> In Fascism as well, there exists the Gracchian fact of two fronts—the left one, comprising of the lower-class urban masses, and the right one, of the nation graded from the peasantry up to ruling classes of society—but

this fact is suppressed by the Napoleonic energy of an individual. This conflict is not, and cannot be, transcended, and it will emerge again, the moment when this iron hand leaves the helm, in the bitter struggles of the Diadochi. For Fascism, too, is a transition. It had its origin in the city mass, as a mass party with noisy agitation and mass oratory (176).

Written in 1933, just following the Nazi accession to power, such analysis clearly referred to the growing importance of Ernst Röhm's SA and their demand for a "second revolution," highly unsettling for conservative supporters of the regime. The need is clearly implied that the left faction be strictly disciplined by the rightist one, so that the masses, which have been tamed outside the party, shall not gain their ascendancy from *within* it. This implication becomes quite clear when Spengler further affirms that a true leader, such as Mussolini (whom Spengler consistently admired) as opposed to a weak pseudo-dictator (such as Hitler, whom Spengler never appreciated), shows his greatness precisely by asserting his authority over his own followers:

> Mussolini...rules truly alone.... The most difficult and the most essential victories of a ruler, are not those won over enemies, but those won over his own supporters...This is the mark of the born ruler. He who does not know this, who cannot or dare not achieve it, floats like a cork on the wave, on top and yet powerless. Perfected Caesarism is dictatorship, yet not the dictatorship of a party, as of one man against all parties, especially his own. Every revolutionary movement reaches victory with a vanguard of praetorians, who are then no longer useful, but only dangerous. The true master is known by the manner in which he dismisses them, ruthless, ungrateful, intent only on his goal...(178).

Ideologically speaking, Spengler should therefore have been quite pleased and impressed with Hitler's actual elimination of the SA as an independent force about a year later, during the Röhm Purge (mid-1934), a "dismissal" which could scarcely have been less "grateful" or more "ruthless," making Il Duce appear almost straitlaced in comparison. Yet far from being impressed, Spengler was disgusted by the event, which made him definitely part ways with Nazism, abandon his last hopes about it.[19] Among those liquidated was Gregor Strasser, the once powerful leader of the more "socialist" wing of the NSDAP, who, "unlike Hitler, never clearly disassociated himself from social experimentation" (Petzold 1978: 212). Paradoxically enough, Spengler long

---

[19] See Hamilton (1971: 158).

sympathized precisely with the "leftist" Strasser, holding the "right-ist" Hitler in contempt. Once again, measured against the yardstick of Spengler's theories, Hitler, if anything, seems more consistently a Spenglerian than Spengler himself. In turning away from Hitler, Spen-gler objectively had to turn away from his own theories, violate his own principles and disregard his own counsels.[20]

Let us take another example of the way Spengler was forced to con-tradict himself in rejecting Nazism: in assiduously preparing the ground for the abolition of democracy and the transition to "Caesarism," Spengler's early writings repeatedly glorified the "man-of-action" and of "destiny," ascribing him with unerring intuition and the ability to leave his positive mark on the world. To him was contrasted the man "who is destined either by the power of his mind or the defect of his blood to be an 'intellectual'…or ideologue," the pitiful "ink-slinger," and "bookworm." Such glorifying of men of action was expressly an apology for authoritarianism, as is evident in the following passage, from *The Decline of the West*:

> Men of theory commit a huge mistake in believing that their place is at the head and not in the train of great events…. Often enough a states-man does not 'know' what he is doing, but that does not prevent him from following with confidence just the one path that leads to success; the political doctrinaire, on the contrary, always knows what should be done, and yet his activity, once it ceases to be limited to paper, is the least successful and therefore the least valuable in history. These intru-sions happen only too frequently in times of uncertainty,… when the ideologue of word or pen is eager to be busy with the actual history of the people instead of with systems. He mistakes his place. He belongs with his principles and programs to no history but the history of a lit-

---

[20] The capricious nature of Spengler's critical stance was not lost upon the Nazis, who found it rather perplexing. Attempting to defend National Socialism from Spen-gler's charges, one Arthur Zweiniger published a short book titled *Spengler in The Third Reich. A Response to Oswald Spengler's 'Years of Decision.'* This text documents the wonder, on the part of the Nazis, that Spengler did not acknowledge the way his doctrines had been vindicated by Nazism. Zweiniger asserted that Spengler's conclu-sions stand "in contradiction to his own facts, to the results of his own inquiries. He obviously fails to recognize his own ideas, once presented to him by historical reality" (Zweiniger 1933: 9–10). Similarly, the author complained that Spengler "does not rec-ognize his own children" (12). In view of this baffling myopia, Zweiniger stated that he will refute the famous philosopher by remaining true to his own teachings, since it is Spengler "who everywhere enters into a conflict with himself, or fails to logically conclude his own assumptions," for had he done so, he would have, by necessity, "vali-dated Adolf Hitler's Third Reich and the entire National Socialist body-of-thought" (13).

erature.... A Plato or a Rousseau not to mention the smaller intellects could build up abstract political structures, but for Alexander, Scipio, Caesar, and Napoleon, with their schemes and battles and settlements, they were entirely without importance. The thinker could discuss destiny if he liked; it was enough for these men to be destiny (Spengler 1928: 17–18).

Yet faced with a real man of action-cum-destiny in Hitler, Spengler could not obey his own injunctions, and had effectively to discard his theories, to move from the history of literature to actual history. Importantly, however, this did not involve any kind of self-critique, a re-thinking of one's old doctrines, to say nothing of acknowledging or regretting one's own responsibility, as one of Germany's foremost anti-democratic thinkers, in bringing Hitler about. Spengler now simply affirmed, with the same apodictic tone which he formerly employed, the very reverse of what he argued before, namely that the man of action is *impulsive and short-sighted* and stands in urgent need of the *wisdom and insight* of the thinker:

> The active person often does not see far. He is being driven further, without knowing the real goal. Had he seen that goal, he might have resisted it, since the logic of destiny never took notice of human wishes. But much more frequently he goes in the wrong way, since he had developed a false idea of things around and within him. It is the great task of the history expert to understand the facts of his time and from these facts to sense, to read, to outline the future, which will come whether we want it or not. Without creative, anticipating, warning, guiding critique, an epoch with such a consciousness like the present one is impossible (Spengler 1980: 14).

So much for the leader's numinous intuition and for the theorist's inherent limitations. Such theoretical turnaround, moreover, remained a mere whim. Spengler was much too devoted to the anti-democratic notion of the leader's infallibility to really revise his teachings, so that in the very same book, constituting a prolonged intervention in world affairs and political preaching, he could simultaneously complain as of old about the pitiful pretension of his fellow intellectuals, meddling in the man-of-action's affairs: "Political dilettantism talked large. Everyone instructed his future dictator what he ought to want. Everyone demanded discipline from the others, because he himself was incapable of discipline" (186).

Perhaps the only point where one can detect a significant ideological disagreement between Spengler's teachings and the official National-Socialist line, concerns racism. Traditionally, much is made of the fact that Spengler was not a biological racist, operating with a more properly Nietzschean definition of race, highlighting "instinct," a "strong nature," personal valor, and so on, rather than genetics. Spengler, to be sure, expressly condemned the Nazis' fixation on racial purity as well as anti-Semitism, and took care to distinguish his use of the term "race" from theirs (203). In retrospect, these are the only points of dissension, which, so to speak, redeem Spengler's position, unlike the many other points in which he disagreed with the Nazis for all the wrong reasons, as when accusing them of being too pacifistic and democratic. Yet, these facts granted, one should not overrate the ethical advantage of Spengler's own race concept, or ascribe it a very great practical significance. The fact that Spengler often encloses the term race in quotation marks, to imply that it is not to be taken as an essentialist attribute but as a cultural one, does not at all mean that he would leave racism bracketed in political reality, too. On the contrary, he harnesses racial rhetoric to spur Germany to conduct a military-economic crusade in defense of the white races against the "colored" ones:

> It is high time for the 'white' world, and for Germany first of all, to reckon with these facts. For behind the world wars and the still ongoing proletarian world-revolution there looms the greatest of all dangers, the colored one, and it will require every bit of 'race' still available among white nations to meet it. Germany...alone has the fact of Prussianism within itself. With this treasure of exemplary Being it can become the educator, perhaps the savior, of the 'white' world (190).

By Germany "educating" the "white" world, Spengler does not mean a cultural mission of submerging the world in the music of Mozart and Beethoven, or spreading the rhymes of *Faust* among Asians and Africans. Spengler's "Faustian man," rather, is a warrior, contemptuous of mere culture, a Roman imperialist rather than a Greek contemplator. His mission is to suppress the two world revolutions, the "colored" and the working-class: "The one comes from below, the second from without: class-war and race-war" (191). This menace is to be met with barbarism—"Barbarism is what I call strong race, that which is eternally bellicose in the type of the beast-of-prey man. It often seems to have been extinguished, but it is crouching, ready to spring, in the soul" (208)—which, in turn, is predominantly a German merit:

> Why are the German people the least worn out of the white world and for that reason the one on which the strongest hope may be placed?

Because its political past has given it no opportunity for wasting its precious blood and its great abilities.... Fine [*tüchtige*] blood, the foundation of every kind of intellectual superiority too, there was and still remains.... 'Race' was asleep in the people, awaiting the waking call of a great age. Here lies, in spite of the destruction of the last decades, a treasure of fine blood such as no other nation possesses. It can be awakened and must be spiritualized to be ready and operative to confront the stupendous challenges before it. But these tasks are already here. The battle for the planet has begun. The pacifism of the liberal century must be overcome if we are to survive.

How deep have the white nations sunk in pacifism? Is the outcry against war an intellectual gesture or a serious abdication from history at the expense of dignity, honor, liberty? Life is war. Can we bid farewell to its meaning and still retain it? (208–10).

It is hence very difficult to tell Spengler's "German task" apart from the Nazi "German task." In light of such harmony with regards to the goal, the question of whether such terms as "race" or "blood" are meant literally or metaphorically seems mere hair-splitting.[21] Notwithstanding formalities, Spengler's position was implicated in Nazism all along the way, from imperialism and race-war, up to eugenics:

19th century medicine...prevents natural selection and thus enhances the decay of the race. The number of incurable mental cases in England and Wales has increased in the last twenty years from 4.6 to 8.6 per thousand. In Germany, the number of the feeble-minded is almost half a million, in the United States significantly over a million.... But to these must be added the huge numbers of mental, spiritual, and physical abnormal people of every kind, the hysterical, spiritual, and nerve cases who can neither give birth nor bear healthy children.... From this degenerate crop springs the revolutionary proletariat, with its hatred born of inferiority, and the drawing-room Bolshevism of the aesthetes and literary people, who enjoy and advertise the charm of such states of mind (Spengler 1980: 206–7).

---

[21] In fact, for a Nazi such as Zweiniger, Spengler's call for a racial war of the whites against the "coloreds" is out of place, not because it falls short of some biological standard or is a half-hearted racism, but because it is *overly*-zealous. Interestingly, Zweiniger (1933: 66–67) saw fit to criticize Spengler's racism, such as it was, as unnecessarily confrontational, when no real *casus belli* for racial conflict exists. He refused to be impressed by the putative danger posed by the colored and was unwilling to have Germany lead a "white" coalition, given that the whites are in any case disunited: "It is untimely and vastly utopian to recommend to us Germans to consider the eventuality of a possible clash between the colored and the white races... All of these nations are deeply interwoven into the spheres of interests of all races. Is it practical politics to broach such a discussion, precisely as a German?"

Nor does he differ from the Nazis with regards to his concept of woman's social role: "A woman of race does not wish to be a 'companion' or a 'lover,' but a mother; and not the mother of one child, of a toy and pastime, but of many: through the pride that large families inspire, through the feeling that infertility is the worst curse, speaks the instinct of a strong race" (204).

If not substantial ideological disagreement with National Socialism concerning race, what Spengler's terminological differences do reflect is his snobbery. Like other elitist, would-be-aristocrats who vacillated between support and critique of fascism (we might mention, among numerous others, Julius Evola, Edgar Jung, Ernst Jünger and Gottfried Benn), Spengler perfectly realized the need to nationalize/neutralize the masses and hence was positively inclined towards fascism, but at the same time found the actual practice of mass politics hard to stomach. For all their desire to see class-struggle transcended, which implied the need to promote an ethos of the nation as united and harmonious facing its external enemies, such people were horrified at the thought of actually being included in this newly united *Volk*, along with the despised rabble. Theirs was primarily what Domenico Losurdo helpfully defined as "vertical racialism," one that classifies the "master race" and the "slave race" *within* a society, distinguishing the superior elite from the base multitude. But Nazism operated simultaneously with an "horizontal racialism," which makes all Arians, regardless of social status, members of the *Volksgemeinschaft* and places them above other races.[22] This was a necessity under modern conditions, which no longer allow one simply to dismiss the masses. The Pandora's Box had already been opened and the demons of the demos cannot just be summoned back into place. So some kind of an alternative ethos must be created to rally the people, to function as an alternative to a mass/class sense of belonging. Such was the objective underpinning of fascist conceptions of the nation, regardless of the subjective rationalizations of its numerous proponents, whether honest or cynical—and their ingenious propositions for Fichtean socialism, bourgeois socialism, national socialism or, indeed, Spengler's own ideal of Prussian socialism. No matter how disdainful of the masses, all these entrenched elitists had themselves courted the populace. They

---

[22] See the edifying distinction between "*razzizzazione orizzontale*" and "*razzizzazione trasversale*" in Losurdo (2004: 823–26, 847–54).

all partook in modern, parliamentary politics, if only to induce the voters to destroy democracy. Yet even such pseudo-equality was irksome to elitists like Spengler. As Walter Struve (1973: 273) observed in his important early study of German inter-wars' elitism: "Spengler was unwilling to accept the largely illusory concessions to the Left that his own works implied must be made. He shied away from the demagoguery that he himself had recommended." Spengler's true ideal was a politics able to repel the masses with force and authority alone, a modern form of what he referred to as Caesarism. Fascism was a necessary compromise, but as such only a second-best solution. Typical of other elitists' inner-dilemma, he desired the *goal*, but not the *means*, the *fascist dictator*, but not the *movement*:

> Mussolini's creative idea was great, and it has had an international effect: it pointed to a possible form of combating Bolshevism. But this form arose out of imitating the enemy and is hence full of dangers: the revolution from below, in part made and participated in by *Untermenschen*... This all belongs to the past. What looks forward to the future is not the being of fascism as a party, but solely and exclusively the figure of its creator (Spengler 1980: 177).

Yet the pre-condition for a dictator, *is* the movement; in the absence of the movement, a dictator would not be one. It is impossible, as the saying goes, to make an omelet without breaking eggs.[23] This explains why Spengler, although never believing Hitler to be the suitable dictator, could nonetheless support him and his party. As he reputedly told his sister, justifying voting for the NSDAP: "Hitler is a bonehead. But the movement must be supported" (Petzold 1978: 211). The undiluted form of authoritarian-liberalism which Spengler idealized, that gives the masses absolutely nothing above the joys of strenuous work and perilous fighting, and which he marketed as socialism, was bound to remain an ideal. Fascism came close enough to fulfilling it, perhaps as close as at all possible. Not even Spengler's role models, the Caesars or the Bismarcks, ruled with the stick alone, and the hailed "Iron Chancellor" was himself guilty of introducing wide scale social measures to arrest socialism. So Spengler was unduly harsh on the Nazis who in truth gave their absolute best to play the part of "Prussian socialists" according to the original script and were fairly successful. And if Hitler

---

[23] Zweiniger (1933: 37) paraphrased Spengler's paradoxical stand with recourse to another idiom: "Wash me, but don't get me wet!"

chose to introduce certain modifications to the script, surely he was only exercising his right as a statesman to ignore the "bookworm" and "the political doctrinaire" and to "be destiny." Nothing much can be said against that; not, at any rate, from a Spenglerian vantage point.

After Fascism: J. S. Schapiro and the Illusive Death of the Dismal Science

In the aftermath of the Second World War, and to a significant extent as a result of the fascist catastrophe, it was not Germany that abandoned its anti-Western prejudices and illusions to finally join the capitalistic West, as numerous liberal German historians would have it, but *the West* which, at least for several decades, somewhat blunted its capitalistic edge, shifting towards a more moderate socioeconomic doctrine. Based on an unprecedented scale of progressive taxation and social services and securities, the welfare state, while doubtlessly motivated by the need to hold communism at bay, was also an attempt to avoid the pitfalls of capitalist fanaticism, and create a "mixed economy" which will acknowledge the right of the political sphere, of democracy, to intervene in the economic domain. Visibly moved, Kurt Schumacher, the first leader of post-War German Social Democracy, who spent nearly the entire Nazi period in concentration camps, summed up the lessons of Nazism, in the first party conference of the SPD, in Hamburg, on May 8, 1946:

> German intellectual history, and German political history and the German economic class interests of the big landowners, have inexorably led to the point, that in the future democracy in Germany must be socialistic or it will be nothing at all. Democracy demands socialism, and socialism demands democracy. For this realization, comrades, we must fight, and we shall fight.

And while it was not Schumacher nor his party who were to lead Germany in the coming years, some such "realization" [*Erkenntnis*] seems to have vitally informed the post War welfarist consensus across much of western Europe. It was thus not simply Germany who learned from the West, but the West that learned a vital lesson from Germany. Yet such was a precarious balance of forces, as the triumphant rise of neo-liberalism throughout the 1980s and into the present testifies. It is befitting that H. A. Turner's influential critique of the notion that capitalism has anything to do with Nazism was published in the mid-1980s, at the very heyday of Reagan's and Thatcher's rule. The historiographic revision of Nazism presenting it as a force against capitalism, thus accompanied and accommodated the rise to power of a capitalism that was no longer willing to assume an apologetic stance and to accept a working compromise with any form of "socialism," however democratic.

The welfare state consensus was founded on an at least implicit recognition that fascism was the product of capitalism gone berserk. I say "implicit" since liberals themselves were understandably reluctant, even immediately after the war, to admit the possibility that the just defeated world-fascism was in some profound respects an extension of capitalist politics and ideology. Thus, making a virtue out of necessity, the transition to the welfare state was often presented not as a departure from classical liberalism but as a continuation, even a logical conclusion, of the liberal line. A typical attempt of that kind was J. Salwyn Schapiro's study *Liberalism and the Challenge of Fascism*, published in 1949, that minimized the ideological damage to liberalism by providing an historical account of liberalism as a fundamentally democratic and, indeed, egalitarian force:

> During the nineteenth century liberalism became the protagonist of political equality, or democracy. In the movement to establish universal, equal suffrage, it was clear... that political democracy would not be the final step in the march toward equality. Once established, political democracy would become a powerful method for applying the principle of equality to economic matters in the interest of the working class (Schapiro 1949: 8–9).

This made post-war social democracy appear a seamless appendage of liberalism, rather than its far-reaching revision, or a painful concession. The bitter struggles between democrats and liberals throughout the 19th century, over the extension of the suffrage, vanished from sight, as if what we have termed "the liberal split" had never existed. This meant that socialist, economically anti-liberal measures could have been described as a mere implementation of the worthy liberal principles: "Therein lies the significance of the rapid growth of the socialist and labor parties, which fell heir to the egalitarian principle first proclaimed by liberalism. The many social reforms in the interest of the working class, moderate and halting at first, but comprehensive and far-reaching today, have been so many steps in the direction of economic equality" (9). The reader of such an account might have found the very *need* for socialism perplexing, given the thorough liberal commitment to democratic and egalitarian measures. So Schapiro gradually unveiled the fact that liberalism in practice was not altogether harmonious with democracy and with economic equality, in truth running into a strong conflict with them. He admitted (67) that "a disturbing contradiction soon loomed up" between theoretical, "legal and moral" equality and actual, "social and economic" inequality, and criticized the "bland concept of 'an invisible hand' of the general good, guiding the crass selfishness of the 'economic man'" (72–73). The gist of all that was to justify the emanating welfare state as a distilled, *superior* form of liberalism, which further carries out the immanent emancipatory logic of liberalism, while discarding its unwholesome, dogmatic, and anachronistic aspects, such as the myopic opposition to state regulation of the economy with a view to economic equality. This implied conclusion became quite explicit in the last chapter, where liberalism was said to culminate in—state socialism. Before "the advent of liberalism," the author maintained (398), "the state had acted in the interest of the economically strong; now it acted in the interest of the economically weak.... It was the liberal state that succeeded in reconciling government with liberty." And, most emphatically: "liberals developed the method of compromise, according to which the propertied classes were given protection against confiscation, and the nonpropertied classes, protection against poverty. The functioning of the liberal state in all its political and social phases can now clearly be seen in the extensive reforms put through by the British labour party" (398–9). Most importantly, this superior social wedlock was brought about, as argued in the book's last page, by fascism, unwittingly playing the matchmaker, drawing liberalism and socialism together, and the dowry that bourgeois liberalism had to bring was renouncing its obsession with economic hegemony:

> Its [bourgeois liberalism's] contributions have been accepted—and forgotten. Those who still cherish its central doctrine of *laissez faire* are regarded as relics of the past that has receded even more in opinion than in time. Yet bourgeois liberalism did perform a historic function the greatness of which merits recognition. It was the fascist threat to parliamentary government and civil society, a heritage from bourgeois liberalism, that solidified the English people in the critical year 1940. And it was the same heritage that, in France, inspired the Resistance movement which led to the creation of the Fourth Republic. In the new pattern of life and thought which is now emerging, in which socialized democracy is in the foreground, bourgeois liberalism is clearly seen as the background (403).

It is not difficult to see why such explanations, while protective of liberalism, could not be more than a transitory line of defense. A reconciliation of liberalism with socialism, while appropriate for the time being, was bound to become an ideological inadequacy in the long run, given the strategic antagonism between them. Schapiro was clearly unjustifiably sanguine in decreeing *laissez faire* over and done with, or in imagining that the inherent contradiction between economic and political liberalism has been forever resolved, rather than tactically postponed. Soon enough, against the welfare-state consensus, capitalist ideologues were being called upon to stress the crucial and unbridgeable *differences* between liberalism and socialism, and to reaffirm the injunction against any political-democratic intervention in the economy. It is a sobering exercise to read Schapiro's depictions of 19th century *laissez faire*, allegedly a gloomy historical episode transcended forever, in the light of the neo-liberal comeback of the late 20th century, and to notice the striking parallels between the two ideologies:

> The social order established by capitalism was stoutly defended by the classical economists, who justified the new inequality as being part of the natural order. Furthermore, they turned the powerful weapon of economic law against the new poor as they did against the old rich, in order to protect the interests of the capitalists. The attitude of the classical economists to the problem of poverty constitutes a somber page in the intellectual history of modern Europe.... They proclaimed the existence of biologic and economic laws that decreed, at the same time, prosperity for the capitalists and mere subsistence to the workers. And these laws, being natural, were enforced by nature herself; they could not be repealed as could man-made statutes by man-chosen parliaments.... Economic law, universal, impersonal, and implacable, was invoked by the classical economists to justify the economic damnation of the working class.... The justice of economic law was never tempered with mercy and was administered with an impersonality as pitiless as was the Calvinist god himself (84–85).

How lucid a description of 19th century "dismal science," but how unwarranted the conviction that such science has dwindled into a mere relic of the past.[24] The socioeconomic lesson that fascism gave

---

[24] A comparable work, in ideological terms, to that of Schapiro, is that of John Weiss (1967). The narrative there unfolded was actually very close to the class explanation of fascism as an extreme expression of upper-class resentment vis-à-vis the growing power of the socialist and democratic masses. As such, it contains numerous descriptions that remain both correct and insightful, for example, a refutation of the idea that fascism was revolutionary and numerous affirmations of the support of bourgeois, indeed

the Western nations proved hardly an abiding one; and bourgeois liberalism was not at all content with remaining a mere background to socialized democracy. The neo-liberal comeback was hence predicated on the notion that fascism was an egalitarian, collectivist attack on capitalism, and therefore no state meddling with capitalism ought to be tolerated.[25] Hence the somewhat belated ideological triumph of the von Miseses and the von Hayeks, who always insisted that Nazism be seen as a collectivist, indeed socialist phenomenon. While a relatively marginal voice throughout the 1950s and '60s, it was their "history" which became the central narrative during the late '70s, throughout the '80s and into the '90s. The lesson of fascism remained, formally, as fresh and unshakable as ever, only that its content was nearly completely reversed: from the anti-fascist imperative "do not let capitalism run amok!" anti-fascism now admonished: "dare not meddle with capitalism, no matter how crazy it behaves!" The liberal split, which

---

capitalistic, sections for fascism. Weiss, however, was conspicuously uncomfortable with the disturbing implications of his own account, namely that fascism was part of the liberal tradition, and hence insisted on its "anti-liberal" character and related it, rather, to a "last gasp of conservatism" (5), a disastrous attempt on the part of the dying forces of the European pre-modern era to repulse the united forces of "liberalism" and "radicalism." This lumping together of largely antagonistic forces permitted Weiss to eschew the implications of the distinctly *liberal* share in the "conservative" reaction. Occasionally, however, he was forced to admit this joint work, but ascribed it, quite like Schapiro, to some destructive, obdurate, *laissez-faire* residues from the past, which did not as such pertain to modern, progressive liberalism, pointing towards the welfare state:

> It should be remembered, however, that in general such supporters of fascism insofar as they were liberal, were so only in the sense, say, that members of the John Birch Society are liberal; i.e., they stood for the values of early nineteenth-century liberalism. Such ossified liberalism is starkly conservative in our time. It opposes representative democracy, trade-unionism, and the social legislation of the modern neoliberal welfare state; and it supports a rigid defence of the rights of private property regardless of social cost (5).

In historical perspective the gratuitous optimism of such a passage cannot but strike the reader, who recognizes in the "ossified liberalism" of the past the very same fashionable and hegemonic liberalism of the present. The impact is doubled by the terminological choice of "neoliberalism" to indicate, of all things, the welfare state as the conclusion of liberal modernity. We now know that neoliberalism can mean something quite different, and far less remote from early 19th century values.

[25] At least, not one that seeks to promote social equality. State interventions or projects aiming at enhancing capitalism, boosting industry or bailing it out in its hours of need, no matter how costly, were never met with nearly as much doctrinaire compunctions on the part of neo-liberals.

for a time appeared to have healed and vanished, reasserted itself with a vengeance. The West, it turns out, will be the West.

We have gone some way towards tracing the intersections between fascism and liberalism. Yet a number of important issues remain to be addressed, and exemplary figures discussed, for the picture to become more rounded. This will be our task in the next chapters.

CHAPTER THREE

ANTI-LIBERAL LIBERALS—I
(MOELLER VAN DEN BRUCK, PROUDHON, CARLYLE)

A focus on fascist ideology, as we have seen, is often employed by modern critics as the most effective means of dislodging the materialistic approach, that alleged a strong link between fascism and capitalism, and installing in its place an idealistic methodology, that tends to shift fascism away from capitalism and into the vicinity of socialism. And yet, by focusing on ideology, I have argued that fascism and liberalism were not antagonistic bodies of thought, and that, moreover, fascism was *at its most liberal* precisely when it came to defending capitalism. Conversely, to the extent that fascism could be described as *anti*-liberal, this was primarily with a view to those political aspects of liberalism that have grown to hamper the capitalist economy and the bourgeois social order. To an extent that should not be underestimated, fascists were socioeconomic liberals exasperated by the implications of political liberalism. Fascism took over from liberalism some of its most pressing ideological concerns and deep seated convictions and obsessions. Fascism, no doubt, exacerbated such liberal legacy, but it did not quite distort it beyond recognition.

The Bourgeois Spirit of the Germanic Ideology

Following the debacle of European fascism, its liberal pedigree became a source of embarrassment. The need, on the part of intellectuals endorsing the liberal order, was to absolve liberalism of any historical complicity with fascism, by delineating an alternative genealogy, that would construe fascism as a non-liberal or even anti-liberal force. An initial response—as the example of the historian J. Salwyn Schapiro and his 1949 book have shown—was to present post-War social democracy as a natural continuation of liberal ideology and policy. Yet in realigning their forces against the Cold War adversary, liberal thinkers adopted a more aggressive position. The increasingly common theoretical response was to strategically present fascism as the rightist counterpart of leftist liberalism-critique, to conflate Nazism and Communism as the twin evils of "totalitarianism," equally the foes of the liberal West. A notable case in point would be Fritz Stern's classical study *The Politics of Cultural Despair: A Study in the Rise of the Germanic Ideology*, published in 1960. The main argument advanced by Stern in his analysis of "the Germanic ideology" was that it consisted of a sustained cultural attack on liberalism and capitalism. The 19th century figures of Paul de Lagarde and Julius Langbehn, and the 20th century one of Arthur Moeller van den Bruck, taken to be the paradigmatic representatives and initiators of said ideology, were repeatedly held to have chastised liberalism above all: "The conservative revolutionaries denounced every aspect of the capitalistic society" (Stern 1961: xviii), their "chief target" being "liberalism" (xix). Or, to the same effect: "the primary target was modernity as embodied in the rational, liberal and capitalistic society" (xxiii). This argument was eventually expanded into the following, general evaluation of Nazi ideology:

> The National Socialist ideology, in motive, form, and content, resembles the Germanic ideology. Their negative views were indistinguishable. For both, liberalism was the chief enemy, an alien and corrosive force... Both were embittered critics of the bourgeois way of life, of the spirit of capitalism and Moeller anticipated the National Socialist belief in Germanic socialism (295).

So, as we were asked to believe, there is no "spirit of capitalism" whatsoever to be traced, say, in the pages of *Mein Kampf*, such as endorsement of the benefits of competition, individual excellence, free entrepreneurship, etc. Only an embittered critique of them. Similarly, if the Nazis rallied against "liberal" institutions such as the parliamentary system, this was motivated merely by cultural despair and a rejection of "the bourgeois way of life." In a highly influential ideological analysis, the possibility was not even allowed for, let alone seriously considered, that there might have been the slightest socioeconomic incentive for the Nazis to defeat the trade unions and exclude the masses from politics, precisely in order to *safeguard* the bourgeoisie and the capitalistic spirit. Nothing of that was allowed to confuse and deter the reader from seeing liberalism as a defenseless victim of fascist aggression. In his 1974 preface, warning against the contemporaneous re-emergence of dangerous rightist, but mostly leftist, utopianism associated with student counterculture, Stern remarked (ix) that, "once again, implicit in the attack on modernity has been the repudiation, the hatred of the West," as if the Nazis had not ritually celebrated themselves as the last barrier of Western civilization in front of Asian-Communist barbarism.[1] Certainly, even had Stern assured his readers, as many other political theorists have been willing to do, that Nazism was a *sui generis* political phenomenon, standing between and opposing both capitalism and socialism, this would have been grossly inaccurate; anti-Marxism, namely, dominated both Nazi theory and practice as compared with an infinitely milder critique, and even that mostly perfunctory, of capitalism. Yet Stern went as far as averring that Nazism was *primarily* anti-capitalist and, moreover, that it could actually be seen as a socialist reaction to capitalism, however Germanic. Indeed, early on (xx), Stern claimed that, "by the end of the nineteenth century, the liberals themselves changed their political philosophy by gradually adopting a paternalistic program," this bearing the regrettable consequence that, "today's political rhetoric is full of confusion concerning the true meaning of liberalism. Amidst this confusion, some critics persist in blaming liberalism for everything they find undesirable in modernity." But Stern's "true meaning of liberalism" emerged as a platonic ideal, upon which actual historical proceedings cannot impinge. It was therefore possible to return to that lofty paradigm without pausing to consider why it was that the liberals themselves felt obliged to change their political philosophy and resort to paternalism.

Furthermore, the Germanic ideology was diagnosed, in the spirit of Nietzsche, as a foul tide of *ressentiment* against the liberal-capitalistic order. Stern (xxi) spoke about the "Ideology of Resentment": "Under the auspicious conditions of declining liberalism, this political organization of resentment erupted time and again." Or, similarly (xxx): "The National Socialists gathered together the millions of malcontents, of whose existence the conservative revolutionaries had for so long spoken, and for whose relief they had designed such dangerous and elusive ideals." Fascism was thereby explained as a slave-revolt, a movement of failures and tormented outsiders exasperated by industrial society. We were told nothing of the fact that, among "those millions of malcontents," the embittered outsiders to industrial society

---

[1] As one scholar states (Fischer 2002: 292), both Italian and German fascists "worried about the condition of Western culture, which they wished to save."

who rallied to Nazism, were the likes of Alfred and Gustav Krupp, Kurt Schröder, Fritz Thyssen and Albert Vögler, i.e., some of the most prominent German industrialists. They, too, were apparently engaged in desperate cultural protest against industrial society. Post-War ideological necessity dictated that capitalism and fascism be dichotomized, that fascism be explained as an anti-capitalist slave-revolt, and Stern obliged.

Yet what about Stern's pioneers of the Germanic Ideology, Lagarde, Langbehn and Moeller? Were not these ideologues, as he argues, "embittered critics of the spirit of capitalism"? Stern had a strong case with regards to the first two, who were typical representatives of 19th century petty bourgeois or old *Mittelstand*, threatened by large-scale industrialization. In Lagarde's *Deutsche Schriften*, in particular, one might find an effusive critique of the precarious "values of industry" as opposed to the wholesome way of life of traditional artisanship [*Handwerk*] and farming. "Only agriculture, livestock breeding, and trade," he insisted, "can make Germany rich, not industry" (Lagarde 1994: 21). He also denounced (111) the reliance on machinery, which de-humanized the worker, and he expressed a longing for a creative and complete life: "No one should be expected, year in and year out, to do no more than supervise a machine which folds and glues envelopes or sharpens needles. With that, one's heart will not be satisfied: humans long for the whole." In *The Communist Manifesto*, in the passages dealing with petty-bourgeois socialism and with "German or 'true' socialism," Engels and Marx provide, some 25 years before Lagarde's publications, a pithy and apposite analysis of his ideological position and the social interests it reflected. I quote just a couple of relevant sentences:

> In countries where modern civilization has become fully developed, a new class of petty bourgeois has been formed, fluctuating between proletariat and bourgeoisie... The individual members of this class,... see the moment approaching when they will completely disappear as an independent section of modern society, to be replaced in manufactures, agriculture and commerce, by labor overseers and stewards.... In Germany, the petty-bourgeois class, a relic of the sixteenth century,... is the real social basis of the existing state of things.... The industrial and political supremacy of the bourgeoisie threatens it with certain destruction; on the one hand, from the concentration of capital; on the other, from the rise of a revolutionary proletariat. 'True' Socialism appeared to kill these two birds with one stone. It spread like an epidemic (2005: 75–80).

It is clear that such an outlook informed certain variants of Nazi ideology, for instance that of Gottfried Feder, the early economist of the Nazi movement, and was also effective in gathering support among sections of the middle classes. It is altogether another question to what extent these anachronistic, anti-industrial positions were central to actual Nazi policies, as opposed to having been politically sidelined (as Feder's own increasing marginalization would suggest). To claim, as Stern did, that this formed the central plank of Nazism, ideologically and practically, is exaggerated as well as unfounded. We could, at this point, embark on a survey of the vast literature on the topic of Nazi economics and its relationship to capitalism, industrialism and modernity. Yet this would run against our own intent to remain largely within the sphere of ideological analysis, to examine what the fascists and proto-fascists themselves wrote and said. And, as it happens, for evidence seriously compromising Stern's theory, we need do no more than consult the youngest among the Germanic Ideologues, Moeller van den Bruck, the one who had, according to Stern, "anticipated the National Socialist belief in Germanic socialism" (295). Let us therefore examine Moeller's position as expressed in his treatise *The Third Reich*, published in 1923, and generally acknowledged as an important text of German fascism. What were his views on liberalism, capitalism and socialism?

Moeller van den Bruck: A Socialist Champion of Capitalism

With Moeller, we have a textbook example of fascist terminological jugglery, whereby concepts are employed in a completely new meaning to achieve a mystifying effect, in the hope of ideologically disarming the opposition and recruiting new support. This is the semantic jumble, familiar from the discussion in the former chapter, where the cards of socialism, liberalism, conservatism, and so on, are conceptually reshuffled, so that one obtains a "socialist" Joker, that actually stands for—capitalism. Why is this at all necessary? Why should a pro-capitalist writing during the early phases of the Weimar Republic embrace socialism, while using the word capitalism with great reserve, if at all? Because, when engaging in a political campaign, it is necessary to consider the market price at which a given concept is currently traded. If, in a given time and place, a term such as "socialism" is greatly unpopular, promoters of a socialist agenda would be well advised to employ this term in moderation in their discourse. Upton Sinclair, the great American socialist writer and activist, realized this fact during his 1934 campaign for governor of California, an experience that he recalled some 17 years later, in a letter to fellow socialist Norman Thomas:

> The American People will take Socialism, but they won't take the label. I certainly proved it in the case of EPIC. Running on the Socialist ticket I got 60,000 votes, and running on the slogan to 'End Poverty in California' I got 879,000. I think we simply have to recognize the fact that our enemies have succeeded in spreading the Big Lie. There is no use attacking it by a front attack, it is much better to out-flank them (Sinclair 1951).

In many European countries during the same time, however, particularly in the aftermath of the First World War, socialism enjoyed a highly positive reputation amongst large segments of the population. By contrast, it was the rivals of socialism who found their creeds devalued, and so, unable to attack socialism *frontally*, they had to try to *out-flank* it. They had to be everywhere on the defensive in order to weather the storm, making concessions to socialism politically, economically and, *terminologically*. Vilfredo Pareto, writing two years before the publication of Moeller's book, astutely expressed this upper-class predicament, in which the values of the left are becoming quasi-hegemonic, so that people of the right are hard pressed to feign conformity with them:

> [T]he fact that a religion has hypocritical supporters is an indication of the faith's power, since men feign belief in something only if it is widely accepted by large numbers of their fellow men.... It is today a sure index of the power of the belief in democracy to see so many people pretending to share the belief, while it is a certain sign of the decline of the belief in aristocracy that among this belief's supporters there remains not one hypocrite (Pareto 1966: 319).

To substitute the term socialism for that of democracy in this quotation, is to clearly perceive the structural necessity underpinning fascist hypocrisy, the reason that so many fascists were driven to endorse socialism, even as they were doing all they could to destroy it. To realize this historical constellation, incidentally, is also to get a sense of how inadequate is the fashionable theory that fascists were genuine and need be taken at their word and that, therefore, a straightforward approach to fascist ideology, freed from undue suspicion, can divulge the secret of fascist politics.

Writing in Germany in the early 1920s, just following the collapse of the old system and amidst the severest of economic and social crises, an outright apology for capitalism, liberalism, or monarchism, would have been as sensible as trying to sell umbrellas to desert dwellers. Overt pro-capitalism and pro-liberalism, therefore, almost completely disappeared from the political discourse of the time. But actual supporters of capitalism did not evaporate; they were merely forced to go temporarily under cover, assume a double identity, preferably the identity of the enemy. In that way, they hoped to profit from the better reputation of the rival's concepts, notably socialism, which, after the October Revolution, seemed for both supporters and antagonists, for better or for worse, to be the force of the future. To put it once more in Sinclair's terms, supporters of capitalism hoped to promote it de facto, without having to brandish the unpopular *label*. Simultaneously, this strategic maneuver rested on the ability to tap into and exploit, with a greater or lesser degree of tactical awareness, the existing traditions of "German or 'true' socialism," as analyzed by Engels and Marx. Calling this a strategy should not be taken to imply complete cynicism, whereby one knows at all times that one is merely pretending. We may presume that, as in dramatic performance, the process of successfully playing a role, even that of a villain, involves a certain degree of identification and appropriation of the persona's character; precisely how deeply such an identification penetrates and how easily, rapidly and completely one can shed this borrowed identify off the stage, can change considerably, from actor to actor. With Spengler, for one, identification with his socialist part was only skin-deep. As long as such obfuscation was objectively necessary and useful, Spengler avidly pretended to be a socialist, as in his *Prussianism and Socialism*—although we have confirmed that he gave socialism a radically capitalistic bent. Once the enemy was defeated and the Nazis were in power, the defensive maneuvers were no longer necessary, in fact they hampered one's progress. The very same ambiguity that was formerly a blessing, became a source of confusion. In an attacking mood, it was now possible to dispense with hypocrisy and attack socialism openly and unflinchingly, as Spengler did in *The Years of Decision*.

Among the many who feigned belief in socialism was Moeller. Let us examine how he plays this part in *The Third Reich*. Moeller (1934) has plenty of good things to say about socialism, while he denigrates liberalism consistently and in the most uncompromising tones. Certainly, at that rhetoric level, Stern was quite right to describe him as anti-liberal. Not only does Moeller encourage the workers to be German socialists, he tells them furthermore (76) that "German socialism is called to play a part in the spiritual and intellectual history of mankind by purging itself of every trace of liberalism," and he declares (113) a "fight against liberalism all along the line." Yet was this unremitting opposition to liberalism indeed all-inclusive? Did it, for example, include a fight against such liberal keystones as private property, individual enterprise, differences of income or hierarchy of labor relations? In other words, does the term liberalism, in Moeller's use, include the capitalist economy? And is he a socialist in the sense of challenging such an economy? For Stern, the answer to both questions was positive. Moeller's anti-liberalism, he insisted, meant an embittered critique of capitalism and the bourgeoisie. And F. A. Hayek (2007: 191), for whom, of course, liberalism is nothing if it is not capitalistic, similarly construed Moeller as a fierce opponent of the liberal order: "As with Spengler, liberalism...is the arch-enemy.... Moeller van den Bruck's Third Reich was intended to give the Germans a socialism adapted to their nature and so it did." This, of course, is the decisive point: if Moeller was anti liberal from a perspective affirmative of both capitalism and the bourgeoisie, then the effort to drive a wedge between his "Germanic ideology" and the liberal-capitalist West must come to naught. The outcome would be the same if Moeller's "Germanic socialism," like Spengler's Prussian one, was a euphemism for imperialistic capitalism. Yet such it was. In no way does it come any closer to socialism in the traditional—i.e., anti-capitalist—sense, than Spengler's visions. I will not go into the details of Moeller's socialism, since this would mean little more than a repeat of what was said above about Spengler's schemes. Socialism for Moeller simply meant: 1) overcoming internal class struggle. Germanic socialism must therefore be weaned from Marxism: "Every people has its own socialism. Marx disturbed German socialism at the very root.... We must now set about making good the mischief he effected" (Moeller 1934: 71); or (76): "Socialism begins where Marxism ends." 2) achieving national unity for the purpose of imperialistic expansion. Certainly, this imperialistic scheme was justified as benefiting the workers, and, in that capacity, could be presented as socialistic:

> [T]he German socialist [i.e., the social democrat]...did not realize that it is even more important to attain a balance between nations than between classes. He never enquired what the crowded nations, who had not the

same scope as the sated nations enjoyed, were to do with the product of their increasing industry. He would not see that it might be the role of a socialist-imperialism to procure them new markets and thus provide work for the worker (73).

But, of course, even assuming that German workers would indeed materially benefit from German imperialism, this would not make it any more socialistic than, say, the British Empire benefiting English workers. And the British Empire was, in fact, explicitly cited as a model for the German future one, just as the British working class was invoked as a model for its German counterpart:

> This same German social democrat who contrived to reconcile pacifism with Darwinism—undisturbed by the reflection that Nature represents a fight for existence in which the victor is the survivor—...would not see that the solution to the over-population problem *is* socialism. He would not ask whether the true system for regulating the production and consumption of an excess population might not be found in imperialism. He repeated parrot-wise that imperialism was a system for the exploitation of foreign countries and, like capital, a matter of profit only.
>
> Yet the thesis might well have been maintained—and brought home to the proletariat—that the possession of the earth is the means indicated for an over-populated country to find means of livelihood: a practical, living, politically workable thesis. By an irony of fate the truth of this has been revealed to the working classes of two countries, France and England, whose populations are decreasing, and has been concealed from the German working man, the inhabitant of an over-populated country (63).

Moeller's anti-Western, anti-capitalist, Germanic socialism, plainly reveals itself as Western, capitalist, imperialism. England and France—resented enemies of Germany though they certainly are, and fierce competitors in the imperialistic "fight for existence" and for "the possession of the earth,"—are brought up not to exemplify some antithesis of the German essence, but rather as providing the model from which to copy. The problem with Germany, according to Moeller, is not that it had hitherto imitated the West and neglected its own special calling, but, on the contrary, that it was naively pursuing its own *Sonderweg*, adrift from the Western main-path:

> In England every stratum of the people is aware that power takes precedence of economics. The trusting German proletariat believed what its social democrat leaders preached: that a day was coming when states and nations would be no more, when all men would posses the earth in

common, and providential economics would care for well-being of the masses (63).

The only potentially socialistic aspect about Moeller's programme is his notion of a planned economy, geared towards imperialism. Surely, this signifies a serious breach with Western, liberal capitalism? For liberal interpreters, at any rate, this was unmistakably the case. George Mosse (1987: 166), not unlike Stern, used this to illustrate the fascist endeavor to form a "third force" in between capitalism and communism, in fact closer to the latter:

> Moeller van den Bruck, whose book *The Third Reich* (1923) was originally entitled *The Third Way*, brought this tradition up to date for a defeated nation: the Germanic mission would transcend all the contradictions inherent in modern life... To be sure, Moeller was pragmatic in his demand for political action, his advocacy of the corporate state, and his desire to institute a planned economy (hence his praise of Lenin's new economic policy).

This sounds ominously anti-capitalistic indeed, linking Moeller's project with that of Lenin. Mosse did not cite Moeller, finding it more convenient to paraphrase him. And this was judiciously done, since Moeller's notion of coordinated economy was in truth closely linked, not to socialism, but to *monopoly capitalism*, which Moeller regarded as the triumphant answer to the doom prophecies of the Marxists:

> Marx had maintained that a collapse of capitalism was imminent and inevitable; both these theories proved untenable. Intelligent capitalist enterprise took the direction of constructive reorganization instead of the line of collapse. Even before the War, trusts and cartels and mergers had been formed to stabilize capitalism, and after the War capitalism seized on the idea of the zones and provinces on which to base a system of planned economics (Moeller 1934: 160).

Given such affirmations of the abiding vitality of capitalism, it is unsurprising that what Moeller praised about Lenin's NEP was actually the perceived dismantling of the revolutionary project and the setting of a course that was as *politically conservative* as it was *economically capitalistic*:

> Russia, where the revolutionary upheaval began, was the first to make concessions to conservatism, to abandon one after another of its utopian doctrines.... An internal economic compromise accompanied the foreign one: free trading was again permitted, markets flourished once more and the famous fairs were renewed. These surrenders to interna-

tional capitalism were unavoidable. They hit the Bolshevist hard, because they were contrary to his economic principles, and involved the admission that the Marxist experiment had broken down (187–8).

"Free trading" and "flourishing markets": is this a language to be expected from a die-hard foe of the liberal-capitalist order, whom Hayek baptized as the "the patron-saint of National Socialism"? The historians—Stern, Mosse—(to say nothing of the capitalist apologist Hayek), are found guilty of neglecting the historical context and applying the idealistic yardstick of "planned economy" (as well, of course, as such abstract notions as socialism and liberalism that they conveniently take for granted, not inquiring after their actual historical content).[2] They then proceed to draw misleading, if ideologically opportune, deductions: since we know that liberalism is capitalistic, then an anti-liberal must be anti-capitalistic, even if his text is shot-through with pro-capitalism; since "planned economy" is a well-known socialist tenet, we can take it that it means, at the very least, a third way between capitalism and communism, if not an outright Leninist path, even though it is expressly grounded on the two phenomena that Lenin, of all socialist theorists, famously analyzed as the distinguishing features of contemporary *capitalism*: monopolies and imperialism.[3]

---

[2] I do not wish to give the impression that Stern and Mosse were at all exceptional in that regard among historians, economists or political scientists. In truth, they represent a very prevalent approach. Numerous scholars, and by no means the less respected or successful ones, have drawn a very similar picture of the Germanic Ideology, even if without normally using that title. As an additional example, one could mention the renowned German historian, Hans Mommsen (2004: 371), who paraphrased the Moellers and Co. to the effect of transforming their ideology into one only *intermittently* and *secondarily* anti-socialist, while *consistently* and *primarily* anti-capitalist, anti-Western, and anti-liberal: "The main-stream of these ideas was directed against Bolshevism and social democracy, although crossings [Übergänge] existed, whereas the front against liberalism and Enlightenment was common to all positions, and as a rule corresponded to the tendency to idealize Russia…The common denominator of these positions consisted of their rejection of Western industrial culture…" In the former page, the author links Moeller's Third Reich concept with a widespread "notion of the corrupt and degenerated capitalistic West." Again: the capitalistic West might indeed have been corrupt and degenerated in Moeller's view, but "free trading" and "flourishing markets" he considered wholesome and vital.

[3] It is interesting to note how, for certain contemporary observers, the implications of Moeller's "planned economy" were clearly different than those of Lenin: in the introduction to the 1934 English translation of *Das dritte Reich*, Mary Agnes Hamilton wrote: "To-day his book,…in its demand, in the name of non-Marxian Socialism, for the totalitarian State which is *the ultimate realization of capitalism*, reads like description" (Moeller 1934: 11; italics added).

Far from hostile to the bourgeois spirit, Moeller's text is *suffused* with such spirit. Hayek was unduly harsh with Moeller, curtly relegating him to the badlands of anti-liberalism. If he had been less concerned with decorum and more with the actual content of Moeller's ideology, he might have discovered several points of contact between himself and "the patron-saint of National Socialism." In his book *The Fatal Conceit*, for example, Hayek dismisses any notion that capitalism is exploitative, by asseverating that, far from being in any way abused by capitalists, proletarians should thank them for their very existence:

> If we ask what men most owe to the moral practices of those who are called the answer is: their very lives.... Most individuals who now make up the proletariat could not have existed before others provided them with means to subsist. Although these folk may *feel* exploited, and politicians may arouse or play on these feelings to gain power, most of the Western proletariat,... owe their existence to opportunities that advanced countries have created for them (Hayek 1988: 130–31).

Though this affirmation would strike some readers as controversial, Moeller, for one, would clearly have subscribed to it: Karl Marx, Moeller argued for his part, "did not see that factories had in fact arisen at the moment of an acute and menacing population crisis, and had come to the rescue of a proletariat whom the country could no longer absorb and who must otherwise have emigrated or perished" (Moeller 1934: 158).[4] This also shows how, for Moeller, if imperialism would be conducted socialistically for the worker's sake, it will merely take this basic drive over from capitalism, which was equally founded to allay the proletariat. There is also an odd harmony between Hayek and Moeller with regard to the critique of socialism as blindly ambitious, in its belief that reality and human nature can be shaped according to ideal precepts of justice and equity. This vain utopianism, Hayek described (1988: 27) as the very "fatal conceit that man is able to shape the world according to his wishes." And Moeller (1934: 232) finds such utopian obduracy no less exasperating: "The revolutionary lives in the illusion that this collapse [of the reactionary's world] gives him the opportunity for giving existence an entirely new set of values according to laws

---

[4] Elsewhere, as Petzold (1978: 112) pointed out, Moeller "characterized the enlistment of the proletariat to the class struggle as downright ungrateful to the employers, since, as a 'surplus' human group, they owed them their very existence."

evolved in his own head which he can compel the present to accept." A fatal conceit, indeed.[5] But beyond such punctual agreements between the intransigent liberal and the Germanic socialist, *Das dritte Reich* is strewn with affirmations of the value of the entrepreneur, defending him from mass resentments, and justifying, in fact, the entire capitalist system. Against radical attacks on capitalists, Moeller affirms (158) the creative value of the entrepreneur: "Marx never even attempted to understand the psychology of the enterprising capitalist.... [H]e left entirely out of account the psychological factors: initiative, energy, imagination. He stereotyped a coarse, contemptuous caricature of a slaveowner which would be sure to appeal to the multitude." This does not sound like the words of an embittered denigrator of the "bourgeois way of life," nor does the following statement, which reads, rather, like a hymn for enterprise:

> But the capitalist possessed not only capital but intelligence, technical mastery, organizing ability, commercial efficiency; he had in fine the power of experience behind him; the proletariat had only the weight of numbers. It was useless for the proletarian to attempt to take over businesses which though dependent on his labour owed nothing to his initiative. We get down to a natural difference between two human types—the director and the workman—each of which is complementary to the other but neither of which can play the other's role. The... proletarian was intellectually unripe for a socialist revolution; because it is the distinguishing mark of a proletarian to be intellectually unripe (147).

Stern, as will be recalled, construed the "Germanic ideology" of Moeller and Co. as the "Ideology of Resentment," targeting "the millions of malcontents, of whose existence the conservative revolutionaries had for so long spoken, and for whose relief they had designed such dangerous and elusive ideals" (xxx). Yet he did the Germanic ideology a great injustice—at least if we take Moeller as its mouthpiece—for

---

[5] Consider, too, Alfredo Rocco's refutation of socialism as a wrongheaded, moralistic utopianism:

In reality the most potent impulse of human actions is in the thrust of individual interest, and to eliminate individual interest from the economic domain is to introduce paralysis into it.... What is the use of constructing a mechanism to achieve a better distribution of wealth, if such mechanism drains the fountains of wealth at the same time? The fundamental error of socialism is to turn private property into a question of justice, whereas it is really a question of utility and social necessity (Rocco 2004: 240).

A more steadfast enunciation of the Hayekian basic creed, would, I think, be difficult to conceive.

in fact, such ideology was fighting shoulder to shoulder with him to stem precisely the dangerous Ideology of Resentment. This leads to a strange situation in which numerous passages in *The Third Reich* could be cited to *refute* Stern's historical thesis while *supporting* his political position. For example, far from spreading rancor among the millions or inciting them to rebel against industrial society, Moeller argues that there is absolutely no reason to be discontented with capitalism since social differences are not unjust or artificial. Workers are neither born into labor, nor coerced to be proletarians, but rather willingly *choose* their employment, and hence have only themselves to blame:

> The proletarian is a proletarian by his own desire.
> It is not the machine, it is not the mechanization of industry, it is not the dependence of wages on capitalist production that makes a man a proletarian; it is the proletarian consciousness (161–62).

Unsatisfied, however, with refuting merely one argument against the legitimacy of the bourgeois order, by assuring that it is based strictly on merit, achievement and the individual's desire to do well, Moeller advances another argument against the idea that proletarians are unjustly treated by society, emphatically affirming that the worker is *born*, not (self-) *made*:

> The spell which binds the proletarian is the spell of birth. As men, as prehistoric men, if you like, we were all originally proletarians, who sat about naked on the bare ground. But a differentiation soon set in; inborn superiority asserted itself, and was inherited as outward privilege. The man who was not sufficiently developed to fit into this social structure as it developed remained at the bottom, he did not rise, he sank.
> He was the proletarian (162).

This is all not very cogent, no doubt, but there is nothing here to ignite resentment, only words to assuage discontent. One would scan such a passage in vain for anti-liberalism. Moeller's account of the natural division of labor under capitalism provides a good opportunity to compare the fascist position with that of classical liberalism, as formulated by the iconic figure of Adam Smith. It is interesting to see how even when Moeller objectively disagrees with classical liberalism, this is done not in attack on the capitalist edifice, but precisely in order to *better defend it*, under radically different historical circumstances. In his seminal apology for the benefits of the division of labor under modern industry, the father of economic liberalism argued, in fact, that such division of labor is not natural but artificial, and that, moreover, it does not reflect the unequal abilities of men but rather *produces* such disparities:

> The difference of natural talents in different men is, in reality, much less than we are aware of; and the very different genius which appears to distinguish men of different professions, when grown up to maturity, is not upon many occasions so much the cause, as the effect of the division of labour. The difference between the most dissimilar characters, between a philosopher and a common street porter, for example, seems to arise not so much from nature, as from habit, custom, and education. When they came into the world, and for the first six or eight years of their existence, they were very much alike, and neither their parents nor play-fellows could perceive any remarkable difference. About that age, or soon after, they come to be employed in very different occupations. The difference of talents comes then to be taken notice of, and widens by degrees, till at last the vanity of the philosopher is willing to acknowledge scarce any resemblance (Smith 1789: 27–28).

Both Smith and Moeller seek to defend the capitalist division of labor. Both justify and approve of its operations; but they do so in diametrically opposed ways: the first by emphasizing the artificial, mechanical way such division works, the latter by grounding it in natural differences. What explains such disparity between Smith's egalitarianism and Moeller's elitism? The answer lies in the historical context of their respective capitalist polemics, and the different social targets of such polemics. For Smith, the representative of the rising bourgeoisie defending the newly conquered terrain against the landed aristocracy, the aim is to discard the naturalistic myths of high- and low birth, which decree humankind's qualities to be inborn and unalterable. The aristocracy relies on such myths to justify its privileges as stemming from the natural, divine order, and to exempt it from work. No amount of work or achievement can make a plebeian the equal of a nobleman. Quite the contrary, the latter's labor distinguishes him for the *worse*, and attest to his ignobility. Smith, bent on showing that it is labor and industry that make a man what he is, will have none of that. He confidently and eloquently elucidates the way the division of labor creates human differences and is the sole source of a man's real value, in that way upholding the bourgeois ethos of industry against the aristocratic ethos of birthright. Yet precisely such an elucidation becomes a source of great danger when, many years later, capitalism has to be defended not against the nobility but against the industrial workers. What formerly was a useful defense of the creative power of industry to transform men and society, now becomes an indictment of the system. Now the workers can, and do, denounce the arbitrary nature of capitalism which, by allotting a person a niche in the division of labor predetermines whether that worker will become a philosopher or a porter, a prosperous, cultivated bourgeois, or a crude proletarian, resembling the "prehistoric man."

What was once an apology, turns into a condemnation. Hence the 19th century bourgeoisie discards the theoretical egalitarianism of Smith to re-embrace a version of neo-aristocratic birthright. It became necessary to defend the capitalist system as natural and reflecting innate abilities, to argue, pace Smith, that genius and talent are the *cause*, not the *effect*, of the division of labor. This is precisely what Moeller— like most 19th century liberals, Social Darwinists and, later, fascists— did. Hence the new cult of the born genius, ubiquitous in bourgeois post-1848 literature, the great men of history and society, from Mill to Nietzsche and beyond. In the teachings of 19th century German national-liberal, Heinrich von Treitschke, we find both justifications of the division of labor side by side, the artificial and the natural. On the one hand, Treitschke virtually admits that the subjugation of the laboring masses to the cultural elite is the outcome of an artificial, and yet indispensable, constellation, as in the following argument:

> [M]ankind is by nature so frail and needy that the immense majority of men, even on the higher levels of culture must always and everywhere devote themselves to bread-winning and the material cares of life. To put it simply: the masses must for ever remain the masses. There would be no culture without kitchen-maids.
>
> Obviously education could never thrive if there was nobody to do the rough work. Millions must plough and forge and dig in order that a few thousands may write and paint and study (Treitschke 1916: 42).

The proletarian here is *made*, and has to facilitate by his or her work the flourishing of culture in the higher social spheres. Social labor is so divided between "the millions" and "the thousands" that culture is sustained. Implicitly, at least, no natural difference between the masses and the elite need exist, since, even supposing that all human beings were perfectly equal, the huge majority would nonetheless have to be subjected to hard work as a precondition for civilization. Yet such cynical acknowledgement of the structural need for modern slavery is a very poor political excuse vis-à-vis those who are meant to serve as slaves (or kitchen-maids). Like numerous other bourgeois spokesmen, Treitschke must thus supplement this justification of class hierarchy by a naturalistic explanation, which presupposes—quite like Moeller—

the *born* proletarian, who can blame only innate inferiority for his or her socioeconomic subordination. An inferiority, moreover, which happens to be racially determined:

> Still more significant is the growth of the population when two different races meet on the same soil. In Austria, for instance, the Slovaks and Vlaks breed like rabbits, and the superior German and Magyar stocks are in danger of being swamped by the rising flood of the proletariat. We see with astonishment that it is precisely to the lowest races that the word 'proletariat' can be applied in its literal meaning.... Our Saxon country folk in Siebenbürgen, who are themselves all of the upper class, have a general term for their servants, derived from the word which means 'menial,' which they use freely in speech, without the least intention of giving offence. This is because all their domestics are Vlaks, or gipsies, and utterly inferior to themselves (226–7).

Culture and nature thus wondrously cooperate, the former needing an abundance of proletarians, and the latter dutifully providing them, in masses. And this justification of the social division of labor as corresponding to natural, racial superiority and inferiority, is the essence of most Social Darwinism, as when the early 20th century American liberal and eugenicist, Lothrop Stoddard, affirmed:

> [W]ithin the higher group itself there exist a relatively large number of very superior individuals, characterized by unusual energy, ability, talent, or genius. It is this élite which leavens the group and initiates progress. Here, again, we see the supreme importance of quality. In no human society has the percentage of really superior individuals ever been large—in fact, their percentage has been always statistically negligible. Their influence, however, has been incalculable. Athens was not made up of Platos or Xenophons: it had its quota of dullards, knaves, and fools...Yet the dynamic power of its élite made Athens the glory of the world, and only when the Athenian stock ceased to produce superiors did Athens sink into insignificance. Thus we see that civilization depends absolutely upon quality, while quality, in turn, depends upon inheritance (Stoddard 1924: 10–11).

Does the doctrine of inborn elitism of the Treitschkes, the Moellers and the Stoddards, reflect the fact that they are all Adam Smith's intellectual and/or moral inferiors? I have no wish to dispute either the first or the second assertion. Yet it is important to realize that we are not dealing here with some fascist or Social Darwinist distortion of liberalism. Quite the contrary, it is a telling historical paradox that, with regard to the issue of the capitalist division of labor, Treitschke, Moeller, and Stoddard are far more representative of the current hegemonic bourgeois-liberal conception than Smith. The latter's egalitarianism reads today as counter-intuitive, heretic, indeed radically anti-bourgeois. His notion that geniuses are produced more or less mechanically, that the philosopher is the porter's equal under favorable circumstances, and that it is only the vanity of the former that declines the kinship, reads like a socialist blasphemy, whereas Stoddard's insistence on the natural gulf separating Plato from the multitude of dullards surrounding him, though perhaps untactfully phrased, agrees with our collective, common-sense notions. Smith's conception flies in the face even of the most hallowed tenet of modern liberalism, equality of opportunity. For he shows us that reality turns on its head the imaginary conceptualization of opportunity as supposedly exploited by merit, talent and effort: it is not, namely, the person of quality who takes advantage of an opportunity; on the contrary, it is the opportunity that an average person receives which turns her willy-nilly into a person of quality, or into a person of the mass. The porter is no less successful than the philosopher in exploiting the opportunity given to him, and that he has indeed taken advantage of it to the full is testified to by the fact that he becomes...a porter. The sacred fire of individualism burns only very dimly in Smith's account of modern industry. Individuality is, at most, the end-product of the division of labor, its final result, not its starting point. Clothes, as the saying goes, make the man; to which we should add, with Smith: but so do machines. Moeller, on the other hand, fully subscribes to the equality-of-opportunities principle. Who is the one who furnishes a more entrenched, systematic and effective defense of capitalism, the illustrious liberal Scott or the German anti-liberal fascist? "It is not the machine," Moeller claims, "it is not the mechanization of industry, it is not the dependence of wages on capitalist production that makes a man a proletarian; it is the proletarian consciousness." The Proletarian, he avows, is the man who could not (on account of a natural insufficiency), or would not (because of a spiritual inclination), exploit the ample opportunities provided by capitalism, "the man who was not sufficiently developed to fit into this social structure." We stand now, ideologically (and practically) much closer to the naturalism of Moeller than to the materialistic, sober vision of Smith. If the criteria for being labeled anti-liberal revolve around a critique of capitalism, than Moeller does not in the least apply. His apologetic efforts on behalf of capitalism, on the other hand, deserve a long-due liberal recognition. From a standpoint shielding capitalism from lower-class unrest, no praise could possibly exaggerate the zeal of such efforts:

Marx called the proletarian revolution 'the independent movement of the overwhelming majority.' Lenin talked of the 'forward-movement of the masses...' The proletarian masses have the ponderous force of a steamroller.... The German proletariat, lacking other leadership than that of its independent party organizations, clings to the class-war idea and finds nothing better to do than to go on tilting against capitalism— naively imagining that smiting German capitalism it is also smiting the capitalism of the world, and that presently communism will be established everywhere (Moeller 1934: 143).

Nor is praise for Nietzsche, the arch adversary of all slave revolts— whom Stern absolves of any part of the Germanic Ideology, and hence of any responsibility for the ideological development of Nazism—lacking. Nietzsche is invoked as the antithesis of Marxist fixation on the mass (151–178) and as a vital forerunner of imperialism (160): "it was Nietzsche...who first used the expression 'world economics,' and saw ahead the 'inevitable common economic administration of the world.'" A Nietzschean free spirit, splendidly above and against *ressentiment*, characterizes the book as a whole and imparts an over-manly aura to its attack on democracy: "Jealousy of power explains this hate of genius, of anyone who is great, who does, singlehanded, things which can never be done by the many.... This jealousy of power explains no less that passion for constitutions which makes power dependent on elections..." (88). Moeller simply refuses to concur with any aspect of the Germanic Ideology as outlined by Stern. As if to counter in advance any notion by future historians that he was motivated by some cultural despair, he proclaims (165) with unconcealed pride: "The man who is prepared for all eventualities is the conservative. It is not his role to despair when others despair; he is there to stand the test when others fail."[6]

In view of what has been said so far in demonstration of Moeller's profound attachment to the bourgeois spirit of economic liberalism, it should come as little surprise that his anti-liberalism "all along the line" was in fact reserved to liberal *politics*. His position in that regard differs so little from that of the other figures discussed, from Donoso to Spengler, that a few short examples would suffice. For all the detestation of the liberals, Moeller is there objectively to save them from their own mischief. Since the problem is democracy and the popular power it involves, the resolute fight against liberalism has nothing to do with a given *liberal party*, or a struggle against specific *liberal*

---

[6] See also Geoff Eley's critical commentary on Stern's thesis (1986: 235–6).

measures. Rather, it can expand without further ado to target *all* parties: "This deadly liberalism is not to be conceived as being the prerogative of any one political party. It originated in a general European party to which it owes its name, but it subsequently exercised its baneful influence on all parties" (77). Anti-liberalism and anti-democracy thus become interchangeable, as if liberalism, precisely, was not smarting under mass democracy for at least fifty years. What is more, since liberalism turns against itself in the form of socialism, conservative anti liberalism in effect *joins* the liberals, no matter how contemptuous, in the fight against those who threaten them from below, those proletarian parties that "smite capitalism." Moeller is the grim sorcerer coming to save the liberal apprentice from the surge of the masses, which the foolish knave himself has let loose:

> The problem of the masses grows urgent.... We find the liberal—who lives on the produce of human labour, or on the produce of trade or on dividends—in *full retreat* before the proletarian who claims that it is he who does the work. The liberal now does his best to *stem the tide* of the masses—*which he himself set in motion*...(138; emphases added).

Examined carefully, this passage discloses a strange, and highly illuminating, paradox. The true objective of Moeller's ideological campaign surfaces above the thick layer of rhetorical fog: liberalism, which Moeller heroically feigns to be "fighting all along the line," has *already been defeated*! It is already "in full retreat before the proletarian"! What could possibly be the point of a resolute fight to the end against an enemy, liberalism, which is dead in the water anyhow? Unless, of course, the *real* fight is conducted against that other, superior enemy that has defeated liberalism: the triumphant, emancipated masses? In truth, had the goal really been the overcoming of liberalism, there would have been no need for a Moeller in the first place, and his Third Reich would have been superfluous; one could have simply joined the ranks of the masses, rejoice in their victory.[7] Instead, Moeller tells us

---

[7] Here, too, an uncanny parallel with Hayek surfaces. The Austrian economist argued that Nazism was first and foremost anti-liberal, indeed that liberalism was the only consistent anathema of Hitler, whereas opposition to socialism and communism, though superficially fierce and violent, was merely an internal strife, between heretics. To both communism and Nazism, argued Hayek (2007: 81), "the real enemy, the man with whom they had nothing in common,...is the liberal of the old type." He then approvingly quotes Eduard Heimann who believed that "Liberalism...has the distinction of being the doctrine most hated by Hitler" (81). But Hayek then adds that, when coming to power, Hitler could do very little to express this implacable hatred since

that they pose an "urgent problem." So *this* is where the shoe hurts. The problem with—contemptible, vile, dangerous—liberalism is not that it poses a threat but that it has been brushed aside. Put differently: liberalism *is* dangerous, yet because of its weakness, not strength. It stands to be discharged, as far as Moeller is concerned, not since it is (economically) exploitative, based on private property or an unjust distribution of wealth, but because it is (politically) foolish, humanistic, suicidal: "Such was German liberalism. Its greatest crime was its crass stupidity" (106). Like his fellow pro-capitalists, Moeller is exasperated by the way the decadent liberal elite leads to its own destruction, the emancipation of the masses hitting them boomerang-like, and for him, too, the paradigmatic historical example is the French Revolution:

> Reason surely never wrought more havoc than in the rationalist circles of France. Everything they did recoiled on themselves. They did it because it was liberal: in the name of the rights of man and the ideal of a liberal state—now transformed into the ideal of a revolutionary state—they were persecuted, dispossessed, exterminated by the *tiers état*, to whom they had been the first to preach its peculiar claim to the rights of man (100).

German liberalism at that time was *already dead*, killed by socialism! Like Moeller, Hayek wants to have his cake and eat it: he avers that the *raison d'être* of Nazism was to do away with liberalism, while at the same time he concedes that such a project was already a *fait accompli* when Hitler became Chancellor. With a little humor, one could turn this ingenious thesis into a novel explanation of the unprecedented violence of the Nazis: coming to power with the firm intent to unleash their wrath on the liberals but finding nothing left to do, they instead unload their fury all the more fiercely on the socialists and communists who so recklessly deprived them of their existential mission.

More seriously, we should note how, in order to sustain his interpretation, Hayek had to draw mythical dichotomies between Nazism and liberalism in defiance of the most rudimentary facts of political reality: "While to the Nazi the communist," he maintained, "and to the communist the Nazi, and to both the socialist, are potential recruits who are made of the right timber,...they both know that there can be no compromise between them and those who really believe in individual freedom" (81). The liberals were thus bathed in an aura of incorruptibility, the only ones immune to the Nazi appeal. The fact that the combined electoral results of socialists and communists, allegedly susceptible to Nazism, remained fairly consistent throughout the meteoric rise of the Nazis (SPD and KPD retained between them a little more than one third of the total vote), whereas the high-principled and liberty-cherishing liberals suffered enormous losses (in 1928, before the first successes of the NSDAP the liberal DVP obtained 8.7 percent of the votes. In November 1932, the last free elections in Weimar, they dwindled to a measly 1.9 percent), was clearly not a deterring factor as far as Hayek was concerned: socialists and communists were made of crooked timber; liberals were beyond any compromise with fascism.

Again, one must wonder: why should a visceral anti-liberal such as Moeller take a resolute stand against the French Revolution, which, according to his own account, had punished liberals so severely? Nor does Moeller fail to register what I have called "the liberal split." He laments the way in which the economy has drifted apart from politics, and underlines the necessity of healing this fissure. Crucially, however, this re-synchronizing is *not* intended in the sense of disciplining the capitalists who have grown too powerful in their autonomous sphere, bringing them back under political control. On the very contrary, the problem is that *politics* has grown too independent, defiant of the capitalist economy, and the resulting need is to bring the *men of business* back into leading political positions, as the following passage, analyzing the crisis of the German parliamentary system, implies:

> The intellectual representatives of the nation, the great businessmen, all who were in any way creatively active, realized that the nation's salvation did not lie in debating-matches, and consequentially held more and more aloof from parliaments. Thus the parliaments fell deeper into disrepute and people went about their daily business ignoring them (127).[8]

The Fascist Failure to Emulate the West

Finally, a few additional remarks on the contradictory way in which Moeller's argument against the Western nations is structured. Here, too, a disparity reveals itself between form and content. Formally, Moeller is bitterly complaining against the subjection of Germany to the Western nations that have won the war, imposing a series of humiliating and debilitating measures on Germany. His aim is to lift the Germans from their submissive position, and kindle them to divest themselves of their parasitic oppressors and re-earn their proper national place. This basic political hostility to the post-War order imposed by the Treaty of Versailles, as well as Moeller's keen interest in Russian culture (he edited the first collection of Dostoyevsky's works in German), can serve as evidence of Moeller's anti-Westernism, just as similarly formal features can testify to his opposition to liberalism or affirmation of socialism. And yet, what such arguments ignore, is the concrete content of Moeller's critique which is far from being anti-Western. His

---

[8] The translation was here altered from "the great capitalists and employers of labour," to "the great businessmen" which accords more with the German original "*großen Unternehmer*" (Moeller 2006: 116).

hostility to the terms dictated by the Western powers does not unfold into a comprehensive disparagement of Western values and political models, but rather, paradoxically and revealingly, into the recurrent claim that the West must largely be *imitated*. The problem of Germany is diagnosed not so much in terms of its pursuing a foreign, Western path, but rather in its failure to do so *properly*. More precisely, Germany *did* pursue the Western example but in an erroneous way, failing to understand how this model in fact functions. The upshot of this misunderstanding is that Germany has become not genuinely Western, but *excessively* so, taking to pernicious extremes measures and ideologies that would have proven, in moderation, rather beneficial. Germany, Moeller frequently complains, has taken the West *at its word*, thus becoming truly and thoroughly liberal, failing to see through the limited, sham-liberalism of the Western nations. In the West, liberalism is wisely used as a means to fence off revolution, by diverting the revolutionary powers of the masses onto the channels of a sham-democracy, thereby neutralizing such powers:

> Liberalism in Europe is one thing, liberalism in Germany another.
>
> When two augurs of the West are met together, they both know what liberalism is: a political trick: the trick with which the upstart society of the *tiers état* was able to swindle the tiresome, remaining plebs out of the promises of 1789. The augurs know what 'liberty' means, that most seductive of the three catchwords with which the champions of the rights of man lured the deluded masses away from their dangerous barricades and shepherded them to the innocuous ballot-box (103).

But whereas the Western powers employ liberalism to bypass revolution, in Germany it leads directly *into* it. Here Moeller's understanding of the German deviation from the Western path, its harmful *Sonderweg*, so to speak, is thrown into strong relief:

> The German people took historically the opposite course from the peoples of the west. France and England began as national states, they progressed as monarchies and after they had their Revolutions got rid of, or limited their monarchies, they established their parliamentary system which they called democracy and which served as a cover for their nationalism. We on the other hand began as a democratic people, maintained ourselves by our monarchy and finally broke our history off with a Revolution which was not so much a national revolution as an international revolution, supposed to be aiming at universal brotherhood and eternal peace (131).

Democracy, in Germany, became the goal instead of the means. A parliamentary system modeled after the Western example, keeping the masses under strict control, would have actually been very useful, but Germany pursued its own, misguided, *literal* democracy:

> The English invented the cabinet and the prime minister, to whom they gave precedence over their lower house, and whom they equipped with almost sovereign powers. The French invented the political clique which manipulated the chambers for its own private ends, which were, however, also the ends of France. It was reserved for the Germans to interpret parliamentism literally, to endow parliament with real powers of control which it then exercised only negatively and obstructively (126).

The ultimate problem with Germany, therefore, is that it is *not* democratic and liberal in a Western sense, but in a German, wrong and naïve misapplication. Hence the answer to the strange dilemma thus formulated by Moeller (112): "Liberalism is the death of nations. What? Was it not the liberal nations who won the War?" The Western nations won because they knew how to be liberal in a sophisticated, moderate and cautious way, always subservient to national interests, a way which Germany could not make its own. This is no peculiarity of Moeller's thought. The complaint against Germany's belated and ill-advised *Sonderweg*, the way it took essentially workable and sound political models and perverted them by taking them literally and unreservedly, was quite recurrent among German rightists, expressed, for example, by another key publicist of the so-called "conservative-revolutionaries," Edgar Julius Jung:

> Whereas in the West democracy was inhibited aristocratically by the conservative bastions of an unwavering social order, with us, the nation of ravenous appetite for technical improvements, of late capitalistic development, of frenzied urbanization and enormous multiplying of the proletariat, it was boundless (Jung 1933: 44).

As we have observed above, Hitler himself entertained similar notions of Germany's inadequate line of development, as compared with the West.[9] In Italy, too, such an explanation of the necessity of curbing

---

[9] Interestingly, already Paul de Lagarde, writing in 1878, expressed admiration for the British parliamentary system, precisely since it remained at all times a tool at the complete disposition of the entrepreneurial and politically responsible gentry, rather than becoming a democratic system of ruling:

> We must make the [German nobles] economically independent [from the Crown], and they will become again, not immediately but quickly enough, what most of their ancestors once were,...they will become gentry [English in the original], the class that made England great, which we completely lack and which alone sustains political life, since having political duties. The English parliament

liberalism *not* on account of its Western, and hence illegitimate, origins, but because of the specific inadequacies of local circumstances was often articulated. The prominent fascist leader Alfredo Rocco thus maintained that the problem with the Italian liberal state was not so much the result of an immanent and universal affliction of the liberal state *per se*, as it was a specifically indigenous symptom. In the Western countries properly speaking, argued Mussolini's minister of justice from 1925 to 1932, liberalism is adequate and productive because it is subservient to national aims: "Outside Italy, and especially in Anglo-Saxon countries, the liberal democratic State has been able to flourish and to achieve great results, because in the social and political conditions of those peoples it found correctives which we do not have. In the Anglo-Saxon countries, and also in France, there is a great national tradition" (Rocco 1931: 17). Quite like Moeller, Jung or Hitler, Rocco laments the absence, in that case in Italy, of checks and balances on mass power: "in England the individualistic and disintegratory spirit of Germanism is counteracted by a rigorous moral education, so that the individual, while theoretically maintaining perfect liberty in the face of the State, knows of himself how to keep it within limits" (17). In anarchistic Italy, by contrast, individualism knew no limits. In order to tame the rebellious masses, the state had no other option but to move from liberalism to fascism:

> All these conditions are lacking in Italy…. [F]oreign rule…, above all, made the State appear for centuries as the instrument of foreign oppression, and in the mass of the Italians gave rise to a profound spirit of distrust and of revolt against public authority…. [E]ven after unity and independence were established, the Italian masses preserved towards the national State the same distrustful and hostile attitude…In these circumstances, the liberal State in Italy could maintain its position only with difficulty…[A]fter the War came a period of total anarchy, in which the State became the shadow of itself…The painful period of anarchy was arrested by the coming of Fascism, which, by restoring order and discipline to the country, was obliged to bring about the transformation of the State…(17).

---

is only valuable as representative of the gentry: only in that capacity does it mean anything: representatives of the people exist in England not at all. The state institution of parliament represents only those who take a real part in the life of the state, only those who rule, and not the ruled…(Lagarde 1994: 22–23).

In a typically fascist roundabout way, Rocco used "individualism" and "anarchy" as euphemisms for *mass agitation* and *mass organization*, namely for phenomena which are very much the *antitheses* of individualism and of anarchy. The real problem was thus *not* the disintegration of the state into its individual atoms, *not* the fact that it became increasingly Anglo-Saxon or French, but the fact that it *failed* to do so, and instead increasingly fell under the sway of the organized class enemy. In Rocco's own words: "This lack of an entity, an ideal, a will of its own, was therefore the characteristic of the liberal and negative State, which was thus incapable of controlling *the real forces* existing in the nation; these forces therefore *organized themselves, lived and prospered* outside the State, and ended by *mastering* it" (16; emphases added). In other words, had the individuals in Italy remained truly atomized and isolated, had they merely pursued their private interests in the anarchic intercourse of market society within the framework of the nation state, there would have been no need for fascism, and Italy might have "flourished and achieved great results," just like its Western counterparts. But since the very opposite happened, since individuals refused to stay atomized and purposefully conflated into "real" and "organized" "*forces*," fascism was "obliged" to intervene and transform the liberal state. Fascists, in summary, by their own admission, would have often preferred to pursue the Western path, but the degree of working-class organization and militancy in their countries did not allow them to do so, forcing them into a national *Sonderweg*.

Outsiders-Insiders: Proudhon and Carlyle

Those post-Second-World-War historians attempting to delineate a genealogy of fascism as distinct from that of capitalism and liberalism, in fact standing in stark opposition to both, were often drawn to two 19th century intellectual figures: Thomas Carlyle, the passionate Victorian prophet lampooning *laissez faire*, the "cash nexus" and the "dismal science" of classical economy, and P. J. Proudhon, who famously and tersely equated *la propriété* with *le vol*. Proudhon was invoked by Zeev Sternhell, for example, to indicate the anarchist-socialist origins of French fascism: both in what concerned Proudhon's own writings and with regards to the legacy he left behind, notably the virulently nationalistic "Cercle Proudhon," which was founded in 1911 to quickly become a busy gathering point for voluble enemies of

French democracy. At all times, Sternhell cites Proudhon as an important source of socialism in countless variants: French socialism (Sternhell 1986: 13, 180, 197), Gallic socialism (57), national socialism (24,
146, 180), true socialism (180), peasant socialism (57), socialism "with
an earthy flavour" (136), new socialism (146), old socialism (180),
warrior socialism (57), communal socialism (146), anti-Marxist socialism (13, 180), pre-Marxist socialism (197), voluntarist socialism (13),
authentic socialism (11), and so on. All these socialisms, it is averred,
were profoundly indebted to the teachings and the spirit of Proudhon.
Conversely, like his "prototypical disciple," Georges Sorel, Proudhon
is imputed to have "contempt for bourgeois and liberal values" (37).

The epithet of "proto-fascism" would, in my view, largely apply to
both Proudhon and Carlyle in terms of the social perspective from
which they wrote as well as the political and economic programs they
advocated. Superficially, moreover, they were passionately antagonistic to capitalism. A closer look, however, reveals that both of them
were strange outsiders indeed to bourgeois society and ideology; their
respective critiques had roots deep within the capitalist camp. Neither
of them envisioned transcending capitalism as a mode of production;
what they wanted was rather to purify capitalism, to preserve it as a
mode of production, while shearing off some of its attributes—political, cultural, socioeconomic—considered insalubrious. With Proudhon, we have an attempt to remould capitalism in the image of the
middle-class, adjust it to the interests of *la classe moyenne*, while Carlyle strove to ennoble capitalism, play the matchmaker in a glorious
matrimony that would fuse the two historically feuding classes, the
bourgeoisie and the aristocracy, into the elite of the future, prepared
for the decisive battle against the "million-headed" dragon of socialism
and democracy. If, in addressing "the Germanic Ideology," I took as
my historiographic point of reference Fritz Stern's influential study, I
will here refer to J. S. Schapiro's book, *Liberalism and the Challenge of
Fascism* (1949), which systematically set out, in two of its chapters, to
make the case that Proudhon and Carlyle were "Heralds of Fascism."

Proudhon: An Anarchist of the Market

Schapiro convincingly argued that Proudhon's writings should be seen
as adumbrating 20th century fascism; being an "inharmonious genius"
Proudhon did not belong in any of the ideological currents of his
time—socialism, conservatism, monarchism, liberalism—and neither

was he a real forefather of anarchism, as often claimed. Rather, he strikingly prefigured the fascist stance in a number of senses. An inventory of these would include, for example: Proudhon's defence of distinctly petty-bourgeois interests, in opposition to those of both capital and labor; the espousal of a dictatorship that would transcend class strife; the increasing glorification of war and of military values; articulation of conservative-traditionalist values, such as the sacredness of the family and a fierce opposition to budding feminism; racism and anti-Semitism; denouncement of finance, and money-lending capital, seen as predominantly Jewish. This cocktail of ideas, while misunderstood by his contemporaries, becomes clear and nameable in light of the fascist experience.

Schapiro's account, however, suffers from two crucial limitations that are interrelated. First, it suffers from the fact that, intent on showing that fascism was an absolute innovation on the horizon of political ideologies and moreover, as the book's title indicated, an innovation *defying* liberalism, the author was not satisfied with merely identifying the "petty-bourgeois" dimension, in and of itself important, of fascism. Rather, he went a step further and *reduced* fascism to this sole aspect, indeed defined it in those terms. He offered the following, compact definition of fascism (which, incidentally, is not unlike that which today, almost six decades later, is subscribed to by numerous historians, particularly those of the "new consensus"):

> It would be a great error to regard fascism as a counterrevolutionary movement directed against the communists, as was that of the reactionaries against the liberals during the first half of the nineteenth century. Fascism is something unique in modern history, in that it is a revolutionary movement of the middle class directed, on the one hand, against the great banks and big business and, on the other hand, against the revolutionary demands of the working class (Schapiro 1949: 365).

Schapiro thus insisted, very much against the evidence he himself skilfully collected and coherently organized, on squeezing fascism into the confines of this petty-bourgeois niche, thereby limiting the potential harm to bourgeois ideology in its entirety. Integral to such reductionism, was the second main problem with Schapiro's explanation, namely the refusal to register the vital importance of the liberal motifs informing Proudhon's worldview, even as such motifs were amply documented by Schapiro himself. For indeed, Proudhon's project of eliminating capitalism was paradoxically steeped in the liberal spirit. The profound indebtedness of his socioeconomic outlook to classical liberalism he in fact readily acknowledged, for example in the follow-ing words, quoted by Schapiro: "I have certainly read Fourier, and have spoken of him more than once in my works; but, upon the whole, I do not think that I owe anything to him. My real masters, those who have caused fertile ideas to spring up in my mind, are three in num-ber: first, the Bible; next, Adam Smith; and last, Hegel" (as quoted in DeGrood 1978, vol. 1: 79).

How strange that an enemy of capitalism should fall back on Adam Smith as his second major influence (indeed, as regards economic questions, arguably the *first*, if we consider that the Bible does not touch on issues pertaining to capitalism)! Yet this evoking of the most important economic liberal is neither coincidental nor incongruent with Proudhon's teachings. From the Bible, Proudhon derived his sense of moral indignation at the ills and injustices of modernity and his appeal to eternal ethical truths, as well as his would-be prophetic, sermonizing style; from Hegel, he derived his method of attempting to reconcile antagonistic forces and yield a superior "synthesis" (leaving aside the issue of whether or not he had mastered the Hegelian dialec-tic. Marx, for one, was convinced he had not); yet it was to the Scot-tish economist that Proudhon owed much of his concrete approach to socioeconomic issues, such as production, property, taxation or eco-nomic individualism. Proudhon, (2007b: 259) in fact, conceived his task as completing the transformation of society along the lines envis-aged by "Adam Smith, whose genius dimly foresaw everything and left us to do everything."

To re-visit Proudhon's anarchism today is to find it in many ways akin to 20th century purist, liberal-cum-libertarian critiques of mod-ern, corporate capitalism as stifling and perverting the genuinely com-petitive spirit of 19th century, small-scale, capitalism. Unlike later day libertarians, however, who idealize the supposedly unhampered cre-ativity of early production, Proudhon's critique was levelled at 19th century capitalism itself. Hence the crucial distinction Proudhon makes, already in his first and most famous book—*What is Property?*—between malignant "property," which must be abolished, and benign "possession," small-scale ownership and production, which is the firm bedrock of civilization:

> Individual possession is the condition of social life...Property is the suicide of society. Possession is within right; property is against right. Suppress property while maintaining possession, and by this simple modification of the principle, you will revolutionize the law, government,

economy, and institutions; you will drive evil from the face of the earth
(Proudhon 1994: 214–15).

The aim was thus, from the start, not to eliminate capitalism but to re-
build it on solid, "just" foundations. Proudhon thus assures Adolphe
Blanqui, the bourgeois political economist who—rightly—defended
him against charges of inciting to destroy the present social order, that
the system he proposes will not do away with capital, since possession
will in fact furnish it with a more steadfast basis than does property:

> Discovering a system of absolute equality in which all existing institu-
> tions, except property, or the sum of the abuses of property, may not
> only find a place but also themselves contribute to equality: individual
> liberty, separation of powers, public ministry, the jury system, adminis-
> trative and judicial organisation, unity and uniformity of education, mar-
> riage, the family, inheritance in direct and collateral succession, the right
> of sale and exchange, the right to make a will, and even birthright—a
> system which, *better than property, assures the formation of capital* and
> maintains the morale of everyone…(11–12; italics added).

As we can see, Proudhon's great passion for equality, emphasized by
him time and again, does not threaten to make a clean sweep of the
non-egalitarian social order, since what it implies is not *actual* equality, either in terms of equal income and possessions or of common
ownership of the means of production, but an ideal of equality *of
conditions* broadly interchangeable with the liberal tenet of equality
of opportunities: "*Equality*," he clarified, consists "only in *equality of
conditions*, that is, *of means*, and not in *equality of well-being*, which
it is the business of the laborers to achieve for themselves, when given
equal means" (211; italics added). This is very much the equivalent of
the liberal notion of individual achievement: "Liberty favors emulation and does not destroy it; in social equality emulation consists in
accomplishing under equal conditions" (213). In Proudhon's use, the
ominous concept of "anarchy" likewise disowned any insurrectionary
connotations. Anarchy à la Proudhon boiled down to an ideal quite
compatible with classical liberal notions of liberty, namely self-rule,
individual freedom and limitations of state intervention of any kind
(considered illegitimate regardless of whether the sovereign making
claims on individuals is a king or the majority of the people). His
notion of "social contract" thus owed in truth very little to Rousseau,
instead echoing the standard liberal-capitalist notions of a working
contract drawn between interested parties, entered into voluntarily

and signed without coercion, hence vouching, so the liberal argument goes, for the absolute freedom of all involved:

> Between contracting parties there is necessarily for each one a real personal interest; it implies that a man bargains with the aim of securing his liberty and his revenue at the same time, without any possible loss.... The contract therefore is essentially reciprocal... The social contract should be freely discussed, individually accepted, signed with their own hands, by all the participants (Proudhon 2007a: 113–14).

Given the liberal logic underpinning Proudhon's approach, it is unsurprising that, like most other classical liberals—or "liberals of the old kind," as Hayek would put it—he soon realized and sharply articulated the incompatibility of his ideal with democracy. He, too, landed on the economic side of the liberal split and consequently sternly prohibited the right of political intervention in the free-contract economy. "*Economic criticism*," he averred, demonstrated "that *political institutions* must be *lost* in *industrial organization*" (126; emphases added). From this he concluded that democratic intervention in industrial-economic matters is as little warranted as any other political intrusion: "Neither monarchy, nor aristocracy, nor even democracy itself,... even though acting in the name of the people, and calling itself the people. No authority, no government, not even popular, that is the Revolution" (126). "The law of the majority," Proudhon makes clear, "is not my law, it is the law of force; hence the government based upon it is not my government; it is government by force." From this follows the idea that "the authority of the suffrage must be renounced: we must give up the vote,... everything in the government of society which rests on the divine must be suppressed, and the whole rebuilt upon the human idea of CONTRACT" (205). In view of Proudhon's idea of the optimal socio-economic order—"free contract in place of arbitrary law; voluntary transactions in place of the control of the State;... *economic unity* in place of *political centralization*" (292; emphases added)—it ought not to astonish us that some so-called "anarcho-capitalists" acknowledge their affinity with Proudhon;[10] nor should it strike us as odd that

---

[10] Per Bylund, for example, writes:
Thus it seems anarcho-capitalists agree with Proudhon in that 'property is theft,' where it is acquired in an illegitimate manner. But they also agree with Proudhon in that 'property is liberty' in the sense that without property, i.e. being robbed of the fruits of one's actions, one is a slave. Anarcho-capitalists thus advocate the

Hayek (1988: 63–64), in a book claiming to unmask "the errors of socialism," should indeed refer to our "Gallic socialist" but *affirmatively*. Proudhon, namely, is invoked *in support* of Hayek's advocacy of restricting governmental intervention to the absolute minimum, which is said to give "scope for the most extraordinary freedom and diversity."

Proudhon tailored capitalism, in its economic and political implications, to suit the interests of the small artisan and property owner. Economically, he proposed small-scale production, undertaken individually, whereby no profit is made nor labor exploited since products are self-produced on one's own farm or workshop and then exchanged only for their equivalents, for other products in which the same amount of labor has been invested. As Marx observed in his many lucid analyses of Proudhon, the latter clung tenaciously to the basic feature of capitalism—commodity production—while wishing to get rid of its unpleasant corollaries, construing them as merely contingent, and hence disposable, side effects.[11] This economic basis was to be shielded from the abuses of government, in thrall to large cartels, on the one hand, and from the democratic infringement of the masses, on the other hand, who might use their power to encroach upon property (or, if one insists, possession) by way of progressive taxation, which Proudhon consistently decried as a form of theft.

To assume that Proudhon, being a proto-fascist, was "on the one hand, against the great banks and big business and, on the other hand, against the revolutionary demands of the working class," (Schapiro 1949: 365) is true, but superficial. And in its implications, it is plainly wrong. It implies a sort of a middle-class middle *path*, that winds precisely in between the two great modern players, big-business capitalism and working-class socialism. Yet in reality, petty-bourgeois fascism, and the example of Proudhon as precursor demonstrates this very well, tilted heavily in favor of the capitalist side, while firmly negating socialism, both evolutionary and revolutionary. Proudhon (2007b: 213) made no secret of the fact that, if forced to choose between the

---

freedom of a stateless society, where each individual has the sovereign right to his body and labor and through this right can pursue his or her own definition of happiness.

[11] Marx (1999: 734) pokes fun, for example, of Proudhon's wish to "abolish capitalist property—by enforcing the eternal laws of property which are themselves based on commodity production!"

evils of capitalism and socialism, he will opt for the former. Thus, in polemics against the socialism of Louis Blanc, he stated: "For my part, I deny your God, your authority, your sovereignty, your judicial State, and all your representative mystifications;...rather than submit to your androgynous democracy, I would support the status quo." Even facing the hateful, concrete *realities* of "the system Guizot" catering to the big bourgeoisie, Proudhon saw in the *projects* of socialism a still greater evil. He declared himself "irreversibly convinced...that communism, republicanism, and all the social, political, and religious utopias which disdain facts and criticism, are *the greatest obstacle* which progress has now to conquer" (227; italics added).

Capitalism, certainly, stood to be amended and purified after a petty-bourgeois fashion; yet, in its basic premises—competition, possession, individual enterprise—it remained at all times the ultimate horizon of human society, corresponding to both morality, science and nature. While a reformed capitalism was to underpin Proudhon's schemes for the future, socialism had no place whatsoever in them. Proudhon was a passionate and lyrical advocate of competition, repeatedly singing its praise, proclaiming it "a principle of social economy, a decree of destiny, a necessity of the human soul," (186) and this in polemics with the socialist project of abolishing competition. In defending the principle of competition from communism and quasi-socialistic democracy, he did not hesitate to rely on bourgeois political economy, on Smith's legacy. While the socialist project was deemed "a contradiction given to the most certain laws of economic science," this same science was vindicated at every turn:

> Everywhere it was necessary to emancipate labor, stimulate genius, and render the manufacturer responsible by arousing a thousand competitors and loading upon him alone the consequences of his indolence, ignorance, and insincerity.... Liberty of industry and commerce figure in our constitutions on a level with political liberty. To this liberty, in short, France owes the growth of her wealth during the last sixty years (185–6).

Proudhon raises the question: "Can competition in labor be abolished?" He provides the typically liberal answer: "It would be as well worth while to ask if personality, liberty, individual responsibility can be suppressed" (209). He also vents the classical concern of the economic liberal that political liberalism would halt the dynamics of capitalism. "The constitutive unit of society," he says (210), "is the workshop," and proceeds to underscore the necessity of excluding any political-democratic meddling with this unit:

> Are not workingmen who vote their regulations and elect their leaders free? It may very likely happen that these voting workingmen will admit no command or difference of pay among them: then, as nothing will have been provided for the satisfaction of industrial capacities, while maintaining political equality, dissolution will penetrate into the workshop, and, in the absence of police intervention, each will return to his own affairs (213).

As these sentences show, it often becomes rather difficult to distinguish Proudhon's "revolutionary" visions of small-scale production from actually existing capitalism, with its hierarchies, chains of command and inequalities. The boundary-lines between possession and property appear quite blurry. Similarly, Proudhon's petty-bourgeois perspective is manifest, among other things, in his opposition to monopolies; yet it is from a liberal point of view that monopolies are censured, not because they are the natural upshot of capitalistic competition, and hence raise a general objection to capitalism, as a socialist would argue, but, on the contrary, because they obstruct capitalist competition: "Monopoly is the natural opposite of competition.... Competition is the vital force which animates the collective being: to destroy it, if such a supposition were possible, would be to kill society" (220). This leads to a strange paradox. As a representative of the interests of small property owners, Proudhon condemns the effects of large concentrations of capital upon small-scale producers, lamenting the fact that the big fish swallow the little ones, driving them out of competition. Yet *compete* they indeed *must*, given that Proudhon's reservations with regards to monopolies are thoroughly *from within* the capitalist camp, not for a second contemplating to cut the root of monopoly which is competition. He is aware of the fact that to condemn monopoly squarely is to condemn competition, too: "monopoly is the inevitable end of competition, which engenders it by a continual denial of itself: this generation of monopoly is already its justification" (221). Yet this justification of *bad* monopoly as the outcome of *good* competition, can just as easily become the condemnation of *good* competition as the source of *bad* monopoly. Hence, to somewhat comical effect, Proudhon is driven to think through a justification of monopoly as well, in and of itself: "Nevertheless this justification would seem of little force and would end only in a more energetic rejection of competition than ever, if monopoly could not in turn posit itself by itself and as a principle" (221). Petty bourgeois though he is, Proudhon thus proceeds to acknowledge fully the legitimate aspect of monopoly and decrees it, too, a "necessity of the human"—i.e., capitalistic—"soul":

> [M]onopoly is…the strongest stimulant of all the steps in progress taken since the beginning of the world…Monopoly is…the dictatorial right accorded by nature to every producer of using his faculties as he pleases, of giving free play to his thought…This right belongs so thoroughly to the essence of liberty that to deny it is to mutilate man in his body, in his soul, and in the exercise of his faculties, and society, which progresses only by the free initiative of individuals, soon lacking explorers, finds itself arrested in its onward march (221–2).

In this passage, the liberal-capitalist contours of Proudhon's economic viewpoint are thrown into a particularly vivid relief. The whole point is to preserve monopoly while alleviating its harmful effects for the small producer, to find a reconciling synthesis between competition and monopoly: "among such animals [bees, ants, etc.], there can be no room for privilege and monopoly…But, humanity being individualized in its plurality, man becomes inevitably a monopolist, since, if not a monopolist, he is nothing; and the social problem is to find out, not how to abolish, but how to reconcile, all monopolies" (230). For the opponent of big business the very essence of man is, how astonishing, monopoly. These passages suffice to demonstrate the inadequacy of the view that Proudhon—and by extension fascism—was a figure in between "big business" and "socialism."

According to Schapiro, the proto-fascism of Proudhon manifested itself in his 1861 book *La Guerre et la Paix*, comprising of a protracted exaltation of war. And he was certainly right. Yet he symptomatically overlooked the extent to which such an approval of war was rooted, not in some proto-fascist ideological novelty, but precisely in the *economic liberalism* underlying Proudhon's outlook, in his affirmation of the *bellum omnium contra omnes* of competition. As the following extract from *The Philosophy of Misery* (2007b) expressively illustrates:

> Now, that is precisely the effect of competition upon industry.… [T]he surest way to extinguish [man's] genius is to deliver him from all solicitude and take away from him the hope of profit and of the social distinction which results from it, by creating around him *peace everywhere, peace always*, and transferring to the State the responsibility of his inertia.
>
> Yes, it must be admitted, in spite of modern quietism,—man's life is a permanent war, war with want, war with nature, war with his fellows, and consequently war with himself (189–90).

Proudhon's social utopia consisted of generalizing the individualistic, entrepreneurial middle class so that competition ceases to be the asset of the few, to become humanity's universal panacea: "I said a little while ago, competition is an exceptional matter, a privilege; now I ask how it is possible for this privilege to coexist with equality of rights?" (202). Interestingly, Proudhon's anarchism, with or without quotation marks, quite like that of his German contemporary, Max Stirner, meant the generalization of the market principle to embrace all spheres of human activity and inter-human relationships. In his ground-breaking anarchistic text, *The Ego and Its Own*, Stirner (1995)—who was a translator of Adam Smith, incidentally—envisaged in commerce and transaction of commodities the unsurpassable expression of individual fulfillment, regarding society as a huge market where all human feelings are subject to the laws of supply and demand just like ordinary goods: "But love is not a commandment, but, like each of my feelings, *my property. Acquire*, that is, purchase, my property, and then I will make it over to you. A church, a nation, a fatherland, a family, etc., that does not know how to acquire my love, I need not love; and I fix the purchase price of my love quite at my pleasure" (259 emphasis in original). Compare this with Proudhon's following reflections, which also strongly foreshadow Nietzsche's atheism:

> Charity! I deny charity; it is mysticism.... I ask all that my products cost me, and only what they cost me: why do you refuse me?...Talk to me of *debt* and *credit*, the only criterion in my eyes of the just and the unjust, of good and evil in society.... God! I know no God; mysticism again. Begin by striking this word from your remarks, if you wish me to listen to you; for three thousand years of experience have taught me that whoever talks to me of God has designs on my liberty or on my purse. How much do you owe me? How much do I owe you? That is my religion and my God (Proudhon 2007b: 229).

The iconoclastic anarchism of these figures thus uncannily echoed the anarchy of market relations, allowed to regulate all human interactions, after the abuses of monopoly and big capital have been abridged and "equality of conditions" generally established, under the aegis of Proudhon's *Bank du Peuple*. Far from being exponents of anti-capitalism, such figures were attempting to distil capitalism in its purest form, and then pursue its logic to its utmost conclusions.

Compared to such ample and profound concord with capitalism, indeed the celebration of market society—tarnished only by certain tactical and ethical misgivings, but none that an "equality of conditions" could not placate—the resolute, comprehensive and vehement nature of Proudhon's opposition to socialism stands out all the more. In my view, there is not a single point on which Proudhon's outlook can come into a dialogue with any kind of socialism, whether revolutionary or reformist-evolutionary. Facing the prospect of a communist revolution which will do away with property, competition and monopoly, Proudhon expressed the strictest of repudiations. Like the economic liberal that he, at bottom, was, he refuted the economic feasibility of such an order, since the motor of competition and individual possession will be switched off. Yet he also discarded communism on moral grounds, as the organized exploitation of the strong by the weak, and in the familiar liberal terms equating economic liberty with individuality, personality and excellence. Under communism, Proudhon averred (1994: 196–7), "the strong work for the weak,...the industrious work for the lazy,...the clever work for the foolish,...and, finally,...man, throwing off his ego, his spontaneity, his genius, and his affections— humbly prostrates himself before the majestic and inflexible community." Evolutionary socialism, however, did not fare any better in the estimation of the Gallic socialist. All of its pillars were systematically battered by Proudhon, from universal suffrage, through trade unions and collective bargaining, to the hope of improving the worker's lot via a more egalitarian distribution of wealth. As Schapiro pointed out (1949: 363), Proudhon's hatred of socialism, which he "regarded as the worst of all social poisons, drove him to advocate anarchy as its very opposite. What he really saw in anarchy was not a solution of social problems but an antidote to socialism." Proudhon's middle-class utopia was to be created through the activities of responsible and far-sighted elite, of "savants"—naturally lead by Proudhon himself and his plans for reform—quite independent of, and if necessary against, the wishes of the masses, which were both unripe to understand it, and, still worse, unworthy to merit it. As already observed, since democracy was most likely to impede the universal competition he idealized, Proudhon denied that the will of the majority had any more value than the will of the monarch, both representing arbitrary imposition of force rather than the scientific implementation of the dictates of "justice," which Proudhon flattered himself to have discovered and sketched out once and for all.[12]

---

[12] Not that he was particularly consistent in this dismissal of the majorities' view: when it suited him, namely, when he could enlist what he felt was the majority's opinion in favour of competition, he did not hesitate to discard "scientific" argumentation and rely rather on the spontaneous intuition of the multitude:

In his unswerving opposition to progressive taxation, Proudhon explicitly drew on Smith. It is interesting to observe, in the following passage, how his anarchistic refusal to abide by any social norms and conventions, was in fact integral to an effort to shield the socially powerful individuals from the supposedly weak ones. The state—the favourite target for anarchistic critique—was frequently attacked not from a socialist point of view, as serviceable to the interests of capitalism, but rather as a mechanism for putting the strong social members under the control of the ineffective ones. This was, once again, an anarchism compatible with the economic-liberal rejection of the socialist welfare state as undercutting the principle of competition, achievement and merit: "The tax belongs to that great family of preventive, coercive, repressive, and vindictive institutions which A. Smith designated by the generic term police, and which is, as I have said, in its original conception, only the reaction of weakness against strength" (Proudhon 2007b: 263).[13]

In summary, if it is indeed true, as Schapiro argued, that Proudhon's writings provide us with untimely mediations on an altogether new political phenomenon, a petty-bourgeois anti capitalism, it is no less true that we get a vital insight into the *liberal underpinning* of precisely such petty-bourgeois outlook, and hence, at a second remove, into the liberal roots of fascism, as opposed to a fascist challenge to liberalism. Yet if Schapiro's account was misleading, it remains a good deal more reliable than that of Sternhell who, some forty years after Schapiro, used Proudhon to trace the allegedly socialist origins of French fascism. For even as he was striving to disengage liberalism from fascism, Schapiro never lost sight of the fact that fascism—and its precursor,

---

The French Revolution was effected for industrial liberty as well as for political liberty: and although France in 1789 had not seen all the consequences of the principle for the realization of which she asked,...she was mistaken neither in her wishes nor in her expectation. Whoever would try to deny it would lose in my eyes the right to criticism: I will never dispute with an adversary who would posit as a principle the spontaneous error of twenty-five millions of men (Proudhon 2007b: 185).

[13] This was very similar to the way that Stirner (1995: 235), in rebuffing an egalitarian redistribution of wealth, did so markedly on behalf of the successful, strong individual, whom society would unjustly strip of his well-earned remuneration, the prize of competition: "Now am I, who am competent for much, perchance to have no advantage over the less competent?...Against competition there rises up the principle of ragamuffin society—*partition*. To be looked upon as a mere *part*, part of society, the individual cannot bear—because he is *more*; his uniqueness puts from it this limited conception."

Proudhon—were fiercely anti-socialist. For Sternhell, set on the task of comprehensively re-evaluating fascism so that it may appear a dissident variant of socialism, this was not nearly enough; he thus overbid past efforts and repeatedly stressed the socialism of Proudhon and of his nationalistic and eventually fascist disciples (a procedure that we will examine more closely in the next chapter, focusing on one of Proudhon's most important disciples, Georges Sorel). Such important differences notwithstanding, both historians were united in ignoring the extent to which Proudhon was an insider to the liberal camp, who, seeing himself as Adam Smith's executor, came to redress and reform the iniquities of the system, not to destroy it. Lastly, Proudhon also sheds light on the important issue of anarchism and anarcho-syndicalism and their relation to fascism, which we will address below. For to treat Proudhon as a seminal figure in the trajectory of anarchism is surprisingly to obtain concrete evidence of *the liberal* origins of anarchism, as opposed to the widespread assumption that anarchism was simply another form of leftist social radicalism, different in its aims and assumptions than socialism, but equally *anti*-liberal.

Carlyle's Critique of Capitalism: from the Cash Nexus to the Lash Nexus

Thomas Carlyle, for his part, could preach, always ardently and at times perceptively, against the "Gospel of Mammonism" and denounce the universal degradation of human relations in industrial society, in a way which appealed to such critics of capitalism as the humanitarian Dickens and the communist Engels. Yet in fact, much of Carlyle's critique ultimately addressed the way capitalism leads to its own destruction, first breeding and then training its grim executioners: democracy, socialism and revolution. In this, certainly, Carlyle went beyond the habitual critique of the economic liberal that we have so far encountered, which disapproves of political liberalism for endangering and encumbering capitalism. Carlyle saw *economic liberalism* as endangering *economic liberalism*, too; unbridled capitalism, that is, unleashes in Carlyle's view the forces that will ultimately make capitalistic production, and the social class system upon which such production rests, impossible. In that respect, Carlyle reveals himself a more far-sighted and sophisticated defender of the capitalist system, than the dogmatic advocates of *laissez faire*, who insist on having capitalism undiluted at any cost, even that of jeopardizing the future of capitalism. Carlyle repeatedly decries, not so much the inhumanity or cruelty of capitalist exploitation, as its *stupidity*. This is very similar to the exasperation of the economic liberal in the face of political liberalism "foolishly" opening the floodgates of social democracy, only that Carlyle sees the same imprudence in classical economy as well. "The sage of Chelsea," as Carlyle was called, finds the practices of *laissez faire* at once too *lenient*, and too *harsh*. Too lenient, in that capitalism politically emancipates the worker, makes her work wholly a matter of voluntary contract, and deludes itself into thinking that such voluntarism, grounded solely in economic interest, can serve as an abiding basis for extracting labor. Carlyle's horizon was militantly elitist and un-egalitarian, not primarily in a cultural sense, but *above all* in terms of the division of labor.[14] He saw in slavery the ideal relationship between employer and employee, since the permanent contract between the two sides pre-empts the danger of a future disengagement, whether revolutionary or evolutionary. He commended slavery as a supremely natural arrangement whereby the slave was compelled to do the work befitting his abilities:

---

[14] I say with purpose "above all," since Carlyle was contemptuous of art as divorced from the "practical," i.e., social question, and saw in such aestheticism an inane occupation. He expressly dismissed "high art" and in 1867, interestingly prophesized that it will disappear within 50 years as a serious factor, leaving commercial, mass culture a sole player. This prospect did not worry him in the least since, like the Marxist *in reverse* that he was, he did not see any purpose for an elitist cultural superstructure, no matter how many "masterpieces" it might produce, unless it be organically linked to an elitist socioeconomic base:

> First, then, with regard to Art, Poetry and the like, which at present is esteemed the supreme of aims for vocal genius, I hope my literary *Aristos* will pause, and seriously make question before embarking on that; and perhaps will end...by devoting his divine faculty to something far higher, far more vital to us. Poetry? It is not pleasant singing that we want, but wise and earnest speaking: 'Art,' 'High Art' &c. are very fine and ornamental, but only to persons sitting at their ease: to persons still wrestling with deadly chaos, and still fighting for dubious existence, they are a mockery rather (Carlyle 1867: 27–28).

"Deadly chaos," moreover, was unmistakably a social affliction, as is made clear in the same text (52): "This Practical hero, Aristocrat by nature, and standing face to face and hand to hand, all his days, in life-battle with practical Chaos (with dirt, disorder, nomadism, disobedience, folly and confusion), slowly coercing it into Cosmos." This position in cultural matters pre-figures Nietzsche's critique of "high art" when it ceases to be socially functional, as I have elsewhere attempted to analyze (Landa 2007: esp. 97–107), as well as that of Nietzsche's disciple, and hence Carlyle's disciple at a second-remove, Oswald Spengler, pronouncing the end of culture and the commencement of an era of Caesarism. For all these figures, "culture" loses all interest and sense unless serviceable in underpinning socioeconomic hierarchy.

> [W]ith regard to the West Indies, it may be laid down as a principle, which no eloquence in Exeter Hall, or Westminster Hall, or elsewhere, can invalidate or hide, except for a short time only, That no Black man who will not work according to what ability the gods have given him for working, has the smallest right to eat pumpkin, or to any fraction of land that will grow pumpkin, however plentiful such land may be; but has an indisputable and perpetual *right* to be compelled, by the real proprietors of said land, to do competent work for his living. This is the everlasting duty of all men, black or white, who are born into this world (Carlyle 1869b: 299).

As can be seen, if Carlyle solemnly repudiated the cash-nexus, it was only to passionately uphold the *lash*-nexus. Vis-à-vis the leniency of political liberalism, Carlyle thus expressed the habitual anxiety that the social order will disintegrate. The problem with capitalistic labor relations—which Carlyle referred to as "nomadic servitude"—is not so much that they exist, as that they *cannot survive*. Those who have been foolish enough to emancipate the slaves in the West Indies, he pointed out, should not marvel at the fact that their own laborers at home are becoming increasingly unmanageable. The abolition of slavery, of political subjugation of labor, leads inexorably to democracy and socialism, since slavery is the "*taproot*" of civilization:

> One always rather likes the Nigger... The Almighty Maker has appointed him to be a Servant.... The whole world rises in shrieks against you, on hearing of such a thing:—yet the whole world... listens, year after year, for above a generation back, to 'disastrous strikes,' 'merciless lockouts' and other details of the nomadic scheme of servitude; nay is becoming thoroughly disquieted about its own too lofty-minded flunkeys, mutinous maid-servants... and the kindred phenomena on every hand: but it will be long before the fool of a world open its eyes to the taproot of all that, to the fond notion, in short, That servantship and mastership, on the nomadic principle, was ever, or will ever be, except for brief periods, possible among human creatures (Carlyle 1867: 5–6).

And the remedy Carlyle had in mind was quite clear: re-establishing slave-like, permanent servitude. This would be one of the most urgent tasks of the heroic capitalist of the future, the Captain of Industry: "In or out of Parliament, our Practical hero will find no end of work ready for him. It is he that has to recivilise, out of its now utter savagery, the world of Industry... To change *nomadic* contract into *permanent*" (35).

On the other hand, capitalism is too harsh in that it over-exploits the worker, alienates him, and hence incites rebellion. This is the rather unspectacular source of Carlyle's concern for the well-being of workers. Behind the irascible, thundering tone of Carlyle's rhetoric, so different from the dry and dispassionate discourse of the classical economists, often hides in fact a greater *moderation*. Capitalism would be better served by restraining *laissez faire*:

> In Rome and Athens,…it was not by loud voting and debating of many, but by wise insight and ordering of a few that the work was done. So is it ever, so will it ever be…. Democracy,…is the consummation of No-government and *Laissez-faire*. It may be natural for our Europe at present; but cannot be the ultimatum of it. Not towards the impossibility, 'self-government' of a multitude by a multitude; but towards some possibility, government by the wisest, does bewildered Europe struggle. The blessedest possibility: not misgovernment, not *Laissez-faire*, but veritable government! (Carlyle 1869a: 74).

Ironically, what Carlyle condemns about economic liberalism is not the political disempowering of the masses but precisely the reverse, their political *empowerment*, the way *laissez faire* recklessly leads, quite in spite of itself, to democracy and the rule of the multitude, destroying elitism. Thus, instead of simply anti-liberalism, what we have is another powerful articulation of the liberal split. Those who economically exploit the worker and fend off any political, governmental regulation, neglect to consider the long-term effects of such elimination of the political. They fail to see that, by selfishly evacuating the political arena they leave it unprotected, free to be occupied by the working class. This abdication of their political duties will lead either to hateful democracy or, still worse, to revolution. "Cost what it may, by one means or another," stated Carlyle (76), "the toiling multitudes of this perplexed, over-crowded Europe must and will find governors. '*Laissez-faire*, Leave them to do'? The thing they will *do*, if so left, is too frightful to think of! It has been *done* once, in sight of the whole earth, in these generations: can it need to be done a second time?" What is at stake is thus the very survival of capitalist society, which the capitalists, fixated on squeezing immediate gains, short-sightedly lay on the line. Carlyle, by contrast, emerges as the true guardian of the existing social order: "we will advise Society not to talk at all about what she exists for; but rather with her whole industry to exist, to try how she can keep existing! That is her best plan." Abandoning *laissez faire*, for Carlyle, is thus a matter of life and death for class society, which he aims to preserve. For if society, "by cruel chance, did come to exist only for protection of breeches-pocket property, she would lose very soon the gift of protecting even that, and find her career in our lower world on the point of terminating!" (80).

Nietzsche, who for all his avowed contempt at the Scottish writer was enormously influenced by him, particularly—but not only—with regards to social and political matters, even to the point of plagiarism,[15] pondered this same predicament and reached similar conclusions. It was essential, Nietzsche once wrote (1988, vol. 2: 681–2), to take care "of the well-being of the worker as well, of his physical and spiritual satisfaction, *in order that* he and his descendants will continue to work for our descendants... The *exploitation* of the worker was, as one now understands, a stupidity, a ruthless enterprise at the cost of the future, which endangered society". In addressing Carlyle's goals, on that point as on many others, Schapiro's account was much more dependable than the conclusions he ultimately drew:

> Like the fascists, Carlyle believed that these evils could be cured by state control of economic life, which would result in making the workers more productive and more contented at the same time. A worker having security, receiving good wages, and living in a comfortable home would work harder for his employer, fight better for the state, and serve loyally the 'noble Few' who ruled him (Schapiro 1949: 394).

And this, indeed, is the whole point of the willingness of fascism to disobey the injunctions of *laissez faire*: not out of revolutionary enthusiasm, but to forestall revolution; not to challenge capitalism, but to steady its ship; not to facilitate the classless society, but to entrench class divisions; not to eliminate exploitation but to ensure its endurance. In short, to take care of the worker's well being "*in order that* he and his descendants will continue to work for our descendants." This was the gist of the matter, for Carlyle, for Nietzsche, and for the fascists

---

[15] Consider, for example, the closing section of Carlyle's *Chartism* (1839), titled "Impossible," in which he analyzes the working-class problem in Europe and proposes the solution of mass emigration, with Nietzsche's section from *Daybreak* (1881), titled "The Impossible Class," in which he analyzes the working-class problem in Europe and proposes the solution of mass emigration. And this "parallel" is by no means an isolated instance. Nietzsche's recurrent thoughts about militarizing relations with the workers ("The workers should learn to feel like soldiers," or "culture that rests on a military basis still towers above all so-called industrial culture") reads like a paraphrase of Carlyle's notions about a nation universally drilled into obedience and military discipline. Among the many remarkable points of convergence not directly having to do with sociopolitical issues, one could mention Nietzsche's *Jasagen zum Leben* as an echo of Carlyle's notion of "Everlasting Yea" from *Sartor Resartus*, or Nietzsche's *Gay Science* as a rejoinder to Carlyle's critique of the "dismal science."

following their trail (in objective terms, and regardless of the existence or absence of direct influence). Ultimately, the alliance of the Captains of Industry with the aristocratic heroes in a dictatorship against the masses, attests to Carlyle's position firmly within the capitalist camp. The ultimate enemy of such anti-capitalists was anti-capitalism. Carlyle was described by Schapiro (372) as the only famous Victorian Briton "who was not, in any sense of the word, a liberal." How strange then, and how instructive, that the anti-liberal Carlyle, this "prefascist" outsider, comes to save the capitalist system from going down the drain because of the capitalists' own combination of political naiveté and economic selfishness, "that unhappy wedlock of Philanthropic Liberalism and the Dismal Science," which has "wrought huge woe for us, and for the poor civilized world, in these days!" (1869b: 299). Schapiro's prophet of "revolutionary" fascism thus comes in truth to cement order and disperse the forces of anarchy. He assures the heroic few fighting against anarchy, that ultimate victory will be theirs:

> For everywhere in this Universe,... Anti-Anarchy is silently on the increase, at all moments: Anarchy not, but contrariwise; having the whole Universe forever set against it; pushing it slowly, at all moments, towards suicide and annihilation. To Anarchy, however million-headed, there is no victory possible. Patience, silence, diligence, ye chosen of the world! (Carlyle 1867: 50).

Yet according to Schapiro, fascism, as will be recalled, was decidedly *not* counterrevolutionary, not a force on the side of the established order, but against it, "something unique in modern history, in that it is a revolutionary movement of the middle class" (1949: 365). So either Schapiro inadequately defined fascism, or he misunderstood Carlyle. I would argue that the former is the case. Carlyle's writings unmistakably foreshadow Fascism, but they show us, pace Schapiro's liberal narrative, that fascism was indeed in its mainspring *counter-revolutionary*, and that, moreover, it cannot be reduced to a middle class movement, divorced from capitalism, or representing a very specific, parochial, petty-bourgeois interpretation of capitalism. In fact, the tenor of Carlyle's discourse is unequivocally aristocratic, although the more numerous middle class, "aristocratic by nature," are to buttress the efforts of the tiny elite:

> Aristocracy by title, by fortune and position, who can doubt but there are still precious possibilities among the chosen of that class? And if that fail us, there is still, we hope, the unclassed Aristocracy by nature, not inconsiderable in numbers, and supreme in faculty, in wisdom, human

talent, nobleness and courage, 'who derive their patent of nobility direct from Almighty God' (Carlyle 1867: 24).

Carlyle's burning lava of all encompassing social critique soon congeals around the traditional pillars of the social order, shoring it up. He does not come to revolutionize but to conserve. In the face of mass democracy, "amid the thickest welter of surrounding gluttony and baseness," while the millions "are noisily living a mere beaverish or doglike" life and everywhere there is "bottomless anarchy from shore to shore," the internal, upper-class feuds of the past are negligible (24). He brokers a union of the historically antagonistic classes, capitalists and aristocrats, and urges them to close ranks, in fact to fuse into each other by way of intermarriage:

> This Industrial hero…is already almost an Aristocrat by class…. [H]e is already by intermarriage and otherwise coming into contact with the Aristocracy by title…He cannot do better than unite with this naturally noble kind of Aristocrat by title; the Industrial noble and this one are brothers born; called and impelled to cooperate and go together. Their united result is what we want from both. And the Noble of the Future… will have grown out of both (34–35).

If anything, Carlyle—in juxtaposition with Proudhon—illustrates how fascism was a coalition of counterrevolutionary forces, the broad union of the propertied classes. He longs (52) to see the "Aristocrat by title…coalescing nobly with his two Brothers, the Aristocrats by nature," namely the "teaching aristocrat," a form of heroic intellectual spreading the gospel among the few—of which Carlyle clearly considered himself the prototype—and the "Industrial," "Practical hero." From their coalition, Carlyle expects a wondrous reversal of the democratic tide: "Were there but three Aristocrats of each sort in the whole of Britain, what beneficent unreported 'Parliamenta,'—actual human consultations and earnest deliberations, responsible to no 'Buncombe,' disturbed by no Penny Editor,—on what the whole Nine were earnest to see done!" There is no suggestion, here or elsewhere, of a privileged role for the middle class in this Parliamenta; no special prerogative reserved, say, for the small artisan vis-à-vis the Captain of Industry. The scheme is politically anti-liberal to the hilt, without a doubt, but it is everywhere committed to capitalism (whereby "capitalism" is understood—here as elsewhere—as a mode of production in the Marxist sense, broader and more primordial than merely one of its possible expressions, laissez faire). Schapiro himself, in fact, contradicted his own emphasis on the middle class as the core of fascism, by describing the diverse clientele of what he considered the major pre-fascist statesman, Louis Napoleon, as well as by pointing to the one item on the agenda about which they were all in agreement—the defense of property from revolution:

> Louis Napoleon's appeal had a far more solid basis in that the propertied classes saw in him a powerful force able and willing to make use of a dictatorial government to save them from social revolution. He gained the solid support of all who feared a social revolution: property owners great and small, aristocrats, capitalists, peasant proprietors, shopkeepers, and professionals; Catholics, who dreaded a revival of attacks on the church by a socialist Reign of Terror; and people generally, who recoiled with horror at the prospect of class war (Schapiro 1949: 316).

Pre-fascism, as Schapiro encountered in real history, and which he forthrightly described, declined the kinship to the fascism he theoretically defined. History, according to his own account, does not confirm a petty-bourgeois prevalence, but rather registers the flocking together of "property owners great and small"; it does not bear out the thesis of a "revolutionary movement" directed against both "big business and the banks" and "the demands of the working class," but rather delineates "a dictatorial government" to save "all who feared a social revolution." Nor did Schapiro entertain any illusions about Bonapartism in power, as if it somehow then preferred the petty-bourgeois Proudhonists to the aristocratic-cum-industrialist, Carlylean constituency. Quite the contrary, he showed that Louis Napoleon allied himself from the very beginning with the latter, with the interests of Capital, which bitterly disappointed the great hopes Proudhon invested in him, while setting off a period of unprecedented growth of French industry. Bonapartist populism and paternalistic Saint-Simonism were rhetorical, not substantial; they created the semblance of a "new" power above the classes, but not a new politics above classes. Within the pre-fascist coalition it was the Carlyle line, so to speak, that swiftly predominated in practice, relegating *Mittelstand* aspirations to a secondary plane. Schapiro thus stated (325) that, "the class that benefited most from the Second Empire was the *bourgeoisie*," and that "Napoleon did all in his power to encourage commerce and industry which won for the government the powerful support of the new moneyed class." This pro-capitalism was so accentuated, that the Second Empire in its later phase, from 1867 up to the end, was dubbed *l'Empire libéral*. Schapiro's tale was more trustworthy than the storyteller; there was a dissonance between his predetermined conclusions and what he actually *saw*, and faithfully documented. Despite the evidence of a broad, anti-mass coalition in defense of property, a coalition which stems from the mainstream of Western society and culture, Schapiro concluded that fascism was some heretic movement, an absolute novelty, and above all, an *anti liberal* one. With great erudition and with a skillfully interwoven narrative, he demonstrated that liberalism and democracy were at loggerheads throughout the 19th century; he showed that bourgeois liberalism was in practice dictatorial and cynical (see his excellent account of the *Système Guizot*, as well as the class despotism embraced by the British liberals, cloaked in pseudo-scientific guises and in philanthropic phrases); he also laid bare the dictatorial option that was built into bourgeois liberal rule. But he recoiled from drawing the inevitable conclusions from all that, namely that dictatorship is, at the very least, a *potential* line of liberal development, one possible denouement of the liberal contradiction. Instead, he went on, in the epilogue, to praise "the historic importance of bourgeois liberalism," which he identified in the peaceful facilitating of the move to the "socialist liberalism" taking shape in the immediate post-War period. Fascism, by contrast, was deemed a mere "challenge to liberalism," an outside phenomena, an aberration.

This apologetic matrix assumes its sharpest contours with reference to the two paradigmatic protagonists of Schapiro's story, Carlyle and J. S. Mill, the first described as the odd anti-liberal, the black sheep of Victorian England, the second as the "pioneer of democratic liberalism," (256) pointing towards the smooth and satisfactory resolution of the liberal contradictions. Yet, in my view, the trajectories of these two figures call for a rather different interpretation, carrying vastly different implications for our historical understanding of the relationship between liberalism and fascism. Both Mill and Carlyle were initially treading the same tortuous path, grappling with the liberal dilemma of how, if at all, the bourgeois class might preserve its freedoms and hegemony under mass democracy. Both expressed this quandary in terms of uncommon, superior individuals, on the verge of being engulfed by the indifferent many. Notice the similarity of language in the following formulations of this idea: Carlyle first (1867: 34): "And all eyes shall yet see them *better*; and the heroic Few, who are the salt of the earth, shall at length see them *well*. With results for everybody. A great 'work' indeed; the greatness of which beggars all others!" And for Mill (1905: 120–1), equally, "these few" outstanding individuals "are the salt of the earth; without them, human life would become a stagnant pool.... Persons of genius are, *ex termini, more* individual than any other people." This is the objective, elitist, starting point, the common problem posed by democracy, and which both Carlyle and Mill had to resolve, one way or another. If Mill, particularly the later one, opted for democracy, while Carlyle outlined a proto-fascist solution, this was not because Carlyle idiosyncratically defied the logic of liberalism, while Mill pursued it to the end. On the contrary. It is an edifying fact that Mill ultimately resolved the contradiction between political and economic liberalism by *bailing out* of economic liberalism, by abandoning to an increasing degree the tenets of *laissez faire* which he at first abided by, and by envisioning nothing less than a comprehensive *alternative to capitalism*. On that account, as well, we should trust Schapiro's *tale*:

> Mill realized, rather vaguely it is true, that political democracy was inadequate unless a new economic system was established in harmony with its egalitarian ideals.... Mill began to speculate on the possibilities of abolishing the capitalist system and became a convert to socialism (Schapiro 1949: 274–5).

Of the two, it was Carlyle who remained the more consistent pro-capitalist. For all his critique of the capitalist system he never bailed out of it, but remained its unswerving champion, defending it at all costs (by defending, I include his propositions for reform, which were meant to save the system, not transcend it). Hence the paradox that Carlyle, the consistent and implacable foe of *laissez faire*, could produce an alternative, proto-fascist program, which was in many respects similar to that embraced by someone like Pareto, the consistent and implacable *champion* of *laissez faire*. Such objective agreement was finally possible because both Carlyle and Pareto were defending the same capitalist system and the property relations attendant on it, notwithstanding the vast disagreements about the precise doctrine according to which this system should be administered. By contrast, Mill, the erstwhile "dismal scientist," crucially departed from economic liberalism, preferring a political one. It was he who was forced to stray out of the main road and seek novel, unheard of, solutions, which would have earned him the wrath and contempt of his liberal intellectual forefathers (and of his biological father, James). Thus, in the final account, Mill, too, like Carlyle, was an outsider-insider to liberalism.

Already in the 20th century, Mill—in his *later* phase, significantly— was acknowledged as a trailblazer of so-called Social Liberalism, a political stream in English politics which, while professing liberalism, understood it as decisively closer to socialism than to capitalism. We can exemplify this by sampling the judgment of one of its leading representatives, Leonard Trelawney Hobhouse:

> As [Mill] advanced in life, however, he became more and more dissatisfied with the whole structure of a system which left the mass of the population in the position of wage-earners, while the minority lived on rents, profits, and the interest on invested capital. He came to look forward to a co-operative organization of society...in which the surplus products of industry would be distributed among the producers. In middle life voluntary co-operation appeared to him the best means to this end, but towards the close he recognized that his change of views was such as, on the whole, to rank him with the Socialists, and the brief exposition of the Socialist ideal given in his Autobiography remains perhaps the best summary statement of Liberal Socialism that we possess (Hobhouse 1919: 114–15).

"Social" or "New" Liberals thus landed very much on the *political side* of the liberal split, abandoning classical economic liberalism altogether or demoting it to a secondary plane, where it had at all times to be compliant with the overarching political and social goals. And this understanding of liberalism as above all a political complex of rights and liberties and a defense of democracy, meant that such liberalism was apt to ally itself with the very antipode of capitalism, i.e., socialism, at least ideologically if not outright politically. In 1900, for example, amid the Second Boer War, John Lawrence Hammond (1900: 210), an eminent liberal journalist, found in socialism a worthy ally against the imperialism of Lord Salisbury's government, in which Joseph Chamberlain, the Liberal Unionist, served as Colonial Secretary: "The courageous and consistent opposition to the war maintained by the Labour members is significant and encouraging." It is also highly instructive how, in 1927, in direct polemic against George Bernard Shaw's defense of Mussolini as an allegedly anti-oligarchic man-of-the-people, the left-liberal newspaper *The Manchester Guardian*, in an unsigned column, reminded the Irish playwright that Mussolini was a "capitalist, not a socialist" (in Salvemini and Shaw 1997: 136). Even more to the point, it insisted that liberalism, which Shaw proclaimed his perennial enemy, was no longer the docile attendant of capitalism as it was during the 19th century. It succinctly maintained that someone who still believes today in unlimited *laissez faire* "is not a liberal but a Rip Van Winkle" (137). Gaetano Salvemini's definition of liberalism, also against Shaw,

is perhaps most instructive of the way Mill's legacy was overwhelmingly that of a *political*, as opposed to *economic*, liberalism:

> *Democracy*, or as they say in England, *liberalism*, is that doctrine which
> affirms that all citizens have a right to the same freedoms: freedom of
> expression, freedom of the press, of association, of assembly, of religion;
> freedom to work, to strike, to travel; *habeas corpus*; the right to control
> public administration through representatives elected for that purpose
> (144; emphases added).

Such liberalism, of course, rendered not only compatible but *interchangeable* with democracy, could not but have found itself firmly
opposed to fascism, and fairly close to socialism. But it should not
cover from view the momentous historical reality of the liberal split,
which Salvemini on that occasion ignored, and which *The Manchester
Guardian* regarded as a *fait accompli*, from which no turning back was
possible. That such rift has not been truly patched is evident today,
in an age when democracy and liberalism are anything but identical,
when the right of elected representatives to control public affairs, particularly economic ones, is *de facto* if not *de jure* exceedingly restricted,
and in which *laissez-faire* capitalism is the hegemonic ideology (or at
least *has been* hegemonic, until the 2008 economic crash, whose long-
term practical and ideological implications are obviously not yet clear).
A model neo-liberal such as Hayek (1988: 52), while seeing himself as
an old Whig in the tradition of Tocqueville and Lord Acton, took care
to distance himself, not only from "all contemporary Americans who
call themselves 'liberals,'" but also from the "Benthamite tradition,
represented and continued by John Stuart Mill and the later English
Liberal Party," all of whom he associated, rather, with a socialist mode
of thinking. For their part, had they been resuscitated in today's reality, Salvemini and the columnists of *The Manchester Guardian* would
themselves likely have felt like Rip Van Winkles, facing an unfamiliar world; or, alternatively, like travelers back in time, witnessing the
revival of an epoch they believed was gone for ever, where liberalism
had meant plenty of "dismal science" and only very small doses of
"democracy."

CHAPTER FOUR

ANTI-LIBERAL LIBERALS—II
(SCHMITT, SOREL)

Carl Schmitt: A Democratic Anti-Liberal?

In addressing the problematic of fascist anti-liberalism, a symptomatic case in point is that of Carl Schmitt, one of the brightest intellectuals to have aligned himself with fascism, sometimes considered one of the three major political thinkers of the 20th century alongside (the liberal) Hannah Arendt and (the communist) Antonio Gramsci. So a consideration of Schmitt's ideas will be indispensable for our purposes. The standard interpretation of Schmitt underscores his intractable hostility to liberalism; so insistent has been this view, that Schmitt's thought has even experienced an unlikely revival in the post-War period precisely among not a few left-wing critics of liberalism. They believe they have found in the German theoretician of law and politics a brother of arms of sorts, the enemy, perhaps, as the title of a left-wing biography of Schmitt has it (Balakrishnan 2002), but one from whose writings a vital criticism of liberalism can be gleaned, to subsequently augment, however critically and selectively, their own anti-liberal polemics. On the liberal side, too, Schmitt is invariably portrayed as an out-and-out anti-liberal and often, what is more, as an idiosyncratic *democrat*. I provide just two examples:

> Critique of liberalism has a long tradition. However, those launching critical attacks against liberalism frequently turn out to be liberals themselves... Carl Schmitt's critique of liberalism is different. His polemic does not fit into the tradition of liberal self-criticism.... Schmitt systematically undermines the liberal principle of the rule of law. He wants it to be replaced by an authoritarian version of democracy, a democracy based on the substantial 'homogeneity' of the collective unity of the people rather than one resting upon the principles of participatory republicanism. Although Schmitt until 1933 opposed the Nazi party, his ardent anti-liberalism entails from the outset the potential for fascism (Bielefeldt 1998: 23).

Similarly, Shadia B. Drury (1999: 82) argued that Schmitt promoted "the idea that liberalism and democracy are incompatible, and that the latter is preferable to the former." Such a broad consensus vis-à-vis a pivotal thinker such as Schmitt thus appears to designate a solid, unquestionable anti-liberal stronghold within fascist thought. And yet, in my view, the standard interpretation is profoundly mistaken and needs to be radically redressed. Far from being utterly alien to the liberal tradition, Schmitt's critique of liberalism ought to be seen, indeed, as "liberal self-criticism," but from the radical right. Schmitt furnishes a paradigmatic illustration of the split of liberalism I have been outlining, whereby political liberalism is severely criticized, to the point of being jettisoned altogether, because it burdens capitalism and imperialism and boosts up democracy and socialism. I maintain that in their basic definition of Schmitt's position with regards to liberalism and democracy, Bielefeldt and Drury have got it quite wrong: I agree with Drury that Schmitt considered liberalism and democracy incompatible, but I think it is evident that he thought *the former* preferable to the latter. What he envisaged in dictatorship, and what facilitated his embrace of Nazism, was a way of discarding democracy—homogenous or otherwise—and preserving the capitalist and imperialist core of liberalism. To be sure, Schmitt himself did a lot to abet the subsequent confusion, since he could not quite openly state his aims and had to find roundabout ways of justifying this maneuver and camouflaging its real motives. In this he was not alone, but rather reflected the intrinsic necessity of fascism to employ double talk and diverse strategies of dissimulation.

Schmitt's Adaptation of Classical Liberalism

Many analyses of Schmitt's works are handicapped by insufficient attention to the historical specificity of such texts. Thus, rather than someone who was grappling with an acute historical conundrum, the menace of mass democracy in a very specific time and place from the standpoint of the upper classes, Schmitt is often discussed as if he was a detached political scientist deftly juggling such abstractions as politics, liberalism, democracy, will of the people, and so on. Such synchronic notions are then extracted from their original context and projected onto our own times. This prevalent idealistic attitude was prefigured by Paul Hirst, when *Telos* was still happy to call itself "a nice leftist journal" (Piccone and Ulmen 1987: 3): "Because [Schmitt's] thinking about concrete political situations is not governed by any dogmatic political alternative, it exhibits a *peculiar objectivity*" (Hirst 1987: 16; italics added). This idealism is compounded by an interrelated lack of awareness of the fundamental esotericism of Schmitt's rhetoric; there is very little willing-ness to consider the possibility that Schmitt was not wearing his heart on his sleeve. Instead, interpreters recurrently take him at face value: an unwise thing to do, when dealing with one who belonged to two groups of people not exactly known for their guilelessness: a *fascist*, to start with, and a fascist *lawyer*, to boot. We thus need to contextualize Schmitt, who was operating not in our social and political constellation but in his, which was drastically different.

Schmitt underlined the powerlessness of political liberalism to cope with democracy, specifically *mass* democracy, and consequently the need to break out of this impasse by recourse to dictatorship, that would establish once and for all who is the sovereign, who is the one who can decide on the *Ausnahmezustand*, the state of emergency (literally: state of exception), and define the relevant "friend-enemy" groupings. The entire set of fundamental questions raised by Schmitt and the well-known answers he provided, derived from this historical predicament. And since Schmitt approaches this quandary as a jurist and grapples with the legalistic implications of the move to dictatorship, he becomes the personification of the upper classes' dilemma explained by Engels and Gumplowicz, that sees them legally confined within the—politi-cally liberal—straitjacket they themselves ordered made. "The parties of order," according to Engels (1895), "are perishing under the legal conditions created by themselves,...in the end there is nothing left for them to do but themselves break through this dire legality.... Breach of the constitution, dictatorship...!" And for Gumplowicz, the bour-geoisie finds "the yoke of legal logic about its neck and must submit to its ideas," until, "from this unbearable condition," it appeals "to the despotic might of reaction" (1899: 149–150). The straitjacket is thus torn asunder, and Schmitt, quite from within the system, indeed from its very headquarters, provides an exquisitely erudite and sophisticated juristic counsel on how to do so. Schmitt was not the ultimate outsider portrayed by liberals, not a sworn enemy of liberalism, nor a "peculiarly objective" observer, but one of those upper-class travellers on board the liberal vessel, who was made anxious by the stormy waters of mass democracy and driven to consider what might best be ditched to get the ship steadied. Overboard goes political liberalism.

Far from being a *democratic critic* of *liberal politics*, in his analysis of "the crisis of parliamentarianism," Schmitt displayed striking parallels with the standard, 19th century *liberal critique* of *democratic politics*. Schmitt did not deny the value of political liberalism as such, but claimed that it had by then become historically outmoded and hence due to be replaced. And why, according to Schmitt, did it become obsolete? Is it because, as another conventional reading of Schmitt has it, liberalism is founded on discussion and rational decision-making, whereas an irascible fascist and totalitarian of Schmitt's ilk rather prefers clear-cut decisions and emphatic actions that defy the rational? In truth, Schmitt charged political liberalism, i.e., parliamentarianism, with being, or more precisely with becoming, an irrational system of ruling. It did *once*—in its 19th century heyday—involve reasoned discussion and dialogue between opposing ideas, leading to one argument prevailing over another. And this was the time when parliamentarianism was *useful* as well as *meaningful,* living up to its name which of course implies *talking,* convincing, reasoning. The problem, for Schmitt, is that this was no longer the case, that parliament had regretfully *ceased to function* as a locus of rational discussion. This fissure, symptomatically, he blamed on the advance of mass democracy. With the entry of the masses onto the political scene, reasoned discussion was at an end. Now parliament was a mere site of power struggles, a vulgar brawl of selfish, sectarian interests, disguised as discussion:

> Discussion means an exchange of opinion that is governed by the purpose of persuading one's opponent through *rational arguments* of the truth or justice of something... To discussion belong shared convictions as premises, the willingness to be persuaded, independence of party ties, freedom from selfish interests. Most people *today* would regard such disinterestedness as scarcely possible.... The situation of parliamentarism is so critical *today* because the *development of modern mass democracy* has made argumentative public discussion an empty formality.... The parties... do not face each other today discussing opinions, but as social or economic power-groups calculating their mutual interests and opportunities for power, and they actually agree compromises and coalitions on this basis (Schmitt 1988: 5–6; italics added).[1]

Schmitt was wistful for the days of classical liberalism when an elite of wise men was ruling the state, setting argument against counter-argument until the best decision had been reached, and he bemoaned the fact that the masses had perverted this into a thinly veiled power-game. The class logic of such position is manifest. A democratic opponent of liberalism would have advanced the criticism that under liberal

---

[1] I introduce small changes to the translation, relying on the German original: Schmitt (1985).

democracy and its pluralistic veneer, under the cover of "the rule of the people," the bourgeoisie is still able to wield the state apparatus for its own advantage. This is a leftist argument familiar to modern ears, and there were similar voices heard in Schmitt's days, if surely to a lesser extent, given that liberal democracy at that time was a much livelier and indeed literally more *re-publican* affair as compared to our own, jaded, political era. Conversely, those—not all too numerous—contemporary German liberals who did support the Weimar Republic, the so-called *Vernunftrepublikaner*, often did so precisely on the grounds that the republic was *not truly* democratic, that a liberal elite was in reality covertly running the show. So argued such figures as Max Weber, Hugo Preuss and Friedrich Naumann. But Schmitt, explicitly referring to their elitist justification of democracy, was not so sanguine:

> Whether parliament actually possesses the capacity to build a political elite has since become very questionable. *Today* one would certainly not think so optimistically about this selection instrument; many would regard such hope as already outmoded... But worse and destroying almost every hope, in a few states, parliamentarism has already produced a situation in which all public business has become an object of spoils and compromise for the parties and their followers, and politics, far from being the concern of an elite, has become the despised business of a rather dubious class of persons (4; italics added).

Schmitt thus opposed the Weimar Republic not because it is was still liberally conducted, behind the masses' back, by an elite, but precisely because it *escaped* the elites' control. He shared with Weber and the liberal democrats the ideal of elite rule; he was in that respect just as liberal as they were, but he disagreed with them that political liberalism can still be manipulated to the elites advantage. Here, he insisted, all *hope* is nearly lost. But *their* hope was also *his*. If they accepted the Republic as *pseudo*-democratic, he rejected it as *genuinely* so:

> Never mind. If someone still believes in parliamentarism, he will at least have to offer new arguments for it. A reference to Friedrich Naumann, Hugo Preuss and Max Weber is *no longer* sufficient. With all respect for these men, no one *today* would share their hope that through parliament the education of a political elite is readily guaranteed (7; italics added).

If, "today," parliament can "no longer" be trusted, when was it a source of "hope" and "optimism"? Schmitt's anti-democratic and pro-liberal ideals can best be gauged by contrasting his two historical points of reference: if, on the bad side of parliamentary rule stands modern mass democracy, such as exists in post-War Germany, on the good side stand the cabinets at the times preceding the extension of the suffrage, where a bourgeois elite exercised political power:

> Who still believes in this kind of openness? And in parliament as its greatest platform?
> The arguments of Burke, Bentham, Guizot, and John Stuart Mill are thus antiquated *today*. The numerous definitions...in which parliamentarism appears as essentially 'government by discussion' [originally in English] must accordingly also count as 'moldy' (7; italics added).

Notice again the historical character of the argument: the reasons provided by classical 19th century liberalism are "antiquated today." They are not, that is, inherently inadequate, and were quite relevant to describe the parliamentary rule of their own times. But *today*, faced with the historical phenomenon of mass democracy, they have forfeited the legitimacy they once contained, and have become "moldy." Schmitt's narrative was strewn with such indications of underlying nostalgia for the liberalism that once was but is alas no longer: he spoke (8; italics added) of "the belief in parliament which *once actually existed* and which one *no longer* finds *today*." And: "*today*...it is *no longer* a question of persuading one's opponent of the truth or justice of an opinion but rather of winning a majority in order to govern with it" (7; italics added). The entire text is under the sign of an historical analysis, brought to bear on a specifically modern, 20th century, predicament, as the very title indicates: "The Spiritual-Historical Condition of *Today's* [*heutigen*] Parliamentarianism." Such recurrent "that-was-then / this-is-now" constructions underscore Schmitt's conviction that political liberalism, legitimate in the past, has run its course. To say that "Schmitt systematically undermines the liberal principle of the rule of law" is misleading inasmuch as, for Schmitt, political liberalism of the good kind *has already been undermined*, made a mockery of, under the grotesque disfiguration of mass democracy. And the positive historical counter-example—what a strange predilection on the part of a sworn anti-liberal!—is the classical liberalism preceding its mass degradation, where discussion was allegedly still worthy of its name:

> The much discussed crisis of parliamentarianism lies...in the fact that today, as a result of the development of mass democracy, the belief in such principles is lost. The classical political liberals and pioneers of continental parliamentarianism were still completely convinced not only that public

discussion is an anti-dote against political corruption, but also of the moral value and the superiority of parliament. The typical representative of such belief is Guizot, a typical liberal of the times of Louis-Philippe. Parliament is for him a place where in public discussion, through argument and counter-argument, the truth and the just are most safely to be found (Schmitt 1994: 60).

Schmitt's positive—if "moldy" and "obsolete"—model of parliamentary rule is Guizot's, the same French liberal who had given his name to the notorious *Système Guizot*, which became a synonym for the tight-fisted, self-serving and hypocritical rule of a small bourgeois minority (suffrage was based on some 200,000 voters). Schmitt discounted the fact that mid-19th century parliamentarianism was just as motivated by selfish interests and just as party-biased as in the early 20th century, only that back then it was only *one* group whose perspective was represented and only *one party* that was able to voice its "selfish interests." Naturally, the fact that the bourgeoisie was able to rule supreme without having to take into consideration the majority of the population, made its process of decision-making much smoother and its discourse considerably more homogenous. It is a great deal easier, certainly, to convince one's interlocutor of the rightness of one's position, if those engaged in dialogue share the same social and economic interests and those who do not are excluded from the conversation. But this hardly means that their discussion is more serious and genuine than the much more thorny interchange between social forces, indeed parties, representing clashing interests. Clearly, the move from the first stage of parliamentarism, to the second, would have been welcomed by a *democratic anti-liberal*, as Schmitt allegedly is, as a marked progress, not a retreat. And all democrats indeed, whatever their misgivings about liberal democracy, did not wish to revert back to the times of Burke, Guizot, or Bentham. It is illuminating to compare Schmitt's take on Guizot with that of Tocqueville, himself hardly a passionate champion of mass democracy, in fact its famous critic, who nonetheless found the exclusive practices of the Guizot-clique the antithesis of meaningful politics and true discussion:

> In a political life thus composed and led, what was most lacking…was political life itself. Such life could hardly emerge or survive within the sphere delineated for it by the constitution: the old aristocracy had been defeated, and the people were excluded. As every matter was settled by the members of one class, in accordance with their interests and points

of view, no battlefield could be found on which great parties might wage war. This peculiar homogeneity of position, interest, and consequentially of point of view which prevailed in what M. Guizot had called the legal country, deprived parliamentary debates of all originality, all reality, and so of all true passion. I have spent ten years of my life in the company of truly great minds who were in constant state of agitation without ever really becoming heated, and who expended all their perspicacity in the vain search for subjects on which they could seriously disagree (Tocqueville 1997: 9–10).

It is as if Tocqueville's words were written in anticipated retort to Schmitt's claims, even to the point of deconstructing the alleged political value Schmitt ascribed to the homogeneity of classical liberal politics as opposed to the crippling heterogeneity of mass politics. For Tocqueville, precisely in such heterogeneity, in the clash of real "interests" and of "great parties," lies the essence of genuine politics, whereas the homogeneity of Guizot's constellation is a token of a simulacra of politics, a mock-discussion, indeed a literally bogus *parlia*ment. It is a telling measure of the staunch *classical political liberalism* underpinning Schmitt's position and of its stringent *negation of democracy* that Tocqueville appears by comparison a *radical democrat* and an incisive *critic of classical political liberalism*. Where Tocqueville sees "lack of politics," Schmitt identifies genuine parliamentarianism; and where Tocqueville sees the potential for a true political "battlefield" upon which a real, red-blooded clash of interests may unfold, Schmitt complains that the masses have made "an empty formality" out of "public discussion."

The Hyper-Politics of Weimar

This analysis, incidentally, also belies the notion, oddly widespread among leftists, that Schmitt advanced a useful critique of the liberal "end of politics":

> Schmitt's thought serves as a warning against the dangers of complacency that a triumphant liberalism entails.... It should shatter the illusions of all those who believe that the blurring of frontiers between Left and Right... constitute progress in the enlightened march of humanity towards a... cosmopolitan democracy.... When we take a look at the current state of democratic politics through a Schmittian lens, we realize how much the process of neutralization and depoliticization, already noticed by Schmitt, has progressed. Does not one of the most fashionable discourses nowadays proclaim the 'end of politics'? (Mouffe 1999a: 2–3)

But Schmitt, in truth, rather denounced the liberal *beginning of politics.* Liberalism he found problematic, not because it defused and muzzled politics, but because it opened up the political Pandora's box in the first place. The hateful Weimar Republic was, for Schmitt, as for most liberals and conservatives, *hyper*-political, stretched to the limit by clashing political segments and interests. The problem was not any elimination of the friend-enemy divisions, but an intolerable multiplication of such lines, and, even more importantly, a division of the friend-enemy along the wrong, *class* lines (in Chapter 6, I address in greater detail the class-logic behind Schmitt's famous friend-enemy distinction. In a nutshell: it was meant not to revitalize or restore the dignity of the political, but to de-legitimize socialist politics and place it below the national one.[2]) As an example of this repudiation of political pluralism, we can examine the following passage, in which Schmitt (1994: 215) criticizes the German democratic procedure. The beginning sounds, admittedly, somewhat akin to modern-day left-wing critiques of liberal democracy as a hollow process whereby the voters are being deftly maneuvered into channels pre-arranged from above: "Five party lists appear, formed in a most secretive, occult way, dictated by five organizations. The masses proceed, so to speak, into five already standing fencings, and the statistical record of this process is called 'election.' But what is it, in truth?" And yet, as the continuation of the discussion makes perfectly clear, Schmitt's whole point was to denounce this process *not* as leading to a political vacuum, *not* as making the masses choose between fake alternatives, but, quite the opposite, as impossibly multiplying their choices between very real and sharply defined alternatives:

> In truth, it is a downright grotesque option between five *utterly contra-dictory* systems,... five *antithetical worldviews, state forms, and economic systems*..., for example between atheism and Christianity, between social-ism and capitalism, between monarchy and republic, between Moscow, Rome, Wittenberg, Geneva, and The Brown House [the building housing the National Socialist headquarters in Munich] and other *incompatible such friend-enemy alternatives*...! (215; italics added).

This political pluralism thus *prevents* the masses from becoming unified and homogenous: "Such a process only means that the people's

---

[2] This is also the conclusion of Hardt and Negri (2004: 6) as well as that of Wolin (2006: 247).

will is immediately and at its spring diverted into five channels and flows in five different directions, so that it can *never flow together in a single stream*" (215; italics added). The upshot of political liberalism is thus not a depoliticization but a social implosion, a pernicious proliferation of antagonisms of all sorts. Schmitt—exasperated by this pluralism of interests, namely by a real and operating democracy—was the one preaching neutralization and "blurring of frontiers between Left and Right." In Schmitt's quintessential analysis of "The Age of Neutralizations and Depoliticizations," a 1929 lecture added to the 1932 edition of *The Concept of The Political*, it is evident that the defect of the modern, liberal state, is that it *is unable* and *unwilling* to eliminate the Left-Right schism:

> [O]ne and the same state cannot accommodate two contradictory economic systems, i.e., capitalism and communism are mutually exclusive. The Soviet state has realized the maxim *cujus regio ejus oeconomia* [meaning: whoever rules a given territory decides on the economy.[3]]... Essential here is that a homogenous economic state conforms to economic thinking.... In an economic age, a state which does not claim to understand and direct economic relations must declare itself neutral with respect to political questions and decisions and thereby renounce its claim to rule.
>
> Now it is remarkable that the European liberal state of the nineteenth century could portray itself as a *stato neutrale ed agnostico* and could see its existential legitimation precisely in its neutrality (Schmitt 2007: 88).

The liberal state must thus "renounce its claim to rule," since it does *not* homogenize politics and still worse, economics; it leaves un-decided the all-important modern conflict between capitalism and communism. And if Schmitt wished for a dictatorial Germany to emulate the Soviet example and forcefully eradicate one side of the economic schism, he clearly did not wish to see *capitalism* disappear.

To look at current politics "through a Schmittian lens," is therefore to find it all in all satisfactorily homogenous, having restored the unity of interests and shared perspective upon which an elite can fruitfully reason and discuss. What one finds, in other words, is a condition not unlike that which prevailed under the complacent and triumphantly liberal *Système Guizot* whose engulfment by mass democracy Schmitt lamented. The parliamentarian crisis, along with mass democracy, has been contained. Liberalism, in the form of neo-liberalism, has shaken

---

[3] This follows Leo Strauss' notes to Schmitt (2007).

itself out of its democratic stupor, to regain its former, elitist vigour. The ongoing neo-liberal depoliticizing which we have been witnessing over the last 30 years, is not something to be criticized *with* Schmitt as much as it is a token, as it were, of a successful Schmittianizing of politics. This is evident in a number of ways, from the far reaching neutralization of internal social struggles throughout the western, liberal world, through the handing of political and economic decisions to small elites of so-called experts, unelected and unaccountable to the masses. Last but not least, it is evident in the way foreign politics has been conducted by the great Western powers, uncannily reproducing the ideal Schmittian pattern of a radicalization of the struggle between states and peoples, the *Us vs. Them* warfare, perhaps best encapsulated in the "clash of civilizations" and "the axis of evil" tropes. This is the fundamental mistake in extrapolating Schmitt's critique of the liberalism of *his times* to our own neo-liberal age.[4] One imagines Schmitt as providing a critique of the liberal practice of liquefying political antagonisms into some sort of bland, lukewarm, hegemonic porridge. Yet the liberalism that he fought against was not lukewarm, but *red hot* (and red indeed, in more than one sense).

From Donoso to Schmitt: the Introduction of Demagoguery

So far, I have analyzed the ideological core of Schmitt's position, which is elitist and anti-democratic in the extreme, while harking back to the liberalism preceding the fall of universal suffrage. And yet this core, while not particularly difficult to discern, was not openly admitted by Schmitt who, on the contrary, took care to envelop it in layers of rhetoric. Overtly, Schmitt frequently spoke *in favor of democracy* and *against liberalism*. So those, like liberal critics and left-wing admirers, who would rather take Schmitt at face value, can indeed use such outward layers to portray him as a democratic anti-liberal, whom they respectively

---

[4] Such extrapolation, by the way, also discounts Schmitt's own emphasis on the purely contextual and circumstantial significance of political concepts. The following statement, for example, should serve as a caveat to those wishing to apply his ideas in vastly different times and constellations: "all political concepts, terms and images have a polemical meaning. They are focused on a specific conflict and are bound to a concrete situation; the result…is a friend-enemy grouping, and they turn into empty and ghostlike abstractions when this situation disappears" (Schmitt 2007: 30). Schmitt's understood historiography, similarly, as inextricably embedded in the context of *the present*: "all historical knowledge is knowledge of the present,…such knowledge obtains its light and intensity from the present and in the most profound sense only serves the present…" (81).

condemn or praise. But why did Schmitt bother to encrypt his position, and how can its essence be distinguished from its appearance?

We can begin to address this duplicity by comparing Schmitt to one of his major influences, the 19th century Spanish proponent of dictatorship, Juan Donoso Cortés. Both political thinkers, confronted by the revolutionary upheaval of their times, envisage the same solution: a decisive move from political liberalism to authoritarianism because political liberalism can not take on the socialist challenge with any resolution, caught up in futile, endless discussions. For both, political liberalism has to be eliminated since it breeds the mortal enemy of the hierarchical state in the form of socialism. Both endorse dictatorship, but Donoso is perfectly straightforward about its anti-democratic character; indeed, the whole point of eliminating political liberalism is to impede the socialist-democratic rule of the people. Schmitt, on the other hand, without distancing himself from Donoso's positions, nevertheless introduces an element totally absent in Donoso, by grounding his own apology for dictatorship on the odd claim that it will be democratic. The rule of liberalism, he contended, is only a sham democracy, so its elimination and the move to a dictatorship might be perfectly compatible with democracy; in fact it will only usher in the true "rule of the people." In the context of elucidating Donoso, Schmitt thus argued (1950: 36) that "dictatorship is the antithesis not of democracy but of discussion." But this is definitely not the way Donoso saw things. For him the problem with liberal "discussion" was that it 1) opened the dam gates of authority and tradition which 2) started the flood of reasoning and discussing that 3) culminated in democracy and socialism. The reasons behind Donoso's bid to terminate liberal discussion, which he puts in the mouth of "democratic socialism" dialoguing with "liberalism," are vividly explained in the following passage:

> When you incite me to discuss, I forgive you, for you know not what you do; discussion, the universal dissolvent,...already eliminated your adversaries and will now eliminate you... [A]gainst discussion neither industry nor the coat of arms are of help; 'disussion' is the title under which death travels when it does not wish to get identified and goes incognito (Donoso 1851: 203).

Donoso was not so much against liberal political freedom per se—in fact, as mentioned above, as long as it remained the restricted asset of the upper classes, he was himself a liberal—but only because, as the 1848 revolutions traumatically exemplify, it leads, quite in spite of itself, to the advance of democratic socialism. As Nietzsche (1990: 106) would put it some decades later, certain taboos are better not broken, certain questions better left un-broached: "The stupidity, fundamentally the instinct degeneration which is the cause of *every* stupidity today, lies in the existence of a labour question at all. About certain things *one does not ask questions*: first imperative of instinct." Donoso's anti-liberal misgivings in any event exclusively concerned *political* liberalism, metonymically referred to as "discussion." Notice the highly instructive way in which "discussion" is said to overwhelm "industry"! And while it is true, as Schmitt pointed out, that Donoso became infinitely contemptuous of liberalism, and expressed himself much more respectfully about socialism, this was only because he considered socialism to be the real, deadly enemy, whereas liberalism was merely the foolish knave and the irresolute weakling who plays into the enemy's hands. The battle of Armageddon will be waged between the people and socialism, on the one side, and the elite and God, on the other:

> The liberal school, enemy at the same time of darkness and of light, has chosen for itself a God-knows-what uncertain twilight zone between the illuminated regions and the murky ones, between the eternal shadows and the divine auroras. Placed in this nameless region it embarked on the enterprise of governing without the people and without God, an extravagant and impossible enterprise: its days are numbered, for on one side of the horizon God is emerging, and on the other side the people. No one can say where it would be on the tremendous day of battle, when the field would be covered by the Catholic phalanxes and those of socialism (Donoso 1851: 206).

Liberalism is incomparably weaker and less consistent than socialism, but for that very reason also incomparably *less evil*. It is caught indeed between God and Satan, which is an uncomfortable spot to be in, but democratic socialism is an outright emanation of Satan: "The socialist schools, an abstraction of the barbaric multitudes which support them, examined according to their theoreticians and teachers, are much better placed than the liberal school... Socialism is powerful for no other reason than for being a satanic theology" (201). Therefore, for all his contempt for liberalism, there is no question whatsoever that Donoso was first and foremost anti-democratic and anti-socialist, and anti-liberal only since liberalism forms the antechamber of democratic socialism. For that reason, he did not exclude a political alliance with liberalism, in fact chastised the conservatives of his time, for *failing to* unite with the liberals to create a solid front against democracy, hence increasing the ranks of Satan, a fact of which Schmitt, moreover, was quite conscious:

Noteworthy and typical for Donoso's outlook is his evaluation of Prussian conservatism. This political orientation, which must have best appealed to him because of its monarchic and counterrevolutionary convictions, he judges very coldly. He sees it in a dangerous situation: as a reaction-ary party it distances itself from the liberal bourgeoisie, which is hence driven to align itself with the democrats; had it been less reactionary and somewhat more tolerant, it would have been able to establish in Prussia a more or less durable, at any rate well-ordered government (Schmitt 1950: 56).[5]

Having re-capitulated Donoso's position, it becomes clear how capri-cious it was on Schmitt's part to suggest that Donoso's authoritarianism was anti-liberal, but not anti-democratic. But what is the reason for this divergence? How could a "homogenous" democrat like Schmitt, eager to put at the state's helm the "collective unity of the people," rely so heavily and admiringly on an ultraist anti-democrat like Donoso, who feared nothing more than precisely such popular rule? In truth, however, Schmitt was just as staunchly anti-democratic as his Spanish role model and the difference is merely the introduction of social dema-goguery into his argument, made necessary by the different historical circumstances under which he was writing. Schmitt, in fact, made it a point to acclaim the political realism of his tutor, one not bound to any idealistic fixations:

Donoso's judgment constantly adjusted to the changing situation of for-eign affairs, since he was anything but the Don Quixote of an abstract principle. His perception of the realities of foreign politics was excep-tionally acute, his adaptability, in spite of rhetorical theses, astounding (59–60).

And clearly it would be wrong to ascribe any such quixotism to Donoso's German pupil, or to underestimate his own "adaptability" and skill in exploiting "rhetorical theses." Donoso, living at the time preceding

---

[5] Schmitt's appreciation of Donoso's political realism, contradicts the attempt of liberals to portray him as a die-hard "conservative," fanatically opposed to even a dialogue with liberalism, to say nothing of an alliance:

Schmitt's German version of conservatism, which shared so much with Nazism, has no direct links with American thought. Yet residues of his ideas can nonethe-less be detected in the ways in which conservatives today fight for their objectives. Liberals think of politics as a means; conservatives as an end.... Liberals think of conservatives as potential future allies; conservatives treat liberals as unworthy of recognition (Wolfe 2004).

Whether correct or not in describing the position of American conservatives, this cer-tainly does *not* apply to Schmitt himself, who was far more pragmatically committed to the bourgeois order than most liberals are willing to acknowledge.

the mature challenge of mass democracy, felt no need to disguise his anti-popular sentiment nor exhibit any hesitation when equating the people's rule with Satanism. But Schmitt was writing in a period when the prospect of an open, anti-popular dictatorship was rather meager. Democracy was not an ideal to be taken lightly, much less to openly flout. He was therefore compelled, like most fascists, to gain some popular support for his dictatorship, to present it as a legitimate expression of The People's will, a much more organic and coherent expression than the fragmented politics of liberalism.

Leo Strauss, who understood something about the difference between what one *avows* and what one *means*, realized that for all his attacks on liberalism, what really concerned Schmitt was the democratic rise of the masses. It was they who constituted the true enemy. In an early (1932) review of Schmitt's *The Concept of the Political*, Strauss thus perceptively argued that "what *ultimately* matters to Schmitt is not the battle against liberalism." Rather,

> in order to gain a free line of fire, with a sweep of the hand [the mortal enemies] wave aside…the [liberal] neutral who lingers in the middle, interrupting the view of the enemy. The polemics against liberalism can therefore only signify a concomitant or preparatory action; it is meant to clear the field for the battle of decision between 'the spirit of technicity,' the 'mass faith that inspires an antireligious, this-worldly activism' and the opposite spirit and faith, which, as it seems, still has no name (in Meier 1995: 118).[6]

Let it also be noted that Schmitt, for his part, had clearly recognized himself in Strauss' interpretation. He is thus reported to have recommended Strauss' review to one of his confidants, Günther Krauss, who worked under him in 1932–33: "You've got to read that. He saw through me and X-rayed me as nobody else has" (xvii).

Fascism: Cui Bono?

Apropos Leo Strauss, Schmitt was well aware of the long exoteric tradition of "the political arcane," that of advertising to the people reassuring falsehoods, while esoterically keeping the cards close to the chest, a tradition which he saw in operation under all political forms, monarchy

---

[6] Consider, also, John McCormick's (1997: 5) informed emphasis on the fact that Schmitt's "main intellectual-political nemesis" was not liberalism, but socialism. Liberalism, he adds, became a target for criticism in the first place because it had "weakened Germany's position vis-à-vis socialism internally and internationally."

and aristocracy, as well as *democracy and dictatorship*. As he described unsentimentally in his book *The Dictatorship*, such esotericism was no deplorable aberration to be fought against but, for those who wished to run a state, an objective, timeless necessity:

> For the state certain measures are always necessary, in order to create an appearance of freedom, if only to calm the people, simulacra, decorative constitutions [*Einrichtungen*]. In contrast to such external, ostensible motives, the *Arcana Reipublicae* are the internal driving forces of the state (Schmitt 2006: 14).[7]

The question was thus simply how best to manipulate the people. Shadia B. Drury (1999: 83) underscored the fact that Schmitt regarded the need to feign an allegiance to democracy as a modern political must: "Even though democracy is self-refuting, it has remained the most irresistible political force in European history. Every political movement that hopes to succeed must present itself in democratic guise—liberalism, Marxism, and socialism have done just that." Precisely from this correct observation follows the necessity, which Schmitt must have felt, for fascism and dictatorship to follow suit and brandish "democracy." In view of this, it is all the more striking that Drury—habitually a judicious observer and one perfectly positioned to appreciate esotericism, which she has done in general very usefully with regards to Strauss—neglected to consider the possibility that Schmitt's "democracy" might have been a mere "guise." Instead, she took him at his word and concluded a marked preference on his part for democracy over liberalism.[8] Guided by such strategic considerations, Schmitt portrayed the move to a dictatorship, indeed a fascist one, as a development from which the people *can only benefit*:

> That fascism dispenses with elections and hates and despises the whole 'elezionismo,' is not un-democratic but anti-liberal and springs from the correct realization that today's methods of secret individual voting threaten to privatize everything that pertains to the state and everything political, to completely drive the people as a unity out of the public sphere (the sovereign vanishes in the polling booth), and to degrade the will-formation of the state to the sum total of secret and private individual wills, that is, in reality, to uncontrollable mass desires and resentments....

---

[7] See also the former and the next page, for a distinction between two main different forms of political esotericism, the *Arcana imperii* (that characterizes "normal times") and the *Arcana dominationis* (prevalent under the dictatorial state-of-exception).

[8] Then again, the fact that Drury herself is a committed liberal might explain her disinclination to treat Schmitt cynically in that respect.

> The equation between democracy and secret individual voting is 19th century liberalism and not democracy (Schmitt 1994: 126).

Schmitt did all he could to dress the wolf of fascism in democratic, sheep's clothing, simultaneously vouching for the anti-liberalism of fascism. But the historical and contemporary truth, as he knew all too well, was diametrically opposed: 19th century liberalism, which Schmitt essentially approved of but discarded since it was no longer practicable, rested precisely on the alleged "homogeneity" afforded by an exclusive elite rule which, quite like fascism in that regard, saw and promoted itself as identical with the good of "the nation," "the people," or "the state." For that very reason, 19th century bourgeois liberalism by no means wished to expand the suffrage, and see the sovereign (that is: the liberal elite) vanish in the polling booth. But Schmitt was content to overlook the tenacious popular struggle to obtain universal suffrage, conducted largely *against* the liberal bourgeoisie, and topped this off by labeling such suffrage un-democratic and liberal. Similarly, Schmitt was painfully aware of the fact that "secret individual voting" does not culminate in a privatization of the political or in a mere aggregate of disparate individual atoms. He realized that this process rather leads to the formation of powerful *collectives*, uniting large groups and classes, as he himself described, for example in the passages quoted above. But that is precisely what makes voting so threatening from an elitist point of view. Homogenous democracy, distilling the will of "the people as a unity," is a *contradictio in adiecto*, at least as long as a class society exists. That is precisely why any attempt at such homogenization without transcending class can only come about by way of a political exclusion, which classical liberalism achieved by keeping the suffrage strictly limited, and which fascism accomplished by abolishing it altogether (as well as with liberal recourse to the paraphernalia of the *Arcana Reipublicae*). Schmitt, as a rule, kept silent about this class character which liberal democracy bears, and tried to present it as a mere mathematical formula, devoid of any social content. As in the following passage:

> The parlance that is common today rests in truth on the fact that, since the 19th century, the 'people' became ever larger, and incorporated the *mass*, which was excluded as a matter of course from the old, classical democracy. *Quantitatively*, the participation in political life expanded evermore; that was the democratic progress. The demand for the franchise of woman, the demand to lower the age required for voting, everything which *increased the number* of those entitled to vote was consequently called 'democratic' (25; emphases added, except for the word 'mass').

Notice the way Schmitt attempted to reduce "the democratic progress" to a mere matter of quantity, as implicitly opposed to quality. He conveniently left out the obvious and crucial fact that, with the gradual entry of "the masses" into politics, entered new social elements, new classes, from the lower middle classes right down to the working classes, which clearly involved more than a mere increase in the number of voters. Glaringly symptomatic is the way that, in recalling the progressive stages of democratic expansion, Schmitt neglected to mention the most central struggle, namely for the lowering and eventual elimination of property restrictions, while remembering the infinitely less vital issue of the voters' ages: that is, an issue which does not bear directly on allocation of social power between *classes*; a Freudian slip, perhaps, but more properly a *Machiavellian* one. This small omission permitted Schmitt to unfold his further argument against liberal democracy, to the effect that abolishing it would entail no qualitative loss for the people, no real democratic setback, and merely contravene the liberal insistence on numbers, a claim which recurred in numerous fascist narratives. Consider, for example, Moeller van den Bruck's claim (1934: 118) that "Democracy does not depend on the form of the state but on the share which the people take in the working of the state."

In his critique of liberalism and apologia for dictatorship, Schmitt, like other fascists, unwittingly reproduced the arguments of the German anti-revolutionaries of 1848, whose claims to represent the people's interests against the liberal revolution Engels and Marx scathingly dismantled in *The Communist Manifesto*:

> The fight of the German and, especially, of the Prussian bourgeoisie against feudal aristocracy and absolute monarchy, in other words, the liberal movement, became more earnest.
>
> By this, the long-wished for opportunity was offered to 'true socialism' of confronting the political movement with the socialist demands, of hurling the traditional anathemas against liberalism, against representative government, against bourgeois competition, bourgeois freedom of the press, bourgeois legislation, bourgeois liberty and equality, and of preaching to the masses that they had nothing to gain, and everything to lose, by this bourgeois movement (Engels and Marx 2005: 78–79).

Very similar indeed was the gist of Schmitt's anti-liberal polemic, with the obvious differences that it came already from within the bourgeois camp and, secondly, claimed to represent not "true socialism" (other fascists copiously employed this ideologeme: from Spengler and Jünger to Reventlow) but "true democracy." In a 1929 text dealing with "The Being and Becoming of the Fascist State," Schmitt (1994: 129) went as far as arguing that dictatorship will by necessity defend the weak from the capitalists: "Only a weak state is a capitalistic servant of private property. Every strong state—if it is truly a higher third force and not simply identical with the economically strong—demonstrates its real power not against the weak, but against the socially and economically powerful." This, once again, suggests an anti-liberal position from the left, which upbraids the economic subservience of liberalism to capitalism, at the expense of the people. But these are merely the exoteric trappings of Schmitt's argument, the demagogic façade, behind which hides a keen commitment precisely to the capitalist order. This esoteric truth can be intimated by the spurious nature of Schmitt's assurances regarding the benign nature of fascism vis-à-vis the working class. To be sure, as Schmitt claims and as every leftist critic of liberalism would agree, political liberalism favors the capitalist class over the working class. Yet from this, it certainly does not follow that a dictatorship will improve the workers' lot or enhance their power. Under bourgeois political liberalism the workers enjoy a variety of means—parties, unions, freedom of organization and of expression, and so on and so forth—which, while certainly imperfect and limited in power, are still highly valuable in facing the capitalist class, and constitute a thorn in the flesh of "the economically strong," who therefore urge the state to blunt the edge of these tools as much as possible if not confiscate them altogether. As Schmitt himself obliquely admitted in the same text:

> In highly industrialized states...the internal political condition is completely dominated by the phenomenon of 'a structure of social equilibrium' between capital and labor, employers and employees.... If today in highly developed states, employers and employees face each other with roughly equal social power and neither of these groups can impose a radical decision on the other without a dreadful civil war, then social decisions and fundamental constitutional changes become impossible through legal means (127).

This account of the "social equilibrium"—which Schmitt also attributed to Otto Bauer, a key figure within so-called Austro-Marxism—clearly means that under dictatorship the balance might be turned *both* ways. A strong state might, indeed, serve to strengthen the workers at the capitalists' cost, but it might also serve to tilt the balance in the capitalists' favor. And surely a dictatorship like Mussolini's, whose first move, in fact the precondition for its accession to power, was to eliminate the working class as an independent sociopolitical factor, can only cynically be commended as one that will serve the employees, most particularly in a country such as Germany, where the organized power of the workers was arguably at an historical peak. In Austria, too, the "weak,"—i.e., liberal-democratic—state which Otto Bauer supported, allowed the socialists, by way of their democratic majorities, to wrest from capitalism unprecedented gains for the workers and, in what has gone down in history as "red Vienna," erect a groundbreaking system of public housing, healthcare, education, leisure activities, etc. These achievements, financed by heavily progressive taxation, expose Schmitt's commitment to "the economically powerful," who were eager to see the "equilibrium" shift their way. And indeed, it was the cessation of political liberalism under Dollfuss and the transition to the Austro-fascist *strong state*, that permitted the employers to reinstate a classically liberal economic policy of cuts in public spending, a balancing of the budget and support for business, under the financial advice of no other than Ludwig von Mises. Both these historical examples demonstrate vividly what was really at stake in the choice between the "weak," liberal-democratic state, and the "strong," fascist one, and who were the respective beneficiaries of each one.

Repelling the Democratic Pickpocket

There is still the possibility that such reasoning does Schmitt an injustice by overestimating his political and social acumen. Maybe the famed jurist was in reality infinitely more ingenuous and less shrewd than he is usually considered, and hence sincerely believed that fascism would inevitably improve the workers' position and endow them with greater social power? Yet there is no reason to doubt Schmitt's well-earned reputation, for a cunning jurist he indeed was. He knew well enough that political liberalism under mass democracy does not simply play into the hands of the capitalists and the propertied classes. In common with economic liberals, he clearly appreciated the challenges from below which such a system entailed. Going in fact beyond a mere appreciation of these dangers, he proceeded, if briefly, to analyze and conceptualize them. Let us examine a short essay, "Democracy and Finance," written in 1927, that is two years before his just quoted exposition of the fascist state. In this text, Schmitt (1994: 97; italics added) uncharacteristically addressed the economic issue directly, elucidating the inherent tension between modern mass democracy and finance, that is, a vital plank of liberal economics. Schmitt, at the very start, actually argued that "the terrain on which *the momentous split* [*Zwiespalt*] between liberalism and democracy is most strongly manifested, is finance." Where did Schmitt identify this split? Did he, as a democratic critic of the weak, pseudo-democratic state would have done, point to the way that political liberalism panders to the interests of the economically strong at the expense of the weak? Not at all. Quite as an economic liberal would have argued, Schmitt described the way 20th century mass democracy, unlike 19th century parliamentarianism in which the suffrage was still limited along property lines, makes substantial inroads into the property of the wealthy by progressive taxation, imposed and favored by the majority of the poor:

> As soon as economic categories take the place of political concepts, and economic contrasts associated with a Marxist understanding of class endanger democratic homogeneity, all notions of 'finance' are changed... According to the conventional, in their historical roots part feudal [*ständisch*] part liberal-bourgeois convictions, the one who pays taxes, must also be the one who authorises them and controls their administration.... The famous liberal saying 'no taxation without representation' is only meaningful if the reverse is also true (97–98).

This, namely, is the ideal situation from a classically liberal point of view. "No taxation without representation; no representation without taxation": a tenet that any member of the Guizot cabinet would have emphatically subscribed to. But this "democratic homogeneity" is disrupted by economic conflicts and a Marxist concept of class. Schmitt's ideal of democratic homogeneity boils down to *class society* preceding *the political enfranchisement of the masses*. But in "the mass democracy of modern industrial states," Schmitt affirms, "such simple contexts and attributions can no longer be sustained." Once the masses are granted entry into the polling booth, such homogeneity goes down the drain, and the sovereign is lost in the crowd:

> The 'people,' that is the majority which legislates on taxation, prescribes also to the outvoted minority taxes and social expenses. This is certainly something substantially different from the old notion, that taxes are, in a banal phrasing, self-evidently to be collected only 'out of one's own pocket.' Today... the very notion... of 'one's own pocket' has lost its class [*ständisch*] or its individualistic simplicity.... Since here, too, 'the people,' that is, the voting majority, which 'authorizes' taxes and expenses and 'the people,' that is, the taxpayers, those who in economic reality actually pay them, are no longer conclusively the same quantities (98).

These complaints are classical liberal economics of the 19th century, voicing their gravest anxieties vis-à-vis mass democracy dipping its countless fingered hand into the bourgeois' pocket, and were the basis of its sternest opposition to universal suffrage. They might have been copied down from any number of liberal texts. So here, the demagogic nature of Schmitt's assurances that a fascist dictatorship will endorse the "economically weak" is unceremoniously unveiled. Schmitt plainly recognized how a weak state *does not* seamlessly serve the capitalists, and knew that a strong one, a fascist one above all, would eliminate the irksome split between mass democracy and finance in the latter's favor. The democratic homogeneity of the past simply meant that the majority were excluded from politics, and hence class antagonisms—which certainly were not lacking under feudal and liberal-bourgeois conditions—disappeared from sight. Under a Schmittian dictatorship, therefore, "the people" will be again united, that is, will again consist of those same taxpayers who at present have to share representation with the majority. Notice the way Schmitt put the word "authorize" in quotation marks, suggesting the illegitimate nature of the imposition of taxes by the masses.

In conclusion, it can be seen how, squarely against Heiner Bielefeldt's interpretation, quoted above, Schmitt's opposition to the Weimar Republic was not really motivated by "ardent anti-liberalism" and by the desire to establish a "democracy based on the substantial 'homogeneity' of the collective unity of the people." In truth, it concealed the desire rather to return to the liberal *status quo ante*, before "the people" got insupportably puffed up. Equally, Chantal Mouffe turns Schmitt on his head when she affirms (1999b: 43) that he "had nothing but contempt for the constraints imposed by liberal institutions on the democratic will of the people." As I attempted to show, the very opposite was the case: Schmitt's whole maneuver was aimed at bursting the constraints imposed *by the democratic will of the people* on liberal institutions. But he saw fit, consummate legal expert that he was, to disguise these esoteric intentions, and broadcast—exoterically—the good news that fascism suits democracy much more so than political liberalism. Like his role model Donoso, and like a great number of outright liberals, Schmitt was anti-liberal only in the political sense—and even that only if we ignore the dictatorial loophole that was implicit in the liberal conception from Locke onwards—but not at odds with liberalism as a socioeconomic system. Schmitt was thus anti-liberal indeed, but in a very liberal way.

He embraced dictatorship to avert the triumph and rescind the gains, political and *hence* economical, of popular democracy.[9]

The Strange Case of Georges Sorel

The last anti-liberal liberal whose ideas I wish to examine is Georges Sorel, who has been traditionally assigned an important place in the genealogy of fascism. My historiographic point of reference in this case is the Israeli historian, Zeev Sternhell, for whom the fin-de-siècle French political thinker represents well-nigh the ideological founder of fascism, the one who had triggered the all-important "anti-materialist revision of Marxism" from which the "fascist synthesis" has emerged. The confrontation with Sorel's ideas will thus afford us the proper occasion to deal critically with Sternhell's highly influential theory of fascism and proto-fascism, which has been responsible, perhaps more than any other single scholarly factor, for a far-reaching transubstantiation of the mainstream historiographic understanding of fascism.

The undeniable merits of Sternhell's studies notwithstanding—above all the fact that they have helped to expand the habitual scholarly focus to seriously include the French intellectual and political tradition, thereby showing that fascism was a pan-European phenomenon, rather than a mere local accident—the theoretical framework he proposed has proven problematical. Fascism, he argued, was not the exclusively right-wing political current it was thought to be, it was "neither right nor left," and in fact in its original impulse much *more indebted to the left*. It had inspired a new school of ideological interpretation that denies the class content formerly ascribed to fascism, and assumes that ideology was the central part of fascist politics rather than any social or material concern, without in reality providing the necessary

---

[9] As part of an overall effort to depict fascism as a force apart from capitalism, Michael Mann underplays Schmitt's commitment to capitalism. Schmitt's emphasis, according to Mann was on "the state" and on "order" (see Mann 2004: 75–77). But it was clearly not Schmitt's concern, for he could have had both, and in abundance, in a Bolshevik Germany, emulating the Soviet lead. But *such* order and *such* state were his nightmare. The abstract ideals of state and order were thus only meaningful as subservient to the concrete aims of capitalism and imperialistic expansion. Let us not forget, against the attempt to downplay the centrality of the economical to Schmitt, and by extension to fascism, his categorical statement that "the terrain on which *the momentous split* between liberalism and democracy is most strongly manifested, is finance."

evidence to justify such sweeping revision. My misgivings concerning such framework have, in general, little to do with the facts presented, but rather with their arrangement and signification. Sternhell—somewhat like Schapiro, whose theories have accompanied our discussion of Proudhon and Carlyle—is one of those historians from whom one can learn a great deal on the condition that their overarching interpretation of the material is taken with a sizeable grain of salt.

The Crisis of Socialism?

So what was Sternhell's account of "the birth of fascist ideology," the title of one of his books, and what role did Sorel play in it? In grasping the gist of Sternhell's story, it is useful to begin by saying that, in its fundamental outlines, it is diametrically opposed to the one I have been unfolding: in my version of history, fascism was mainly the product of a long-term crisis of liberalism, and a response to the advances of socialism—revolutionary *as well as* democratic (this, as we shall shortly see, is a very important point, particularly with regard to Sternhell's theories). Fascism was enveloped in the logic and contradictions of liberalism, erupting at an apex of the liberal predicament, as a form of the latter's denouement (which is *not* to say a pre-determined or inevitable outcome). Sternhell, on the very contrary, claimed that fascism[10] was born as a result of *the triumph of liberalism* and *the crisis of socialism*. How did liberalism triumph, and how did socialism lose? On account of democracy. Democracy, which Sternhell usually identifies with liberalism, gradually expanded to create a widespread political consensus, blurring the formerly sharp lines of class antagonism and hence eliminating the permanent foreboding of a revolutionary flare-up from which classical socialism nourished and on which it based its hope for a radical social transformation. Instead of defying the bourgeois establishment, Marxist parties, under the revisionist influence of the likes of Eduard Bernstein in Germany, Saverio Merlino in Italy and Jean Jaurès in France, were engulfed by the establishment, becoming merely one

---

[10] Or at least fascist ideology, and in Sternhell's account fascist ideology and its political practice are virtually exchangeable, the latter becoming a kind of imperfect application of the firmly established ideological tenets. In fact, it is boldly maintained that fascist praxis was distinctly *less* opportunistic and accommodating than that of other major ideologies, such as liberalism and socialism: "Like any other movement, the fascist movement too engaged in different compromises; and yet, in the case of fascism, the correspondence between ideology and practice is the highest" (Sternhell: 1988a: 42).

more player on the parliamentarian stage, if slightly to the left. Hence, in a nutshell, the crisis of socialism / Marxism. "At the beginning of the [20th] century," Sternhell avers (1986: 85), "liberal democracy had become the guardian of the established order, a veritable citadel of conservatism." Or, in greater detail:

> The revision of Marxism…in fact meant the acceptance of the capital-ist and bourgeois order…. The revolutionary Marxist principle steadily eroded and the socialist parties accepted, without exception, the verdict of liberal democracy…. In that way was formed a liberal political culture, resting on the principles of the liberal revolutions of the 17th- and 18th centuries (Sternhell 1988a: 10).[11]

And how did fascism evolve out of this socialist crisis, and the bour-geois-liberal triumph? At the margins of the socialist parties remained the ultra leftists, stick-in-the-mud revolutionaries who would have absolutely nothing to do with capitalism and the rule of the bourgeoisie. This minority, "which refuses to accept the capitalist order," would, in turn, divide into two dissident branches: Leninists, who would uphold the violent revolution, but now in the name of the proletariat, to be carried out by a small avant-garde of professional revolutionaries, and Sorelians, who "opened up a new revolutionary course" (23). From this latter branch would spring fascism. Sorel, of course, would be their key figure. Initially believing in the power of the proletariat, he would embrace the illusive option of revolutionary syndicalism. Soon enough, however, he and his disciples would understand that such hopes were unfounded, and turn to develop a "new socialism, of Marxist origins, which keeps taking distance from proletarian socialism and evolves into a socialism of the entire society" (23–24). Being to the left not only of official, reformist socialism, but of the complacent proletariat itself, Sorel, and by extension the proto-fascists, were ultimately logically forced to abandon the working class and replace it as carrier of the revolution by the nation. "Sorelians," Sternhell writes (26), "remain committed to their revolutionary positions, after the proletariat has withdrawn from them: between a revolution without a proletariat and a proletariat with-out a revolution, they chose revolution. Therefore, this will already be a national revolution." Combined with the organic, tribal nationalism which evolves roughly at the same time (end of the 19th century, start of the 20th), and receives quintessential expression in the writings of

---

[11] Cf. also Sternhell (1994: 15–17).

such intellectuals as Maurice Barrès or Enrico Corradini, these two main components would form the "national socialist" synthesis, i.e., fascism: "Thus develops in France of the late 19th century a synthesis of tribal, Darwinist nationalism, with a social radicalism which develops into a sort of anti-Marxist socialism, and in many ways already post-Marxist: this synthesis takes the name of national socialism" (19–20). This united national socialist front had provided the intransigent revolutionaries with a new and effective platform from which to launch their "assault" on the bourgeois, liberal, capitalist order, after Marxism had failed to deliver the goods: "He who abides by the elimination of the bourgeois order...is forced to devise a new weapon...since...the Marxist weapon...is no longer effective for the current campaign... This is the meaning of Sorel's rectification of Marxism" (24–25).

Sternhell's account of the bourgeois-liberal hegemony exasperating the revolutionary Sorelians and driving them to seek new outlets for their radical zeal is interchangeable with the earlier argument of Eugen Weber. For Weber (1964: 32), too, Sorel had "to adjust the conventional Marxist analysis... It was naïve, thought Sorel, to put your trust in the gradual proletarization of a society which, contrary to the predictions the *Communist Manifesto* had made in 1848, was becoming increasingly bourgeois and ever less inclined to desperate revolution."

But was society indeed "becoming increasingly bourgeois"? Weber, and Sternhell in his wake,[12] dramatically exaggerated the extent of the crisis of orthodox Marxism and of the gains made by the bourgeois-liberal forces. As far as Marxism is concerned, we have already seen how a Marxist as orthodox as Engels could, as late as 1895, ooze optimism with regards to the future of Marxism *within* a parliamentarian, bourgeois, "legal" framework. Far from consternated by the delay in the revolutionary Day of Judgment, Engels was worried that the socialists would take to the streets to conduct an armed struggle made impractical under modern warfare techniques, and thereby jeopardize

---

[12] Indeed, in the early sixties, Weber—whom Sternhell mentioned in the "Acknowledgments" section of *Neither Right nor Left*—already outlined, one by one, all the main features of the Sternhellian interpretation of fascism, from the insistence on fascism as revolutionary and implementing a variant of socialism, through the presentation of fascism as anti-liberal, and down to the claim that fascism needs to be taken seriously as an ideology, discarding cynicism and materialistic deconstruction. Notice the similarity even in formulation: "my objectivity," said Weber, "consists of taking Fascists and national Socialists *at their word*" (1964: 3; italics added). Weber even anticipated Sternhell's focus on France as a major laboratory of fascist ideology, including the stress on Sorel as a pivotal thinker.

the political power they were daily accruing through democracy. A quick reminder:

> The parties of order, as they call themselves, are perishing under the legal conditions created by themselves...whereas we, under this legality, get firm muscles and rosy cheeks and look like life eternal. And if *we* are not so crazy as to let ourselves be driven to street fighting in order to please them, then in the end there is nothing left for them to do but themselves break through this dire legality (Engels 1895).

Engels was here perhaps overly sanguine, not foreseeing the difficulties and limitations of such a legal way of action from a radically socialist point of view, and surely he would have sharply disapproved of many of the concessions and accommodations of Bernstein and Co. Yet from here, to conclude a fatal demise of Marxist potency, both actual and theoretical, is clearly unwarranted. And Marx himself, while never quite as optimistic as Engels about the possibility of transforming capitalism by using the political apparatus of bourgeois democracy, regarded from the very beginning (i.e., *The Communist Manifesto*) working inside parliaments a vital facet of socialist strategy, indeed whenever necessary *alongside* the bourgeoisie. "In Germany," Engels and Marx (2005: 88) averred, the communists "fight with the bourgeoisie whenever it acts in a revolutionary way, against the absolute monarchy, the feudal squirearchy, and the petty bourgeoisie." Similarly, they stated that "the first step in the revolution by the working class is to raise the proletariat to the position of ruling class, *to win the battle of democracy*. The proletariat will use its political supremacy to wrest, *by degrees*, all capital from the bourgeoisie, to centralize all instruments of production in the hands of the state, i.e., of the proletariat organized as the ruling class" (69; emphases added). Marx never fundamentally altered this initial conception, and if he dissented from the practice of the German Socialists, as expressed most famously in his 1875 *Critique of the Gotha Programme*, this was done in concrete disagreement with the tactics and aims formulated by the Lassalleans and their accommodation to Bismarck's state, and not in principled refutation of party action.[13]

---

[13] Not even Lenin, for that matter, to whom Sternhell imputes a despairing of the revolutionary potential of the proletariat, would have subscribed to socialism as achieved strictly by direct, violent revolutionary methods. On the contrary, he attacked at length—most notably in his *Left-Wing Communism: an Infantile Disorder*—precisely those ultra-leftists who would dispense with parliamentary work, which he regarded as absolutely vital in preparing the masses for revolution. He said (1920), for example, that "the Bolsheviks *could not have* preserved (let alone strengthened and developed)

This was the vantage point of many, though not all, socialists. And they were not alone in this assessment of democracy. We have seen how numerous bourgeois liberals and conservatives, for their part, were exasperated by the democratic empowerment of socialism and the frustrating intervention in economic liberalism. We have seen that for such people, opposition to political liberalism was a form of defending capitalism. The narrative of liberalism triumphant, attacked by desperate socialist-cum-fascist renegades, therefore discounts the fact that the democratic power of socialist parties, the "non-revolutionary" demands of organized workers, were nearly as disturbing from a capitalist point of view as the possibility of revolution.[14] This was the crisis, precisely, of liberalism, which fascism came to solve by creating, objectively, *a new kind of liberalism*, not socialism. For fascism (and Nazism) did not merely wish to vanquish socialism as *revolutionary enemy*; it was equally concerned about socialism as a *democratic partner*.

Among these liberals frustrated by democracy was Pareto—who, incidentally, admired Sorel and was appreciated in return—as well as Gaetano Mosca. I analyzed Pareto's position in detail above, and now turn to Mosca for a reminder of the basic liberal predicament, faced with democracy once it veers in a socialist direction, and by no means in a strictly revolutionary sense. "The bourgeoisie," Mosca affirmed

---

the core of the revolutionary party of the proletariat, had they not upheld, in a most strenuous struggle, the viewpoint that it was *obligatory* to combine legal and illegal forms of struggle, and that it was *obligatory* to participate even in a most reactionary parliament." Elsewhere in the same text, Lenin claimed that to repudiate the party principle as the opposition would like "is tantamount to completely disarming the proletariat in *the interests of the bourgeoisie*." This goes to refute any notion of Leninism as extolling the solitary work of desperadoes who can dispense with the masses or work aloof from the existing political frameworks. Lenin expressly embraced Engel's position in that matter, concerning the need for patient and tactical action, and quoted him against those ultra leftists who "are Communists if 'communism will be introduced' the day after tomorrow. If that is not immediately possible, they are not Communists."

[14] There are, to be sure, serious inconsistencies in Sternhell's discussion of the rapport between liberalism and democracy. At times (1988a: 10) he insisted that, by the start of the 20th century, they had successfully merged into each other, leaving their feuds in the past: "Toward the end of the 19th century the processes of the adjustment of liberalism to political democratization...had matured. Within the new mass society, liberal democracy had become a fact." Elsewhere (1994: 13), however, he affirmed that such fusion was actually far from smooth: "It was with tremendous difficulty that liberalism, adopting the principle of political equality, developed into liberal democracy. This was one of the main aspects of the crisis of the turn of the century as of the those of the interwar period." The second observation, however, essentially remains a pro-forma caveat, carrying little or no weight within Sternhell's overall narrative. Which means that, despite the said "tremendous difficulty" experienced by liberalism, it is from within socialism, not liberalism, that fascism is reputed to have emerged.

(1939: 392), "has been, in a sense, the prisoner not only of its democratic principles but also of its liberal principles." "Slave to its own preconceptions," he elsewhere elaborates, "the European bourgeoisie has fought socialism all along with its right hand tied and its left hand far from free. Instead of fighting socialism openly, [they accepted] compromises that were sometimes, nay almost always, undignified and harmful" (479). The main upshot of attributing to Sorel such a central role in the spadework for fascism is to distinguish, purportedly, the *leftist, radical* origins of fascism. For indeed, virtually alone among thinkers of importance who have been associated with fascism, Sorel is traditionally thought of as a man of the left. Yet this attempt at tracing the genesis of fascism back to a Sorelian eureka moment is heavily flawed. If Mussolini did not conceal his admiration for Sorel, neither did he make any secret of his profound debt to Pareto. So the overriding focus on Sorel is as arbitrary as it is functional. For with Pareto and Mosca—two thinkers who were once often centrally linked with fascism but are currently mentioned only marginally—the leftist background of fascism fades; instead of a link with radical anarcho-syndicalism via Sorel, one finds a link to *laissez-faire* capitalism. And *such* a family tree is obviously not what the mainstream of scholarship was out to draw. Hence, symptomatically, their role was drastically downplayed, by both Weber and Sternhell: the former ignored them altogether and the latter mentioned them in passing and always from a certain distance, as it were, as vague influences over the thought of the "new," "post-Marxist socialists," without explaining their teachings directly and in detail. This yielded a fuzzy portrayal which prevents an identification of the precise, i.e., largely liberal and pro-capitalistic, contours of their "anti-democratic" thought. Pareto and Mosca, instead, were associated with the development of "revolutionary syndicalism" (Sternhell 1986: 34).

Painting the Roses Red: Sorel's Post-Liberalism

This reflects a peculiar quality of Sternhell's analysis that works with a painting brush which, like those of the Queen of Hearts' card servants in *Alice's Adventures in Wonderland*, paints white roses, red. Whatever he touches is prone to turn "socialistic": Not only Proudhon, who sometimes has been described as a socialist, but also Nietzsche, Le Bon, and Pareto: they all influenced, we are told, the birth of "Sorel's ethical socialism" (Sternhell 1986: 34). Sorel's teachings thus form, a priori, a highly lucrative node, tying leftist radicalism with fascism, and attesting to the birth of a new socialism. But are they a reliable foundation, too? As happens with many other figures who are sometimes seen as proto-fascists—from Carlyle and Nietzsche to Pareto and Mosca—there are vast disagreements as to what extent, if at all, Sorel could be legitimately so described. At the other extreme from Sternhell are those, like Michel Charzat (1983), who refuse any connection whatsoever, whether personal or ideological. Still others have had misgivings less about the proto-fascist contribution Sternhell attributed to Sorel (although they doubted its degree and its centrality), but questioned the identification of Sorel with French revolutionary syndicalism in general. Jacques Julliard, for example, argued compellingly that Sorel was not only a dissident with regards to orthodox Marxism and socialism, but also within the ranks of the syndicalists themselves. Never more than an intellectual outsider to the actual syndicalist movement, "a solitaire," Sorel is not to be substituted for the general syndicalist tendency or doctrine. Thus, the attempt to categorically prove a link to syndicalism via the figure of Sorel and his disciples is debatable (Julliard 1984: 858–9). Be that as it may, and although I fully subscribe to Julliard's admonition that a handful of intellectuals ought not to stand for a vast social movement, the great usefulness of Sorel's thought for the fascists cannot be disputed. Whether appropriated or misappropriated, his ideas proved seminal for the fascist project. Here, Sternhell is on safe ground. I would therefore proceed from the terms he suggested, accepting Sorel's objective proto-fascism. Yet I will attempt to understand the reasons behind the fascist enthusiasm for Sorel: what precisely was it in his teachings that so stimulated Mussolini and his companions? My aim, in other words, will be to inquire whether this incontestable Sorelian contribution to fascist ideology could indeed be described as one of a revolutionary opposition to the bourgeoisie, to liberalism and to capitalism. Does it indeed testify to the originally leftist thrust of fascism, to the fact that "the growth of fascist ideology," in Sternhell's words (1986: 119), "was the chief manifestation of the tremendous difficulty that socialism experienced in responding to the challenge of capitalism"?

Let us consider, to start with, the question of socialism turning democratic, which allegedly signified a clear-cut triumph for the bourgeois order and the forces of conservatism. Sternhell did not only make this point a cornerstone of his theory, on numerous occasions emphasizing the triumph of the bourgeoisie *over* socialism *through* democracy; he did this, moreover, expressly in Sorel's name. To Sorel, he claimed, the

Dreyfus Affair represented an "enormous hoax"; the proletariat had once again been deceived by its political leaders into becoming "the bourgeoisie's watchdog," unwittingly rescuing "its own exploiters, its own oppressors." Given such shameless manipulation, Sorel came to a "simple" conclusion: "since democracy and the bourgeoisie are inseparable and since democracy is the most effective offensive weapon the bourgeoisie has invented, democracy has to be overthrown in order to destroy bourgeois society" (18–19). All this is Sorel as paraphrased by Sternhell. But now let us allow Sorel himself to speak on the matter, from *Reflections on Violence*:

> Conservatives are not deceived when they see in compromises which lead to collective contracts, and in corporative particularism, the means of avoiding the Marxian revolution; but they escape one danger only to fall into another, and they run the risk of being devoured by Parliamentary Socialism (Sorel 1972: 90).

How strange to hear Sorel, the main witness summoned by the revisionist prosecution to implicate socialism, providing decisive evidence to refute its case! Far from sharing the conviction that "liberal democracy had become…a veritable citadel of conservatism" (Sternhell 1986: 85) and that "democracy was simply a swamp in which socialism had become bogged down" (Sternhell 1994: 24), Sorel insisted that it was socialism that was "devouring," no less, its conservative antagonists, and that parliaments were the seat of the irreverent banquet. Far from seeing democracy as a lethal weapon in bourgeois hands, Sorel repeatedly decried the weakness and stupidity of the bourgeoisie which, for fear of revolution and a violent clash with the socialists, allows itself to be intimidated and extorted by the democratic socialists. Jaurès' pernicious methods of democratic socialism, argued Sorel (1972: 85), "suppose an entirely dislocated middle-class society—rich classes who have lost all sentiment of their class interest." How different indeed is this from the vanquishing, sly bourgeoisie, manipulating the proletariat at will which *Sternhell's Sorel* was loathing? Admittedly, Sorel did consider the Dreyfus Affair an enormous hoax, but *against* the gullible bourgeoisie. For that reason, he speculated (86) on "a great extension of proletarian violence, which would make the revolutionary reality evident to the middle-class and would disgust them with the humanitarian platitudes with which Jaurès lulls them to sleep." Clearly, therefore, Sorel does not consider Jaurès the "bourgeoisie's watchdog," as Sternhell would have it; in Sorel's eyes, the socialist leader looks much more like a wolf in sheep's clothing, or a snake hypnotizing its prey, "lulling" and then "devouring."

Similarly, Sternhell asserted that the liberal order was doing fine not merely politically, having domesticated the socialist opposition, but also economically, with capitalism prospering in an unprecedented fashion. This was underscored as part of the claim that the revolutionary Sorelians were frustrated by the fact that capitalism did not weaken and, given the failure of Marxism to produce the longed for demolition of capitalism, sought alternative ways of bringing it down. In *The Birth of Fascist Ideology*, for example, it was argued that "the capitalist economy...was in excellent shape," and "had shown itself capable of adapting to all conditions of production," thus forcing the dissidents who were determined "to destroy bourgeois society" to forge a new, "antimaterialist form of socialism" which would artificially ignite the class struggle with recourse to the irrational power of myths: "This was the very original solution Sorel proposed for overcoming and superseding the crisis of Marxism" (Sternhell 1994: 23–24).[15] Yet Sorel himself did not in the least share this appreciation of economic prosperity and capitalist ascendancy. Quite the opposite is true: he tirelessly complained about the fact that capitalism, forced to compromise with socialism, was losing its momentum and entering a phase of dismaying *stagnation*. Sorel's starting point is the assumption that the Western world, under the combined effect of a democratic socialism and a weakened, anemic middle class which cannot defend capitalism, has entered into a phase of "economic decadence," a term which he repeats on numerous occasions. Under such conditions the growth of capitalism is severely hindered, and the rules of the liberal economy are systematically violated: "Parliamentary Socialism would like to combine with the moralists, the Church, and the democracy, with the common aim of impending the capitalist movement; and, in view of middle-class cowardice, that would not perhaps be impossible" (Sorel 1972: 93). Similarly, according to Sorel, Jaurès "saw that this upper-middle class

---

[15] Or, to the same effect:
   This...point is an important one. Toward the middle of the last decade of the nineteenth century there began in Europe—and particularly in Germany and France—a period of rapid economic growth, and this situation contributed to the stagnation of orthodox Marxism and to the emergence, in France and Italy, of the two characteristic forms of revisionism... Reformism and Sorelian syndicalism were thus the consequence of the ideological inadequacy of Marxism and its inability to provide a realistic theoretical response to the questions raised by the new economic situation. Hence, the radicalism represented by revolutionary syndicalism resulted not from an economic crisis but from a situation of relative prosperity (Sternhell 1986: 267).

was terribly ignorant, gapingly stupid, politically absolutely impotent; he recognized that with people who understand nothing of the principles of capitalist economics it is easy to contrive a policy of compromise on the basis of an extremely broad socialism" (85).

In economic terms, Sorel consistently speaks like an advocate of *laissez faire* who rises against the bourgeoisie precisely since it has neglected its economically liberal duties and fatally acquiesced in diluting capitalism.[16] Sorel was thus not so much an enemy of capitalism, as he was an enemy of a *weak capitalism*, given to seeking compromises with parliamentary socialism which breed a kind of mixed, decadent economy. For classical 19th century capitalism, by contrast, preceding the democratic fall, he felt unreserved admiration, precisely from a professedly "Marxist" point of view:

> The middle class with which Marx was familiar in England was still...animated by their conquering, insatiable, and pitiless spirit, which had characterized at the beginning of modern times the creators of new industries... [W]e should always bear in mind this similarity between the capitalist type and the warrior type; it was for very good reasons that men who directed gigantic enterprises were named *captains of industry*. This type is still found today in all its purity in the United States: there are found the indomitable energy, the audacity based on a just appreciation of its strength, the cold calculation of interests, which are the qualities of great generals and great capitalists (89).

This shows how misconceived was Weber's contention (1964: 13) that fascism shared with socialism "an opposition to liberalism defined on the economic plane as the application of competitive *laissez- faire*." With regards to Sorel, who for Weber is quite an important figure, this is entirely wrong, for he infinitely preferred *laissez faire* to the watered-down capitalism of the 20th century. In fact, Sorel's espousal of a bellicose working-class stance, which rejects all compromises with the bourgeoisie, was intimately bound with this strange predilection, on the part of a self-proclaimed "socialist," for liberal economics. One of the functions of proletarian violence was to shake the bourgeoisie from its stupor, encourage it to rebuff all economic advances on the part of

---

[16] Nor is the standard liberal complaint from the point of view of the "tax payer" lacking, the one who has to finance the social reforms which the "state socialists," aided by finance capital, bring about. Sorel (1972: 222) disgustedly referred to Clemenceau who, "replying to Millerad, told him that in introducing the bill to establish old age pensions, without concerning himself with where the money was to come from, he had not 'acted as a statesman nor even as a responsible person.'"

the democratic socialists and thus allow capitalism to regain its former "indomitable energy." This allocates to the working class the surprising task of restoring the glories of capitalism. Sorel (1972: 90) asks: how can the syndicalists "hope to give back to the middle class an ardor which is spent?" And answers: "it is here that the rôle of violence in history appears to us as singularly great, for it can, in an indirect manner, so operate on the middle class as to awaken them to a sense of their own class sentiment." In fact, in view of the pervasiveness of this notion, one cannot help wondering if this was not the *main* function of working-class militancy as envisioned by Sorel, over and above any putative boost to the prospects of the revolution. I provide a couple of further examples: "Proletarian violence...can compel the capitalist class to remain firm in the industrial war; if a united and revolutionary proletariat confronts a rich middle class, eager for conquest, capitalist society would have reached its historical perfection" (92). Sorel (91) speculates that, if it will be possible to bring home to the employers the fact "that they have nothing to gain by works which promote social peace, or by democracy," then there would be "some chance that they may get back a part of their energy, and that moderate or conservative economics may appear as absurd to them as they appeared to Marx." To Marx? Surely Sorel would have better said to Smith, Burke, Malthus or any other thinker of classical political economy? By getting capitalism back on its feet, the working class will not only have reinvigorated production and guaranteed the validity of Marx's theories, it will also have secured the future of civilization, rescued it from sinking into barbarism:

> Everything may be saved, if the proletariat, by their use of violence, manage to...restore to the middle class something of its former energy.... Proletarian violence...appears thus as a very fine and very heroic thing; it is at the service of the immemorial interests of civilization; it is not perhaps the most appropriate method of obtaining immediate material advantages, but it may save the world from barbarism (98).

This concern for middle-class regeneration and for the pristine strength of capitalism is not a cursory feature but a crimson thread running through Sorel's thought, anti-bourgeois, anti-liberal, and anti-capitalist though it may be. It is thus not difficult to perceive, and commentators have in fact not overlooked it. Jeremy Jennings (1999: x), for example, correctly observed that "the interpretation that underpins much of the economic argument of *Reflections on Violence* is that Marxism is a form of 'Manchesterianism' (i.e. classical liberal economics)." Yet for historians whose argument hinges on Sorel having been a fierce revolutionary opponent of the bourgeoisie and of capitalism, this perforce becomes invisible, as in the case of Weber, or present-absent, in Sternhell. All Weber saw was adamant, if maverick, socialism. He thus reversed Sorel's position by stating that he was reacting against "a society which was becoming increasingly bourgeois." Sternhell, for his part, did not ignore this aspect. But he was forced to keep it in impossible subordination to his thesis of Sorelian "anti-capitalism," a complicated maneuver that bore the most striking paradoxes and flights of narrative logic. Thus, after making Sorelian ultra-leftism and opposition to the bourgeoisie the premise of his studies, and indeed the very claim which lends them a revisionist and iconoclastic value against the old and allegedly misguided materialistic notions, Sternhell in fact introduced evidence severely undercutting his own theoretical construct. In his earlier works, especially in *Neither Right nor Left*, the pro-capitalism of Sorel and his followers is *almost* completely absent. I stress the word "almost" with purpose, for on rare occasions Sternhell revealed himself to be aware of the capitalist affiliation of the Sorelians, and yet seemed disinclined to acknowledge the proper theoretical and ideological import of this fact. Consider the following passage, from the 1988 introduction to the Hebrew translation of *Neither Right nor Left*. Here, the anti-capitalism of fascist and proto-fascist ideologies is stated in terms that cannot be more emphatic, and placed at the very ideological nucleus around which their different variants revolve:

> Anti-Marxism, *anti-capitalism* and anti-liberalism are the common denominator of *all variants* of this rebellion, and well express its essence: the negation of 'materialism.'
> So it came about that different schools of thought, in some respects standing far apart from each other but united in *rejecting the liberal order*, formed a kind of crown around the hard core of fascist thought (Sternhell 1988b: 25; emphases added).

It is thus plainly enough impressed upon the reader that "all fascism" is both anti-liberal and anti-capitalist, a presupposition which will henceforth underpin the discussion. And yet, sporadically, remarkable gaps open up, in effect overruling this very premise. For example, on page 261 of the same edition, Sternhell sees fit to point out a fact hardly compatible with his own theoretical guidelines. He writes: "Here it is necessary to clarify a key point for the understanding of the social and economic system of European fascism: the fascists never objected either to private property or ... to the idea of profit as the motor of economic activity." One cannot but wonder why this clarification is undertaken precisely "here," so late in the book, rather than, for example, in the very introduction; is the acceptance of property and profit a mere nuance, an afterthought, which can be randomly mentioned? And shortly afterwards, this "clarification" assumes even sharper contours; suddenly, the reader is informed that the fascist regime is in fact "not only based on a compromise with capitalism and the acceptance of its principles, but that it also means to perpetuate the system" (263).[17] So what's it to be? If fascists were invariably "anti-capitalist" how could they be involved at the same time in nothing less than the "perpetuation" of capitalism? And is it meaningful to introduce as "rejecting the liberal order" those who were keenly interested in upholding capitalism? Does not capitalism form a part, and not a negligible one, of such order?

If, in *Neither Right nor Left*, such admissions of the pro-capitalist essence of fascism are confined to random, timid concessions, relegated to the depths of the text, in Sternhell's next major study, *The Birth of Fascist Ideology*, they claim a central place. Already at the introduction, and then recurrently throughout the text, the fact is underlined that Sorelianism and proto-fascism were actually anti-liberal *only* in the political sense, and that they did not—repeat, not—challenge capitalism. I sample a few instances: Sorel, it is asserted was "proclaiming the perpetual validity of capitalism," developing "a theory of moral and spiritual revolution that would fail to touch the bases of capitalism" (Sternhell 1994: 21). The Sorelians are unambiguously associated with "the liberal economy" and with "Manchesterian economics" (22), which recognize "the laws of capitalist economics as having a permanent value" (25). It is further asserted that Sorelians and *liberists* (the Italian term for "free marketers"), "were in complete agreement on the most extreme principles of economic liberalism" (45). And the author goes on to "stress this fundamental aspect of Sorelian thought: the revolutionary struggle depends on a market economy; it is determined by the most absolute economic liberalism. ... But, at the same time, Sorel advocated the destruction of *political* liberalism" (45–46). These, indeed, are remarkable statements and the liberal affinity of proto-fascist thought becomes unmistakable in Sternhell's exposition—in an objective, factual sense, as opposed to the historian's thesis, an exposition which is therefore often

---

[17] Cf. the English edition of the book (Sternhell 1986: 199–201).

highly instructive. The evidence does not point to a "new socialism" but to a new liberalism, resulting, precisely, from a liberal split between politics and economics. Consider the following quotation the book includes, from Arturo Labriola, the important syndicalist theoretician, who exclaimed in 1905: "A class liberalism! That's what syndicalism is!" (22). Or the judgment pronounced by another important syndicalist thinker, Enrico Leone, also cited in the book (147–8), that working-class socialism needs to become an "integral liberalism," whereby political equality would be finally attained by allowing the mechanism of the market to operate without any sort of political intervention!

And yet, the narrative continues to vacillate; the historian, that is, does not consider it necessary to revise his explanatory framework, in agreement with the abundant evidence of the pro-capitalist and economically liberal convictions of the proto-fascists and the fascists. They still remain, for him, fervent opponents of the bourgeois order, staunch anti-liberals and indeed, anti-capitalists, as when, in conclusion of the first chapter on Sorel, the following is tortuously affirmed:

> The fate of civilization and not that of the proletariat or the nation preoccupied Sorel..... For that reason this revolution never touched the foundations of capitalist economy. Sorel's anticapitalism was limited strictly to the political, intellectual, and moral aspects of the liberal and bourgeois system; he never tried to question the foundations, principles and competitive mechanisms of the capitalist economy (90–91).

But how can someone be defined as anti-capitalist who does not "touch the capitalist foundations"? You cannot, as an Indian saying goes, take one part of a fowl for cooking and leave the other part to lay eggs. Moreover, such admittance that Sorel and his disciples were not interested in ousting capitalism, still falls short of fully facing up to the implications of such insights. For it is inaccurate to say that Sorel "did not touch the foundations of capitalism"; he certainly *did* touch them, he did put his intellectual muscle power behind them, but in order to *prop capitalism up*. This is a subtle but significant nuance: Sorel was not some cultural critic, too starry-eyed to notice the economy, too absorbed in questions of morals and cultural dynamics to take stock of the materialistic, economic domain and therefore, allegedly, limiting his critique "strictly to the political, intellectual, and moral aspects of the liberal and bourgeois system." Far from it: civilization and morals, in Sorel, are *predicated* on capitalism. He thus actively assists and wishes to rejuvenate market society, resolve its prolonged crisis, rekindle the

entrepreneurial middle class. There is a fundamental economic motivation behind Sorelianism in both Sorel and his followers, which is *at
least as important* as the moral and cultural considerations. Indeed, if
Sorel concentrates his attack only on "the political, intellectual, and moral
aspects of the liberal and bourgeois system" this is precisely because such
aspects he judged to be working *against* "the capitalist foundations."

This concern for the economic base—Sorel, in that respect, did appear
to have internalized Marx's lessons, albeit to turn them against the
Marxist project—belies the idealistic (in the philosophical-theoretical
sense of the term) effort by Sternhell to isolate some strictly cultural-
philosophical focal point of fascism, from which all else allegedly
followed. The insistence on the primacy of ideology is of paramount
importance for Sternhell since it underpins the bid to refute the traditional class analysis, which posits the centrality of social and economic
conflicts. "There can be no doubt," Sternhell avows (3), "that the crystal-
lization of ideology preceded the buildup of political power and laid the
groundwork for political action." And at the centre of this ideology, it is
further argued, was no tangible socioeconomic interest, but a concern
far more illusive: anti-materialism: "At its most fundamental essence,
fascist ideology constitutes a revolt against materialism" (Sternhell
1988a: 9).[18] Not so; for Sternhell himself in effect concedes the centrality
of economic concerns. At one point—in a chapter written together with
the co-author Mario Sznajder—one can even read about "the primacy
of economics" in the worldview of the Italian Sorelians (Sternhell 1994:
143). How could such economic primacy, no less, be reconciled and find
its place within the anti-materialistic core of fascism? "Ideology," thus,
may have preceded "political action," but it itself had been preceded
by "economics." The real causal sequence, if anything, thus appears to
have been the following: 1) *economic concern* for the health of capitalism
which *then* produced 2) a proto-fascist *ideology*—covering such tropes
as the crisis of civilization, myth, violence, etc., which *then* leads to 3)
political action—namely, fascism.

We can begin to appreciate why there existed mutual admiration
between the Italian advocate of free trade, Pareto, and the French
anti-capitalist, die-hard revolutionary, Sorel. Their antithetical political
positions notwithstanding, in terms of what they actually wanted to

---

[18] Or, from *The Birth of Fascist Ideology*: "In its essence, Fascist thought was a rejection of the value known in the culture of the time as materialism" (Sternhell 1994: 7).

see socio-economically materialized, there is surprisingly a profound harmony. Both wished to see a strong and revitalized capitalism, unburdened by socialistic demands and compromises, a middle class recuperating its virile determination and fighting socialism with all its powers, and, on the other side, a working class making no demands whatsoever on the capitalist state, being perfectly satisfied with whatever the "economic logic" of capitalism is kind enough to allot it. That Pareto wished for this from an anti socialist point of view, whereas Sorel had the perfect alibi of wishing for such a state of things from a leftist—nay, ultra leftist—position, and in order to salvage Marxism, is at bottom a semantic difference, not a substantial one. If we wish, we may call *Pareto* an ultra leftist and *Sorel* a rightist liberal, without in the least affecting things. If two waiters offer us the same cream and cherries dessert, what does it matter if the one recommends it on account of the delicious cream, and the other on account of the splendid cherries? And is this, after all, the real, anti-climactic sense, of being "neither right nor left"? Or does the difference, perchance, lie in the fact that Sorel, unlike Pareto, ultimately wished to see the triumphant proletariat usher in a new world order? Yet Sorel's utopia, as I shall elaborate shortly, was not at all the classless society traditionally dreamed of by the anti-capitalists, a free association of producers, but an hierarchical society where industrial production is brought to still higher levels of efficiency, and where workers are subjugated to the demands of production much more stringently than under the present, lax system of state socialism. And besides, given that the myth of the political strike is above rational or practical critique as usually conceived of, a mere reason to *act* in a certain way—namely, rebuff reforms and improvements and not expect anything from capitalism—there is little reason to suppose that the proletariat will actually be able to defeat capitalism with such an ideological weapon, especially as it will be confronted with a revitalized, militant capitalism, ready to fight with all the might it possesses. Indeed, a paltry practical perspective, such as Engels adopted, will show the workers the likelihood that they will lose all their material assets and political power by the violent insurrection, which stands no chance of overcoming the military might at the disposal of the bourgeoisie. As early as 1901, Jean Jaurès, a favorite target of Sorel's heated polemics, embodying the "anti-Marxist" socialism he so despised, was equally clear sighted about the prospects of the Sorelian, go-for-broke strategy:

The supporters of the general strike...are obliged, it should be well realized, *to succeed at the first attempt.* If a general strike, once turning to
revolutionary violence, fails, it will leave the capitalist system in place, but
now armed with an implacable fury. The fear of the managers and also
of a great part of the masses would set off long years of reaction. And
the proletariat would be for a long time unarmed, crushed, enchained
(Jaurès 2008: 116).

The experience of actual "Sorelian" fascism is soon to establish precisely
such balance of forces as foreseen by Engels and Jaurès (befittingly, with
most Sorelians on the side of the middle-class strikebreakers). So the
working-class' line of action recommended by Sorel was from the start
likely to result in a loss of all the materialist and social gains of the
workers and bring them back to the point where they started, facing
a capitalism as ruthless and as untainted as it was at the beginning of
the 19th century. But what of that loss, if proletarian martyrdom will
prevent civilization from sinking into the barbarism of economic decadence and universal happiness? Undeniably, one can construe this as
attesting to the principled "anti-materialism" of the Sorelians and their
aloof contempt for worldly gains; the problem is that such injunction
to snub material value was confined to the proletariat whereas capitalist
production was certainly not meant to shuffle off its mortal coil.

It is understood that Sorel's recurrent claim to represent the real
spirit of Marxism against its annulment by professional socialists
was utterly unfounded. In 1880, Marx flatly rejected the doctrinaire
opposition of Guesde and Lafargue to all reformism and their insistence that only a proletarian revolution is a feasible strategy, calling it
revolutionary phrase-mongering and famously telling Lafargue that, if
that be Marxism, then "ce qu'il y a de certain c'est que moi, je ne suis
pas Marxiste" ["what is certain, is that I myself am not a Marxist"] (as
quoted in Evans 1975: 48). This would apply with a vengeance to Sorel,
who not only rejected any improvements in the worker's lot as counter-
revolutionary, but topped that off with an insistence that socialism must
actively contribute to the perfect health of its class antagonist, see to it
that it is brought up from its knees and bounces again with renewed
vigor around the ring, before it could punch him down definitively. And
if Sorel admired Lenin as a man who demonstrated the veracity of his
theories regarding the advantage of violent struggle, this was a purely
one-sided affair, as Lenin's characterization of Sorel as "the professor
of confusion" demonstrates. And Lenin's following words (1920) seem
almost as if they were written in answer to Sorel, and certainly apply

to him: "the 'Left' Communists have a great deal to say in praise of us Bolsheviks. One sometimes feels like telling them to praise us less and to try to get a better knowledge of the Bolsheviks' tactics."

An instructive confirmation of the fact that Sorelian tactics did not constitute a menace from a state-capitalist point of view, is unlikely furnished by a contemporary observer who was quite *fearful of syndicalism*, namely Pareto's great Italian counterpart in contriving elite theories, Gaetano Mosca. For Mosca (1939: 480), writing in the aftermath of the First World War and on the verge of fascism, "the syndicalist peril" is a source of great concern; indeed, he considers it the worst possible scenario in post-War Italy. Crucially, however, syndicalism is *not* understood in the Sorelian sense of stringent working-class asceticism and an obdurate boycotting of parliament (nor in the form of a potential fascist take over). The whole danger of syndicalism lies in the eventuality that it will forcefully intervene in the parliamentary system, indeed legally hijack the system and monopolize it, for the purpose of imposing a classical mode of state socialism:

> We need not spend many words in describing the dangers of the...syndicalist, or unionist, solution. A chamber possessing sovereign powers and *participating* in *lawmaking* as the legal mouthpiece of class syndicate would supply the best possible basis for the organization of sovereignty intermediate between the individual and the state, which is perhaps the most serious threat to society... *By means of their representatives*, the unions themselves can...paralyze every effort of the state to free itself of its tutelage.... [I]t is not far-fetched to assume that the syndicalist chamber...could, by *marshalling a compact and disciplined vote*, exert great influence upon *elections* to chambers constituted on the present basis of individual representation (488–9; emphases added).

A judicious and knowledgeable political observer as Mosca thus identifies the syndicalist peril precisely in its *legal, parliamentary, political* and *democratic* potential. Not a word is wasted on the prospect of a vague general strike, the utopian possibility—which Mosca, surely, would have heartily welcomed—that the unions shall substitute a hazy, ultra-leftist myth, for their tangible political power. Mosca—like Pareto, and like Sorel—sees a very potent democratic socialism and a bourgeois capitalism in dire straits.[19]

---

[19] In passing, it should be noted how Mosca (like Pareto, as discussed above), in expressing such anxieties, betrayed the hollowness of his own polemical contention that elites always rule and hence democracy is impossible, in effect conceding that democracy is a feasible option, indeed an imminent danger.

Sorel's Campaign against the Bourgeoisie… and the Polynesian Savages

The fundamental objective disagreements with Marxism notwithstanding, it still remains interesting that Sorel converted to Marxism in the first place—which he did at he start of the 1890s—and felt an affinity with Marx, to the point of seeing himself as continuing his real legacy. By the same token, the fact still needs to be accounted for that, being at bottom an economic liberal, Sorel nonetheless departed from the liberal main road and did not become a conventional, straightforward apologist for market economics, which would perhaps have been the most natural outcome for a man of his credo. The answer to this rather perplexing ideological choice should not, at any rate, be conceived in terms of cynicism à la Spengler, who more or less consciously assumed the socialist identity in order to try and destroy socialism from within. Sorel was not a cynic or an infiltrator, so to speak, to the socialist ranks. His Marxism was—as far as one can judge, or rather intuit—sincerely felt, and this is confirmed by his late praise of Lenin which ends with the passionate denunciation of the liberal democracies, equally heartfelt. A comparable clear-cut and overt endorsement by Sorel of fascism and of Mussolini is not available, despite some second-hand testimonies; on the contrary, there is some evidence that he lamented the power of the fascists—even as he acknowledged and was impressed by it—and through its social demagoguery saw a force employed to break socialism, with the consent of the bourgeois elites.[20]

It appears as if, in ultra-leftist socialism and, later, Bolshevism, Sorel envisaged, no matter how paradoxically, a form of *rescuing* the kernel and the ideals of economic liberalism, albeit not necessarily under the bourgeois rule. Shlomo Sand correctly characterized Sorel as a "liberal conservative oddly attracted to Marxism."[21] This should be complemented by the realization that Sorel's Marxism remained oddly embedded in liberalism and conservatism. For he never had to renounce his economic liberalism in order to espouse Marxism. On the contrary: given the fact that classical 19th century liberalism seemed to decay irretrievably and disgracefully interbreed with state—alias: "official," "parliamentary," "democratic," "professional"—socialism, which Sorel so detested, there appeared little hope that capitalism will be rescued

---

[20] See Charzat 1983: 41–42.
[21] Sand 1993: 89.

by the emasculated bourgeoisie. This was precisely the dreaded crisis of civilization, the chronic phase of economic decadence. Yet in Marxism, understood ingeniously as a form of *laissez faire*, Sorel envisaged an unlikely solution to this predicament, a way of halting the disintegration of the liberal economy, first by compelling the bourgeoisie to regain its heroic qualities, and second, if syndicalism would eventually win, by heralding an era of heroic industry, motivated by idealism and a fanatic commitment to an ever-growing increase of production. The role of true Marxism as a surrogate capitalism is plainly enough stated, for example, in *Introduction to the Modern Economy*:

> The Marxists see things differently [from the advocates of state socialism], since they are convinced that socialism does not have as its premise the stopping or the slowing down of the revolutionary movement of the modern economy, but rather that it should supplant capitalism once the latter is no longer capable of conducting such movement at a sufficiently rapid pace (Sorel 1903: 112).

Marxism was thus conceived not as the antithesis to, but as the perfection of, capitalism. It is equally telling that, even as Sorel praised Lenin as a hero of socialism, he urged him not to discard the legacy of capitalism:

> In order to give to Russian socialism a basis which a Marxist (such as Lenin) may regard as secure, a stupendous effort of intelligence is required: the latter must be in a position to demonstrate to the directors of production the value of certain rules derived from the experiences of a *highly developed capitalism*.... In order that Russian socialism become a stable economy, it is necessary that the intelligence of the revolutionaries be very nimble, very well informed, and very free from prejudices (Sorel 1972: 281–2; italics added).

We can once more appreciate how Sorel did not move to the far-left because he despaired of socialism living up to expectations; he never had any belief in socialism, or, more correctly, never really *desired* to see socialism realized. Like Nietzsche who greatly influenced him, he envisioned socialism as a universal stagnation, the dystopian rule of mediocrity, the obliteration of great art, heroism and the warrior virtues, amid a "barbaric" world of consumer hedonism. That socialism might procure the masses a higher standard of living, as one would put it today, a safe and comfortable life, with less work and more leisure and gains, was for him an argument *against* such an order. His starting point, rather, was the exasperation at the deadlock of (economic) liberalism, from which he hoped to escape via Marxism-Manchesterianism. In the words of Michel Charzat (1983: 47), Sorel "prefers the rule of a liberal bourgeoisie to that of state socialism" since he was a "classical liberal *and* revolutionary in politics."

Mutatis mutandis, this last observation lends considerable support to our pivotal argument concerning the split of economic and political liberalism. For whereas the majority of the liberals of the time feared the consequences of radical politics, democratic as well as revolutionary, for a capitalist economy, Sorel shared only the former concern, namely with respect to parliamentary socialism. By contrast, he welcomed working-class intransigence as a force *for* economic liberalism. Herein is a vital insight into the evasive substance of his ideological stance. Hence, Sorel's "anti-materialist revision of Marxism" was not, ultimately, a theoretical construction meant to succour socialism, but to succour liberalism; it is strange, but nonetheless true, that in ultra-leftism Sorel saw a way of ensuring a renaissance of the era of "the captains of industry" against the age of the passive-nihilistic "last man," prophesized by Nietzsche. This also sheds light on Sorel's ever-present cultural attacks on the bourgeoisie, which Sternhell makes a great deal of. Attentively read, however, such attacks usually reveal themselves to be directed rather at mass society and culture. It is not exaggerated to say that "the bourgeoisie" in Sorel's use is generally a codename for the masses. What he lampoons has very little do with bourgeois civilization insofar as it is capitalistic, in fact targeting the very opposite tendency, the renunciation of capitalist production, and the perceived sliding back into primitivism. This idiosyncratic use of terms, whereby capitalist production is lauded as "working class" while mass consumption is vilified as "bourgeois," is illustrated in the following passage. Sorel, drawing an analogy between the development of the Benedictine orders and the modern economic world, describes the way that members of such orders "have ceased to be workers grouped in a quasi-capitalist workshop" to become "bourgeois, retired from world affairs" and dedicated to "the cooperation of consumption which suits everybody." An analogy on which he further elaborates:

> This *perversion of capitalism*, which ceases to be industrial to return to its usurious origins, has a great importance in history since it marks the moment in which man abandons the notion *painfully acquired* that he is a producer, in order to return to the idea of the Polynesian savages, who view in man above all a consumer, who works only accidentally. It is the honor of Marxism to have founded all its sociological investigations on

the consideration of production and thus to have made clear that an abyss separates serious socialism from all the bourgeois caricatures which take as the basis of their theories the distribution of riches and consumption (Sorel 1903: 125).

And while the indigenous Polynesians might possibly be described as savages, particularly in early 20th century European terms, surely only the most flexible of taxonomies would classify them together with the modern bourgeois? In fact, Sorel's imagery of savagery and of barbarism was grafted onto a repudiation of the modern, complacent, and pleasure-seeking masses, quite in line with contemporary critiques of mass culture, as elaborated by countless middle-class theorists. In *The Illusions of Progress*, for example, Sorel advances a classical "cultural-pessimist" analysis of the way modern mass culture retrogrades into savagery by catering to the lowest tastes and preferring "entertainment" over art which "educates" or which "affirms power" (the Nietzschean affinity is evident):

> It is therefore not impossible that the future of refined societies immersed in decadence will resemble the remote past of the savages.... The arts that entertain are the only ones which the savages truly know; they manifest a taste at times quite remarkable in their dances, their songs, their costumes, but their magical nest eggs [*magots*] appear to us prodigiously grotesque. In the course of civilization, men did not cease to invent new ways of amusing themselves, and it often happened that the educational arts and those which should have affirmed power were corrupted under the influence of the ideas generated by the entertaining arts (Sorel 1911: 318–19).

This critique of mass society also featured importantly in the writings of Sorel's closest disciple, Édouard Berth, who accused official socialism of "arousing in the workers the most unhealthy sentiments: a taste for destruction, an appetite for enjoyment and well-being, an aspiration...to be rid of anything that constrains passions, instincts, and vices" (as quoted by Sternhell 1994: 121.) Notice the way that the supposedly ultra-revolutionary Sorelians and preachers of violence, censure precisely the worker's "taste for destruction." Given that much of the assault on bourgeois culture is actually directed at the working (and playing) masses, it makes sense that Berth should have found the actual French bourgeoisie, allegedly in the process of rediscovering its spiritual and bellicose values, worthy of admiration and be driven to seek an alliance with them rather than with the hedonistic workers. The "bourgeois renaissance," Sternhell informs us, discussing Berth's views (1994: 122), "took place not only independently of the proletarian renaissance, which never happened, but also despite the proletariat's slow but continuous slide into degeneracy.... [T]he roles had been reversed: the bourgeoisie had snatched the torch of the revolution out of the tremulous hand of the proletariat. The new force for progress was the bourgeoisie." This is very instructive: the real carriers of the anti-bourgeois revolt are *the bourgeoisie*, and their ultra-radical march is checked and hampered by *the proletariat*. And yet Sternhell notices no conflict between the data he assembles and his general interpretive matrix, that consistently posits the Sorelians as anti-bourgeois. This ties into another question: if the root of fascist ideology is Sorel, what were *Sorel's* own roots? Just Marx? Wasn't he deeply influenced by the thought of bourgeois, anti-socialist, anti-democratic figures—among them not a few important liberals, or liberal-conservatives—such as Proudhon (who was, besides Marx, Sorel's strongest "socialist" influence), Tocqueville, Taine, Renan, Bergson, Le Bon, Nietzsche, William James, von Hartmann, Pareto and Croce? This partial list of Sorel's intellectual sources and interlocutors should in itself suffice to cast heavy doubts about the allegedly anti-bourgeois character of his thought.[22] To bear Sorel's intellectual background in mind is to realize that he was in truth considerably more indebted—intellectually, philosophically and economically—to the bourgeois-liberal *right*, than to the pro-proletarian *left*. "At the beginning of [Sorel's] 'long march,'" Sternhell symptomatically states (1994: 28), "one finds Marxism"; in the very next page, however, he himself points out that in the early 1890s Sorel, by then over forty, was actually "a new adherent to the cause." So Marxism, in fact, was not Sorel's first station. What is more, before this belated conversion to Marxism, Sorel had been *a liberal*, a fact which is not pointed out. Sorel was hardly the Big Bang of fascism, hardly the great constitutive moment in its genesis, but merely one more sequel in a long and intricate chain of events.

The fact that the Sorelians denigrated "bourgeois" (read: mass) consumption and fetishized "proletarian" (read: capitalist) production, understood not as a means of satisfying concrete human needs but as an end in itself, to be pursued at the cost of human, or in truth, *workers'* comfort and gratification, is a cultural phenomenon that agrees profoundly with the economic, capitalist drive for the accumulation of profit for its own sake. The upshot of this, as in so much (proto)-fascist thought, was to elevate work into a sacred activity and sentimentally sing its praises, and to see workers, too, as admirable precisely since

---

[22] Cf. Salvemini 1969: 375.

they were indispensable in turning the ideal of work into a palpable and profitable reality and inasmuch as they didn't "degenerately" shirk their sacred mission and duty. With a rhetorical sleight-of-hand, and possibly with a measure of self deception, this appreciation of work—"hard, long, fatiguing" work, as Spengler put it—could be promoted as socialistic. But Spengler at least acknowledged the fact that such socialism was the very reverse of Marx's, representing a noble, Prussian alternative, predicated on "the *dignity* of hard work," whereas Sorel ascribed this veneration of toil to "serious socialism," genuinely Marxist, whose merit was allegedly to focus on production, as if the true socialist utopia, as envisioned by Marx (1991: 958–9), did not revolve precisely around the opposite quest to eliminate the yoke of forced labor: "The realm of freedom really begins only where labour determined by necessity and external expediency ends."

Behind the superficially ultra-leftist, anti-bourgeois conception of Sorel lurked in reality a quintessential version of the bourgeois work ethic. But the signifiers were conveniently reversed, so now it was possible to vex indignant against the bourgeois tendency of the modern masses to shun hard work. Thus, when looked at closely, Sorel's myth of the general strike, at the very heart of his revisionist conception, is rather a myth of *general work*. He is not at all after an ethic of leisure and pleasure, but after a stringent work ethic, revolving around the workers' selfless sacrifices and a passionate commitment to industrial progress:

> The question must be stated otherwise than Renan put it; do there exist among the workmen forces…which could combine with the ethics of good work, so that in our days, which seem to many people to presage the darkest future, this ethic may acquire all the authority necessary to lead society along the path of economic progress…. The idea of the general strike…bends all the energies of the mind to that condition necessary to the realization of a workshop carried on by free men, eagerly seeking the betterment of industry; we have thus recognized that there are great resemblances between the sentiments aroused by the idea of the general strike and those which are necessary to bring about a continued progress in methods of production (Sorel 1972: 247–8).

Such passion for work involves no material gain for the workers; Sorel maintains (227), for instance, that "men who devote themselves to the revolutionary cause know that they must always remain poor." He approvingly quotes Renan, saying that "the soldier of Napoleon was well aware that he will always be a poor man, but he felt that the epic in which he was taking part would be eternal, that he would live in the glory of France." And he then asks (247) whether there is "an economic epic capable of stimulating the enthusiasm of the workers." Sorel is very fond of drawing parallels to the world of industry from the world of war, particularly from the French soldiers at the time of the revolution,[23] who were fighting so well against the European Coalition because they saw the cause of the revolution as their own individual goal, rather than a superficial motivation externally imposed by an alienating authority. The workers-soldiers of the future would therefore sacrifice themselves upon the field of the workshop for the greater glory of industry: "Economic progress goes far beyond the individual life, and profits future generations more than those who create it" (247). The attraction of such a worker militia for any capitalist is not difficult to see, a fact which Sorel seemed to realize all too well. "Work and obedience," he says (1903: 119), "are the two columns of the Benedictine edifice just as they are of the capitalist edifice. St Benedict has all the foresight of a great boss [patron] whose concern is to guarantee the prosperity of a vast and durable enterprise." This objective affinity provides the link to the fascist appropriation, whether Sorel as an author would certify by such a reading of his text and find it pleasing, or not. No wonder, too, that Sorel's ideas proved attractive in the eyes of the German so-called conservative revolutionaries, including people like Schmitt, Jünger, Spengler, Hans Zehrer, Michael Freund, and so on, who were keenly interested in inculcating an aesthetical, ascetic, and quasi-religious notion of work.[24] This conception of work, which Sorel by no means invented, but was one of countless bourgeois intellectuals who gave expression to it, found a memorable culmination in the infamous motto *Arbeit macht frei*. Such a credo sits well with capitalism but not with socialism whose goal is precisely to get *free*, to the greater possible extent, *from* work.[25]

It is important to realize that Sorel's vision of economic progress inspired by the warlike virtues, in which the worker produces devot-

---

[23] Less so, incidentally, from Napoleon's soldiers, precisely since at his time the ethic of personal abnegation was counterfeited by a logic of personal gain and decorations.

[24] A very useful discussion of Sorel's influence in German right-wing circles in the years leading up to the Nazi takeover is provided by Buckmiller (1985).

[25] Richard Wolin (2003) provides an excellent analysis of another important fascist thinker keen on accentuating "the joy of work," Martin Heidegger. I have also discussed Heidegger's quest to spiritualize work (Landa 2008: esp. 120–124).

edly and proudly, without an eye to a reward, is expressly founded on an *individualistic*, and by implication *liberal*, conception:

> In the wars of Liberty each soldier considered himself as an *individual* having something important to do in the battle, instead of looking upon himself as simply one part of the military mechanism committed to the supreme direction of a leader.... Battles under these conditions could then no longer be likened to games of chess in which each man is comparable to a pawn; they became collections of heroic exploits accomplished by individuals under the influence of an extraordinary enthusiasm (Sorel 1972: 239; emphasis in the original).

Sorel equally emphasizes (241) that "the working class groups who are eager for the general strike...picture the Revolution as an immense uprising which yet may be called individualistic...the revolutionary Syndicalists desire to exalt the individuality of the life of the producer," and he contrasts (243) the "passionate individualism" of the Syndicalists, with the meek subordination of the workers "who have been educated by politicians." Here, as well, we must register the disparity between Sorel's original text and Sternhell's paraphrasing of it. The latter, sticking to the dictates of the anti-liberalism matrix, insisted that the rebellion of the proto-fascists was in general unreservedly anti-individualistic, "the individual had no value in himself" (Sternhell 1986: 33). And Sorel was certainly not treated as an exception:

> Sorel saw individualism as the root of evil, and on this point he never changed his opinion. In fact, he continued to be violently anti-individualistic even when he had long since ceased to be a Marxist in the orthodox sense. Revolutionary syndicalism was a form of anti-individualism... (68–69).[26]

Read attentively, however, Sorel (much like his countryman Proudhon, "the Gallic socialist," to whom he was greatly indebted), should provide ample reason to ponder the link of certain varieties of anarchism not simply or even primarily to the left but to the liberal tradition as well. On that point too, if we trust the tale and not the teller, Sternhell's exposition proves highly informative, since what objectively stands out is not really the socialism of the anarcho-syndicalism but rather the *liberismo*

---

[26] Jacques Julliard (1984: 855), in an early critique, doubted this alleged anti-individualism attributed not only to Sorel, but also to another important figure in Sternhell's narrative, Maurice Barrès. Julliard pointed out the insufficiency of attaching the epithet of anti-individualism to the author of the exceedingly narcissist book "The Cult of the Self."

of so many of them. This *liberist* footing of syndicalism, especially in its theoretical manifestations, was illuminatingly inspected by Antonio Gramsci in his *Prison Notebooks*, who suggested considering "to what degree theoretical syndicalism derives...from the economic doctrines of free trade—i.e. *in the last analysis from liberalism*. Hence it should be considered whether economism, in its most developed form, is not a direct descendant of liberalism" (2000; italics added).[27] Such affinity Gramsci underscored in both ideological as well personal terms: "The nexus between free-trade ideology and theoretical syndicalism is particularly evident in Italy, where the admiration of syndicalists like Lanzillo & Co. for Pareto is well known." At the same time, Gramsci exposed the objective serviceability of Sorelian syndicalism to capitalism. He identified this pliancy precisely in what syndicalism subjectively perceived as its most radical feature, namely its opposition to political action. In that crucial respect, Gramsci judiciously observed, the liberal master was infinitely shrewder and more practical than the syndicalist pupil. Liberal economics, he maintained, is never just a set of doctrinaire, intransigent assumptions on the best way an economy should function, aloof from politics. On the contrary, it is always a political project, striving to become hegemonic and use the state to implement its program:

> [L]aissez-faire...is a form of state 'regulation'... It is a deliberate policy, conscious of its own ends, and not the spontaneous, automatic expression of economic facts. Consequently, *laissez-faire* liberalism is a political programme, designed to change...a state's ruling personnel, and to change the economic programme of the state itself—in other words the distribution of the national income.

These lucid observations, made during the 1930s, were amply born out several decades later, when the neo-liberal return to *laissez-faire* in Europe and the US was undertaken as a distinctly political project, indeed changing the state's "ruling personnel" and its "economic programme" in order to affect the "distribution of the national income."[28] Theoretical syndicalism, by contrast, naively accepts the liberal theoretical separation between the economic and the political spheres at face value, and hence renounces political struggle. Economic "autonomy," which for the liberals is a concrete goal that must be obtained by way of

---

[27] This is from the 13th notebook, on Machiavelli's politics, written between 1932 and 1934. For the Italian original, see Gramsci 2007, vol. 3: 1589–90.

[28] For an insightful account of this political initiative in global perspective, see Harvey (2005).

concerted political action, was for the syndicalists a sacred tenet, which should not be contaminated by political action. We might say that the *ideal condition* of the pragmatic liberals became the *unconditional ideal* of the intransigent syndicalists. Hence, while an extremely efficient political tool at the hands of the bourgeoisie, "economism" became a debilitating and counter-productive ideology for the workers. "The case of theoretical syndicalism," Gramsci argued (2000), "is different. Here we are dealing with a subaltern group, which is prevented by this theory from ever becoming dominant… It is undeniable that in it, the independence and autonomy of the subaltern group which it claims to represent are in fact sacrificed to the intellectual hegemony of the ruling class, since precisely theoretical syndicalism is merely an aspect of *laissez-faire* liberalism."

Strikers or Strikebreakers?

As a consequence of such insights it becomes clear that, even if we choose to go along with the all-important role ascribed to Sorel in shaping fascist ideology, there is no need to automatically accept the concomitant assumption, namely that with and through the author of *Reflections on Violence*, fascism was indeed imbued with an ideology neither right nor left. In other words, that Sorel himself was a man of paradoxes, attempting to concoct an improbable blend of antagonistic schools of thought, does not prove that *fascism* was such a synthesis, too. If indeed Sorel was a thinker of both left and right, what did fascism take from him? Sorel's "leftism," such as it was, was above all his encouragement of working-class radicalism, the endorsing of the general strike as the ultimate weapon of class struggle. Now, is this an ideological or practical tenet which can be identified in fascism, which of all political movements, was the most uncompromising enemy of working-class radicalism, and the diligent breaker of strikes, any strikes, let alone general ones? Hence a Sorelian legacy—a "leftist" one at any rate—cannot have played more than an ephemeral role in fascism. If a Sorelian imprint on fascism can be identified surely it is in those aspects of his thought which were right, not left? Such right-wing features would include his cult of violence, his celebration of myths and of the irrational, his swashbuckler notions of heroism, his contempt for material achievements, indeed particularly *for workers*, as a "bourgeois" weakness, his hatred of democracy and his concern to emancipate production from its burdens, and his opposition to socialism in nearly every variant—with the notable exception of "socialism" which is utterly committed to capitalism. Surely, these were the reasons that Sorel's teachings were greeted with such enthusiasm by people who should have been disgusted and alarmed by the notion of the general strike.

A good example of this paradox is Pareto, who embraced Sorelian myths, while consternated about the growing power of the working class and the helplessness of the ruling elites. The reason for that was simple: working-class activism was ever escalating in Pareto's Italy, a fact of which he was acutely aware.[29] The workers, hence, clearly did not need any irrationalist theorist to show them where their interests lie, nor suggest to them the weapon of striking. In that regard, if Sorel did no good, he certainly did little harm, either. Conversely, his theories of myth and the appeal to the irrational proved such an exciting novelty, because Pareto immediately recognized in them the promise of changing the grounds of workers' activities, redirecting them from defending their interests onto the terrain of what he called "sentiments" or "residues." This seemed to reveal an unexpected path of escape from the dead-end of democracy. Now, it appeared, one could appeal to the sentiments of the masses to shepherd them against their interests. In such terms, in fact, was perceived the peculiar attribute of the statesman, that of being able to sell the masses a social policy in the best interest of the rulers. Sorel insisted (1972: 50) that "contemporary myths" are revolutionary, leading "men to prepare themselves for a combat which will destroy the existing state of things." Yet this was an unfounded opinion since myths, as Pareto and others of his class realized, can just as well, or perhaps better, serve to *sustain* the existing order. Sorel should have known better himself, since just a few pages before he had referred to Renan's understanding of the irrational as underpinning perfectly conservative causes throughout history. He thus spoke (43–44) of "the extraordinary virtues shown by the Romans who resigned themselves to a frightful inequality and who suffered so much to conquer the world," or of the Greek "belief in glory" which enabled "a selection...from the swarming masses of humanity." And why should not a *modern* myth equally serve to reconcile the masses to "frightful inequality," and drive them to "conquer the world"?

---

[29] A fact, incidentally, also confirmed by Sternhell (1994: 53–54), again in clear dissonance with the alleged "triumph-of-liberalism" matrix, supposing the peaceful cessation of the class struggle. He thus writes about the reality, in both France and Germany during the first decade of the 20th century, of unprecedented worker's unrest and strike waves, bringing "terrible hardship," and seeing "social tensions" reaching "their climax."

Quite independently of Sorel, the ruling classes of the late 19th and early 20th century were looking desperately for new popular myths and narratives which might sustain their hegemony, when the influence of religion was weakening. So when the French ultra-leftist handed them the myth of the general strike, they said "no, thank you" as far as the content of the gift was concerned, but eagerly accepted the wrapping. Salvemini, on this matter, is still very useful:

> Fascist revolutionary syndicalism is mere humbug.... What Fascist doctrine has in common with Sorel is not syndicalism, but the dislike of parliamentary institutions, the advocacy of violent direct action...and the methods of exciting the emotions of the mob through myths in order to be able to exploit those emotions for ends anything but mythical. But these doctrines were not invented by Sorel and they have no essential connexion with the real syndicalist doctrine (Salvemini 1969: 373–75).

And the same applied when Sorel was embraced by the German (proto)-fascists; they, too, adhered to the formal aspects of his doctrine and discarded the content, at least insofar that it was socially radical. Carl Schmitt, one of the first to introduce in Germany the ideas of the French anarcho-syndicalist, was unambiguous about the social value of the Sorelian myth, which certainly did not lie precisely in its power to ignite strikes:

> The theory of myth is the most powerful symptom of the decline of the relative rationalism of parliamentary thought. If anarchist authors [besides Sorel, Schmitt refers to Bakunin and Proudhon] have discovered the importance of the mythical from an opposition to authority and unity, then they have also cooperated in establishing the foundation of another authority, however unwillingly, an authority based on the new feeling for order, discipline, and hierarchy (Schmitt 1988: 76).[30]

Another important and authoritative confirmation of this view from within the fascist camp is provided by Giovanni Gentile, perhaps *the* philosophical voice of Italian fascism. In 1928, retrospectively equipping fascism with "a doctrine" and reflecting on the rise of the movement, Gentile saluted the beneficial impact of Sorel's syndicalist ideas at the start of the 20th century. He saw them as an idealist force helping to

---

[30] Buckmiller (1985) draws attention in several places to this purely formalist way in which the German right-wing had adapted Sorel's ideas (see page 56 with relation to Schmitt, as well as 59, 61). The piece is also significant in stressing that among those truly interested in class struggle and ready to wield the weapon of striking, namely the German left-wing, Sorel's impact had been negligible. He was either ignored, as in the case of Rosa Luxemburg, or dismissed as "confused" and "bourgeois" by the likes of Anton Pannekoek and Gustav Eckstein (cf. 52–53).

shake Italians out of their materialistic and hedonistic daze. Two main aspects were singled out in which Sorelianism had been beneficial in transforming Italian socialism. The first, indeed, is the vibrant intransigence of its proletarian action as opposed to moderate, reformist socialism. Here, the one-time liberal and exemplary *Bildungsbürger* awkwardly goes through the motions of working-class radicalism:

> (1) the rejection of that strategy of foolish and deceptive collaboration of socialism with the parliamentary democracy of the liberal State. In so doing, socialism succeeded only in betraying the proletariat as well as the liberal State (Gentile 2007: 12).

Sorel's second contribution was said to be the substitution of action motivated by myths, for the otherwise materialistic conception of socialism:

> (2) [As opposed to standard socialism, the proletariat found in syndicalism] a faith in a moral reality, exquisitely ideal (or 'mythic,' as was said at the time), for which one would be prepared to live, die, and sacrifice oneself, even to the point of using violence whenever violence was necessary to destroy an established order to create another (12).

To those who are willing to take him at his word, Gentile must indeed appear a radical Sorelian revolutionary, rejecting the humiliating compromises with liberalism and prepared to use violence to overturn the capitalist order. And yet, just a few pages further on, when depicting the situation in post-War Italy in which the workers were growing ever defiant, the tribute to the radical aspect of Sorel's legacy reveals itself as mere lip service. Suddenly, Gentile laments the fact that the workers had indeed *ceased* to compromise with the liberal State and to collaborate with parliamentary democracy, and proceeded to threaten it with a revolution, in the process even going to the length of interfering—heaven forbid!—with economic life:

> The ganglia of economic life appeared thoroughly impaired. Work stoppage followed work stoppage.... A sense of revolution permeated the atmosphere which the weak ruling class felt impotent to resist. Ground was gradually ceded and accommodations made with the leaders of the socialist movement. Under [Giolitti],...there was sedition among the employees of the State and the occupation of the factories by workers; the very economic organism of the administration of the State was mortally wounded (15–16).

Sorel, the anarchist, is swiftly transformed into Pareto, the economic liberal bemoaning the inability of political liberalism to shield "the ganglia of economic life" from working-class harm. Militant, independent, intransigent, violent, proletarian action may have been Sorel's panacea, but they are certainly Gentile's nightmare. "Work stoppages," which should have thrilled a Sorelian, mortify him. What remains useful of Sorel is only the second contribution, that which extols the readiness of the worker "to live, die, and sacrifice oneself, even using violence to destroy an established order to create another." Yet the order that will be destroyed in the name of the Sorelian myth will not be that of economic liberalism. On the contrary, Mussolini, the lion, will subdue the "seditious employees" and liberate the "occupied factories," where Giolitti, the fox, had compromised. This, under fascism, is what Sorelian violence boiled down to (if indeed it was ever really meant to become a different kind of food).

We ought to briefly remind ourselves, finally, that this discussion is not a strictly theoretical affair, addressing the past only. It entails a commentary on present political affairs, which might have highly practical implications. Sternhell's theories (as well as those of a great number of other historians, from Talmon to Mosse and Furet) can be ironically turned against themselves, put to uses that would doubtlessly displease Sternhell. Something of that kind had occurred when Jean-Marie Le Pen, perhaps the single most important (covertly) neo-fascist politician of post-War Europe, cavalierly dismissed allegations of fascism by appealing to the following logic: "I always condemned communism, national-socialism and fascism. Incidentally, I define all of them as leftist movements that were spawned by the French Revolution" (as interviewed by Primor 2002). The leader of the *FN*, possibly having caught the gist of the Sternhellian revision that caused some uproar in France at the time of publication, here sounds almost like an amateur historian, wishing to ingratiate himself with the doyens of "the new consensus." This provides a small but pregnant illustration of how such revisionist theses, whether this is intended or not, can end up delivering an alibi to right-wing people, who see themselves absolved from the charge of extending the fascist legacy *because* they are right-wing! Left-wing admirers of Rousseau, by contrast, would be well advised to consult their lawyer. This revisiting of Sorel, however, refutes such a convenient pretext: *pace* revisionism, it has shown how the path which was treaded by the Sorelians, the fascists, the Nazis, and, ultimately, by our modern-day Le Pens, is one that stretches distinctly along the right flank of modern history.

CHAPTER FIVE

LIBERALISM AND FASCISM BETWEEN MYTHS AND REALITY—I

Liberal Myth No. 1: Fascism as Tyranny of the Majority

One of the most widely employed pieces of weaponry in the arsenal of liberal anti-fascism is the use of fascism as an object lesson of the dangers of democracy. Democracy, so the argument goes, because its practitioners rely on courting public opinion and catering to the great number, easily transforms into demagoguery and dictatorship. Fascism, in that account, is just a particularly pernicious manifestation of the populism inherent in the democratic system of ruling. Commencing her discussion of totalitarianism, Hannah Arendt thus invoked a long tradition of anti-democratic literature:

> Eminent European scholars and statesmen had predicted, from the early nineteenth century onward, the rise of the mass man and the coming of a mass age. A whole éérature on mass behavior and mass psychology had demonstrated and popularized the wisdom, so familiar to the ancients, of the affinity between democracy and dictatorship, between mob rule and tyranny. They had prepared certain politically conscious and over-conscious sections of the Western educated world for the emergence of demagogues, for gullibility, superstition, and brutality (Arendt 1960: 316).

The celebrated cultural historian, George Mosse, stated such an "affinity between democracy and dictatorship" even more boldly. "The French Revolution," he maintained (1989: 20), "stood at the beginning of a democratization of politics which climaxed in twentieth-century fascism." Similarly, the French Revolution "set the tone and the example for a new mass politics whose real triumph came only after the First World War" (7). Mosse spoke (14) of the "theory of democratic leadership adopted by Hitler and Mussolini" and asserted (16) that "Fascism and the French Revolution, each in its own way, saw itself as a democratic movement directed against the establishment."[1] The

---

[1] To be sure, apparently in awareness of the enormity of these claims, Mosse attempted to create for himself a kind of an alibi, leave behind an escape opening.

examples for this line of interpretation could be multiplied many times over. Such theoretical constructions, that trace back the origins of fascism to democracy, do not particularly flatter democracy, still less *mass* democracy. Between the lines, at least, there is a lesson implied in such readings of history: if democracy we must have, then let us take care that it be influenced as little as possible by the masses, and guided as far as possible by wise and responsible people, indeed not unlike those "eminent scholars and statesmen," whom Arendt mentioned. The best remedy to the pitfalls of democracy involves the curbing of its populist dimension, the guaranteeing of a democracy of quality, standing on a solid liberal base rather than a shaky populist one.

Tocqueville's Predictions: A Self-Fulfilling Prophecy?

Ritually, the credit goes to such discerning critics of the "tyranny of the majority" as J. S. Mill, Tocqueville, and even Nietzsche, praised by one commentator (Stackelberg 2002: 312–13) as "a clairvoyant critic of impending totalitarianism who warned of both fascism and communism." A good example of this explanation is provided by Robert O. Paxton, in his recent book on fascism. Very early, the author contends that the historical novelty of fascism consisted precisely in its ability to rally mass support behind right-wing politics. This unlikely socio-political configuration upset the calculations of traditional class analysts, such as Engels. Paxton quotes Engels from his 1895 introduction to Marx's *The Class Struggles in France*, the same text referred to above (first Chapter), in which Engels spoke about the conservative forces that will be compelled to break the law in order to stem the parliamentary rise of social democracy. Yet for Paxton, this text, far from

---

Thus, he formally took care to qualify "the bond" between fascism and the French Revolution by occasionally insisting that he is not referring to the political *content* of the two movements but only to their outward *manifestations*, their common stress on careful liturgy and political symbolism, etc. A close reading of his argument, which for reasons of space I cannot undertake here, would show however that Mosse by no means highlighted strictly formal resemblances (which would have been a rather futile exercise in any event, somewhat like underscoring the outward similarity between Adolf Hitler and Charlie Chaplin). Rather, the recurrent emphasis on the *democratic impetus* of both movements, on the desire on the part of both fascists and French radicals to bring the masses into the political arena, is surely a crucial claim for a bond of *political content*, not mere choreographic form. The reader thus learns from Mosse that both movements were democratic, revolutionary, massified and anti-bourgeois. For what concerns their alleged *differences*, we must use our imagination.

containing any important foresight, reveals the *blind spot* of Engels' perspective. Paxton writes:

> While Engels thus expected that the Left's enemies would launch a pre-emptive attack, he could not imagine in 1895 that this might win mass approval. Dictatorship against the Left amidst popular enthusiasm— that was the unexpected combination that fascism would manage to put together one short generation later (Paxton 2004: 3).

While Engels' is thus humbled, Paxton chooses a predictable figure, upon which to bestow the honors of quasi-prophetic insight:

> There were only a few glimmers of premonition. One came from an inquisitive young French aristocrat, Alexis de Tocqueville. Although Tocqueville found much to admire on his visit to the United States in 1831, he was troubled by the majority's power in a democracy to impose conformity by social pressure, in the absence of an independent social elite (3–4).

Tocqueville, indeed, is conventionally held up as the prototype of the enlightened, moderate, liberal-conservative critic of democratic excess, who was able to predict the main features of the tyranny of the majority, which he discussed in his landmark study, *Democracy in America*.[2] Much of Tocqueville's vast reputation rests in fact on this claim to a forewarning of the totalitarian degeneration of democracy. F. A. Hayek's celebrated diagnosis of the putative emergence of Nazism out of democratic-socialistic demagoguery, *The Road to Serfdom*, was written in conscious emulation of Tocqueville and its very title was borrowed from him.[3] And yet, upon a closer examination of his position, Tocqueville reveals himself an unhappy choice for such lavish praise. In fact, one must doubt not only the value of Tocqueville's predictions as such, exaggerated beyond proportion to their actual merit, but also, and perhaps more importantly, the degree of wisdom and even commitment he actually displayed in fighting and preventing "tyrannies."

---

[2] Tocqueville's foresight has become nearly legendary. A chapter in a recent book (Boesche 2006) on the French liberal is tellingly titled: "Why Could Tocqueville Predict So Well?"

[3] See Hayek (2007: 256). Similarly, in *The Hitler of History*, the conservative historian John Lukacs (1998) appealed to Tocqueville in highlighting the demagoguery of Hitler, advancing the view that the latter was not a "dictator" but a "populist," a thesis which he subsequently expanded into a general critique of democracy in *Democracy and Populism: Fear and Hatred* (2005).

To read Tocqueville's specific warnings against the tyranny of the majority in *Democracy in America*, is to find little in them that is pertinent for fascism. Some of Tocqueville's admonitions, in fact, seem singularly *in*adequate when juxtaposed with the experience of fascism. For instance, he sees a great danger in the fact that American functionaries are *overly independent*, as compared to the situation obtaining in Europe:

> In general the American functionaries are far more independent than the French civil officers within the sphere which is prescribed to them. Sometimes, even, they are allowed by the popular authority to exceed those bounds; and as they are protected by the opinion, and backed by the co-operation, of the majority, they venture upon such manifestations of their power as astonish a European. By this means habits are formed in the heart of a free country which may some day prove fatal to its liberties (Tocqueville 1899: 266).

It is difficult to see how such pointers might have helped their conscientious readers to either understand or counter fascism, which was not characterized precisely by extending the functionaries' freedom of action. If anything, such independence on their part commends itself as a factor that might have beneficially diluted the totalitarianism of fascism. Nor is there great prophylactic insight when Tocqueville argues that, under the majority's yoke, physical oppression becomes obsolete:

> Democratic republics have deprived despotism of its physical instruments.... Fetters and headsmen were the coarse instruments which tyranny formerly employed; but the civilization of our age has refined the arts of despotism...Under the absolute sway of an individual despot the body was attacked in order to subdue the soul, and the soul escaped the blows which were directed against it and rose superior to the attempt; but such is not the course adopted by tyranny in democratic republics; there the body is left free, and the soul is enslaved (267–8).

Whether or not this applies to the situation in democracies, in America or elsewhere, it scarcely sheds light on the dangers of fascism, which certainly did not care to "leave the body free" so that the soul might be all the more effectively subdued by the grinding force of public opinion. For reasons such as these, I entirely agree with Robert A. Dahl's contention (2003: 134–5) that Tocqueville was "dead wrong" in assuming an inherent tendency on the part of democracy to transform itself into an authoritarian or a totalitarian system and that "the Nazi takeover," specifically, "bore no relation to the Tocquevillean scenario."

But I suggest that our scrutiny of Tocqueville ought to go deeper than that. For on other occasions, his inquietudes, far from simply missing their target—if the target is the fascist potential incubated in democracies—seem to anticipate the habitual complaints *of fascists*, regarding the demise of excellence and individuality in a society leveled down and handed over to the dominion of the mediocre many: "The moral authority of the majority is partly based upon the notion that there is more intelligence and more wisdom in a great number of men collected together than in a single individual, and that the quantity of legislators is more important than their quality" (Tocqueville 1899: 259). None other than Hitler (1941: 666–7), for example, expressed analogous apprehension about the effects of such displacement of quality by quantity, stating, for instance, that "Marxism, indeed, presents itself as the perfection of the Jew's attempt at excluding the overwhelming importance of the personality in all domains of human life and of replacing it by the number of the masses. To this corresponds politically the parliamentary form of government." And both Hitler and Mussolini, surely, would have nodded with vigorous assent had they read Tocqueville's lines (1899: 270) in which he listed, as one of the "effects of the tyranny of the majority," the fact that "they check the development of leading characters."

Be that as it may, there is more to Tocqueville than mere social theory. One should not forget, particularly when assessing his contribution to an understanding of fascism, that he was not simply a detached observer of social affairs but a political actor as well, and one who was personally involved in a political and social drama which bears heavily on the experience of fascism, namely the establishment and management of the short-lived French Second Republic. This republic, in turn, was abolished by a coup d'état ushering in a despotic regime that is seen by many as proto-fascist: the "Second Empire" of Napoleon the Third. To read his celebrated *Souvenirs* of the 1848 revolution with 20th century fascism in mind, particularly the trajectory of the short-lived Weimar Republic, is to get a feeling of déjà vu, though projected onto the future. If Tocqueville indeed possessed a unique understanding of the pitfalls of democracy, this did not help him to advocate a course of action conducive to the survival of the republic and to the prevention of (proto-)fascism. On the contrary, he seemed to have pre-figured the basic weaknesses, blunders and strategic miscalculations of those who, nearly a century later, succumbed to Nazism. Anachronistically examined, Tocqueville thus emerges as a *Sisyphean* rather than a *Sibylline* figure. He was so busy with upholding "order," repelling the forces of radicalism and subduing its demagogic political representatives, the Montagnards and the socialists, that he objectively weakened the republic when it came to facing its enemies from the right. To be sure, he did not wish to see Louis-Napoleon installed in power, and was repelled by the prospect of such "bastard monarchy, despised by all the enlightened classes, hostile to liberty, and controlled by intriguers, adventurers and lackeys" (Tocqueville 1997: 201). Yet such insight was expressly relegated to a secondary plane by the overriding fear of the greater, more pressing evil, that of social radicalism. In his own words:

> I was, I confess, much more concerned with putting a powerful leader quickly at the head of the Republic than with drafting a perfect republican constitution. At that time we were under the divided, vacillating rule of the Executive committee, socialism was at our doors, and we were drawing near to the days of June, all of which should not be forgotten (178).

Never more than a *Vernunftrepublikaner* before the term was coined, someone whose acceptance and defense of the republic was animated by no republican—to say nothing of democratic—zeal, but rather by *ad hoc* considerations and the lack of an alternative ("I sincerely desired to maintain the Republic...because I saw nothing either ready or fit to put in its place" [201]), he closely anticipated the outlook and actions of those German conservatives who, while not necessarily appreciative of Hitler, nevertheless paved his path by ever restricting and diminishing the authority and the status of the Weimar Republic. They have in common with Tocqueville a primary concern for isolating, squeezing out and shutting down the forces of the left, whereas the forces of the right are gradually assigned an ever-greater role. Would a German moderate conservative, reflecting on his part during the Weimar-Republic days, not have chosen similar phrases to those that follow, to describe and defend his position?

> The conservatives were not content that the administration should simply be vigorous; they wanted to use our victory to impose repressive preventive laws. We ourselves felt the need to move in that direction although not wishing to go as far as they.
>
> For my part, I believed that it was wise and necessary to make great concessions to the fears and legitimate resentments of the nation. And that, after such a violent revolution, the only way to save freedom was

to restrict it.[4] My colleagues agreed with me. Accordingly we introduced the following measures: a law to suspend the clubs, another to suppress the vagaries of the press with even more energy than had been used under the Monarchy; and a third to regularize the state of siege.

'Your law establishes a military dictatorship,' they shouted at us.

'Yes,' replied Dufaure, 'it is a dictatorship, but a parliamentary one. No private rights can prevail over the inalienable right of society to save itself...'

...We have undertaken to save the Republic with the help of parties who do not love it (220-21).

Even if we accept Tocqueville's account of himself as a fighter, however reluctant, on the republic's behalf, it still must be admitted that his tactics, far from achieving their strategic goal, proved futile, if not outright counterproductive. Clear foresight, at any rate, does not seem to have blessed such choice of weapons and allies. Nor were the consequences of such policies terribly difficult to foresee. Thus, shortly following the repressive measures adopted by Tocqueville's government, one of their direct political victims, the socialist disciple of Fourier, Victor Prosper Considérant, ironically wrote Tocqueville from his exile in Belgium:

My dear Tocqueville,

...You are good for two or three months perhaps, and the pure *Whites* who will follow you may last for six months at the longest. Both of you, it is true, will have perfectly deserved what you will infallibly get a little sooner or a little later. But let us talk no more politics and respect the very legal, loyal and Odilon Barrotesque state of siege (212).

This Montagnard appears to have had a better inkling of what the immediate future holds for Tocqueville and his faction, who fancied they might stay afloat with their tactics of repression of the left and appeasement of the right. He realized that the Tocquevilleans, so to speak, were bound soon to give way before a more resolute counter-revolutionary force (though he was deluding himself in assuming that this reactionary power would in turn be swept aside in favor, apparently, of a left-wing comeback, which of course never came about).

---

[4] This is written, apparently, *not* with a view to June 1848, during which the workers clashed violently with the bourgeoisie, but to June 1849, during which largely non-violent demonstrations by the mostly petty-bourgeois critics of the government took place.

In all this, it is important to realize, there was no gap between theory and praxis; Tocqueville, that is, did not betray his liberal convictions or fail to act on his principles. The problem, it seems, was rather that he *acted on* their logic and fought to stave off the tyranny of the majority. Yet such consistency, far from equipping him with a useful platform from which to fight embryonic fascism, forcefully drove him down the slope, into an escalation of ever more restricting safety measures, from the regularization of the state of siege to a tightened censorship to the persecution of political dissidents to the elimination of universal suffrage (that last, a measure taken on May 1850, after a still more conservative government had been formed). The active participation in this process made Tocqueville, no matter how unwillingly, an accomplice in the piecemeal dismantling of the democratic republic. Like the sworn enemies of socialism during the times of the Weimar Republic, or during the period in which Italian fascism bought its ticket to power by stemming anarchism, Tocqueville, a supremely intelligent observer and wonderfully lucid writer though he was, dogmatically clung to terms such as "order" and "national good" which he automatically identified with the interests of the upper classes against the "demagogic" and "ridiculous" "agitation" from below. Nor were such measures, in the final account, ineffective. They did prove safe in that socialism in France was completely squashed, and order was emphatically restored. The tyranny of the majority was successfully countervailed and the outcome was...paving the road for a rudimentary form of fascism. This demonstrates that an "affinity between democracy and dictatorship" (Arendt) certainly exists, and that democracy can indeed "climax" in fascism (Mosse), but an affinity and climax of the kind that existed between the emancipation of American slaves and the formation of the Ku Klux Klan.

Such a course of action, Tocqueville consciously pursued in spite of the obvious dangers. He never doubted: radical republicanism was more menacing in his eyes than the counter-revolution. The following passage, which deals with the period between June 1848 and June 1849, amply verifies this:

> The reactionary movement triggered off by the days of June [1848] continues to gain momentum in the nation; all the elections demonstrate this, and there are a thousand other signs. Even the government, while regarding this movement with apprehension, is in some degree carried along by it. The monarchical parties regain hope and unite. On the other

hand, many republicans who have been with us so far begin to with-draw towards the Mountain.... Without wishing to be carried away by the monarchical parties, I have no hesitation in voting with them on all measures designed to re-establish order and discipline in society and to strike down the revolutionary and Socialist party (278).

This quotation also contains an important clue about Tocqueville's stance in relation to the notion of "the tyranny of the majority" and to "democracy" in general. Tocqueville was by no means an intractable opponent of the majority's rule. Here, as well, idealism would be a poor guide into historical realities. Tocqueville was intrinsically nei-ther a pro- nor an anti-democrat, neither for nor against the majority. His *intrinsic concern* was with the abiding supremacy of the proper-tied classes in times of social upheaval; *this* overriding preoccupation, not any idealistic conviction, pragmatically determined his subsequent political decisions. To the extent that "democracy" is compatible with the interests of property it is acceptable, indeed it might be an indis-pensable means to hold demands that are more radical, at bay, and to forestall the danger of the revolution. To the extent, however, that the majority espouses socialism, it becomes tyrannical. Thus, in a political text written in October 1847, Tocqueville warns the complacent bour-geois elite of the July Monarchy that their exclusive rule is precarious since it exposes property to the attacks of the disenfranchised classes. He therefore espouses a gradual expansion of the suffrage and political measures to alleviate the sufferings of the lower classes, but he does so in the hope that such measures may obviate the revolutionary danger and with the clear caveat, that property and its attendant social hier-archy will thereby not be infringed upon. He therefore recommends in conclusion:

> 1. Extending little by little the circle of political rights, in a way which will go beyond the limits of the middle class...2. [G]uaranteeing the poor every legal equality and every welfare *compatible with the existence of individual right to property and the inequality of conditions attendant on it* [*l'inégalité des conditions qui en decoulé*]. Because that which, in this matter, had been honesty and justice, now becomes *necessity and prudence* (Tocqueville 1866: 518–19; italics added).

This is the material kernel of Tocqueville's position, and by extension, of no small part of the propertied classes of his times. And herein lies the difficulty, which had puzzled many observers, of deciding whether he was a conservative-aristocrat or a liberal-democrat. For he was obviously both of these: to the extent that democracy conserves property, Tocqueville was a democrat; to the extent that it imperils property, he was conservative. And this pragmatic rather than idealistic coordinator, accounts for the wavering position of the French ruling classes vis-à-vis democracy and universal suffrage throughout the days of the Second Republic. As long as universal suffrage serves property and chastises socialism, as it did ever since the elections of April 1848, the ruling classes go along with it. But the moment universal suffrage turns the tide and breathes fresh life into the left-wing republican forces, it outlives its usefulness. Thus, the elections of March and April 1850 proved to be the last before the universal suffrage was curtailed, in May 1850. A similar logic underpins Tocqueville's own approach to the majority. Turned against property, seeking to tamper with that fundamental algorithm, the majority is unmistakably and terrifyingly tyrannical, banishing individuals and ousting responsible classes: "I felt that we were caught in one of those great democratic floods that drown those individuals, and those parties too, who try to build dikes to hold them" (Tocqueville 1997: 77). Speaking before a sympathetic public in rural France, Tocqueville states (89): "There are those who mean by a republic a dictatorship exercised in the name of freedom; who think that the Republic should not only change political institutions, but reshape society itself;...I am not that kind of Republican." But as long as the majority endorses the cause of property (known also as the cause of "order," "society," "law," "tradition," and so on and so forth), Tocqueville reveals himself contented and reassured in its midst:

> I had a sense of happiness I had never known before. For this was the first time since I entered public life that I felt myself moving with the current of a majority in the only direction that my tastes, reason and conscience would approve, and that was a new and delightful sensation to me. To... make the clear will of the people of France triumph over the passions and desires of the Paris working men, and in this way to conquer demagogy by democracy, such was my only design (105–6).

For this, indeed, is the proverbial *moral majority*. And here we arrive at the heart of the matter, with regards to Tocqueville's notion of the tyranny of the majority and its implications for fascism: the point is not only that fascism was hardly sustained, let alone brought to power, by the majority: in Italy it began decisively as the paramilitary force of the *squadristi*, operating outside, and against, democracy, and in Germany, at the peak of its electoral success, the *NSDAP* had won

37.4% of the votes, which by some margin falls short of constituting "the majority." But such mathematical considerations aside, those who *did* rally behind Nazism and supply it with the bulk of its votes, came predominantly from the upper and the middle classes and the peasants,[5] and this coalition of social forces was a majority that Tocqueville, far from criticizing, was intimately *bound* to:

> There was something which immediately struck me with astonished plea-sure. For although some sort of demagogic agitation prevailed among the workers in the towns, in the country all the landowners, whatever their origin, antecedents, education, or means, had come together and seemed to form a single unit...Neither jealousy nor pride separated the peasant from the rich man any longer, or the bourgeois from the gentleman; instead there was mutual confidence, respect and goodwill. Ownership constituted a sort of fraternity linking all who had anything; the rich-est were the elder brothers and the less prosperous the younger; but all thought themselves brothers, having a common inheritance to defend (87).

Read with fascism in mind, these lines seem indeed uncannily predic-tive, yet not quite in the sense celebrated by Tocqueville's admirers. If *this* anti-socialist front, indeed, is what we should understand under "the tyranny of the majority," then we ought to recognize *in Tocqueville* one of its members, a happy atom in the organic unity of the resur-gent *Volk*, rather than its lofty critic, a proud member of the stalwart countryside, marching against the radicalism of the urban, industrial locus: Paris, in Tocqueville's case, Berlin, in that of German fascism.[6] That the fellow-traveler Tocqueville would not have gone all the

---

[5] As empirically demonstrated, for example, by Richard Hamilton, in his cogent study, *Who Voted for Hitler?* (1982), that dispelled the traditional notion of a predom-inantly "petty bourgeois" electoral support for the Nazis. According to Hamilton's findings, the Nazi urban constituency resembled a reversed pyramid, where support was disproportionally high among the upper classes, and subsequently and consis-tently diminished the "lower" one descended down the social ladder, from the inter-mediate levels of consent of the lower middle classes, right down to the lowest harvests (again: not in absolute but in proportional terms) among the working class. "Support for the National Socialists," Hamilton argued, "in most towns varied directly with the class level of the district. The 'best districts' gave Hitler and his party the strongest sup-port" (421). This pyramidal structure, however, did not hold true in the countryside, where the division was predominantly along lines of religious conviction: Catholics brought the Nazis meager returns, while Protestants, regardless of social or income level, were overwhelmingly supportive.

[6] Again a pattern which Hamilton ratified with regards to Nazism: as he showed, the bigger the town—Berlin, Hamburg—the lowest tended to be the percentage of the Nazi vote; while conversely, the smaller—less industrial, less radical, less "modern"— the town, the greater the percentage of the Nazi vote was likely to be.

distance with them, is beyond doubt; but he was very far from sounding a clear alarm against such social forces. As a useful counterexample to the reflexive crediting of Tocqueville with anti-fascist insight, we may quote J. S. Schapiro's good query, from the aftermath of the Second World War:

> Why was de Tocqueville so much concerned about the tyranny of the majority? It was a recurrent theme in his writings, as it was in those of John Stuart Mill...[T]he history of democratic government has proved their fears to have been groundless.... With the advent of totalitarianism in recent years, the great danger has been the tyranny of the organized minority, a danger all too real, which was not foreseen by the pioneer of democratic liberalism (Schapiro 1949: 301).

This is a sound and much-needed qualification of Tocqueville's alleged prescience. But it remains incomplete unless we realize that Tocqueville did not merely neglect to consider the danger of the minority rule: he was *part* of that danger, having contributed, by his policies and social alliances, to make it more acute. In the words of a rare critic of Tocqueville, he supported "a legalized state of emergency, meant to prohibit any dissension on the part of a class of workers, against which all measures are be taken, in order to conjure away the extreme dangers of which this class is the cause" (Le Cour Grandmaison 2002: 290). Tocqueville, it seems, had not so much foreseen the *horrors* of fascism, as he had prefigured some of its *methods*. A still more somber irony in marshalling Tocqueville against fascism concerns what an otherwise very sympathetic observer describes as "his embrace of war and empire" (Boesche 2006: 109), his advocacy of the colonization of Algeria as a necessary measure if French national honor and its international prominence were to be vindicated. In his colonialist zeal, Tocqueville did not shrink from pressing some very drastic measures, such as the systematic destruction of the natives' economy as a precondition for their military subjugation, and went as far as outlining racial segregation between the French settlers and the Arabs.[7] Such, needless to say, are not the antecedents one would normally look for in the curriculum vitae of a prescient anti-fascist.

---

[7] Le Cour Grandmaison's book (2005) contains highly useful information and analysis (esp. 98–114; 318–19). See also: Losurdo's incisive deconstruction of Tocqeuville's reputation as moderate and enlightened (2005: 224–37; 284–90; 321–2); and Boesche (2006: 109–125).

Tocqueville's belligerent and expansionist foreign policy outlook cannot be separated from his understanding of internal social policies, allegedly benign and moderate. We should rather stress the symbiosis—indeed, one that would come to typify fascist practice—between imperialism abroad and severe social repression at home, embodied in the figure of the French general Cavaignac, whom Tocqueville supported almost unreservedly. Combating the insurgents of the 1848 June revolution, Cavaignac introduced in France the ruthless repressive methods he and other French military men first used in fighting the Arab "rebels" in North Africa, and which were unprecedented in the history of European civil wars. In that way, the struggle against the actual Algerian Bedouins, in aims and methods, was transferred onto Paris, against the figurative "Bedouins of the metropolis" (Le Cour Grandmaison 2005: 308). In fact, as Jennifer Pitts argues in an informative study of 19th century liberalism, Tocqueville's support for the colonization of Algeria was intimately bound with his unease facing the prospect of domestic democratization, and what he perceived as a general decline of the cohesiveness of the French nation, its ongoing disintegration into mere private individuals. In imperialist and military ventures, Tocqueville envisaged a powerful way to counterbalance such processes:

> In addition to attempting to recover France's true history for practical purposes, Tocqueville proposed two means of resisting the individualism and anomie that plagued France…The first entailed great enterprises that require action and sacrifice by the entire nation, political projects that forced individuals out of their private spaces and into the realm of concerted action…Tocqueville's second solution was to promote action that would engender in the people a sense of national greatness…. Both strategies invited imperial exploits (and their celebration), and Tocqueville often implied that pursuit of glory through conquest would generate the political dynamics of an involved citizenry and a strong nation (Pitts 2005: 194).

The analogies between such projects of nation building and the fascist one are, I trust, evident enough. We need only underline the apparent paradox that such a project was endorsed not by a sworn anti-liberal denigrating modern individualism, but by one of the leading European liberals of the century. This is an irony that we shall explore in greater detail in section 2 of the present chapter (2nd myth) and section 2 of the next chapter (4th myth).

Moreover, Tocqueville's criticism of the pioneering biological race theories of his protégé Joseph Arthur Gobineau notwithstanding, his

own thinking was shot through with racist motifs, albeit ones relying more on nurture than on nature. As cogently demonstrated by
Domenico Losurdo, Tocqueville was a firm believer in the superiority
of the European races, claiming, for example, that "the man located by
us, on account of his vices and ignorance, at the lowest grade of the
social scale, is still the first among the savages" (as quoted in Losurdo
2005: 225). Such a vantage point led him, in his correspondence with
American acquaintances, to express severe apprehensions regarding
the consequences of racial miscegenation in the United States.[8] Finally,
and not less ominously when bearing fascism in mind, Tocqueville
theorized about what he called "the revolutionary sickness," as caused
by a distinct "new race" of deprived people, all sharing "the same
physiognomy, the same passions, the same character." This "virus" had
erupted during the French Revolution and kept on spreading all over
the "civilized parts of the earth" ever since (as quoted in Losurdo 2005:
269). Considering such a set of concepts, it is not surprising that Ernst
Nolte (1984: 593) suggested that Tocqueville's "historico-philosophical
premise was far less removed from that of Gobineau than what might
be presumed, and was...in no way simply opposed to it," a view which
Losurdo attenuates, but does not discard.

From Malthus to Mises: Dictatorship as a Necessary Evil

A far cry from the "glimmers of premonition" coming from "an
inquisitive young French aristocrat," Tocqueville appears closer to
embodying—illustriously, no doubt—the liberal lineage of fascism. So
was Tocqueville unsuitably chosen for the role of the prescient liberal
critic of democracy as the breeding ground of fascist tyranny? The
problem, I would suggest, is not with the actor but with the role itself,
not with the casting crew but with the script. Tocqueville is no isolated case within the liberal tradition, a mere unfortunate exception
which cannot invalidate, and might in fact ratify, a wholesome rule.
On the contrary, we should see Tocqueville, in his views, his predictions and his actions, as representing the liberal norm. For that reason,
other possible candidates would not give us a significantly better performance in the role of the prescient liberal. Let us audition a figure
nearly as authoritative and as influential within the liberal tradition

---

[8] See Losurdo (2005: 224–228).

as Tocqueville, that of Thomas Malthus. Malthus, much earlier than his French counterpart, explicitly linked together mass influence and despotism, quite in Arendt's terms. He wrote (1992: 244) about "the tendency of mobs to produce tyranny," affirming that "A mob...is of all monsters the most fatal to freedom. It fosters a prevailing tyranny, and engenders one where it was not." This is an auspicious start, no doubt. And yet, on closer examination, it turns out that the tyranny which is allegedly fostered by the mob is not really the tyranny *of* the mob, but a tyranny *against* the mob:

> The pressure of distress on the lower classes of people, together with the habit of attributing this distress to their rulers, appears to me to be the rock of defence, the castle, the guardian spirit of despotism. It affords to the tyrant the fatal and unanswerable plea of necessity.... While any dissatisfied man of talents has power to persuade the lower classes of people that all their poverty and distress arise solely from the iniquity of the government, it is evident that the seeds of fresh discontents and fresh revolutions are continually sowing.... Are we to be surprised that, under such circumstances, *the majority of well-disposed people*, finding that a government with proper restrictions is unable to support itself against the revolutionary spirit, and weary and exhausted with perpetual change to which they can see no end, should give up the struggle in despair, and *throw themselves into the arms of the first power which can afford them protection against the horrors of anarchy*? (244; emphases added).

Thus, the mob is held responsible for tyranny in roughly the same way that an unruly wife is held responsible for the thrashing she gets, after she has driven her naturally peaceful and orderly husband into fits of anger, and left him no other choice but to reach for the whip. The tyranny is thus exercised against the mob, supported by the same moral majority that Tocqueville identified with, "the majority of well-disposed people," the trustworthy friends of order and property. And, also like Tocqueville, though Malthus would have much preferred to avoid such despotic measures, he has no hesitation whatsoever about their necessity, expediency and morality, once faced by a mob clamoring for food:

> The country gentlemen were perhaps too easily convinced that existing circumstances called upon them to give up some of the most valuable privileges of Englishmen; but, as far as they were really convinced of this obligation, they acted consistently with the clearest rule of morality.... The patriot,... would be called upon...to submit to very great oppression, rather than give the slightest countenance to a popular tumult, the members of which...were persuaded that the destruction of the Parliament,

the Lord Mayor, and the monopolizers, would make bread cheap, and
that a revolution would enable them all to support their families. In this
case, it is more the ignorance and delusion of the lower classes of people
that occasions the oppression, than the actual disposition of the government to tyranny (246–7).

A theory of counter-revolution is thus inherent in Malthus' liberalism:
"As a friend to freedom, and an enemy to large standing armies, it is
with extreme reluctance that I am compelled to acknowledge that, had
it not been for the organized force in the country, the distresses of the
people during the late scarcities,... might have driven them to commit
the most dreadful outrages" (244–5). Military dictatorship, under such
circumstances, is regrettable as it is justified: "If political discontents
were blended with the cries of hunger, and a revolution were to take
place by the instrumentality of a mob clamouring for want of food,
the consequences would be unceasing change and unceasing carnage,
the bloody career of which nothing but the establishment of some
complete despotism could arrest" (245). Having scientifically proven
to his own satisfaction—and to that of several generations of liberals—
that the laws of commerce can tolerate just as little interference as
"the laws of nature," that government can do absolutely nothing to
relieve poverty and hunger since (248) "distributing the produce of the
taxes to the poorer classes of society, according to the plan proposed
by Mr. [Thomas] Paine would only aggravate the situation," Malthus
confines the sphere of politics strictly within the limits of propertied
interests. Ideally, the government should do absolutely *nothing*, apart
from educating the poor about the way "the regular market" functions,
so as to remove any seditious notions from their minds and counter
any "delusive arguments on equality" (245). The people must learn to
starve—for nothing less is at stake—while respecting the rule of law.
Otherwise, government must be entitled to do *everything* in defense of
the well-disposed people against the mob. Malthus, like Tocqueville,
hence does not warn against fascist dictatorship as much as he *pre-
figures* it. Fascism, under such light, is definitely an evil, but sometimes a *necessary* one, under conditions of mass society. In Malthus'
prophetic words:

> I cannot yet think so meanly of the country gentlemen of England as to
> believe they would have given up a part of their birthright of liberty, if
> they had not been actuated by a real and genuine fear that it was then
> in greater danger from the people than from the crown. They appear to
> surrender themselves to government on condition of being protected

from the mob; but they never would have made this melancholy and disheartening surrender, if such a mob had not existed either in reality or in imagination (245).

But the mob, alas, exists.

Things are not different where a salient 20th century liberal as Ludwig von Mises is concerned. Mises prefers the peaceful reign of capitalism, where the masses acquiesce to the dictates of the market, but like Malthus and Tocqueville, against the interference of the mob, he does not shy away from approving of despotism, in that case no longer *potentially* fascist but actually so. Writing in 1927, Mises thus affirms:

> It cannot be denied that Fascism and similar movements aiming at the establishment of dictatorships are full of the best intentions and that their intervention has, for the moment, saved European civilization. The merit that Fascism has thereby won for itself will live on eternally in history. But... Fascism was an emergency makeshift. To view it as something more would be a fatal error (Mises 2002: 51).

As if echoing Malthus' notion of the well-disposed people, Mises asserts that, subjectively at least, fascists are "full of the best intentions." Their dictatorship is undertaken in defense, however misguided, of the liberal civilization. Such basic disposition and a benign, if subterranean liberal influence, seems to Mises to vouch for a relatively civilized and moderate denouement of fascism. He thus ventures the following, sanguine prediction:

> *Fascism will never succeed as completely as Russian Bolshevism in freeing itself from the power of liberal ideas.* Only under the fresh impression of the murders and atrocities perpetrated by the supporters of the Soviets were Germans and Italians able to block out the remembrance of the traditional restraints of justice and morality and find the impulse to bloody counteraction. The deeds of the Fascists and of other parties corresponding to them were emotional reflex actions evoked by indignation at the deeds of the Bolsheviks and Communists. As soon as the first flush of anger had passed, their policy took a more moderate course and will probably become even more so with the passage of time. *This moderation is the result of the fact that traditional liberal views still continue to have an unconscious influence on the Fascists* (49; emphases added).

Remarkably, despite being of partly Jewish descent, Mises' class-affiliation predominates, and he is driven to excuse the deeds, not only of Italian fascists, but also of German ones. In justification of tyranny, Mises invokes—like Malthus and Tocqueville—the horrors of violent revolution: "the deeds of the Bolsheviks." Yet like them, he is exasperated

not only by revolution but also by perfectly democratic and legal intervention in the market, that illegitimately appeals to government to
redistribute wealth in opposition to commercial-cum-natural laws.
And F. A. Hayek, equally, clearly preferred the dictatorial, but liberal, Pinochet, over the thoroughly democratic, but moderately anti-
capitalist, Allende, as he unabashedly informed a Chilean interviewer
in 1981, amid the liberal rule of Pinochet:

> At times it is necessary for a country to have, for a time, some form or
> other of dictatorial power. As you will understand, it is possible for a
> dictator to govern in a liberal way. And it is also possible for a democ-
> racy to govern with a total lack of liberalism. Personally I prefer a lib-
> eral dictator to democratic government lacking liberalism. My personal
> impression—and this is valid for South America—is that in Chile, for
> example, we will witness a transition from a dictatorial government to
> a liberal government. And during this transition it may be necessary to
> maintain certain dictatorial powers, not as something permanent, but as
> a temporary arrangement (Hayek 1981).

But this, in truth, is hardly a matter of personal preference on the part
of Hayek, or Mises. Both were, in that respect, worthy heirs to the
classical liberal tradition which, fairly consistently, regarded a capitalist dictatorship as preferable not only to an anti-capitalist dictatorship
but also to an anti-capitalist *democracy*. This stance has therefore very
little to do with the liberal defense of "the rule of law" against revolutionary lawbreakers. The very reverse is the case: the rule of law is
justified strictly as *defending liberalism*, and upon neglecting to do so it
becomes automatically null and void: "temporarily," Hayek and Mises
carefully add, for a period of "transition": until, that is, some sense
is knocked into the rule of law and it realigns itself with capitalism
(which may, by the way, require some time: Pinochet, for example,
had been in power longer than Hitler). It does not occur to these liberals—or more probably it does, and is the whole point behind their
argument—that under such terms dictatorship can never in fact *be*
"temporary" or "transitional": it is a *permanent* condition, at one time
overt, at another covert. It is permanent because one can scarcely argue
that after having outlawed, imprisoned, tortured and killed thousands
of one's democratic opponents—as Pinochet did—one can simply re-
establish democracy: one can hardly shoot somebody's legs and then
tell him, well, this has been a merely provisional measure, now go
on with you, you are now free to run again! But even assuming that
democracy can somehow run again, or even walk, it is certain that it

will not get very far. The rifle is put back in the dictator's pocket, to disappear from sight. But everybody knows that it is still there, and that it might be taken out again, with all legitimacy as far as a Hayek is concerned, the moment the democrat falls back into error, and acts "illiberally," against capitalism. You are perfectly *free*, says the "liberal dictator" to the democrat, to do precisely as I *dictate*.

This basic dictatorial instinct, putting capitalism above the law or making it interchangeable with it, pertains to the very DNA of liberalism, therefore preceding not only the revolutionary menace of the Bolsheviks but even the French Revolution. It can be traced as far back as John Locke, for whom—as seen above (Chapter 1)—any political encroaching on property is *ipso facto* a violation of natural right, regardless of whether or not it follows a legal procedure or enjoys a political consensus. And Bolshevism, indeed, was hardly the primary issue in pre-fascist Italy, pre-Nazi Germany, and still less, pre-fascist Austria, Mises own homeland; in all these countries, what was immediately at stake was the newly gained political and economic power of the organized workers, which allowed them to seize part of the possessions of the propertied without their consent. That might explain why Mises felt little discomfiture about becoming the economic advisor during the so-called Austro-fascist regime of Dollfuss, which abolished democracy in that country not because it was revolutionary but because it favored social-democracy, ushering in vast social legislation and public expenditure partly at the rich taxpayer's expense.

Croce: the Paradoxes of the Fascist Diet

Our last candidate for the role of the liberal critic of the linkage between democracy and tyranny is one of the most eminent and often cited representatives of Italian anti-fascism, the liberal philosopher Benedetto Croce. In his case, however, there can be little talk about "prescience" and "premonition," since he was formulating his critique well after fascism had been firmly installed in power. The terms of his argument, however, would be perfectly familiar. Writing in 1943, Croce (1943: 94) recapitulates the liberal reproach: "democracy runs a perilous and headstrong career, which, by the help of a demagogue and a mystical faith in 'the people' or 'the masses,' leads to tyranny and the rule of the sword." With Croce, however, the contradictions of this kind of exegesis are thrown into a vivid relief when his theory is juxtaposed with the actual position he took when fascism was busily inaugurating "the rule of the sword." For at the time that fascism was avidly destroying the workers' organizations throughout Italy and beating its way to power, Croce was a benevolent observer, in fact lending his immense intellectual prestige to sanctioning the cause of fascism. Thus, in an article in *La Stampa* in May 1924, he approved of the Blackshirts' "futurist"

> determination to come out in the streets and impose one's ideas, stopping the mouths of those who disagree and braving riots, that thirst for novelty and the eagerness to break with every tradition, that glorification of youth, so typical of Futurism, which appealed to the homecoming soldiers disgusted by the squabbles of the old parties and their listlessness before the violence and sabotage raging against the nation and the State" (Croce, as quoted in Hamilton 1971: 43)

For between 1922 and Matteotti's murder in June 1924, Croce was anti-democratic not because it leads to *fascism*, but because it leads to *anarchy*. Fascism, by contrast, he regarded as an indispensable stopgap, saving Italy from ruin: "The heart of Fascism," Croce affirmed in February 1924, "is love of Italy; it is the feeling of her salvation, the salvation of the State; it is the just conviction that the State without authority is no State at all" (44). Fascism was a bitter but indispensable remedy, a savior of Italy after the weakly, decadent liberals could not maintain order, and an anti-dote to democratic-anarchistic excess. The problem emerged later, when fascism refused to recognize its limited value precisely as an emergency solution and pretended to become a permanent one. The fascists did the invaluable, if "negative" work of eliminating the challenge of organized and militant labor, but then refused to let the liberals take it from there and accomplish the "positive" task of national "regeneration." Fascism should have accommodated liberalism, should have furnished "a bridge of passage for the restoration of a more severe liberal regime, in the context of a stronger state" (Croce, as quoted in Rizi 2003: 70). In basically the same sense as Mises', Croce was grateful for the historical merit of fascism in saving civilization, but warned against this turning into anything more than a makeshift solution. There were of course numerous other liberals and conservatives who initially supported fascism, with greater or lesser enthusiasm, as a *means*, without regarding it as the *end*, and who departed from the fascists once it became clear that they were unwilling to dismount the stage on cue or at least play their part precisely according to the liberal-conservative scenario. Some of these fellow travelers eventually evolved into vital and insightful critics of fascism, willing to recognize their own part in bringing fascism about and atone for it. But there is little trace of such self-critique in Croce. In fact, even after his critical turn, he continued to congratulate himself for having realized the necessity of fascism as a response to liberal frailty and decadence, and thus, implicitly at least, for having made the right choice in initially backing fascism. Writing in 1933, Croce unfolded a thinly veiled apology for his past political alignments and underscored his acumen in identifying the need for fascist "reaction," as against those who, shortsightedly, were willing to have none of it:

> When this danger threatens, the danger of 'a relapse into anarchy' as it is called, the primary and fundamental human need for social order reacts against it and reacts in a one-sided way in the form of self-interest and violence.
>
> All reaction is preceded by an absolute or relative weakness of men's moral nature. Sometimes this consists...in a decadence and corruption of the 'governing' or 'political' classes...Those who suffer by the reaction are generally led by their sufferings to interpret the harshness of the state, which is no longer representative, as treachery and hostility, nor are their feelings and consequent illusions unnatural. But those among them [like Croce, obviously] whose moral consciousness has not been weakened, or has quickly regained its strength, are more ready to blame themselves or, what comes to the same thing, their party, as responsible. In the resulting reaction they do not see harshness and sinister motives, or not these only, but mainly an objective necessity (Croce 1933b: 59).

Fascism was therefore both inevitable and requisite, "an objective necessity," following the unwarranted concessions made by Italian liberalism to anarchy, and Croce was altogether justified in recognizing such condition and facilitating the recovery of the social order. The problem was that fascism was not satisfied with merely fulfilling this vital first aid function and, aspiring to be more, it overstepped its legitimate domain and outlived its usefulness:

> Since reaction restores a social order, which had broken down and revindicates the state's fundamental and permanent function, its character and value is sheerly political. Its direct purpose is accomplished in the repression of violence and anarchy and in the restoration of state authority. Another purpose it cannot directly pursue but only negatively facilitate, by enforcing privation or what the doctors call 'diet.'...For regeneration is a task alien to the very nature of reaction because opposite and complementary to the one it is performing (60–61).

The political and ethical limits of Croce's anti-fascism reveal themselves forcefully when compared with the position of another anti-fascist who began as a supporter, the German Lutheran pastor, Martin Niemöller. Initially a typical conservative anti-democrat who rallied to

Hitler, Niemöller evolved into a famous opponent of the regime. But this process entailed a severe and penetrating self-critique, beautifully encapsulated in the celebrated poem, "First They Came...":

> In Germany, they came first for the Communists, and I didn't speak up because I wasn't a Communist;
>   And then they came for the trade unionists, and I didn't speak up because I wasn't a trade unionist;
>   And then they came for the Jews, and I didn't speak up because I wasn't a Jew;
>   And then...they came for me...And by that time there was no one left to speak up.

For Niemöller, thus, fascism was wrong from the very beginning, to be discarded root and branch. But for Croce, fascism was *not* wrong when it came for the communists and the trade unionists. To them it administered a much needed—castor-oil?—"diet." Fascism only went wrong when it came for Croce and his liberal companions, and demanded that they toe the line culturally and politically. As long as the fascist bulldog was attacking the socialists, it was an impressive sort of animal, egged on by the liberal onlooker; but when the same animal showed its teeth to the liberal, it became a nasty, ugly beast.

In lieu of self-critique, Croce ingeniously subscribed to the liberal tradition that blames democracy for the rise of tyranny. But was not democracy the anarchistic illness that fascism was called upon to cure in the first place? Presently, democracy was portrayed as the force that *engenders* fascist tyranny, which meant that Croce could feel that his misgivings about democracy were largely vindicated. Mysteriously, silently, without a word of explanation, fascism, the erstwhile cure for democratic excess became the very disease such excess allegedly breeds. This maneuver relieved Croce of the painful need for self-introspection and the reevaluation of his role as a leading intellectual who, during the crucial period in which the fascist tyranny was gaining momentum, took a position which even an extremely sympathetic political biographer as Fabio Rizi (2003: 50) could not but describe as "critical benevolence." Equipped with the liberal theory of democracy as leading to fascism, Croce could argue that the intellectual elite, with himself obviously at its hub, could and should remain the safe guardian of liberty, protecting it from the irrationality and gullibility of the masses:

Popular education, which the liberal nineteenth century enthusiastically inaugurated, has not fulfilled the hope of making the masses politically intelligent. They have become more the prey of emotional propaganda, drawing its strength from passion and imagination; and woe to them if the propagandist slogan had been true that 'the fate of the people is in their own hands.' What the people wants is not truth but some myth which flatters their feelings, and the first and unwelcome truth they need to be taught is to distrust the demagogues who excite and intoxicate them. By what means and to what depths the last and latest of their demagogues has degraded the Italian people, we all know (Croce 1951: 90).

The fact that Croce himself had fallen prey to the fascist demagoguery, precisely at a time that its mass support was fairly limited, had no place in such later reckoning (the text was written after Mussolini's fall). Even following Matteotti's murder, Croce was very slow to disengage himself from Mussolini. Though bent on clearing Croce's somewhat dubious reputation, Rizi nevertheless admits (2003: 67) that Croce "was not about to vote against the government," and that he "believed Mussolini" and "trusted" his promise that he would from now on commit himself to the "re-establishment of freedom." But such personal complicity was later on suppressed; now it was only a matter of "the masses" who stood to be "taught to distrust the demagogues who excite and intoxicate them." Croce entertained no doubts whatsoever neither that the masses require such political education, nor that he was the indicated person to provide it. In that respect, he also presented a highly questionable depiction of popular education under 19th century liberalism. To start with, in Italy, as elsewhere, such education was hardly "enthusiastically inaugurated" by the liberals. As a less complacent historian of Italy has noted (Duggan 1994: 154), there existed "a deep ambivalence towards popular schooling among the Italian middle classes." Croce's further claim, that the aim of liberal education was to "make the masses politically intelligent," might be accepted only on the proviso that we understand that "political intelligence," on liberal-bourgeois terms, consisted in making the masses *predisposed*, rather than *resilient* to authoritarianism: "National loyalty and the ethic of work were the two main themes of popular education. One school song spoke of how the children would, when adults, 'rise up, as warrior cohorts,' to fight for the king, and 'die, fair Italy, for thee'" (155). We can easily see how a liberal education of *this* kind must have been, if anything, a contribution to fascism. Yet Croce, far from reassessing the patronizing role of the liberal elites and scrutinizing their lead, merely prescribed a larger and more concentrated dose of their political intelligence. Given that mass democracy constitutes the danger, it was only logical that the main thing to be avoided was entrusting "the fate of the people in their own hands." The solution to the chronic susceptibility of the mass was envisioned in terms of an elevated democracy, guided by adroit and responsible intellectuals:

> The only course then is to put our trust in that part of the ruling elite which is scientifically educated, which can look facts boldly in the face and be guided by them in its relations with the other parties. We must trust the class called the 'intellectuals,' as Hegel acknowledged by call-ing them the 'universal class' or 'the unclassed.'...Certainly such a class will not ruin the selfish interests of the elite, but it will make the most of their other interests which conform to the general good and will pre-vent dictatorships and tyrannies; as an aristo-democracy it will manage, by opening its ranks, to renew and rejuvenate itself constantly (Croce 1951: 90).

The case of Croce is significant in that, on the one hand, he represents the liberal *theoretician* of fascism, advancing all the core arguments of that tradition, while, in his person and activities, as a liberal *politician*, he provides a vivid *refutation* of such a theoretical compound. This gives rise to telling and somewhat amusing paradoxes. For example, in his important work, *History of Europe in The Nineteenth Century*, pub-lished in 1932, Croce, in the capacity of a liberal theoretician and critic of fascism, which he esoterically refers to under the coded, generic term of "activism," is one of the first to encapsulate the liberal interpretation of fascism in a nutshell. There is, to start with, the emphasis on mass irrationality, the "activists" looking "eagerly to the 'masses,' that is, not to the people but to the swarm—blind and impulsive or sensitive to impulses—of the mob, a cheering and howling beast that any man of audacity can move to his own ends" (Croce 1933a: 341). Secondly, Croce anticipates the liberal entwining of fascism and communism, as the joint foes of liberalism, the reverse sides of the same coin, imitating and even flowing into each other. "Communism," Croce writes (353), is "another bitter enemy of liberalism," indeed "on a par with activism, with which it is often merged." And there is, naturally, the attempt at a mythical dichotomization of fascism and liberalism, the claim that their complete antagonism forms the very heart of the political schism and provides the key to the understanding of its nature. Croce asks (342): "What was, in its innermost nature, this ideal of activism which was taking form and consistency in the soul of Europe?" and answers, like so many liberal interpreters in the years and decades to come: "above everything it fought and loathed liberalism." To support such claim, Croce further argues that liberalism was "the only element" which activism, "ready as it was to receive all other elements and to enter into every alliance, including that with Catholicism and the Church—it never received, and with which it never allied itself."

Croce should have known better, however, since he himself, as a *liberal politician*, and his Liberal Party, entered into quite concrete and irrefutable political alliances with fascism. As Rizi observes (2003: 40), with regards to the 1921 elections: "With the aim of weakening both the Socialists and the Popolari, the old leader [Giolitti] encouraged the formation of national blocs, an electoral alliance consisting of the Liberals, the Democrats, and a new protagonist in Italian politics, the Fascists." Similarly (62), in 1924, the "undeniable popularity of Mussolini... persuaded the liberal and moderate political groups to accept Mussolini's invitation to fight the next election under the same banner and to join the government list as candidates." Croce, who was a member of the Liberal Party and served as a minister under Giolitti, and who personally supported such alliances, should thus have refrained from formulating the opposition between liberalism and activism on such categorical terms. In the process, Croce also failed to do justice to the fact that the Catholic *Popolari*, in truth, were less reconciliatory towards fascism than the Liberals, and that they were the "only constitutional party that did not support the Acerbo bill," a highly important and controversial 1923 modification to the rules of government formation, that soon allowed fascism to dominate parliament (Duggan 1994: 208). As a result, and while perfectly willing to align himself with Croce and his party members, Mussolini expelled the *Popolari* from his cabinet. Nor was the later fascist settlement with the Church out of line with age-old liberal aspirations. As Christopher Duggan (226–7) observes: "The resolution of the Roman question... allowed fascism to realise the dream long harboured by the liberal state of using the Church as an instrument for securing mass political consent." But the later ideological necessities once again outweighed actual historical events in Croce's account. In addition to such concrete coalitions, Croce was well familiar with the potential and actual fusion of liberalism into fascism, personified by the choices of his close friend and colleague, Giovanni Gentile, who supported Mussolini and eventually joined the fascist party, seeing in the *Duce* the genuine interpreter of "liberalism as I understand it and as the men of the glorious right who led Italy in the Risorgimento understood it" (Gentile in a letter to Mussolini, as quoted in Hamilton 1971: 42). While Croce and Gentile soon fell apart, both politically and personally, because of this move, there was clearly no justification on Croce's part to ignore such alignments and assert the existence of a hermetic separation and a deadly hostility between fascism and liberalism. And there were numerous other indications to counter such legendary dichotomy. Rizi (2003: 52) is again useful: "in 1923 the official Liberal association of Turin became dominated by businessmen who supported fascism without any reservation."

In Croce's liberal theory there is, however, an element that will be conspicuously absent in later liberal interpretations of fascism. Whether this is to be ascribed to Croce's indisputable calibre as a thinker, or to his personal experiences, or to the fact that at that early stage the liberal ideologemes had not yet coagulated into a set of clichés, he did not simply posit liberalism and fascism as opposites. For even as he affirmed their radical enmity, Croce implicitly recognized the affinities between liberalism and fascism and, I think, went as far as pointing out their *common origin*, or at least, the roots of fascism in liberalism. This he did by portraying fascism as a demonic, exaggerated, emanation of "liberty." The "original impulse" of activism, Croce claimed (1933a: 342), "was nothing other than the principle of liberty, so intrinsic in the modern world that it is not in any way possible to do without it." Intriguingly, Croce attempted to define activism as the pursuit of liberty "deprived of its moral soul," an aimless, boundless "translation and reduction" of the ethical ideal of liberty, becoming a "mournful parody," a "substantial perversion of the love of liberty, a devil-worship taking the place of that of God, and yet still a religion, the celebration of a black mass, but still a mass. And if it hates liberalism, that is because the devil is a *simia Dei*; if it still exerts a certain attraction, it is similar to that of the fallen angel" (342). The obvious apologetic intent and the vague, idealistic language notwithstanding, these strike me as rare and profound insights, of some importance for our discussion and which we should do well to ponder, especially coming from a major liberal philosopher. We shall return to address these in the next section, dealing with the relationship between fascism and individualism.

Liberal Myth No. 2:
Collectivist Liberalism, Individualist Fascism?[9]

We are accustomed to thinking about individualism in terms of liberalism—the liberal proverbial concern for securing individual fulfillment and well-being—and pro-capitalism—the "rampant individualism" of market society. This individualism, in turn, is attacked by the enemies of the capitalist-liberal order, conservatives, fascists and socialists, who espouse a collectivist alternative, the first two in the shape of the organic community of the past, the second in that of the free association of the future. Fascist ideologues have often contributed to enhance such conceptual dichotomy, by brandishing their anti-individualism as the definitive token of their anti-liberalism. Thus, for Alfredo Rocco, the fact that fascism regards the individual as a means to a higher, state-national end, provides the categorical refutation/overcoming of the liberal legacy—exemplified by Kant—which sees in the individual the end itself. He writes:

> In that respect, the anti-thesis between the fascist conception and the liberal-democratic-socialist conception, appears—and is—absolute and total.... For liberalism (as for democracy and socialism) society does not have goals which are not those of the individuals [*singoli*] who compose it in a given moment. For fascism, society has its own aims, historical and immanent, of conservation, expansion, perfection, which are distinct from the aims of the individuals [*singoli individui*] which temporarily compose it, and which might be in conflict with the aims of the individuals (Rocco 2004: 237).

Those mainstream historians who are prepared to take fascism at its word, indeed who turn such naïveté into a methodological principle, usually buy into such claims as an integral part of the bargain, stressing this "innovative" aspect of fascism in a way which would have pleased a Rocco. "Fascist ideology," Zeev Sternhell characteristically writes (1994: 6), "expressed a revolutionary aspiration based on a rejection of individualism, whether liberal or Marxist, as it created the elements of a new and original political culture. This political culture, communal, anti-individualistic,...wished to...provide a solution to

---

[9] The discussion in this section incorporates material which firstly appeared in Landa (2008a).

the atomization of society...and the alienation of the individual in a free Market society."

An historical inquiry, however, does not warrant such simplistic and prevalent taxonomy. In truth, individualism was, from the very start—that is, from its violent eruption onto the scenes of political and ideological debate, during the French Revolution—a highly ambivalent concept, by no means identical with liberalism, still less with capitalism. On that score, as well, epistemological idealism has been the source of much confusion, and is long due to be replaced by a dialectical and historical approach. It should be realized that terms such as "individualism" or "collectivism" are, in and of themselves, devoid of political meaning, whether radical or conservative, left or right, socialist or capitalist. It is only the historical content poured into such signifiers, that lends them their concrete ideological import. Let us take, to start with, the imagery of society as a family, an intimate union between human beings, which is set against the alienation and selfishness of mere "individuals." The understanding of society as a family is habitually associated with the "anti-modern," conservative-cum-fascist response to the strife of modern society, upholding a mode of communal, harmonious existence. Fascism is hence imbued with an anti-liberal and anti-capitalist mentality, offering a kind of haven from capitalist tribulation in the bosom of quasi-familial hierarchy, dispensing mutual, if distinct, rights, duties and responsibilities. Yet the metaphor of society as a family can function to sustain *capitalism*, not the isolated individual. This in fact has been the historical origin of this image, at least as far as the conservative discourse is concerned. We can verify this by re-visiting the theories of a primogenitor of conservatism, Edmund Burke. In a constitutive conservative text, *Reflections on the Revolution in France*, Burke writes about society as a family, his descriptions replete with the rhetoric of "warmth" and "affection":

> A spirit of innovation is generally the result of a *selfish* temper, and confined views. People will not look forward to posterity, who never look backward to their ancestors. Besides, the people of England well know, that the idea of inheritance furnishes a sure principle of conservation, and a sure principle of transmission...Whatever advantages are obtained by a state proceeding on these maxims, *are locked fast as in a sort of family settlement*; grasped as in a kind of mortmain for ever....
> In this choice of inheritance we have given to our frame of polity the image of a *relation in blood*; binding up the constitution of our country with our *dearest domestick ties*; adopting our fundamental laws into the bosom of our *family affections*; keeping inseparable, and cherishing *with the warmth* of all their combined and mutually reflected charities, our

state our hearths, our sepulchres, and our altars (Burke 1826, vol. 5: 78–80; italics added).

Elsewhere, Burke underscores the idea that a conservative society, as exists in England, is embedded in *partnership*, a supra-individual bond, as opposed to the selfish chaos of individualism, championed by the radicals on the other side of the Channel:

> It is a partnership in all science; a partnership in all art; a partnership in every virtue, and in all perfection. As the ends of such a partnership cannot be obtained in many generations, it becomes a partnership not only between those who are living, but between those who are living, those who are dead, and those who are to be born. Each contract of each particular state is but a clause in the great primaeval contract of eternal society, linking the lower with the higher natures,...each in their appointed place.... The municipal corporations of that universal kingdom are not morally at liberty at their pleasure, and on their speculations of a contingent improvement, wholly to separate and tear asunder the bands of their subordinate community, and to dissolve it into an unsocial, uncivil, unconnected chaos of elementary principles (184).

We are thus all bound to each other in ties of familial obligation, warmth, affection, partnership, organic affiliation, and so on and so forth. But the whole point behind this "domestic" embedding of society is to make it a safe and habitable place *for property*, not for the ailing individual chastised by capitalist coldness. Our familial belonging, as far as Burke is concerned, is precisely that which prohibits the part from disengaging itself from the whole, the children from challenging the patriarch, the lower classes from raising against the higher ones. Individualism is all on the side of radical social egalitarianism, upsetting the family hierarchy in favor of the poor. That such a notion is explicitly opposed to the revolutionary happenings in France and Rousseau's notion of the social contract is well known. But it would be deeply mistaken to assume that Burke—talking for example about "mutually reflected charities"—is merely warning, like a good *Pater familias*, against the destruction and fratricide entailed by revolutionary upheaval and that he endorses, instead, benevolent welfare measures on the part of those family members who are more thriving. In fact, such domesticity as Burke conceived of, was meant to absolve the rich of all responsibility for the poor, and safeguard their property not only from revolution but also from any demands for social amelioration. "Warmth" in such discourse simply means that the poor should be sentimentally attached to the interests of the rich. The rich, for their part, are to proceed according to quite different, and distinctly more lukewarm, criteria. As becomes clear on reading Burke's *Thoughts and Details on Scarcity*—written in 1895, five years after the *Reflections*—familial society prefigures not the welfare state but the neoliberal one:

> [I]n my opinion, there is no way of preventing this evil...but manfully to resist the very first idea, speculative or practical, that it is within the competence of government, taken as government, or even of the rich, as rich, to supply to the poor, those necessaries which it has pleased the Divine Providence for a while to with-hold from them. We, the people, ought to be made sensible, that it is not in breaking the laws of commerce, which are the laws of nature, and consequently the laws of God, that we are to place our hope of softening the Divine displeasure to remove any calamity under which we suffer, or which hangs over us (Burke 1826, vol. 7: 404).

Family conduct is thus "warm" from the bottom upwards, but radiates cold "manliness" and sober resistance to all "softening" from the top downwards. Vis-à-vis their masters' property, and privileges, the poor are to show "affection"; vis-à-vis their servants' "calamity," the rich are to follow "the eternal laws of commerce." The patriarch, in Burke's metaphor, is conspicuously relieved of the duty of providing for his protégés. Familial imagery is thus anything but anti-capitalist.[10] The veneer of "warmth" and "affection" conceals implacable coldness; the language itself, examined closely, is quite forbidding: "*locked fast* in a sort of family settlement," "*grasped* as in a kind of mortmain *for ever*," "*subordinate* community," etc.

Interestingly, the self-proclaimed "anti-liberal" fascist, Rocco, un-wittingly restated both these aspects of Burke's theory, the positive and negative one. Positively, he made a great deal of the fascist "organic" conception, presenting it as a true transcending of the liberal horizon. His theory is supposed to be original, whereas it might in fact have

---

[10] The same ambiguity in fact characterized Burke's commitment to "tradition" in its entirety: he was a traditionalist, namely, only when faced with demands of an egalitarian nature. But to the extent that tradition was seen to stand in the way of economic liberalism, he revealed himself considerably less inclined to consult "those who are dead," or stick with reverence to "the great primaeval contract of eternal society." Thus, in his capacity as a Whig Member of Parliament, he led the liberal legislation that, in 1772, discarded age-old laws and customs that regulated markets against middlemen and profiteering in food. In the words of the historians Hay and Rogers (1997: 97): "Burke's view had become the view of Parliament...The legitimacy of many popular customs and claims, most of them rooted in ancient law and practice, came to be redefined in élite discourse as usurpation, archaic ignorance, immorality, even criminality" (see also 98, 110–11). A highly mechanical "organicism," indeed.

been copied down from Burke: "For the old, atomistic and mechanical concept of society and the state, which is the basis of the liberal, democratic, and socialistic doctrine, fascism substitutes an organic and historical conception" (Rocco 2004: 237). Quite like Burke, he emphasized (236) the bond between the living and the dead, society being "not a sum of individuals, but a succession of generations." Yet this "positive" emphasis on the social fabric transcending individuals, deterred Rocco just as little as it did Burke, his objective forerunner, from championing a "negative" economic-liberal domain, where individual enterprise and the rules of the economy must be generally adhered to and where notions of "justice" would be out of place: "to eliminate individual interest from the economic domain," Rocco the anti-liberal emphasizes (240), "is to introduce paralysis into it.... The fundamental error of socialism is to turn private property into a question of justice, whereas it is really a question of utility and social necessity."

If Burke's social theories are anything to go by, capitalism is a big family, collectivist through and through, while "rampant individualism" is strictly revolutionary. Conversely, let us not forget that metaphors of familial obligations were not current only on the conservative side of the social divide, the revolutionaries espousing a "mechanical" notion of humanity, joined together strictly on the basis of contract and interest. Far from it, the French Revolution employed quintessential familial imagery, exemplified most centrally in the notion of the brotherhood of all men, the famous *fraternité*. But *this* was a "domestic" notion wedded to egalitarianism, not capitalistic privilege and property. So the question, historically understood, should not be posed in terms of whether society was imagined along family lines, but what did such lines imply: equality or hierarchy? Exclusive property or mutual accountability? Patriarchy or brotherhood?

The same indecision that obtains with regards to the family, pervades the associated concept of individualism. One of the commonest and presumably most clear-cut indications of the fascist rejection of liberalism is its anti-individualism. Yet this becomes a highly questionable assumption upon closer examination of both fascist *and* liberal ideology and practice. We should be wary of simplifying either fascism or liberalism: instead of the outright celebration of individualism generally ascribed to the latter, and of the outright denigration of individualism ascribed to the former, I would argue that both fascism and liberalism were in fact shot through with irresolvable ambivalence in their approach to individualism. What is more, the fascist ambivalence was largely an exacerbation of the contradictions of liberalism in coming to terms with individualism.

For Burke, at a very early stage of the debate, individualism signifies a revolutionary, chaotic tidal wave, threatening to overwhelm the established order. Individualism is radical and challenges capitalism, which, in turn, is construed as organic and collectivist. But throughout the course of the 19th century a different ideologeme establishes itself as a liberal staple, to the point that it is today almost intuitively coupled with liberalism: individualism as a cherished and precious phenomenon, a delicate and rare plant, assailed by the rude and anonymous mediocrity of the collectivist "masses." For canonical liberal thinkers such as Constant, Guizot, Tocqueville or J. S. Mill, the individual becomes largely synonymous with the liberty and creativity afforded by capitalism, an individuality which thrives upon diversity, and hence *in*equality, whereas socialism envisions the grim uniformity of a leveled down society, forcefully obliterating the differences—individual ones, after all—between the talented and the indifferent, the industrious and the idle, the rich and the poor. Individual excellence pitted against mass homogeneity: the reader will be too familiar with this ideologeme to require illustration.[11] And yet, such appreciation of and concern for the individual as a thing of rarity, already contain the elusive fact that liberalism does not stand up for every individual but, even on its own terms, only for a minority of strong, successful ones. The rest are—at best—the mediocre multitude. These numerous individuals, by definition the great majority, are valuable only as building bricks, human tools that are necessary to permit great works, or, indeed, utterly useless, even counterproductive, mere obstacles standing in the path of individual greatness, the weak parasites who make economic and moral demands on the strong and weigh down their progress. It is at that point that liberal individualism is driven to a paradoxical embrace with its alleged antithesis: collectivism. Individual happiness and prosperity cannot form the true ideal of liberalism since they would logically lead to equal diffusion of individual happiness among the masses, if not directly to the preference of most individu-

---

[11] For a very instructive discussion of the move from Burkean denunciation of individualism to a liberal celebration of individual distinction, see Losurdo (2005: 195–204).

als' welfare over the triumph of the gifted minority. This means that individual accomplishment and satisfaction is only superficially and intermittently elevated as the end: in fact, it must be constantly justified by an appeal to some other, "higher," supra-individual, collective aim, say, culture, civilization, society or any other comparable notion. Take the 19th century American liberal, William Graham Sumner:

> Let it be understood that we cannot go outside this alternative: liberty, inequality, survival of the fittest; not-liberty, equality, survival of the unfittest. The former carries society forward and favors all its best members; the latter carries society downwards and favors all its worst members (as quoted in Hofstadter 1960: 51).

Notice how, surreptitiously, "society" has nudged the individual aside and appropriated the central place for itself, while the individuals must subordinate their interests, even their very right to exist, to those of this superior entity. "Society" becomes the ultimate yardstick, and it requires individual sacrifices; it expects that some, in truth many, perhaps even most individuals will *not* survive, since they are unfit. This is the paradox of *liberal collectivism* which one liberal thinker after another runs up against. Rocco (2004: 237) was possibly deluding himself and certainly his readers when ascertaining that the readiness to sacrifice the individual is a distinctive innovation of fascist doctrine, an historical breakthrough in political and social theory: "Hence the possibility, which the dominant doctrines do not conceive of, of the sacrifice, even total one, of the individual to society." In truth, he rather highlighted a conviction quite prevalent among liberals, if not necessarily Kant. For example, Pareto:

> All species of living beings would degenerate without the operation of selection. The human race cannot escape this law. Humanitarians may be able to close their eyes to this truth, deliberately ignoring it, but this can in no way alter the facts. In every race reject-elements are produced which must be eliminated by selection. The grief and suffering caused by this are the price which has to be paid for the improvement of the race. *This is one of the many cases in which the good of the individual is in opposition to the good of the species* (Pareto 1966: 159; italics added).

"The species," indeed "the race," thus unmistakably precede the individual, and in case of a conflict of interests, it is the individual who must give way. A true individualist would have said, let "the race" rot if a single one of its members has to be eliminated. The Talmudic saying, "Whoever destroys a soul, it is considered as if he destroyed an entire world. And whoever saves a life, it is considered as if he saved an entire world,"[12] expresses genuine individualism. But Pareto is not an individualist; he is a liberal. And liberal, too, is Nietzsche, albeit after his own, elegiac, fashion:

> Through Christianity, the individual was made so important, so absolute, that he could no longer be sacrificed: but the species endure only through human sacrifice—All 'souls' became equal before God: but this is precisely the most dangerous of all possible evaluations! If one regards individuals as equals one calls the species into question, one encourages a way of life that leads to the ruin of the species: Christianity is the counterprinciple to the principle of *selection*.... The species requires that the ill-constituted, weak, degenerate, perish: but it was precisely to them that Christianity turned as a conserving force (Nietzsche 1968: 142).

Or, finally, Herbert Spencer:

> The poverty of the incapable, the distresses that come upon the imprudent, the starvation of the idle, and those shoulderings aside of the weak by the strong,... are the decrees of a large, far-seeing benevolence.... It seems hard that a labourer incapacitated by sickness from competing with his stronger fellows, should have to bear the resulting privations. It seems hard that widows and orphans should be left to struggle for life or death. Nevertheless, when regarded not separately, but in connection with the interests of universal humanity, these harsh fatalities are seen to be full of the highest beneficence—the same beneficence which brings to early graves the children of diseased parents, and singles out the low-spirited, the intemperate, and the debilitated as the victims of an epidemic (Spencer 1851: 323).

The ultraist liberal, Spencer, hence takes care to regard human beings "not separately,"—i.e., as individuals—but from a collective point-of-view, that of "universal humanity," which demands and prospers upon such sacrifices. The individual in liberalism is thus *not* sanctified but, on the very contrary, dispensable and subservient: to "the economy," "the species," "society," "humanity," "life" (in Nietzsche and comparable thinkers who might be described as vitalist liberals) or, last but not least in discussing the affinity and continuities between liberalism and fascism, to "the race." Liberalism, in short, is Janus-faced when

---

[12] Jerusalem Talmud, Sanhedrin 4:8 (37a). There are two formulations of this idea in the Talmudic literature, the one just quoted and another one, that refers only to the people of Israel (Babylonian Talmud, Sanhedrin 37a). I prefer the one with universal application (indeed, the application here could not be but universal, given that the sentence is embedded in the story of Abel's murder).

addressing individualism: "the individual" will come first when confronted with *mass* society; but "society" will come first, when confronted with the demands of *mass* individuals. During the 1980s and under Margaret Thatcher's magical touch, society did an implacable disappearing act when faced by the demands of mass individuals, the poor, the homeless, the unemployed: "there is no such thing as society. There are individual men and women." But she did not in the least contradict her fellow liberals, who underscored the supremacy of the collective: she merely rehearsed the standard liberal point of view vis-à-vis the welfare state, a "society" understood as mass well-being:

> I think we've been through a period where too many people have been given to understand that if they have a problem, it's the government's job to cope with it. 'I have a problem, I'll get a grant.' 'I'm homeless, the government must house me.' They're casting their problem on society. And, you know, there is no such thing as society. There are individual men and women, and there are families.[13]

But liberal "society" does assert its existence, frequently with some vehemence, whenever mass individuals are called upon *to sacrifice*. As was vividly demonstrated when no other than Thatcher sent numerous "individuals" away from their "families" and to the remote Falklands / Malvinas islands, to fight and die for England. Was Thatcher a rampant individualist or was she a rabid collectivist? Considered idealistically, this is a nut to break one's teeth on; considered historically and materially, the answer is as simple as it is dialectical: she was neither, and both.

Fascism largely inherits this oscillation from liberalism. It vacillates irretrievably between individualism and collectivism, and for quite similar reasons to those that underpinned the liberal indeterminacy. But just as standard historiography emphasizes the pro-individualistic aspect of liberalism, marginalizing its manifold opposition to individualism, so too does it one-sidedly exaggerate the anti-individualist current in fascism, and almost completely overlooks its endorsement of individualism. The result is a skewed portrayal of liberalism as individualistic, and an equally partial account of fascism as anti-individualistic, which, combined, create the effect of a dramatic antagonism between the two political ideologies. To redress these twofold

---

[13] Prime Minister Margaret Thatcher, talking to *Woman's Own Magazine*, October 31, 1987.

misrepresentations is to acquire a balanced notion of the profound analogies between them.

The rejection of individualism by fascists has been so amply documented that a repetition of such arguments would be superfluous. Naturally, pages could be filled with examples of fascists denigrating individualism. What we do need to do, if briefly, is to show that this anti-individualism quite often echoed the liberal predicament. We have already observed above how Hitler, in rejecting individualism, did so recurrently from the point of view of the superior collective, the race, the nation, or, quite explicitly and tellingly, the demands of industry. "What would become of a factory," he asked, "which does not possess a tight organization, in which every worker comes to work when its suits him, and does only the work which entertains him. Without organization, without coercion, and so without individual sacrifices it would not function. Life is a continuous renunciation of individual liberty." Hitler, qua anti-individual, demands sacrifices, from an essentially *liberal point of view*. That he justified such measures as benefiting the supra individual entities of the German *Volk*, or the Aryan race, or the species, does not in the least contradict the liberal logic as expressed by a Spencer, a Pareto, or a Sumner, all of whom believed in the supremacy of the collective, unless it be the egalitarian mass. Hitler's language may be more blunt, the formulations whetted, but the ideas contain no heresy: "I strive towards a condition in which each individual knows: he lives and dies for the preservation of the species! The task is to teach man that he deserves the greatest admiration if he does something special to preserve the life of the species" (as quoted in Picker 2003: 111). In this and other instances, Hitler, if anything, seems to draw the liberal logic to its ultimate consequences, attempting to distill from it a system of breeding and a generalized normative pattern. Giovanni Gentile, similarly, wished to subordinate the individual to "the sound organism of a State," on the express grounds that individualism in Italy was historically aligned with *the Left*:

> The Left moved from the individual to the State; the Right from the State to the individual.... The Left made the individual the center and the basis of rights and initiatives—that any regime of liberty was required to respect and guarantee. The persons of the Right, on the other hand,...were firm and in agreement concerning the notion that one could not speak of liberty without speaking of the State (Gentile 2007: 7).

The logic of liberal collectivism is again manifest: individualism must be subordinate to collectivism since it is egalitarian, and because, by making each individual an end in itself and attributing to him inalienable rights, it rules out the imperative of individual sacrifice: "The individual has a law, a goal, through which he discovers his proper value, and for which sacrifice is necessary, with the individual forfeiting private comforts and daily interests, and, should it be necessary, his life" (5). Gentile attests to the liberal-fascist affinity not only thematically, but also personally, given that he was an important liberal recruit of Mussolini, and regarded fascism a perfected form of liberalism.

In view of this complex situation, an ideological scrutiny of liberalism cannot become truly radical if it merely promotes a "collectivist" stance to counter liberal individualism. What is actually called for is a defense of the individual *from* liberalism, an exposure of the way liberalism has uttered the name of the individual in vain. An excellent place to start doing so is to hark back to a somewhat neglected author, at least as far as anti-fascism is concerned, namely the Austro-Hungarian novelist and playwright Ödön von Horváth. I consider Horváth one of the most perceptive contemporary critics of National Socialism; Horváth early identified its menace and dealt with it incisively throughout his literary career, from *Sladek der schwarze Reichswehrmann* (1929) and *Italienische Nacht* (1930), up to the later masterpieces *Jugend ohne Gott* and *Ein Kind unserer Zeit* written in 1938, the year of his premature death. Horváth's exemplary complex of insights—psychological, moral, social and political—into the nature of National Socialism deserves a separate and detailed discussion. Here I wish merely to highlight a moment from *Ein Kind unserer Zeit* (A Child of Our Time). The novel espouses an uncompromising, do or die defense of the individual, demanding to protect her by all means necessary, no matter how ruthless: the novel's protagonist, a young man who starts the novel as a fascist soldier and ends it as a committed anti-fascist, proclaims, after his ideological conversion:

> I don't care about what should happen, I only care about what must not happen.
> It must not be, that the individual shall play no role, be it the last of salesgirls.
> And anyone who argues against that, ought to be exterminated—skin and hair! (Horváth 2001: 123).

This hero indeed eliminates the anti-individualist representative of fascism. The individual is the highest value; to sacrifice him or her is the highest evil. The vital point, however, is that such extremist individualism does not take its place, as might be expected, alongside liberalism.

On the very contrary, it identifies the enemy of the individual *in* liberalism: in the form of the highly placed businessman who had fired a dispensable worker:

> 'Please, please,' [says the businessman] 'since Miss Anna could no longer correctly perform her service we naturally had to cut her down. Do not forget that we are a big firm and consequentially bear a great responsibility.'
> 'To whom?' [asks the hero]
> 'We have around 240 people to take care of, employees, artists and the like—in that circumstances no one can ask of us to worry about each individual.'
> 'Why not?'
> 'Because the individual no longer plays a role.'
> I stare at him.
> No role?
> I said the same once—
> How stupid, how stupid!
> 'We must stay profitable,' he goes on, 'the competitive business struggle is also a war, sir, and a war as is well known cannot be won with kid gloves' (118).

Concluding this dialogue, the hero grabs the business representative of the military-industrial complex and throws him over into the ditch:

> His glasses, I picked up and threw after him. So he could see the mud better.
> Now he could see for himself, if the individual plays no role.
> I feel very good.
> For anyone who goes about saying that the individual doesn't count, should be dispatched (121).

Thus Horváth, elegantly, unceremoniously, and without dwelling on matters of political theory, cuts the Gordian knot: in the name of individualism, the liberal/fascist order is symbolically eradicated. As if in rejoinder to Nietzsche's above quoted view that equality of souls before God is "the most dangerous of all possible evaluations!" since being the "counterprinciple to the principle of *selection*," Horváth appeals precisely to the Christian standard, to a God that cares for each and everyone, to offset the unholy alliance between Nazism and liberalism, as an early dialogue, between a still fascist protagonist and a nurse, shows:

'God knows everything, listens to everything and leaves no individual out of sight, day and night, since He has plans for everyone.'
'For every single individual?'
She stares at me widely:
'Naturally,' she says (46).[14]

Liberal Individualism against Mass Democracy

This is fascism as anti-individualistic: a familiar trope, examined from a somewhat different angle. But Fascism, as we maintained, also inherited from liberalism a celebration of the individual's value, an aspect that standard historiography virtually suppresses. And on the face of it, rightly so, for how could one possibly tie together, for instance, the Nazi project of "the people's community," with the cherished liberal value of individualism? To imagine, however, that the *Volksgemeinschaft* was an expression of the anonymous collective, may have some justification from an abstract and philosophical point of view, but it would mean to work in a timeless vacuum, ignoring the concrete and historical significance of the project. *Historically understood*, the *Volksgemeinschaft* meant in no small measure the effort to *preserve individualism* vis-à-vis the perceived anonymity and leveling down of mass society, a social constellation devised to save the threatened genius from the masses.

Here we should be very discerning when approaching the "antiliberal" effusion of fascist rhetoric: liberalism—understood above all as *political democracy*—was denigrated not so much because it privileged the individual at the expense of the collective, but because it ostensibly meant the collectivist *elimination of* the individual. The individualistic critique of democracy was one of the most fundamental and commonplace features of Nazi ideology. The critique of democracy as mediocrity was no expression of Teutonic backwardness but quite

---

[14] To find Horváth protecting the individual *from* liberalism is no 20th century innovation. Already during the 17th century, as C. B. Macpherson pointed out, support for individual rights came not from the constitutive liberal, John Locke, but rather from the Levellers, who might be seen in some respects as proto-socialists: "Locke's constitutionalism [was] a defense of the rights of expanding property rather than of the rights of the individual against the state. That this is the real meaning of Locke's constitutionalism is suggested by the significant fact that Locke did not think it desirable (whereas the Levellers in the *Agreement of the People* had thought it essential) to reserve some rights to the individual as against any parliament or government. No individual rights are directly protected in Locke's state" (Macpherson 1964: 257).

integral to liberal thought proper, which, as early as John Stuart Mill, found itself brooding over the dangers presented by political liberalism to economic liberalism. Majority decisions, favoring the masses, were seen as inveighing upon the rights and restricting the creativity of the enterprising individual. And at least on that score, *on analyzing the basic problem*, we should not be shocked (or maybe we should?) to find Mill and Hitler expressing quite interchangeable views. Innovative individuals, Mill tells us (1905: 120), are "the salt of the earth; without them, human life would become a stagnant pool. Not only is it they who introduce good things which did not before exist; it is they who keep up life in those which already existed." And the future *Führer*, for his part, "agrees" in *Mein Kampf*: "Thus all inventions are the result of the creative ability of some person. All these persons themselves, whether willingly or unwillingly, are more or less great benefactors to all men. Later on their activity gives to millions, even billions of human beings aids for alleviating the execution of their struggle for life" (Hitler 1941: 664). The problem, however, for Mill (1905: 123), is that the unthankful many join to limit the scope of action of their handful of benefactors: "Persons of genius, it is true, are, and are always likely to be, a small minority; but in order to have them, it is necessary to preserve the soil in which they grow... [T]he general tendency of things throughout the world is to render mediocrity the ascendant power among mankind... The only power deserving the name is that of masses, and of governments while they make themselves the organ of the tendencies and instincts of the masses." Hitler, on that point too, displays concord and goes on to recommend a remedy, in the form of the *völkische Staat*:

> The folkish State has to care for the welfare of its citizens by acknowledging the significance of the value of the person in all and everything and thus introducing in all domains that highest degree of productive efficiency which grants the individual also the highest degree of participation.
> The folkish State, therefore, has to free the entire leadership especially the highest, that means the political leadership from the parliamentary principle of the decision by majority, that means decision by the masses, in order to establish firmly in its place the right of the person (Hitler 1941: 669).

The fascist elimination of political liberalism is thus envisaged as a measure taken in programmatic defense of the individual. That Mill would have vehemently rejected such a "solution" cannot be doubted, yet the common predicament facing both the lofty liberal and the frightful fascist is likewise obvious (I have argued above, that Mill eventually indicated a way out of the liberal impasse by contemplating disposing of capitalism altogether, a move which for Hitler was clearly out of the question). Nor is Hitler's paradoxical concept to be dismissed, as is often done, as a piece of sophistry produced by the alleged *Halbbildung*, vulgarity and other idiosyncrasies of a backward, provincial mind. It rather represented, and herein lies its true historical significance, a staple of "respectable" anti-democratic thinking, developed by some of the most erudite and sophisticated European intellectuals. The abolition of majority decision was presented conventionally as a measure taken to promote, not undermine, the individual initiative in politics and the individual's power to decide. Democracy, it was said, was a form of politics shunning individual responsibility by shifting it onto the others, or, in Heidegger's jargon, onto *das Man*—as explained in *Being and Time*:

> The 'they' is everywhere present, but in such a way, that it always sneaks away whenever Dasein presses for a decision. Yet because the 'they' pretends to judge and to decide everything, it takes the responsibility away from the particular Dasein. The 'they' manages, as it were, to have 'them' always invoking it. It can account for everything most easily, since it is nobody who needs to answer for anything. It was always the 'they' and yet it can be said that it was 'nobody' (Heidegger 1967: 127).[15]

Or, as another existentialist friend of the individual and foe of the mass, Karl Jaspers, claimed (1999: 51), democracy signifies the elimination of true leadership and accountability. It brings forward many occasional *Führers*, in the plural, doing, as it were, part-time jobs, but not a singular, commanding *Führer*: "The man is seldom found who truly assumes responsibility. The multitude of incidental leaders are accustomed not to take decisions on their own. Appeals, controls, committee-resolutions—everyone passes responsibility on to the next person. In the background ultimately stands the authority of the people as the mass, which appears to take decisions through elections." And who is a leader worthy of the name if not a *single* individual? As Luigi Pirandello—a supporter of Italian fascism—puts it, via one of his characters:

---

[15] Heidegger is notoriously difficult to translate, and yet I was unsatisfied with available English translations of this particular passage.

> But do you know what is the real cause of our ills, of this our affliction? Democracy, my dear, democracy, that is the rule of the majority. Since when power is in the hands of one alone, this one knows that he is one and that he must satisfy many; but when the many govern, and think only of satisfying themselves, then we have the most stupid and hideous tyranny of all: tyranny masquerading as liberty (Pirandello 1993: 146).

All different ways of saying the same thing. So Hitler and other fascist dictators merely stepped in to execute what wide sections of their countries' elites felt was necessary, in the process contributing their own formulations of the guiding idea, hardly more crude or less logical:

> First and most of all that which gave me food for thought was the visible lack of responsibility on the part of any single individual. Parliament makes a decision the consequences of which may be ever so devastating—nobody is responsible for it, nobody can ever be called to account.... Is it at all possible to make a wavering majority of people ever responsible? Is not the very idea of all responsibility closely connected with the individual? (Hitler 1941: 100–101)

And from this, Hitler draws the practical consequences:

> The state must be built...upon the principle of personality. There must be no decisions by majority, but only responsible persons, and the word 'council' is once more reduced to its original meaning. At every man's side there stand councilors, indeed, but *one man decides*.... Even then one will not be able to do without those corporations which today we call parliaments. Their councilors will then actually give counsel, but responsibility can and must be borne always only by *one* man and thus he alone can and must have the authority and right of command (669–70).

Personality was therefore a hallowed tenet for most fascists, even if they did not understand it in terms of an isolated, abstract individual, a mere number rushing herd-like to the ballots. Liberalism was consistently attacked in the name of *genuine individualism*; democracy meant precisely the loss of individuality, becoming one of the "voting cattle," as Nietzsche contemptuously put it.[16] Those who waved the banner of the individual against the masses thus found their way almost naturally into the anti-democratic, authoritarian camp, and

---

[16] Across the Atlantic, interchangeable voices could be heard: "In the democratic forms of government," maintained the early 20th century, American social Darwinist, Madison Grant (1936: 5), "the operation of universal suffrage tends toward the selection of the average man for public office rather than the man qualified by birth, education and integrity....The tendency in a democracy is toward a standardization of type and a diminution of the influence of genius."

quite often into the fascist one. Take the case of Alfred Baeumler, one of the leading philosophers in the Nazi state. Writing in 1927, Baeumler appeals to Kierkegaard and Nietzsche in order to criticize democracy as a manifestation of *pseudo*-individualism, where the personality is in truth absorbed into the collective, forfeiting all self-assertion and resolution. Interestingly, this is done in explicit taking-of-distance from the *Gemeinschaft*-idea:

> This is what Kierkegaard's critique of liberalism addresses: modern man argues, that is, he thinks and speaks anonymously, albeit with his name underneath. The entire age becomes a committee. One sets the principle of the 'community' on the throne, and expects it to provide deliverance.... The community-ideal functions in our times negatively, it is an excuse, a diversion: it ostensibly strengthens the individual through the grouping, but it weakens man ethically... Here sounds [Nietzsche's] saying that might have been Kierkegaard's: public opinions equal private idleness. [The treatise[17]] begins with the sentence, that each human is a unique wonder, and is one big protest against the leveling-down of modern man...(Baeumler 1937: 93–94).

Baeumler, importantly, goes on to clarify what distinguishes a genuine, positive *Gemeinschaft* from a fake one: namely, that the former must find its sustenance in *individualism*. The *Gemeinschaft* as a conglomerate of mere numbers, *a mass*, ought therefore absolutely not to be confused with its projected opposite, the *Volksgemeinschaft*, a meaningful, genuine bond between individuals: "'Only when the separate individual has gained an ethical position in spite of the entire world, will it be possible to speak about a true coming together...' Kierkegaard saw his historic mission in re-discovering the category 'the individual,' and imprinting it on the age" (93). This crucial Nazi distinction between a fake community of numbers and quantity and the genuine item based on quality was continuously emphasized by Heidegger in his most overtly Nazi texts. Contrary to what many scholars claim, Heidegger in his Nazi "phase" never simply dispensed with the value of the individual, which he had upheld in his earlier, pre-political, phase. Far from it, he was at pains to underscore the abiding importance of the individual as the precondition for the *Volksgemeinschaft*:

> 'We!'—so speaks some anonymous crowd as well. 'We!'—so too shouts some rebelling mass, so too boasts the bowling club. 'We!'—so too

---

[17] Baeumler refers to Nietzsche's *Schopenhauer as Educator*.

conspires a gang of bandits...The 'we,'...even in the sense of the genuine community, does not simply and unconditionally take pre-cedence...There are things that are essential and decisive for a com-munity, and precisely these things arise not in the community, but in the self-controlled force and solitude of an individual (Heidegger 1998: 51–52).

National Socialism is thus for Heidegger, just as it was for Baeumler, not an elimination of individual independency and authenticity but its *ultimate expression*:

> We are *authentically* ourselves only when deciding, which we do each one on his own. It appears as if only thereafter the individuals are pressed together in numbers. But it is not so.... When deciding, each one is *so* separated from the others as it is at all possible to be sepa-rated.... Friendship grows only out of the utmost inner independence of each individual, which is certainly something quite different from ego-ism (58–59).

So when an apologetic interpreter, seeking to disentangle Heidegger's philosophy from fascist thought, argues that his "descriptions of Dasein—especially the descriptions of the relationship between Dasein and its community—are actually more consistent with liberal views of the self than with communitarian interpretations," he unwittingly characterizes not some redeeming feature, uniquely Heideggerian, but a commonplace of Nazism (Salem-Wiseman 2003: 533–557). That Nazi "collectivism" is quite compatible with an ardent defense, at least a rhetorical one, of the individual, is true not only of the—arguably less representative—philosophies of Heidegger or Baeumler, but even of the biological race theories of someone like Hans F. K. Günther (1929: 302), one of the most popular and influential race "experts" of the Third Reich. Günther could thus highlight the personality inherent in certain, superior, races, threatened by mass society: "The industrial era now allowed even men of decidedly inferior hereditary capacity to increase. Large scale industry could find a use primarily for people to whom the proud individuality of the Nordic human being was alien, for people to whom life in the mass was not spiritually repulsive, or was even congenial."[18] Finally, two typical examples from the literature

---

[18] Nor are Günther's notions any exception within the tradition of "Anglo-Saxon" racism. However counter-intuitively, this tradition was in general wedded to a staunch defense of individualism. The Aryans, as far back as Gobineau, were celebrated as lib-eral and individualistic (cf. Losurdo 2005: 268). And for Madison Grant (1936: 228),

of the *Freikorps*: "One more time can each one of you be an individual, and not confine his soul. But already the mass is coming, to overwhelm us from east and west...At an end is knightly soldiery, at an end the span of earthly space, at an end the boundlessness of individual spirit" (Dwinger 1935: 436). And Hans Zöberlein (1940: 20–21), the SA combatant and future leader of a *Werwolf* unit, derides popular democracy in the name of the outstanding individual, under siege: "From now on the people govern themselves! So says every political buffoon...There are no more distinctions, all human beings are equal, all are now brothers. No one may keep himself apart, or he will be slain."

Protecting the Individuality... of the Nation

In this light we should also understand the fierce Nazi polemic against Descartes. Emmanuel Faye (2005: 27–33) is right to claim that Heidegger never really delivered the systematic philosophical refutation of the *cogito* as he promised to do in *Being and Time*, but he is misguided in taking this to mean a straightforward negation of the individual. Rather, what such philosophers as Baeumler or Heidegger did, was to play out the individual of such proto-existentialists as Kierkegaard and Nietzsche—a passionate, one of its kind, concrete being—against the universalistic, cold, disembodied, abstractly rational being they ascribed to Descartes.[19] Nazism, for them, signified a

---

the aristocratic "Nordic race" differs from the "democratic," "Eastern and Asiatic" Alpine one, in that it is "domineering, individualistic, self-reliant and jealous of their personal freedom." Grant (12) also anticipated the fascist attempt to shelter individualism from egalitarian democracy: "Associated with this advance of democracy and the transfer of power from the higher to the lower races, from the intellectual to the plebeian class, we find the spread of socialism and the recrudescence of obsolete religious forms. Although these phenomena appear to be contradictory, they are in reality closely related since both represent reactions from the intense individualism which a century ago was eminently characteristic of Americans." Worthy of citation is also the view expressed in the British journal *Jewry ueber Alles*, published form 1919 to 1925 by the far-right group The Britons: "with Jewry the tribe is the unit, with White people every adult is a responsible individual; a Jew is not an individual—he is only a bit of his tribe" (Pearlman 2004: 241).

[19] Faye's account would be more appropriate with regards to another Nazi critic of Descartes, Franz Böhm, who was less emphatic about individual value, instead advocating in a more "conservative" fashion the German recuperation of medieval communal integrity as opposed to the French celebration of individualistic modernity. See, for example, his article 'Ewiger Cartesianismus?' in the Nazi organ *Volk im Werden* (Böhm 1937).

higher form of individualism, *alive and authentic*, not *dead and fake*. It is in that sense that nationalism, indeed a militant and aggressive one, was seen as the proper political *expression of individualism* as opposed to pacifistic democracy. The unique, irreducible, passionate individual can only be maimed and mutilated within the mechanistic framework of a universalistic, timeless doctrine, turning the individual into an abstract phantom. *Nationalism* was the union *of individuals* asserting their right to themselves, rebelling against the dictates of universal uniformity. In agreement with the doctrines of Stirner and Nietzsche, a self-respecting individual is anything but a peaceful, law-abiding and norm-cherishing person. Democracy and universal morality are the chastity belt, which the genuine individual casts off with disgust.

Nietzsche is often invoked, in the wake of Walter Kaufmann's post-Second-World-War works, as the positive, individualistic, counter-example to fascist/Nazi nationalism, as typically embodied by the wayward apprentice, Heidegger: "Nietzsche appropriated Greek values in the spirit of individual autonomy and self-overcoming, Heidegger did so in the name of the community and of the *Volk*" (Bambach 2003: 74). But was Nietzsche careful to imply that this right for self expression is *only individual* and ceases to apply when it comes to the nation? Not at all, for he too asserted the inalienable right of *national* self-assertion. In *The Will to Power*, for example:

> At least a people might just as well designate as a right its need to conquer, its lust for power, whether by means of arms or by trade, commerce and colonization—the right to grow, perhaps. A society that definitely and *instinctively* gives up war and conquest is in decline: it is ripe for democracy and the rule of shopkeepers (Nietzsche 1968: 386).[20]

---

[20] The alleged difference between Nietzsche, the "good European" and liberal, and Heidegger, the mythic German and fascist, is very superficial. "Nietzsche," Bambach argues (2003: 80), "rejects German nationalism and racism and affirms instead the solitary existence of one who, like Zarathustra, lives on mountains, apart from the mass." Yet was not Nietzsche, too, keenly interested in reaching the masses? Zarathustra may start on the lofty mountains of proud individualism, but he by no means *remains* there: he immediately descends and mingles with humanity, and it is surely no coincidence that he first goes to the marketplace to proclaim the *Übermensch*! "A book for none and all," is a paradox that reveals much about the strange predicament of Nietzsche and other self-styled "aristocrats," such as Jünger or Spengler, stuck between the need to exclude/banish the masses and the need to include/contain them. For an excellent discussion of Nietzsche's attitude to Germany, which was far less prohibitive than conventionally assumed, see Losurdo (2004: 818, 843).

Stefan Zweig usefully conceptualizes the linkage between the alleged antitheses, individualism and nationalism. Writing in 1925, Zweig shows how nationalism can be an expression of individualism in an epoch of relentless mass—or, in Heideggerian terms, *das Man*—rule (including a quasi Heideggerian emphasis on Europe as the modern Greece, which must repel the levelling tides which come from both America and the USSR):

> The *individual* customs of *the peoples* keep wearing away, the costumes become uniform, the manners international.... It already becomes more difficult to count the peculiarities of the nations and the cultures than that which they have in common. *Consequences*: the end of all individuality, even in outward appearance...Unconsciously, an identity of souls is formed, a mass-soul...Europe still remains the *last bulwark of individualism* and possibly the wild spasm of the peoples, *that inflated nationalism*, despite all its violence, is to an extent a feverish, unconscious rebellion, a last desperate attempt, to resist the leveling down.... But the genius of sobriety is already at work to erase Europe, the last Greece of history, from the annals of time (I quote from several places from Zweig [1990]; emphases added, except for the word "consequences").

For Zweig, the only possible remedy was similar to the one that Heidegger would prescribe about two years later, in *Being and Time*: "Flight, flight into ourselves. One cannot save what is individual in the world, one can only defend the individual within oneself" (38). Unlike the Heideggers and the Bauemlers, Zweig would never embrace the solution of the *individual Volksgemeinschaft*, an option, it has to be said, which was barred to him in any event, and a project of which he eventually became just one of *a mass* of victims, sharing a *mass-soul* in a way he had never imagined possible. In that respect, the closing pages of *The World of Yesterday*, in which Zweig, the desolate exile, contemplates his defeat at the hands of a few world politicians, disclose a startling and deeply moving change of perspective as compared with the aloof contempt at the uncultured multitude from *The Monotonization of the World*. Formerly a proud member of an elite, feeling himself victimized by the masses, Zweig (1947: 323) now becomes a particle of the masses, terrorized by the elite: "My destiny lay in their hands, no longer in mine. They destroyed or spared us helpless ones, they permitted freedom or compelled slavery, and for millions they determined peace or war. And there in my room I sat like everybody else, defenceless as a fly, helpless as a snail, while life and death, my innermost ego, and my future were at stake."

The Führerprinzip *or Self-Glorification?*

Yet what about the cult of the leader? Surely, this was the unsurpassable negation of the liberal concept of the individual, the slav-
ish self-effacement before authority? Not quite; here, too, fascism and
liberalism are far less antagonistic than commonly presumed. The
worship of the fascist leader ought to be understood in some fundamental sense as the projected vindication of the individual amidst the
anonymity of modernity, the heroic triumph of the great man, "the
genius," dear to classical liberalism. By conveying absolute powers
on him, the idea was not to abolish one's selfhood, to melt into the
collective, nor to "escape from freedom." The leader was, rather, the
fetishized form of individualism, the re-entrance of the great man into
history. As Heidegger claims (1998: 85): "And yet the birth-hour of
Albrecht Dürer and the death-hour of Friedrich the Great are history.
When a dog perishes or a cat has a litter of kittens this is no history,
unless an old aunt makes a story of it."[21] Or, in a very unambiguous
formulation (83): "How is it with the revolutions of the propeller? It
may turn for days—nothing genuinely happens. But certainly, when
the plane takes the *Führer* from Munich to Mussolini in Venice, then
history occurs." This fetishization of the individual explains much
about the common fantasy of using the *Führer* as a proxy to express
one's own individuality. The *Führer/Duce* were perceived as means of
self-expression. Hence the tragicomic misunderstandings that arose
once the leader had failed to meet the expectations. The *herd* should
indeed be tamed, but naturally these people hardly regarded *themselves* as docilely marching amidst the sheep. Hence Heidegger, who
saw himself as the philosopher-king of the new Reich, the one "leading the leader" [*den Führer führen*] later complained to Ernst Jünger
that Hitler had let him down and hence owed him an apology.[22] And
D'Annunzio, under pressure from Mussolini's regime to toe the line,
magnanimously asserted: "From the day of my birth I alone have been
my leader...It is you who must rid yourself of supporters who are leading you astray" (Quoted in Hamilton 1971: 48). And Spengler (1961:
186), shortly before distancing himself from National Socialism, complained about the petty rebelliousness of his fellow writers: "Political

---

[21] In German, the word for "history" and "story" is the same (*Geschichte*), which
facilitates Heidegger's pun.
[22] See Wolin (2003: 181).

dilettantism talked large. Everyone instructed his future dictator what he ought to want. Everyone demanded discipline from the others, because he himself was incapable of discipline." Such authors never seriously contemplated an abolition of selfhood. They rather imagined the leader as an ally, a patron of culture, philosophy and the arts, shielding them from the barbarian masses. In the succinct words of Pirandello: "There must be a Caesar and an Octavian for there to be a Virgil" (Quoted in Hamilton 1971: 45).

The fascist cult of the leader is significant historically not as an antithesis of liberal individualism, but in revealing its latent truth, the paradoxical fact that liberal individualism is *exclusive*; it mysteriously tends to be absorbed into purportedly special, unique human beings, leaving untouched the great majority. "Individuality," "creativity," "liberty," "genius" etc., are not for everyone. As Mill himself declared (1905: 121): "Persons of genius are, *ex vi termini, more* individual than any other people." And John Carey (1992: 201), reflecting on the prejudices of the British intelligentsia at the turn of the 19th century, hits the nail of liberal individualism on its head: "an uneasy situation emerges, in which some human beings are individuals, but most are not." Liberal individualism was not a common feature but by definition a luxury article, reserved for the few.[23] Hence the fascist leader is not to be seen as an elimination of the liberal individual by the hands of the vengeful collective, but as "the individual" canalized appropriately into a single, overshadowing individual. As another illustrious sympathizer of fascism, W. B. Yeats, had told a confidante, Mussolini "represented the rise of the individual man as against...the anti-human party machine" (in Foster 2005: 468). A view to which Yeats' biographer, successfully interpellated by the liberal, commonsense rendition of history, adds the apologetic caveat, that Yeats admired fascism "in terms which might not be immediately recognizable nowadays," given that a view of Mussolini as a vindication of the individual and not the party "seems, in retrospect, to have interpreted the movement exactly

---

[23] A paradox that can be traced back to the very origins of liberalism, in 17th-century England. Consider Locke's contradictory stance, as summarized by C. B. Macpherson (1964: 261–2): "full individuality for some was produced by consuming the individuality of others.... [T]he individuality [Locke] championed was at the same time a denial of individuality.... The greatness of seventeenth-century liberalism was its assertion of the free rational individual as the criterion of the good society; its tragedy was that this very assertion was necessarily a denial of individualism to half the nation."

the wrong way around" (Foster 468). That these terms are no longer recognizable today has a lot to do with the liberal historiographic
hegemony, and vouches for the success of the *Verfremdungseffekt* it has
been consistently employing. Yeats, however, was hardly "wrong"; it is
we, "nowadays," who have largely *unlearned* the true nature of fascism.
To re-learn a dialectical insight into its nature, we can welcome some
help from an unexpected quarter: the theories of Benedetto Croce.
As I earlier remarked, while laying emphatic stress on the enmity and
incompatibility between "activism" (a generic term Croce employs for
modern and hyper-modern reactionary phenomena, indeed "reactionary modernism" before the term was coined, the core of which is patently
fascism) and liberalism, Croce nonetheless admitted their common
root, suggesting that activism effectively springs from liberalism:

> What was, in its innermost nature, this ideal of activism which was tak-
> ing form and consistency in the soul of Europe? Notwithstanding that
> above everything it fought and loathed liberalism,... notwithstanding
> this, and indeed because of this, its original impulse was nothing other
> than the principle of liberty, so intrinsic in the modern world that it is
> not in any way possible to do without it (Croce 1933a: 342).

Having established this historical context—forcefully underscoring
the objective affinity between liberalism and fascism, indeed the relationship of paternity between them—Croce fervently insists on the
fundamental perversion of liberalism at the hands of its demonic off-
spring. Liberalism is attributed a moral core, whereas its emanation
is amoral, depriving "liberty...of its moral soul," extracting it "from
its venerable tradition," and leaving nothing "but action for action's
sake, innovation for the sake of innovation, and fighting for the fight's
sake," the "upshot" being "activism." Croce eagerly calls attention to
the unbridgeable distance between liberalism and activism and is at
pains to assert their relentless antagonism. But it is doubtful whether
he did enough to demonstrate that the heart of liberalism, i.e., capitalism, truly has a moral soul, and that the imperative of accumulation
for accumulation's sake, the overriding drive to extract profit is, in
any sense, less blind, self-sufficient and "activist" than the belligerent,
spasmodic eruptions of fascism. Be that as it may, his own words are
surely as damning of liberalism as anything we might add. Fascism, he
for all purposes concedes, is liberalism gone wild, fascist individualism
taking the liberal principles to their extreme limits:

That this deviation of the impetus towards liberty leads to or tends to the opposite of liberty, and to modes of reaction, *lies entirely within the logic of its procedure*, for it leads to the *domination of the individual over individuals*, to the enslavement of others and therefore of itself, *to the depression of personality*, which in the beginning it had *fooled itself into thinking it might potentiate*, whereas by unbridling it and depriving it of moral consciousness, it deprives it of its inner life and sends it along the path to perdition (343; emphases added).

Croce's vision is as acute as it is pessimistic: activism perverts liberalism, but at the same time liberalism leads seemingly ineluctably to activism. At bottom, Croce fails to indicate a way out of this modern aporia: he suggests reverting to the premise, to the pursuit of liberty when it still allegedly possessed a moral soul. And yet, by his own account, this is precisely the starting point where activism/fascism had begun its pernicious march.

CHAPTER SIX

LIBERALISM AND FASCISM BETWEEN
MYTHS AND REALITY—II

Liberal Myth No. 3:
The Origins of the Fascist "Big Lie": Totalitarian or Liberal?[1]

One of the most striking, as well as most unsavory, features of fascism was what Hitler famously referred to in *Mein Kampf* as *"die große Lüge,"* the "big lie." Namely, the fascist radical "instrumentalization of truth" (Paxton 2004: 18), its recourse to unbounded propaganda and mass manipulation, personified by the quintessential, at any rate most pernicious, spin doctor of all times, Dr. Joseph Goebbels. Yet this is no fascist invention. Here, as in other respects, the fascists took to the extreme pre-existing developments. During the troubled 20th century, it became habitual in the West to distinguish between totalitarian societies, whether of the right or the left, and liberal-democratic ones. The former were characterized by Hannah Arendt as signifying the thorough subordination of *truth* to *politics* through the systematic exploitation of propaganda,[2] whereas the latter were characterized, to use Karl Popper's well-known definition in its broadest sense, as "open societies," in two main regards: firstly, a discursive, scientific one: liberal societies are sustained by free, pluralistic circulation of knowledge, excluding any monopoly on truth and, through reasoned discussion, arriving at approximations of the truth, thus facilitating the progress of science and knowledge. This discursive "openness" implies a second, political dimension: liberal societies presuppose the democratic control of the voters over politics, which, in turn, presupposes transparency. While such seamless coupling of liberalism and the liberal frame of mind with openness, transparency, and the unhindered pursuit of truth is doubtlessly politically serviceable, it ignores the fact that liberal society, in its own way, poses serious obstacles to a genuinely free and transparent discussion, and not simply because liberal principles and

---

[1] This section incorporates material which firstly appeared in Landa (2008b).
[2] This was the argument advanced in her "Truth and Politics" (Arendt 1993).

procedures are not always followed to the letter. In addition to such deviations, we need to be cognizant of the structural confines of the liberal discourse itself that, precisely *because* it is liberal, sets limits to a truly open society.

King Demos and his Enemies

In historical perspective, the crucial structural limit was none other than the entry of the masses into political life, indeed the formation of a modern, mass society. Those laying their hopes on the triumph of the masses felt that laying their cards on the table was both inevitable as well as desirable. Communism, for instance, as long as it remained an oppositional force, celebrated discursive openness, a message pithily and defiantly conveyed in the following lines from *The Communist Manifesto*: "The Communists disdain to conceal their views and aims. They openly declare that their ends can be attained only by the forcible overthrow of all existing social conditions" (Engels and Marx 2005: 89). Yet for the social and political eite who stood to lose from the advances in mass power, an elite which at that stage—the post 1848 era—was in most West European countries strongly if not predominantly liberal, there was much to "conceal." The need to deceive the masses and sell them, at best, half-truths formed a formidable obstacle to any genuinely open discussion and uninhibited circulation of knowledge. This is a rocky conundrum, into which had bumped all major liberal thinkers. Thus, some of the most celebrated representatives of 19th century liberalism, such as J. S. Mill and Alexis de Tocqueville, have advanced the notion of the "tyranny of the majority," to conceptualize the dangers to freedom and individuality posed by democratic societies. Today, as was analyzed above, it has become commonplace to interpret these caveats essentially as prophetic warnings against the hazards of fascism: the possibility that democracy, on account of the sentimentality, fickleness and irresponsibility of the mass voters, will degenerate and fall into the hands of demagogues, etc. But for people like Mill or Tocqueville, the danger of the majority was not some future one, awaiting democracy, but something they already detected *in the present*, something inseparable from the way democracy functions. In such accounts, democracy is not—or is not simply—a potential prelude to a tyranny, it is *already* tyrannical. This is particularly so in a democracy in which the masses are allowed to dominate thanks to their greater number. The point is not simply that such masses might choose to abandon democracy and opt for a tyrant instead. Rather, the masses in themselves *constitute such a tyrant*, if a collective one. In the words of Mill:

> [T]he general tendency of things throughout the world is to render mediocrity the ascendant power among mankind. In ancient history, in the middle ages, and in a diminishing degree through the long transition from feudality to the present time, the individual was a power in himself; and if he had either great talents or a high social position, he was a considerable power. At present individuals are lost in the crowd. In politics it is almost a triviality to say that public opinion now rules the world. The only power deserving the name is that of masses, and of governments while they make themselves the organ of the tendencies and instincts of masses.... No government by a democracy or a numerous aristocracy, either in its political acts or in the opinions, qualities, and tone of mind which it fosters, ever did or could rise above mediocrity, except in so far as the sovereign Many have let themselves be guided (which in their best times they always have done) by the counsels and influence of a more highly gifted and instructed One or Few (Mill 1905: 123–4).

Notice the fact that, for Mill, modernity does not signify an advance of liberty and individualism, which nonetheless harbours certain pitfalls. On the contrary, democratic modernity—precisely inasmuch as it is massified signifies a *retrogression*. It is decidedly *less* individualistic, and, we might add, *less* open—as concerns its narrowing of intellectual horizons and the chronic mediocrity of the "tone of mind" it imposes—than preceding political systems.[3] This opinion again reflects the historical fact that classical liberalism and democracy were anything but an harmonious unit, that liberals for the most part doggedly resisted the expansion of democracy to the masses, and insisted on limited, *propertied* democracy, so to speak. The growing pressure from the masses, precisely qua democratic, was seen as endangering freedom in both a cultural sense, given that such masses were less educated (hence Mill, for one, wished to create a democracy in which the educated are awarded multiple votes) and economically, given that now the masses could impose severe restrictions on the entrepreneurial freedom of their employers, by way of regulating labor conditions, as well as redistribute wealth by way of progressive taxation. Democracy

---

[3] Cf. Losurdo (2005: 201).

is thus, according to classical liberal notions, by no means an open society in any sweeping sense.

Since democracy is a tyranny of sorts, it follows that it must be resisted. King Demos, just like any other repressive ruler, must face the challenge of his subordinates, or more precisely his superiors, since democracy, unlike most of its despotic predecessors, is conceived of as a tyranny *from below*. The *non plus ultra* form of such challenge will be a violent coup d'état by the oppressed minority. The fascist dictatorships of the 20th century, as well as comparable military coups, signified for their supporters in no small measure precisely a return to classical liberalism, a violent expulsion of the intruding Demos from its usurped political, economical and cultural strongholds. In the words of Antonio Salandra, the erstwhile liberal premier of Italy who later lent his support to Mussolini and who defined himself as an "old liberal of the Right": "I believe that liberalism in Italy would be eliminated by democracy, since liberalism and democracy are different if not altogether contrasting, as long as democracy is dominated by socialism" (quoted in Losurdo 1994: 39). But other, more sophisticated and less openly violent methods of fighting the tyranny of the majority were also brought into use (and not even fascism, of course, was simply a reliance on brute force). J. S. Mill, despite his profound misgivings about democracy, explicitly rejected the legitimacy of an elite or a "strong man" "forcibly seizing on the government of the world and making it do his bidding in spite of itself" (Mill 1905: 125). The ideal would be a situation in which "the sovereign Many" recognize the superior wisdom of the few or the one and therefore voluntarily submit themselves to their tutelage:

> The initiation of all wise or noble things, comes and must come from individuals; generally at first from some one individual. The honour and glory of the average man is that he is capable of following that initiative; that he can respond internally to wise and noble things, and be led to them with his eyes open (124–5).

But what happens when "the average man" is not so well-advised? As was the case in earlier anti-despotic campaigns, the opponents of mass democracy were obliged to devise methods in order to disseminate protest behind the ruler's back as well as to attempt to persuade them to do the elites bidding *in spite of themselves*. If not with their "eyes open," the masses should at least be lead with their *eyes shut*. Or, in what would probably be the winning combination, with their *eyes wide shut*. This is the historical precondition for the modern employment of techniques of mass suggestion as well as for the no less distinctly modern revival of esotericism.

Esotericism, Old and New

The writings of the German-American political scientist Leo Strauss are very instructive in that regard. In a series of influential works, beginning with *Persecution and the Art of Writing* (1952), Strauss focused his attention on great thinkers such as Plato, Al Farabi, Maimonides and Machiavelli, all of whom appealed to strategies of dissimulation in order to avoid censorship and persecution: they developed a discursive mode that included an exoteric message, one that flattered the powers that be, alongside an esoteric, cryptic message, that was critical and subversive. In that way, they could keep alive critical thought in times of political oppression. And it is this low-burning critical fire that Strauss, at least at first glance, wishes to fan and keep from extinguishing. At the beginning of the chapter which bears the same title as the book in which it is included, "persecution and the art of writing," he thus speaks about the way, in certain countries, where "freedom is now suppressed," governments manage to gradually sway the population to their side by relentless repetition of their credo combined with a silencing of competing views: "A large section of the people, probably the great majority of the younger generation, accepts the government-sponsored views as true" (Strauss 1952: 22). This creates the impression that Strauss' intervention is meant to draw attention to and sustain discursive ways of countering conventional wisdom as circulated by manipulative governments. Strauss proceeds (24) to give the putative example of "a historian living in a totalitarian country, a generally respected and unsuspected member of the only party in existence," who in fact secretly questions "the soundness of the government-sponsored" doctrines. Such a historian would probably need to "employ a peculiar manner of writing" (Strauss 1988: 222) in order to communicate his dissent, so that he would place the critique "between the lines," bury the subversive message which concerns "the holy war of mankind" beneath an apparently innocuous and tedious prose, which would put the censors and potential persecutors off his track, while enabling only the careful and intelligent readers to profit from the truth (Strauss 1952: 24).

The task of Strauss' historian thus appears wholly compatible with democracy or liberalism under siege, at the same time that it would seem superfluous where no such "totalitarian" oppression exists. In and of itself, such a theory of "a forgotten kind of writing" seems to possess a merely antiquarian interest, nor is it particularly innovative. It is well known that authors living under despotic regimes were forced to encrypt their critique to avoid reprisals, for example, Molière in times of Louis XIV. Thus, such theory may help us to read *past* texts with proper caution, but would seem irrelevant when reading, or indeed writing, contemporary texts (at least where freedom of expression prevails, and Strauss does not express doubts that this is indeed the case in the modern West). The apparently innocuous nature of his subject matter notwithstanding, Strauss became one of the leading political thinkers of his generation, being still today widely regarded as a key philosophical figure informing American politics. Strauss, to wit, far from indulging some appetite for the archaic, actually advocated a modern renaissance of esoteric writing. The authors whom he analyzed were, for him, not simply historical figures but highly actual mentors.[4] However, this was possible only because, notwithstanding appearances to the contrary, Strauss gave esotericism a decidedly *anti*-democratic twist. What really attracted him to esoteric teachings was not their resistance to the persecuting elite, but rather the vision of a powerful mode of bypassing and subverting *majority rule*. The question, for Strauss (1952: 25), is how a man can "perform the miracle of speaking in a publication to a minority, while being silent to the majority of his readers?" In the past, coded writings or secret organizations, such as free masonry, could offer important means of galvanizing emancipatory politics. They could serve to transmit to the public an enlightening message, circumventing the rulers. A famous example would be Machiavelli's *The Prince*: was this treatise written to educate the political elite, or to expose its practices to the public? Did the author educate the rulers or the subjects? Antonio Gramsci, for one, was convinced that the latter was the case. But in a society in which censorship is largely absent, esoteric teaching assumes a decidedly conservative function. Its challenge is to *enlighten and sustain the rulers*, while *circumventing the public*. Where the masses rule, the need of their opponents is to outwit them and to galvanize elitism. The trick is

---

[4] As clarified in the Introduction to *The City and Man*: "It is not self-forgetting and pain-loving antiquarianism nor self-forgetting and intoxicating romanticism which induces us to turn with passionate interest, with unqualified willingness to learn, toward the political thought of classical antiquity. We are impelled to do so by the crisis of our time, the crisis of the West" (Strauss 1978: 1).

to preserve democracy—exoterically—while simultaneously practicing elitism and curbing democracy—esoterically. Even in plain daylight, the masses should remain in the dark. While early esoteric writers often attempted to let the cat out of the bag, their modern disciples apply the same methods to keep the cat well hidden. Esoteric writing, in Strauss, has in truth nothing intrinsic to do with "persecution." He makes clear that it is a permanent and indispensable feature, given the ineradicable and necessary gap between the elite and the mass. He fully endorses the notion of ancient writers, which he paraphrases as follows:

> They believed that the gulf separating 'the wise' and 'the vulgar' was a basic fact of human nature which could not be influenced by any progress of popular education: philosophy, or science, was essentially a privilege of 'the few.' They were convinced that philosophy as such was suspect to, and hated by, the majority of men. Even if they had nothing to fear from any particular political quarter, those who started from that assumption would have been driven to the conclusion that public communication of the philosophic or scientific truth was impossible or undesirable, not only for the time being but for all times (34).[5]

If not really a function of persecution, Strauss' esotericism is intrinsically *elitist*. This explains why esotericism fully retains its relevance amidst "the horrors of mass culture" (Strauss 1968: 6), which in fact invest it with an altogether new sense of purpose and urgency: "Writings," says Strauss (1952: 35), "are naturally accessible to all who can read. Therefore a philosopher...could expound only such opinions as were suitable for the nonphilosophic majority." Universal education and the modern elimination of popular illiteracy poses a serious threat to philosophy. Strauss (33) is not out to change anything in "the faulty construction of the body politic," as "modern philosophers" naïvely wished to do, vainly confident that they will usher in "the republic of universal light." His goal is rather precisely to preserve such body politic and forestall radical change. The subversive quality of esoteric writing, the fight against the oppressive regime, is only an apparent and superficial aspect as far as Strauss' theory is concerned, while elitism is the heart of the matter. I would not say that it forms the hidden, esoteric core of his teaching, for the simple reason that the anti-democratic gospel is

---

[5] Strauss elsewhere (1988: 227) maintains: "Esotericism necessarily follows from the original meaning of philosophy."

virtually all over the place, whereas Strauss points out that the esoteric message as a rule is only stated very rarely in the text, perhaps only once, whereas the exoteric teaching is repeated many times. Given that Strauss' elitist avowals come thick and fast, the reader cannot but conclude that, either this message was not decoded at all, or was decoded very poorly (there is, of course, a third possibility which could not be ruled out on strictly logical grounds: Strauss is in truth a radical democrat, merely *pretending* to endorse elitism). What Strauss does not state very clearly is the exact motivation animating his elitist convictions and practices. Here, perhaps, one can discern some sort of esoteric intent, if not particularly subtle in its execution: he recurrently insists that esoteric philosophers (which are basically of the only worthy kind) have no vested interest in any social arrangement. He protests, for example, against the tendency to "see in the different philosophies, exponents of different societies or classes," that obscured from view "the possibility that all philosophers form a class by themselves" (8–9). Being above such sectarianism or material interests, philosophers, he argues (18), "defended the interests of philosophy and of nothing else." Likewise, he sometimes claims that the truth must be concealed from the vulgar *for their own sake*, so as not to harm them, given that their nature is unphilosophical and that they depend for their peace of mind on the "noble lies" fabricated by the elite. It just so happens, however, that in Strauss' theory the interests of "philosophy" are somehow interchangeable with the interests of "society" as it currently exists, and that therefore philosophy must be extremely cautious not to endanger the social order: "Philosophy or science," Strauss argues (1988: 221), "the highest activity of man, is the attempt to replace opinion about 'all things' by knowledge of 'all things'; but opinion is the element of society; philosophy or science is therefore the attempt to dissolve the element in which society breathes, and thus it endangers society." "Just so!"—would argue someone interested in changing society, for the purposes of getting rid, say, of "persecution," or of eliminating "opinions" which underpin socially unjust or exploitative practices—"That is precisely why popular education is so necessary, and why knowledge must be distributed as widely as possible, so as to enable the masses to improve their position." But Strauss draws the very opposite conclusions. Directly continuing, he maintains:

> Hence philosophy or science must remain the preserve of a small minority, and philosophers and scientists must respect the opinions on which society rests.... Philosophers or scientists who hold this view about the

relation of philosophy or science and society are driven to employ a peculiar manner of writing which would enable them to reveal what they regard as the truth to the few, without endangering the unqualified commitment of the many to the opinions on which society rests (221–2).

Here, as on many other occasions in Strauss' work, his social, indeed class premise, though not stated, becomes evident. It is not, namely, "philosophy" which he really aims to protect, but rather "society." Yet "society" will continue to exist even if its current, and largely mythical basis, will be exposed and modified; "society" will likewise continue to exist if the "opinions" that currently sustain it would be replaced by other "opinions" (which will in fact be closer to "knowledge"). What may, however, *cease* to exist, is *class* society, one that is predicated "on the gulf separating 'the wise' and 'the vulgar.'" And such a change is precisely what Strauss' teachings, at least between the lines, seek to forestall. In the end, "government-sponsored views" are not to be subverted but perpetuated *ad infinitum*, vis-à-vis the masses. And the philosophizing elite must come to know the truth so it might better cooperate in making sure that the government's "opinions" are not challenged by "knowledge."

Modern esoteric theoreticians and politicians thus go through the motions of championing democracy, while covertly, behind the masses' back, critical processes unfold and decisions taken have very little to do with a democratic agenda. It is clear, furthermore, that the minority allegedly oppressed by democracy is anything but powerless. This is a minority, which possesses enormous financial resources and is habitually very well represented in the highest echelons of the political hierarchy. Important decision-makers in the cabinet of George W. Bush junior—such as the former U.S. Deputy Secretary of Defense and president of the World Bank Group, Paul Wolfowitz—were students of Strauss directly or of Strauss' students.[6] It might be argued that Leo Strauss and his legacy signify a very specific deformation of the relationship between democracy and liberalism. That may be correct as far as the premeditation and cynicism of the "neocons" are concerned. But it is no less true that the Straussians invented nothing substantially new, and that they themselves built on the foundations of an existing tradition. And here I do not have in mind that of Plato or Machiavelli. Rather, the niche occupied by the Straussians is none

---

[6] For an informative study of Strauss' influence see Drury (1999).

other than the structural contradiction between democracy and liberalism, mass and elite, that characterizes modernity and which still today
remains unresolved. To the extent that the masses appear to the elite
as a tyrant, liberal democracy cannot be considered an open society.
It remains in the shadow of clandestine action. This is ultimately the
way we need to understand Strauss' highly suggestive affirmation
(1968: 24) that "We must not expect that *liberal* education can ever
become universal education. It will always remain the obligation and
the privilege of a minority" (italics added). It seems hardly a coincidence, that precisely in the two countries that represent most typically
the liberal-democratic tradition—England and the USA—political and
economic power, on the one hand, and covert maneuvering, on the
other hand, are strongly interlaced. Precisely in those countries, such
esoteric *modus operandi* was brought into perfection. As illustrations,
we may single out the British Cecil Rhodes Secret Society, which was
founded in the late 19th century to manage the affairs of the Empire
and which was defined by a well-informed historian as "one of the
most important historical facts of the twentieth century" (Quigley
1981: ix). Another example would be the secret fraternity based in
Yale, *The Order of Skull and Bones*, which has played a prominent role
in shaping generations of the American political ruling class.

In my discussion, above, of John Locke's position, I noted how
already at its incipient stages liberalism required the systematic division between a *knowing and reasoning* leisured "few" and a *believing and obeying* labouring "majority." It is now possible not only to
conceptualize this in terms of the Straussian problematic of mass-
exotericism and elite-esotericism, but also to note that Leo Strauss
himself was perfectly aware of this strategy as applied by Locke.
Precisely in addressing the crucial role of religion in disciplining the
masses, Strauss notes (1988: 205–6) that Locke, a covert atheist, is careful not to expose this truth to the masses for fear of its practical, seditious implications: "We for our part would say that Locke regarded the
two [religious] arguments as altogether weak but that he 'was unwilling to show the weakness' of any argument allegedly proving the existence of God 'since possibly by it some men might be confirmed in the
belief of a God, which is enough to preserve in them true sentiments
of religion and morality.'" For the same reasons, argues Strauss, Locke
also kept the truth of the special social interest served by his theory
concealed, preferring publicly to endorse the notion of the common
good, indeed the good of the people: "For all *practical purposes* it may

therefore be *better to say* that the basis or end of society is not the private interest of each but the public interest, i.e., the interest of the large majority. To quote the motto of the Treatises: *Salus populi suprema lex esto*" (218; emphases added, except from the Latin phrase). Locke is therefore, a devout democrat (wink wink). And Strauss then adds (218), drawing a comparison which is clearly not meant to rebuke the English liberal but to compliment him: "Locke is closer to Machiavelli than he is generally said or thought to be." Classical liberalism was therefore Machiavellian, a statement which, in Strauss' use, was meant to underscore its conscious mastery of esotericism, as opposed to the modern, naïve variant, which truly believes in putting the masses on a par with the ruling elite.[7] Given such historical distinction between the liberalism of the ancient-elitist kind and the modern-massified one, Strauss (1968) can imply that his own conservative position, far from antithetical to liberalism as critics argue, in truth vindicates the sprit of classical liberalism, protects it from modern misuse: "Liberalism is understood here and now in contradistinction to conservatism" (vii), but the "conservatism of our age is identical with what originally was liberalism" (ix). Propositions from which Strauss draws the logical conclusion: "Being liberal in the original sense is so little incompatible with being conservative that generally speaking it goes together with a conservative posture" (x).

Strauss' claim to stand for the spirit of classical liberalism is indeed, "generally speaking," correct. We can confirm this by turning our attention to a leading figure of 19th century liberalism. In his work *The English Constitution*, Walter Bagehot provides a classic formulation of the beneficial division, in English politics, between the symbolic figurehead of the Queen, standing on the stage and drawing the citizens' attention to her majestic gestures, extravagant as they are trifling, and a small group of professionals operating behind the scenes doing, unnoticed and uninterrupted, the job that truly counts:

> The use of the Queen, in a dignified capacity, is incalculable. Without her in England, the present English Government would fail and pass away.... We are a more mixed people than the Athenians, or probably than any political Greeks.... The slaves in ancient times were a separate order; not

---

[7] For more on Locke as a consummate esoteric writer, revolutionarily promoting "the spirit of capitalism" but doing so cautiously, so as not to "inflame popular passion," and thus pretending to be "going with the herd in one's outward professions," see Strauss (1953: 205–209, 246).

ruled by the same laws, or thoughts, as other men. It was not necessary to think of them in making a constitution...The Greek legislator had not to combine in his polity men like the labourers of Somersetshire...*We Have*. We...have whole classes unable to comprehend the idea of a constitution—unable to feel the least attachment to impersonal laws. Most do indeed vaguely know that there are some other institutions besides the Queen, and some rules by which she governs. But a vast number like their minds to dwell more upon her than upon anything else, and therefore she is inestimable. A republic has only difficult ideas in government; a Constitutional Monarchy has an easy idea too; it has a comprehensible element for the vacant many, as well as complex laws and notions for the inquiring few (Bagehot 1891b: 78–81).

Bagehot, to be sure, does not justify his conception of the inevitable opacity of politics on the pretext of the need to pool the wool over the eyes of the masses; not explicitly, at least. Instead, he blames the masses themselves—their chronic gullibility, lack of political comprehension and interest, etc.—for the infeasibility of genuine democracy. And yet he seems to be rather thankful that that is the case. The masses, Bagehot concedes, are aware of the existence of a hidden political sphere, but "like their minds to dwell more upon the Queen than upon anything else, and *therefore* she is *inestimable*." A true democrat, surely, would have argued in the very reverse manner: precisely because—on Bagehot's terms—the Queen distracts the masses from occupying themselves with the details of actual politics, she is a liability to democracy, a hindrance to political transparency. Hence, the Monarchy should be done away with. For Bagehot, however, this precisely constitutes her *inestimable* merit. For the liberal Bagehot, the masses are too dim to grasp the intricate details of true politics and too shallow to take real interest in them. Hence he recommends, for all intents and purposes, a division of politics into two spheres, an exoteric and an esoteric, the first for the masses—"the vacant many"—the second for the elite—"the inquiring few." But other liberals expressly identified the problem in the keen political *interest* of the masses, their persistent effort to intervene in politics and to employ the means of democracy to wrest for themselves social and economic advantages. As Pareto (1966: 139) sullenly observed: "going along to the polling station to vote is a very easy business, and if by so doing one can procure food and shelter, then everybody—especially the unfit, the incompetent and the idle—will rush to do it." In terms quite similar to those of Mill or Tocqueville, Pareto complains about the tyranny of the democratic poor, enslaving the rich minority:

The old maxim, which lies at the heart of the parliamentary system, that taxes have to be subject to the approval of those who have to pay them, has now given way, implicitly or explicitly, to another maxim: taxes have to be approved and imposed by those who do not pay them. Once upon a time, it was the serfs who were mercilessly oppressed; now it is the well-to-do (312).

The French liberal, Gustave Le Bon—notice how universal the conflict between democracy and liberalism is, and how little it recognizes national boundaries—protests against the increased organization and political consciousness of the masses:

The entry of the popular classes into political life—that is to say, in reality, their progressive transformation into governing classes—is one of the most striking characteristics of our epoch of transition.... It is by association that crowds have come to procure ideas with respect to their interests which are very clearly defined if not particularly just, and have arrived at a consciousness of their strength. The masses are founding syndicates before which the authorities capitulate one after the other; they are also founding labour unions, which in spite of all economic laws tend to regulate the conditions of labour and wages.... To-day the claims of the masses are becoming more and more sharply defined...Limitations of the hours of labour, the nationalisation of mines, railways, factories, and the soil, the equal distribution of all products, the elimination of all the upper classes for the benefit of the popular classes, etc., such are these claims (Le Bon 1960: 15–16).

Bagehot, Pareto und Le Bon belong in the same camp, ideologically and analytically. All three are strongly convinced that the masses have no business interfering in business, that political action and democracy must remain strictly separated. If Bagehot is more optimistic than his Italian and French counterparts, it is because he considers that with the English constitutional monarchy such separation is satisfactorily achieved, the Queen "inestimably" sidetracking the masses from politics. Pareto's and Le Bon's considerably gloomier outlook is explained by the fact that they confront the power of the masses not on paper but in reality. The masses, stated Le Bon (15–16), send to parliaments "representatives utterly lacking initiative and independence, and reduced most often to nothing else than the spokesmen of the committees that have chosen them." The cleft between the two spheres, elite and mass, is bridged, politics becomes direct and transparent, no secrets or secluded space remains at the disposal of the liberal politician. And that the latter is obliged to comply with the wishes of the demos, is understood by Le Bon as a "reduction." This demonstrates again how the danger

of democracy from a liberal point of view does not consist primarily
in the prospect of the masses forfeiting their political initiative and
placing it in the hands of a dictator. Quite the contrary: democracy
becomes dangerous in direct proportion to the masses' insistence on
actually *cashing in on* their democratic prerogative. A dictator would,
from that vantage point, appear rather useful, since he might bring
democracy back under control:

> [A]ll the world's masters,... have always been unconscious psychologists,
> possessed of an instinctive and often very sure knowledge of the charac-
> ter of crowds...Napoleon had a marvellous insight into the psychology
> of the masses...A knowledge of the psychology of crowds is to-day the
> last resource of the statesman who wishes not to govern them—that is
> becoming a very difficult matter—but at any rate not to be too much
> governed by them (19).

Pareto, Le Bon and Bagehot are fundamentally of one mind concerning the solution to the ominous blurring of the boundaries between the
public and the political domains: a new separation must be effectuated
either through a) the elimination of democracy (Pareto, for example,
applauds the "March on Rome") or b) the creation of an emotional
politics (or aesthetical one, to put it like Walter Benjamin) which will
employ symbols, rituals, techniques of collective suggestion, etc., to
divert the masses from actual politics, or c) a combination of both. It
is instructive that all these political thinkers, although from different
countries and independently of one another, have reached very similar
practical conclusions. All appealed to the irrational and advocated the
use of propaganda. This they justified, as I mentioned, by accusing the
masses of being incapable of pursuing a rational discussion. Pareto is
famous for his theories of irrational political action which maintained
that humans, especially in the mass, are guided by "sentiments" and
deep-seated tendencies beyond, or below, the ratio—"residues"—rather
than by interests. But liberalism, in fact, could not tell the truth in any
case. The structural necessity *to dissimulate* was on the part of liberals,
and it was they who made a significant contribution to the surge of
irrationality and myths, so characteristic of 20th century politics. The
irrational was purposefully inculcated and gambled upon by the elite.
Rather than a surge of evil coming from the depth of the social id,
what we find is an irrationality trickling down from the social super
ego. Esotericism pertained quite centrally to such political conceptions,
as well as a demand for a monopoly on political knowledge. Let us
again listen to Pareto:

Faith alone strongly moves men to act. Nor is it desirable for the good of society that the mass of men, or even only many of them, should consider social matters scientifically. There is antagonism between the conditions of *action* and those of *knowledge*. This is a further argument serving to demonstrate how little wisdom there is in those people who want everyone, without distinction or discrimination, to participate in knowledge (Pareto 1966: 150).

With Pareto and Le Bon we arrive at the doorstep of a disturbing collusion, which should give us pause to rethink the habitual opposition between open-ended liberalism, and the closures of totalitarianism. For it is important to realize that fascism gained a decisive initial impetus and rationale in the anti-democratic, esoteric core of liberalism. "I have read all of Gustave Le Bon's work, and I do not know how often I have re-read *The Psychology of the Masses*. This is a capital work, to which I still today return," said Mussolini (as quoted in Losurdo 1994: 55). And Goebbels, similarly, was a great admirer of the French sociologist, taking his advice and implementing techniques of modern publicity, like the endless repetition of praise or calumny in the world of politics, selling a political leader in the same way one would promote a chocolate brand.[8] Hitler, for his part, expressly—if only, and significantly, in *private* conversations—saluted the art of lying, of practising oppression while speaking freedom, an art, furthermore, of which he considered *the English* the great masters and role models:

> But how could the English, with 50 million people, possibly rule over their world empire, without being masters in lying. If they truly wanted, as they always claim, to bring the Indians freedom and Indian culture, they would have had to get out of India. Like Goethe's 'Reinhard the fox,' they were pretending up until the last minute. The nerve to do so they got not least from their incredible self-confidence, which made them consider the English people the helmsmen of the world's vessel.
>
> The German people too, if it wishes to occupy a position in the world, must first be educated to be honest only with itself, but, in relation to other peoples, for example the Czechs, to feign just as innocently as the English, rather than making itself everywhere unloved because of its sincerity (in Picker 2003: 317).

Nor should it be imagined that this esotericism is reserved merely for those "bad" liberals who contributed directly to fascism and often joined forces with it; the problem goes much deeper. It is significant

---

[8] Cf. Losurdo 1994: 55–57.

that even those liberals who opposed fascism, often did so not out of a commitment to democracy as such, but precisely under the conviction that genuine democracy *cannot* exist, that elites will always rule, with greater or lesser democratic pretext. Max Weber, for example, lent his support to the Weimar Republic, precisely since he regarded the actual power of the masses as very limited. As Walter Struve (1973: 142) observed, Weber was convinced that democracy "would serve to hold the masses in check and gain their support for the rise of strong leaders.... Weber relied upon the political organization of the masses to reduce direct popular pressures to a minimum." It is therefore hardly surprising that esotericism was a pillar of Weber's notion of democracy:

> The effective exercise of political control always lay, [Weber] argued, in the hands of a few men. They made all of the important political decisions.... "The *demos* itself, in the sense of an inarticulate mass, never 'governs' larger associations; rather it is governed..." Decisions could be made best and most readily by a few individuals.... Responsibility for decisions would be clear, and secrets could be well guarded. Weber viewed secrecy as an essential element in all political rule (122).

The Bid for Apparent Democracy

Given that such strategies of esotericism and suggestion are at the core of liberal democracy, they reach their destructive apex during fascism but do not begin nor conclude with it. What is threatening for liberalism is not necessarily the formal existence of a democracy, but rather the existence of a democracy that escapes the elites' control. As Le Bon (1960: 15) clarifies: "The introduction of universal suffrage, which exercised for a long time but little influence *and which is moreover so easy to direct*, is not, as might be thought, the distinguishing feature of this transference of political power."[9] For Gaetano Mosca—a liberal who contributed ideas to fascism but finally withheld from it his support—the case was not different:

> Democratic institutions may be able to endure for some time yet if, in virtue of them, a certain equilibrium between the various elements in the ruling class can be maintained, if our *apparent* democracy is not

---

[9] Emphasis added. The italicised words are in fact absent in the English translation from which I quote, but are found, for example, in the French, 9th edition of Félix Alcan, 1905, where it reads: "et d'une direction d'abord si facile" (Le Bon 1905: 11).

fatally carried away by logic, its worst enemy, and by the appetites of the lower classes and their leaders, and if it does not attempt to become *real* democracy by combining political equality with economic and cultural equality (Mosca 1939: 335; emphases in the original).

While a firm opponent of *real* democracy, Mosca can perfectly make his peace, indeed make the best of, *apparent* democracy. Again, the esotericism of such politics comes immediately into view. And Mosca neatly outlines this double game of the elites, their anti democracy which must cloak its real nature:

> The democratic system probably has greater powers of self-preservation than other systems. That is because its natural adversaries have to make a show of accepting it if they wish to avoid its consequences to a greater or lesser extent.... The fact...that the natural adversaries of democracy are obliged to pay official homage to it prevents them from openly declaring themselves followers of theories that explicitly deny the possibility of democratic government as commonly understood (333–4).

Pareto, equally, is favorably disposed towards a democracy as long as it is secretly governed by an elite:

> A governing class is present everywhere, even where there is a despot, but the forms under which it appears are widely variable.... In so called democratic governments it is the parliament. But behind the scenes...there are always people who play a very important role in actual government. To be sure they must now and again bend the knee to the whims of ignorant and domineering sovereigns or parliaments, but they are soon back at their tenacious, patient, never-ending work, which is of much the greater consequence.... The sovereign leaves everything to his legal advisers, in some cases not even divining what they are having him do and parliaments today even less than many a shrewd leader or king. And least of all King Demos! And such blindness on his part has at times helped to effect betterments in conditions of living in the face of his prejudices, not to mention much-needed steps in [sic]behalf of national defence. King Demos, good soul, thinks he is following his own devices. In reality he is following the lead of his rulers (Pareto 1935, vol. 4: 1573).

Seen under this light, a nominal democracy can be wholly compatible with the actual rule of the elite. It is only a matter of whether King Demos truly governs, or merely entertains the illusion of doing so, being in reality skilfully steered. For that reason, neither esotericism nor suggestion disappear with the collapse of the fascist, totalitarian dictatorships. In some respects, the maneuvring and veiling become even more efficient. As the insightful Italian critic, Domenico Losurdo, suggests, today's politicians sometimes find the task of managing the mass media less unwieldy than their totalitarian forerunners, a reality which is easily identifiable precisely in Italy of the last 10 or 20 years: "Compared with the two predecessors, fascist and National Socialist, [Silvio Berlusconi] enjoys the advantage, of not having to forcefully conquer his multimedia empires, since he owns them already, and which allow him, assisted by an army of communication experts, to launch his campaign of political marketing, whose effects he can at all times monitor with constant opinion polls" (Losurdo 1994: 56–57). Media and politics melt into one. The role of actors in American politics—from Reagan to Schwarzenegger—seems to confirm this as well. It is not my contention that actors are inherently less capable of being good politicians than people of other professions. Theoretically, it is even possible to construe their presence as a testimony for the increasing influence of the masses in politics in the sense of "democratization" and "popularization." In practice, however, things seem to move in the opposite direction: actors are successful not because they admit the masses into the political ball, but because they leave them outside, where they can at most be spectators. They function not unlike the Queen of England in Bagehot's descriptions, namely as figureheads. Their dramatic talents are desired, not because they know how to interpret mass feelings, but because they know how to dissimulate elite desires. The more attention grabbing their performance on the stage, the more private and secluded are the workings behind the scenes. The discrepancy between Arnold Schwarzenegger the actor and Arnold Schwarzenegger the politician provides a concrete illustration of this point: as an actor, Schwarzenegger was often cast in films highlighting, from a democratic point of view, the sinister gap between democratic appearance and oppressive reality, thereby denouncing the esotericism of modern politics. Films such as *The Running Man* (1987) or *Total Recall* (1990) are ingenious satires on American media and American politics, respectively. Not by accident, both films culminate in a popular revolution. The latter film was based on a story by the quintessential conspiracy theorist of American popular literature, Philip K. Dick, who has done perhaps more than any other writer to problematize the elusive nature of political reality. Surely, however, not even Schwarzenegger's most ardent fans will attribute to him any subversive or divulging qualities as Governor of California.

Liberal Myth No. 4:
Fascism as a Nationalistic Attack on Liberal Cosmopolitanism

In the last couple of decades, it has become fashionable to interpret fascism above all in terms of its overarching nationalism, most paradigmatically in Roger Griffin's influential attempt to define the "fascist minimum" in terms of "palingenetic populist ultra-nationalism."[10] One of the main upshots of such definitions is, once again, to drive a wedge between fascism and liberalism. Fascism is understood as a tide of atavistic tribalism, an aggressive collectivist assault on the individualistic, tolerant, pacifist and moderate liberal frame of mind. This is the familiar trope of the vehement 20th century backlash against the progressive optimism of the liberal 19th century. I propose to re-visit such conventional dichotomy. I wish to argue, firstly, that liberalism was far less opposed to nationalism—indeed, even of an expansionist and aggressive variant—than is commonly assumed and, in continuation, to claim that fascist nationalism was to a significant extent a prolongation of, and an emanation from, the contradictions of the liberal stance.

Liberalism, Nationalism, Imperialism

While certainly gaining in momentum during the latter half of the 19th century and into the 20th, nationalism was not without deeper roots in the immanent logic of liberalism as such. We have seen, in section 2 of Chapter 5, that liberalism did not simply extol individualism as the highest good and that it found it taxing to cope with individualism when expressed by members of the working classes. Such vacillation vis-à-vis individualism, in turn, created the opening for diverse expressions of liberal *collectivisms*. For against the demands and expectations of mass individuals, liberalism regularly appealed to higher, supra individual, collective entities, such as "the species," "the economy," "the race," and so on. Given the class footing of liberal individualism, far from opposed to "collectivism," it necessitated from its very inception the corollary protection of the state. As C. B. Macpherson highlighted, in his magisterial analysis of 17th century embryo-liberalism:

---

[10] See Griffin 1993: 32–39.

> Such an individualism is necessarily collectivism... For it asserts an individuality that can only fully be realized in accumulating property, and therefore only realized by some, and only at the expense of the individuality of the others. To permit such a society to function, political authority must be supreme over individuals; for if it is not, there can be no assurance that the property institutions essential to this kind of individualism will have adequate sanctions.... The wholesale transfer of individual rights was necessary to get sufficient collective force for the protection of property.... Locke's individualism... does not exclude but on the contrary demands the supremacy of the state over the individual. It is not a question of the more individualism, the less collectivism; rather, the more thorough-going the individualism, the more complete the collectivism (Macpherson 1964: 255–6).

Given the hegemony of the liberal discourse such words still sound iconoclastic today, nearly 50 years after their first publication. Andrew Ure, a 19th century English advocate of capitalism, provides us with a further example of how the worker's individualism formed an impediment to industrialism, and therefore had to be domesticated for the benefit of a higher goal. In modern production, he observed, "skilled labour gets progressively superseded, and will, eventually, be replaced by mere overlookers of machines" (Ure 1835: 20). This development was for Ure not only ineluctable but also salutary: "By the infirmity of human nature it happens, that the more skilful the workman, the more *self-willed* and intractable he is apt to become, and, of course, the less fit a component of a mechanical system, in which, by occasional irregularities, he may do great damage to *the whole*" (emphases added). Several decades later, another erratic ally of the individual, Friedrich Nietzsche, confronted a very similar task of doing away with the mass individual's "intractability" and "self-will" and offered his pedagogic services to capitalism:

> I attempt an *economic* justification of virtue. The task is to make man as useful as possible and to approximate him, as far as possible, to an infallible machine: to this end he must be equipped with the values of the machine (he must learn to experience the states in which he works in a mechanically useful way as the supremely valuable states; hence it is necessary to spoil the other states for him as much as possible, as highly dangerous and disreputable).
>
> The first stumbling block is the boredom, the monotony, that all mechanical activity brings with it. To learn to endure this... that is the invaluable task and achievement of higher schooling.... Such an existence perhaps requires a philosophical justification and transfiguration more than any other... (Nietzsche 1968: 473–4).

Whether we consult Nietzsche or Ure, the worker's individualism appears, from an *economic* point of view, not so much the goal as the problem. And "the nation" emerged as one alternative, among a number of collective entities, to which economic liberalism appealed to, in order to subject the (working) individual. The basic framework for liberalism was indeed, from the very start, the nation. Classical political economy did not simply raise the question of how individuals acquire riches; rather, it proceeded to inquire into *the wealth of nations*. As far back as Locke, Mandeville or Smith, the individuals' pursuit of their self-interest may have been considered the motor of economic development but it was very far from turning *the individuals themselves* into the goal. *Private* vice was vindicated on the assumption that it produces *public* virtue.[11] And clearly, in the process of acting as the frenzied, self-centered "bees" generating the prosperity of "the state," "the public," or "the nation," numerous individuals will endure great, indeed acute hardship, and even go under. The nation provided the indispensable playground for capitalism, and individuals were the playthings. John Bowring, a prominent 19th century English liberal, the closest disciple and literary executor of Jeremy Bentham and an early champion of free trade, thus maintained in an 1835 speech in the House of Commons:

> The hand-loom weavers are on the verge of that state beyond which human existence can hardly be sustained, and a very trifling check hurls them into the regions of starvation.... The improvements of machinery,...by superseding manual labour more and more, infallibly bring with them in the transition much of temporary suffering.... The *national good* cannot be purchased but at the expense of some *individual evil*. No advance was ever made in manufactures but at some cost to those who are in the rear (quoted in Marx 1848; italics added).

This again goes to disprove the facile equation of liberalism, even at its heyday, with individualism, which even a critical thinker as Norberto Bobbio (2005: 16) made the foundation of his analysis: "From the individual's point of view, upon which liberalism is premised, the state is a necessary evil: and in being an evil, albeit a necessary one..., it should interfere as little as possible in the sphere of action of individuals." Not

---

[11] "Mercantilist that he was," affirmed Macpherson (1964: 207), "when Locke discussed the purpose of economic activity, it was generally from the point of view of the nation's rather than the individual's wealth."

so: as Bowring instructs us, if the individual in question happens to be a starving weaver then his "point of view" must be subservient to the national one. Equally, according to Bowring, the state ought to pursue a *laissez faire* policy vis-à-vis the weaver's plight but decidedly *not* because of an excessive respect for her "individual sphere of action." On the contrary, the liberal state maintains its unshaken impassivity precisely in deference to the "national good." But this does not go to say that liberalism, in truth, is premised on the national point of view. Rather, the concrete social content at each juncture determines the liberal posture vis-à-vis such notions as "individualism" or "nationalism": to the extent that the "national good" implies acting in favor of the masses of workers, the liberal state defends "individualism"; to the extent that "individualism" implies state intervention on behalf of the workers, the liberal state puts its weight behind "the national good." Bobbio's account simply reproduced the idealistic schemes of traditional political science, eliminating their concrete, class content, which resulted in such generalizations as this: "Without individualism, there can be no liberalism" (9). This is hardly correct. In reality, liberalism can certainly exist *without* mass individualism and can exist *with* it only very uncomfortably.

John Bowring himself, revealingly, went on to act out the *ballo in maschera* in which liberalism was the host and the guests included "individualism" and "nationalism," when he served as the governor of Hong Kong between 1854 and 1859, a time in which he personally played a critical role in the conflagration that lead to the outbreak of the Second Opium War.[12] But Bowring's colonial complicity is by no means an isolated moment within the trajectory of 19th century liberalism. Whatever his personal flaws, which apparently were not few,[13] Bowring's blend of liberalism and colonialism is symptomatic of a much larger tendency. Liberalism and imperialism—the latter an inflated, exacerbated form of *nationalism* (or, if we wish to say it with Roger Griffin, "ultra-nationalism")—were strongly intertwined. This is a long-overlooked collusion which a series of recent books and essays has addressed.[14] A very partial list of relevant figures will include some

---

[12] See Q. S. Tong's (2006) instructive and elegant essay.

[13] He was considered by several contemporaries to be a man with "an inflated sense of self-importance" and "a warmonger," though a brilliant individual (Tong 2006: 134; see also the subsequent discussion in pages 136–7).

[14] For example, Mehta (1999) and Pitts (2005).

of the most prominent thinkers and politicians that the liberal tradition ever produced: Locke, Bentham, the Mills, Tocqueville, Macaulay (there were others, to be sure, who took a critical stance with regards to imperialism: in our immediate context the names of Gladstone and Cobden come to mind, who sharply criticized the proceedings that led to the "Arrow War"). There have been attempts to explain this apparent paradox in terms of the "totalitarian" potential dormant in 19th century liberalism; the oppressive mechanism—famously analyzed by Foucault—of Bentham's Panopticon; the utilitarian subjection of the minority to the "greatest happiness of the greatest number"; the irresistible and blindly oppressive march of "reason" and "progress"; the obsessive belief in teleology, etc. etc. In Uday Singh Mehta's book, in particular, imperialism emerges like a ramification of a huge philosophical undertaking, that liberals participated in because of their epistemological concerns and moral norms. The following statement is typical: "What is latent in the liberal conception of the political is a deep impulse to reform the world" (Mehta 1999: 79). Whatever truth there is in such claims, they are not wholly convincing. It remains difficult, for example, to understand how a fanatic Benthamite, following utilitarian logic to the letter, could possibly end up by subordinating the happiness of hugely populous nations such as the Chinese or the Indian, to the welfare of the incomparably smaller English nation (to say nothing of those liberals' substantial *personal* stake in such policies—either as direct beneficiaries of imperialism, as was the case of Locke, J. S. Mill, or Bowring, or beneficiaries at a second remove, as members of the wealthy elite—in either case forming a still tinier *minority within the minority*). In fact, to read first-hand accounts of colonialist military operations is to find in them a barely-concealed sense of pride and satisfaction over the way a small army was able, with the use of modern artillery, to subdue enormous and vastly inhabited cities. Consider for example the bombardment of Canton, whose aftermath was described by Sir. Laurence Oliphant, the personal secretary of Lord Elgin (appointed British High Commissioner and Plenipotentiary to the Manchu Empire in the aftermath of the *Arrow* Incident):

> Such were the principal features of the view in southerly direction; but its striking element was that impressive silence, that absence of all movement on the part of a population of a million and a half, that lay as though entombed within the city walls, whose very pulsation seemed arrested by the terrors of the night before, and whose only desire, if they

could think at all, appeared to be, that the bare fact of their existence should be forgotten by the conquerors (Oliphant 1860: 97).

There is scarce little "greatest-happiness-of-the-greatest-number" in such a report, by a well-placed observer at the spearhead of liberal Europe. Of course, a utilitarian might justify imperialism, as was often done, on the grounds that it ultimately benefits the Indian or Chinese multitudes. But here it is clearly a case of bending the utilitarian logic to apologize for the satisfaction of the immediate materialistic interests of the few, and not of a truly pedantic observance of the utilitarian catechism. And here, I believe, lies the more substantial explanation of the liberal-imperialist complicity: it has less to do with liberalism getting itself tied into doctrinaire knots, and more with the fact that at the heart of liberalism is capitalism, with its accumulative and expansive imperatives. It is not some peculiarity of the utilitarian logic—which, in fact, contains a truly democratic potential and from which sprang embryonic forms of socialism, notably Robert Owen's—but the logic of economic liberalism as such. Bowring is reputed to have said: "Jesus Christ is Free Trade and Free Trade is Jesus Christ" (Newsinger 2002: 127). And behind the ideology of free trade, with or without Jesus Christ, lies the drive for profit extraction. This is the underlying rationale directing the operations of empire. This is the familiar trope of "making the world safe for business," of "opening up" the world market. Utopian schemes, "deep reformative impulses," teleological convictions and epistemological anxieties, may or may not exist. As Frantz Fanon famously reminded Hegel, what the master "wants from the slave is not recognition but work". J. S. Mill justified the English involvement in the Second Opium War as undergirding free commerce, and Bowring himself, in 1855, "had successfully opened the markets of Siam, though not without a calculated threat of war" (Tong 2006: 144). This appears to explain why still today, long after utilitarianism had been philosophically dethroned, along with other classical 19th century tenets such as progress and reason, the liberal state can not dispense with imperialist, or neo-imperialist, policies, backed up by wars or by "calculated threats" thereof.

Hence, just as vis-à-vis the workers in their own homeland, liberals could sacrifice the happiness and liberty of numerous individuals even as they spoke "on liberty" and praised the value of individualism, so they could, facing foreign populations, evoke the moral grounds of the "white man's burden" or appeal to utilitarian principles. Or indeed, junk the pretense of both principles and injunctions altogether and exploit the loophole that, in dealing with the natives, the norms and standards of civilized whites cease to apply. Thus, a devout Benthamite though he certainly was, Bowring could nonetheless rationalize the sacrifice of the happiness of numerous Chinese and Indians simply by ejecting such "barbarians" out of the human equation: "with barbarous...nations, the words of peace are uttered in vain" (in Tong 2006: 125). The affinities between such conceptions and the fascist worldview, between such *modus operandi* and the fascist one, are hard to overlook. Q. S. Tong's words (145), thinking about "the burning and sacking of Yuan Ming Yuan," one of the world's marvels at the outskirts of Beijing, a criminal act which was "instigated by a prominent utilitarian follower" (Bowring) are very pregnant: "Isn't it a holocaust in the original and true sense of the word that was carried out under the order of an imperial state, a holocaust that almost all major contemporary liberal thinkers failed to respond to?" Or consider the following, hardly less compelling de facto enumeration of the analogies between liberalism and fascism, even though the latter is not mentioned:

> As a general matter, it is liberal and progressive thinkers such as Bentham, both the Mills, and Macaulay, who...endorse *the empire as a legitimate form of political and commercial governance*; who justify and accept its largely *undemocratic* and nonrepresentative structure; who invoke as politically relevant categories such as *history, ethnicity, civilizational hierarchies*, and occasionally *race and blood ties*; and who fashion arguments for the empire's at least temporary necessity and foreseeable prolongation (Mehta 1999: 2; emphases added).

"A Farm is a Fatherland in Miniature"

In addressing another facet of the elective affinity between liberal nationalism and fascism, it is a helpful exercise to consider the following avowal:

> A farm is a fatherland in miniature. One is born there, raised there, brought up with the trees that surround it. In industrial property, nothing speaks to the imagination, to memory, to the moral part of man. One speaks of my ancestors' field, of my fathers' cabin. One never speaks of my fathers' shop or workshop.... In relation to their intellectual qualities, the cultivator enjoys a great superiority over the artisan.... Land binds man to the country where he lives, surrounds his departure from it with obstacles, creates patriotism through interest.... Setting aside its

moral pre-eminence, landed property is favorable to public order by the
very position in which it places its owners. Artisans, crowded into towns,
are at the mercy of the factious, while it is almost impossible to collect
farmers together and therefore to steer them up.

Was this some anti-liberal romanticist, recoiling to the safety of the
medieval village encircled by urban capitalism? Or some backward-
looking, anti-modern fascist, rejecting the benison of industrialism?
In truth, these are words by one of the foremost 19th century French
liberals and champions of commerce, Benjamin Constant (1988: 218).
He evinced preference for land over town: the first rooted, conservative, reasonable, orderly, the second uprooted, less patriotic, crowded,
and "at the mercy of the factious." In short, arguments that will belong
to the standard stock of fascist ideology. Needless to say, such a passage does not testify to an identity between fascist thought and classical liberalism, nor am I suggesting that Constant be added to the
list of proto-fascist thinkers. But it does indicate that the demarcation
line between the two worldviews was considerably more blurry than
habitually imagined; and it shows that such motifs as the exaltation of
the countryside as the bastion of order and tradition and the fear of
the town and the radicalism it harbors, were not simply, as later liberal interpreters would have it, reactionary-conservative myths born
out of irrational phobias and espoused by "the losers" in modernity's
competitive game.[15] Rather, they were rooted in the realities of modern, capitalist class society, and as such were shared, to some extent
or another, by all those on the propertied side—the side of the "well-
disposed people" (Malthus), the "fraternity linking all who had anything" (Tocqueville). Working-class urban radicalism, for example, was
at least as threatening to the successful "liberal" industrialist as it was
to the struggling, and putatively "conservative," small artisan.

Constant may have celebrated the end of armed hostilities between
nations and the obviation of war, which he sanguinely ascribed to the
age of commerce. But he could not for all that dispense with nationalism, which remained the presupposition of capitalist enterprise, precisely by binding together its class hierarchy:

---

[15] A classic example for this line of interpretation is Fritz Stern's emphasis (1961) on
the anti-liberal, anti-capitalist and anti-modern character of 19th century "Germanic
ideology," that would later flow into Nazism. Similarly, in Wolfang Sauer's view
(1967), fascism was "a revolt of the *déclassés*...against industrialization" (417), fascists
having been "losers," who acted "from a position of weakness" (418).

A single individual, through his striking merit, may captivate the crowd; but political bodies, to sustain confidence in them, need to have interests which are clearly in accordance with their duties. *A nation always expects that men grouped together will be guided by their own interests.* It is certain that the love of order, justice and conservation will enjoy a majority among property holders (215–16; italics added).

National interest, moreover, he associated with the interests of the propertied classes:

> Those who are condemned by [poverty] to daily labour, are neither more knowledgeable than children about public affairs, nor more interested than foreigners in national prosperity…I do not wish in any way to wrong the labouring class. As a class it is by no means less patriotic than the others…. Yet the patriotism which gives one the courage to die for one's country is quite different, I believe, from the patriotism which enables one to fully understand its interests (214).

There is a telling ambiguity in these words: the working masses are said, on the one hand, to be too immature and childish to "fully understand" their country's interests. Hence, they should be deprived of the power of partaking in political decision-making. But this paternalism, in truth, is premised on the hurried admission that the workers and the poor simply *do not partake* in their country's interests: they are not "more interested than foreigners in national prosperity." National interests are thus identical with class interests. And therefore the notion of "patriotism" continues to be vital even in an age of commerce. Also significant, of course, is the implicit acknowledgment (313) that this new and shining era—"an age must come in which commerce replaces war. We have reached this age"[16]—will not preclude strife and competition between nations: "foreigners," that is, have just as little a share in national profit as the workers. The new epoch merely—or at least that is what Constant imagines—shifts from a physical to a commercial warfare: "War is all impulse, commerce calculation" (313). But we know, with the aid of hindsight, that this is not a case of either/or, that impulse and calculation can coincide, alternate, and nourish one another.

Constant is also instructive in inadvertently underscoring the fact that individualism, under liberalism, is class structured. Individual freedom is reserved for the bourgeois and the propertied: "commerce,"

---

[16] Cf. also page 325.

he argues (315), "inspires in men a vivid love of individual independence. Commerce supplies their needs, satisfies their desires, without
the intervention of the authorities.... Every time collective power
wishes to meddle with private speculations, it harasses the speculators, every time governments pretend to do our own business, they do
it more incompetently and expensively than we would." Clearly, this
is the individual independence of businessmen, speculators and those
who can satisfy their "needs" and "desires" "without the intervention
of the authorities." It scarcely applies to those "condemned to daily
labor," who can only barely satisfy their "needs," to say nothing of
their "desires," without the authorities' intervention. And in order to
ensure that this pattern of class apportioning of individualism between
the bourgeois and the workers remains stable, that the latter would
not be able to exert pressure upon the authorities to come to their
aid, Constant also underscores (316) the division between economic
freedom and political un-freedom: "[W]e can no longer enjoy the liberty of the ancients, which consisted in an active and constant participation in collective power. Our freedom must consist of peaceful
enjoyment and private independence." Whereby it is obvious that the
latter "freedom" and "enjoyment" obtain only on the assumption that
one is indeed "privately independent." Hence the unmistakable class
nature of Constant's notion of modern freedom, based on the liberal
split between the economic and the political:

> The aim of the ancients was the sharing of social power among the citi-
> zens of the same fatherland: this is what they called liberty. The aim of
> the moderns is the enjoyment of security in private pleasures; and they
> call liberty the guarantees accorded by institutions to these pleasures
> (317).

The problem with such a vision is that it presupposes that "ancient"
democracy will not come to cast its shadow on the "private pleasures" of
the modern propertied classes. But once the liberal division of spheres
and powers between the political and the economic collapses under
popular pressure, liberalism is pushed into a corner: in the period leading up to fascism, such a dilemma is becoming evermore pressing.
And at that crucial historical juncture liberalism resorts to nationalism
to shut out democracy and restore modern freedom. As Christopher
Duggan observed, with relation to the constitutive Italian case:

> Without its material claims, however, what could Italian liberalism rep-
> resent? 'We cannot offer Paradise in heaven, unlike our Catholic col-
> leagues,' declared a leading liberal, Antonio Salandra, in 1913, 'nor can

we offer Paradise on earth, unlike our socialist colleagues.' Instead, he claimed, '*the very essence of Italian liberalism is patriotism*'; and it was in accordance with this belief that Salandra led Italy into the war in May 1915 (Duggan 1994: 188; italics added).

Not only did war violently intrude upon the age of commerce; it undermined another of Constant's classical liberal axioms, namely that state intervention is irreconcilable with economic prosperity: "the manner in which [Italy] had coped with the production demands imposed by over three years of fighting was little short of miraculous.... This astonishing achievement was the result of state planning and regulation on an unprecedented scale" (193). In other words, if classical liberal economics shared with fascism the preoccupation about popular political interference to begin with, then came the First World War which removed some of the theoretical, *laissez-faire* objections, that might have remained. The path for an even larger and more audacious experiment lay wide open. But let us now address this experiment more closely.

Fascism: Patriotism as the Last Refuge of the Liberal

To define fascism primarily in terms of "ultra-nationalism," it must be admitted, is a rather safe bet. Not much can go wrong by underlining the flagrant nationalistic core of fascism. But does it really tell us a whole lot about "the nature of fascism"? In truth, it rather raises another question, and one just as daunting, concerning the "nature of nationalism." For nationalism is another notoriously elusive signifier. As Thomas Mann (1981: 363), pondering the rabid nationalism of the German right, observed: "One forgets, that to deal with the word national is to deal with a completely neutral concept, which can be filled with the most disparate content." So to tell us that fascism was "nationalistic," is hardly enlightening. We must rather ask, what is nationalism of the *fascist variant*? What did it *do*, how did it *function*, what was its *content*? An old interpretation which had come under severe attack, insisted on the need to see the nation as the antidote to class, as the capitalistic and bourgeois retort to the class narrative and the class project of socialism. Thomas Mann, for one, diagnosing what went wrong with the Weimar Republic, was convinced that this and no other was the function of fascist nationalism:

> The social Republic did not believe in itself. After a revolution, which was not a real one, it allowed the spirit of the old to persevere, in schools, universities, courtrooms, offices, instead of letting the spirit of the future

take over. It stood under the pressure of the forces of the past, to which
it believed it must constantly make concessions, to which it constantly
stooped, in what it did and in particular in what it refrained from doing.
And with these forces I mean all that which stands *against the great
principle of socialism* and what can be summarized *under the name of
nationalism* (356; italics added).

It might be argued that Thomas Mann here judged fascism "from outside," from a vantage point which, according to his namesake, the historian and sociologist Michael Mann (2004: 21), "made little sense to
fascists, who rebutted class theories as they did all 'materialism.' Fascists
focused elsewhere." Yet is such a claim dependable? Did fascists indeed
dismiss the centrality of class and turn their attention "elsewhere"? It
turns out that there were quite a few "materialists" and "class theorists"
militating around or within the fascist ranks. Let us first listen to an
eminent political scientist like Gaetano Mosca, writing on the verge of
the move to Italian fascism. To start with, he outlined the insidious rise
of socialism, lamenting the complicity of the elite:

> The ruling classes in a number of European countries were stupid enough
> and cowardly enough to accept the eight-hour day after the World War,
> when the nations had been terribly impoverished and it was urgent to
> intensify labor and production.
>   It is readily understandable that in European society, under such
> psychological and material circumstances, a strong political movement
> should have grown up within the bourgeoisie itself... to realize equality
> and bring the masses into actual participation in the management of the
> state. It is understandable, finally, that the thinkers in the movement
> should [uphold the notion] that neither absolute justice nor real equality
> can be established in this world unless private property is abolished....
> Slave to its own preconceptions, therefore, the European bourgeoisie has
> fought socialism all along with its right hand tied and its left hand far
> from free (Mosca 1939: 478–9).

Socialism hence imperils in the bluntest of manners the class system,
capitalism and private property itself. Even as they radically differ in
evaluating the merit of socialism, Mosca and Thomas Mann perfectly
agree as far as assessing the stakes of the conflict. And they equally
agree with regards to the antithesis of socialism, namely nationalism.
As Mosca's subsequent analysis clarifies:

> A powerful labor union or, a fortiori, a league of labor unions can impose
> its will upon the state.
>   In order to obviate this danger, it is necessary to prevent, at all costs,
> the rise of new sovereignties intermediate *between the individual and*

the state. ... In other words, it is absolutely indispensable that the heads of our present government should at all times receive greater obedience from the members of the unions than the heads of the unions themselves receive. *Devotion to the national interests must always be stronger than devotion to class interests* (481; emphases added).[17]

It is difficult to state the case of nationalism as anti-socialistic more emphatically. And Mosca goes still further and spells out how nationalism operates as a myth, a modern substitute for religion, to counter the class ethos of socialism. I quote at some length, for the following amounts to little less than a definition of nationalism, not in and of itself, as an abstract category, but as a concrete historical phenomenon during late 19th and early 20th century:

Unfortunately, one of the major weaknesses of present-day European society...lies in the relaxation of those forces of moral cohesion which alone are capable of uniting in a consensus of sentiments and ideas all the atoms that make up a people... [E]specially during the last two centuries religion has lost much of its prestige and practical efficacy.... Patriotism, therefore, has been left as the chief factor of moral and intellectual cohesion within the various countries of Europe. Patriotism, too, has generally been combated by socialism as an invention that the ruling classes have devised to prevent the unions of the proletarians of all the world against the bourgeoisie...But having deeper roots than religion in the souls of the modern nations today, patriotism has offered sturdier resistance to the attack of its adversaries.... Patriotism is grounded in the sense of common interests that binds together people who live in the same country, and in the oneness of sentiments and ideas that almost inevitably arises among people who speak the same language, have the same background, share common glories and meet the same fortunes and misfortunes. It satisfies, finally, a yearning of the human soul to love the group to which it belongs above all other groups.

It would be hazardous, and perhaps inconsistent with the facts, to assert that the middle classes in Europe have had any clear or definite awareness of the great moral obstacle that patriotism offers to the progress of socialism. But it is certain, nevertheless, that, beginning with the early years of the twentieth century, a powerful awakening of patriotic feeling was observable in the educated youth of almost all the European countries (481–2).

---

[17] Notice, also, the way that Mosca, precisely from a liberal point of view, does not defend "individuals," but rather is eager to see them exposed to the domination of the state, with no "intermediary" organizations taking up their cause against the liberties of capitalism! This is another instance in support of our analysis of liberalism and individualism.

Mosca, too, is unmistakably a "class theorist." And he discloses the social logic behind, not the emergence of nationalism as such, but the emergence of a *particular kind* of nationalism, which functions in the service and interests of the middle class to contest the grounds against a proletarian, class sense of belonging. This nationalism, one might say, is the *middle-class* sense of *class belonging*. For Mosca, nationalism was clearly one of those "political formulas" which the bourgeoisie was widely inculcating in order to sway the masses away from class. Indeed, in the demise of religion, it became the primary myth, the modern political formula par excellence. This is what crystallizes, objectively, the "palingenetic ultranationalism" of fascist movements, regardless of whether their social bearers "had any clear or definite awareness" of what they were doing or not.

Nationalism is defined significantly by the nature of the internationalism that it rebuffs, or which at least serves as its background. One can be nationalistic from a point of view negating, say, globalization and the demands of such supra-national entities as the *International Monetary Fund*, and one can be nationalistic, as Mosca explains, "to prevent the unions of the proletarians of all the world." Surely, this class logic of nationalism explains much about the fact that today, when the socialist challenge to capitalist hegemony has been drastically downgraded, the social elites—again, no matter with what degree of awareness or premeditation—have moved conspicuously away from palingenetic nationalism towards cosmopolitanism and now embrace the global, capitalist village, whereas the masses of the poor in numerous countries have shifted considerably in support of nationalist agendas, which oppose the universal hegemony of capital.

In other words, defining fascism as nationalism, or an attempt at a national re-birth, is not so much wrong as it simply begs the question: *why* should fascists be interested in the "nation" or wish to see it "reborn"? For Michael Mann, fascist desire was informed by genuinely egalitarian ambitions on the part of people, whether leaders or rank and file, standing somehow outside of the conflict between capital and labor, disgusted with the chronic strife of liberal democracy and seeking to create a cohesive national state above class. In that respect, he carries forward the evermore popular notion of fascism as a third force between capitalism and socialism, being "neither right, nor left." This concept leads to a steady underplaying of the properly anti-egalitarian, elitist, anti-socialist and pro-capitalist nature of fascism, accompanied by a contrasting emphasis on the revolutionary thrust of fascist movements:

> Whereas…other forms of authoritarian regime were staffed by conservatives trying to mobilize and control mass movements, fascism was a populist and 'radical' movement, with a strong 'bottom-up' thrust…Not that class was irrelevant to fascist support. Fascists received disproportionate support from economic sectors liking the message of class transcendence, people from all classes who were working and living outside the main sites of severe class conflict in modern society (Mann 2004: 53).

Ideologically, the main import of Mann's effort is to disentangle fascism from the dynamic of capitalism and its concomitant class struggles and show that it was a distinct ideological-cultural strand. He maintains on numerous occasions that one of the most central features of fascist ideology and politics, indeed possibly their very crux, was an attempt to rise above class: "the 'core constituency' of fascist support can be understood only by taking seriously their aspirations to transcendence, for they were perfectly genuine about it.… Transcendence was actually the central plank of fascism's electoral program" (15). Paradoxically, Mann's effort at undermining the class interpretation of fascism culminates in a quintessential *class theory* of fascism, placing the class struggle at its very centre. Did fascists wished to transcend class strife? Of course they did, but so did the socialists whose explicit goal, after all, was the *classless society*. But fascists clearly did not wish for *such* an end to social strife nor for *such* a unity. Indeed, such a solution was their nightmare scenario. Rather, they longed—sincerely enough—to achieve a harmonious society *with* classes, preserving the hierarchical labor and status division of capitalism with all their attendant benefits. And it is hence that they favored the national resolution. To say, therefore, that fascists were essentially leftists who "lacked a general critique of capitalism (unlike socialists), since they ultimately lacked interest in capitalism and class," (15) is thus a complete misconstruction. Fascists were not interested in class *upheaval*, but keenly interested in the class *system*.[18] Strangely, Mann imagines that he disengages fascism from capitalism by emphasizing the fascist desire to transcend class. Yet does not such desire form, precisely, the *link* between fascism and capitalism? Is there any capitalist who preaches class war? Where is the capitalist who will not vouch for his own enterprise as

---

[18] Dylan Riley (2004: 141), reviewing Mann's book, wittily pointed out the inconsistency of his argument: "the plain fact is that the main activity of their squads was to destroy class-based organizations of the labour movement. It seems a little odd to argue then that fascists viewed the class struggle with distaste; they engaged in it with violent enthusiasm."

one merely enhancing the good of the community, enlarging its riches, strengthening the nation? And is there a liberal who is not interested in transcending class strife? Did German liberals, perchance, differ from their contemporary German fascists in that they wished to kindle social friction? Gustav Stresemann, the outstanding liberal politician of the Weimar Republic, expressed the following wish at the DVP's—the liberal party—conference of 1921:

> Never did a people stood so pure before God and world history, as the German people did in the year 1914.... Back to this unity of national feeling, we have not since found our way.... Our goal must be the reconciliation of all the social classes [Schichten] of the German people. That the mass thinks nationally, it had proven in 1914 (Quoted in Verhey 2000: 13–14).

And if we are to trust the fascist and believe him that he is sincere, why should we turn cynical when it comes to the capitalist or the liberal? Class transcendence, therefore, like nationalism, is a neutral concept. The question is always: transcend class in *what manner* and to *whose advantage*? And here, Mann himself (2004: 15) cannot but admit that, genuine though they certainly were, "in the short space of time allowed them, fascists did tend to backtrack from their original project of transcending class conflict. This 'betrayal' is stressed by class interpretations of fascism and by others doubting the sincerity or consistency of fascist values." My own interpretation, however, in fact gives more credit to the fascists than Mann's, and does not accuse them of "backtracking" or "betraying." For fascists did indeed successfully transcend class conflict, in the only manner they ever desired to. With regards to the speculation that fascists would have pursued a vigorous elimination of class had they not been confined into the "short space of time allowed them," I can only say that the term "short" is relative, and as such appears singularly inadequate to describe the fascist period both objectively and subjectively. Objectively, the fascists had more than enough time to pursue genuine egalitarianism had they wished to do so; subjectively, as far as the countless victims of the fascists were concerned, every second of their reign was clearly one too many.

Mann in fact insists that Hitler, unlike Mussolini who was more obliging to the Italian ruling-class, was bent on eradicating capitalism: "Had [Hitler's] regime lasted much longer, I doubt the Reich economy could still have been called 'capitalist'" (15). As against this rather extravagant speculation, we might cite the opinion of Buchheim and Scherner, two German economic historians who have examined both

Nazi ideology *and* its economic praxis, and come to strikingly different conclusions. For them, the increasing state orchestration of the
German economy was dictated by the necessities of the war economy,
and was by no means intended to become a permanent solution. I
quote their view at some length, for it is a highly useful antidote to
such views as Mann's:

> The foregoing analysis again proves that in the Nazi period enterprises
> continued to shape their actions according to their expectations and that
> the state authorities not only tolerated this behavior, but *bowed to it by
> adapting their contract offers to the wishes of industry....* The behaviour
> of enterprises in all these cases also demonstrated that they *foresaw the
> eventual reduction of interventionism and state demand,* which would
> lead to the *reemergence of a market economy* and to greater foreign com-
> petition.... Thus, *industry itself did not consider the development of the
> Nazi economic system as heading towards central planning and social-
> ism.* Rather, the very important role of the state in the prewar and war
> economy was seen as related to warfare—*and thus temporary.* Although
> there was no guarantee that a postwar German economy would return
> to a more market-like framework—in fact, in a dictatorship such as
> that of the Nazi regime no such guarantee could be really credible—*the
> daily experience of entrepreneurs and managers in their dealings with the
> bureaucracy of the Nazi state obviously led them to that conviction.* There-
> fore they acted accordingly and by doing so found this conviction again
> and again confirmed. For the regime generally tolerated their behavior
> inspired as it was by their regard for the long-term profitability of their
> businesses (Buchheim and Scherner 2006: 405; emphases added).

This assessment is all the more important since it does not in the least
represent the kind of traditional "class analysis" that Mann deprecates.
It is based on an analysis of Nazi economic policies and explores the
assumptions and expectations on the part of both German industrialists and the Nazi elite. Nor does it leave out of consideration the ideological aspect—all-important to Mann—underlying such practices. If
the Nazis went along with the industrialists and refrained from priva-
tizing or enforcing contracts on them, this was not at all on account
of some opportunistic or unavoidable compromise with existing pow-
er-bases but because of *their own ideological commitment to private
property*: "Nazi ideology held entrepreneurship in high regard. Private
property was considered a precondition to developing the creativity of
members of the German race in the best interest of the people" (408),
and Hitler himself "frequently made clear his opposition in principle to
any bureaucratic managing of the economy" (409). In other words, the
"sincerity or consistency of fascist values" which Mann underlines, need

not be "doubted"; it was simply the case that these values themselves were predicated on the indispensability of private property, private enterprise and, therewith, of capitalism. In fact it is Mann who needs to deconstruct Nazi ideology and read into it some hidden plan to get rid of capitalism, thus doubting its consistency, whereas Buchheim and Scherner do no more here than take it *at face value*.

Let it also be observed that, given his left-wing credentials probably without intending it, Mann implicitly furnishes something like a vindication of class society. As in the interpretation of fascism and communism as *frères enemis* (Eugen Weber), or the classic notion of "totalitarianism" left and right, two birds are slain with one stone: if fascism was indeed interested in transcending class, then the problem surely cannot lie in the system of class division itself; it is rather the enemies of class society, those attempting to construct an alternative model to replace the social configuration of capitalism, who pose the threat. Class therefore emerges as the ultimate horizon of "the open society," unless it flirts with chiliastic visions, which will only prove nightmarish. Conversely, to accept the reality of class is to be, by default, anti-fascist. Such an implied apology for class, however, loses its ground once we realize that fascism only aimed to eliminate class *politics*, not class *society*.

A Return to "Grand Politics"

More subtle than Mosca's substitution of national politics for social politics, and already from within the fascist camp, was Carl Schmitt's well-known definition of "the concept of the political" as founded upon the friend-enemy opposition. Schmitt's theories have surprisingly commended themselves over the years to left-wing theorists, most recently Chantal Mouffe, who fancied finding in them an insightful critique of the liberal practice of blunting the edge of political antagonisms and liquefying them into some sort of bland, hegemonic porridge, a dialogue of purported tolerance and understanding. Whether indeed Schmitt's theories can be productively construed as reinvigorating politics in a lukewarm liberal age is a question that needs not concern us here. Important for us is only to realize that in their original context Schmitt's writings were concerned precisely with discrediting *class politics* as an inferior, second-rate version of "the political" in its pure form, namely the conflict between peoples or nations. Liberalism, in other words, was hateful to Schmitt not because it glossed over social conflicts and differences, but because it made an issue of them in the first place.

The whole point of Schmitt's attempt to characterize the political was his dissatisfaction with actual, modern politics, precisely since it signified a protracted struggle between social classes, represented by parties, which undermined the authority of "the state" and the unity of "the nation." This hostility to political liberalism qua *democratic* was, of course, a staple of conservative thought in Germany and elsewhere. The—relative—innovation of Schmitt's position was that instead of denouncing politics altogether as an ignoble and harmful business, Schmitt attempted to *celebrate* politics by *re-defining* its nature. But this was merely a new variation on a familiar theme. When somebody in the Weimar Republic embraced an anti- or un-political stance, he or she was making *a political statement* of the first degree, situating themselves almost automatically in opposition to a quite specific, modern way of doing politics, i.e., democracy, and in support of traditional, authoritarian regimes, which were construed as *pre*-political precisely in that sense. It is no coincidence that the majority of those sympathetic to German fascism were also great admirers of this famous self-proclaimed "last anti-political German," Friedrich Nietzsche (a very short list of whose pro-fascist admirers would include Benn, Jünger, Spengler, Baeumler, Rosenberg, and Heidegger, which goes to show that "the last" of the anti-political lineage he certainly was *not*). The early, conservative Thomas Mann (another Nietzsche admirer, later taking a critical view of him as he did of all anti-democracy), in what was perhaps the apolitical manifesto of the period, neatly sums up this equation of *politics* with *democracy*, implying that authoritarian regimes are simply *not* political:

> I declare with deep conviction, that the German people will never be able to love democracy, simply because it cannot love *politics itself*, and that the much reviled 'authoritarian state' (Obrigkeitsstaat) was and remains the state form appropriate and adequate to the German people, the one which it at bottom wants (Mann 1974: 30; italics added).[19]

Fascism in the eyes of many conservatives (as well, of course, of "conservative revolutionaries") owed much of its appeal precisely to its

---

[19] Consider also Georg Lukács' remark (1950: 64) about "Thomas Mann's thesis, that politics is equivalent to democracy."

elimination of (democratic) politics, and in that sense *fascism itself* could be described as apolitical and anti-political. This ideologeme corresponded to the fascist ideal of being above politics, parties, and classes, and merely serving the Nation. Hence Luigi Pirandello, when interviewed in 1924 about his fascist alignment, could affirm: "I am isolated from the world and have only my work and my art. Politics? I have nothing to do with them and never had anything to do with them," only to continue seamlessly, without noting any contradiction: "If you are referring to my joining the Fascist Party, I can tell you that I did so to help Fascism in its task of renovation and reconstruction" (quoted in Hamilton 1971: 51).

Compared with such traditional positions, Schmitt's innovation was to *extol* the value of the political. But this he did only after making clear that under "the political" in its genuine and elevated form he certainly does *not* mean democracy: democratic party politics was deemed a petty and insidious disfiguration of the political in its Platonic sense, as it were, the *Ur*-opposition between the national friend and the national foe. Schmitt's purpose was to construct an axiological hierarchy, at the top of which is politics in its primary and exalted sense—where *national* entities collide—and which then descends into a series of ever less noble and meaningful political manifestations, where *social* groups and parties are the protagonists:

> The political is the most intense and extreme antagonism, and every concrete antagonism becomes that much more political the closer it approaches the most extreme point, that of the friend-enemy grouping. *Within* the state, as an organized political entity, which in its entirety decides for itself the friend-enemy distinction,... *next to* the primary political decisions... numerous *secondary* concepts of the political emanate.... [O]ne can speak of a state's domestic religious, educational, communal, social policy, and so on.... Finally even more banal forms of politics appear, forms which assume parasite- and caricature-like disfigurations. What remains here from the original friend-enemy grouping is only some sort of antagonistic moment, which manifests itself in all sorts of tactics and practices, competitions and intrigues; and the most peculiar dealings and manipulations are called politics. But the fact that the substance of the political is contained in the context of a concrete antagonism is still expressed in everyday language, even where the awareness of the 'serious case' [*Ernstfalles*] has been entirely lost (Schmitt 2007: 29–30).[20]

---

[20] Here and in the following quotations from the book, I occasionally depart from George Schwab's rendition, relying on the German edition (Schmitt 2002).

The gist of Schmitt's endeavor was to draw his readers' attention away from the concrete social differences which were dividing them and which, in real life, formed the content of their political struggles, and draw them in the direction of "the concept," in truth the *ideal* of the political, a metaphysical opposition between themselves as a nation and other such nations. This was at bottom a theoretical "vindication" of what other conservative-cum-fascist thinkers and politicians, from Spengler to Hitler, were repeatedly emphasizing, namely the primacy of foreign politics over internal affairs, and the need of "the people" to be united in their campaign for national greatness. This is why I claimed that Schmitt's innovation was only a relative one, being in fact integral to the thought and goals of the German elites. And did not Nietzsche, again, show the way? Confronted with the political in its social, democratic, and ultimately *class* sense, Nietzsche is the last "anti-political German":

> The labour question.—The stupidity, fundamentally the instinct degeneration which is the cause of *every* stupidity today, lies in the existence of a labour question at all. About certain things *one does not ask questions*: first imperative of instinct.—I simply cannot see what one wishes to do with the European worker now one has made a question of him.... But what does one *want*?—to ask it again. If one wills an end, one must also will the means to it: if one wants slaves, one is a fool if one educates them to be masters (Nietzsche 1990: 106).

But the same Nietzsche (1992: 97) also audaciously predicted that "only after me there will be *grand politics* on earth." So Schmitt merely recapitulated the distinction between small and great politics, inner and foreign affairs, class and national struggles, always of course in justification of the latter. Just as in Nietzsche, though less straightforwardly and with techniques of dissimulation typical of the good jurist, Schmitt lamented the fact that a "labour question" was historically allowed to exist at all. Behind the matter-of-fact tone in which the following observation is made, a nostalgic yearning can be sensed: "Thus there exists 'social politics' only since a politically noteworthy class put forth its 'social' demands; welfare care, which in early times was administered to the poor and distressed, had not been considered a sociopolitical problem and was also not called such" (Schmitt 2007: 30). And just as in Mosca, the labour question was to take the back seat position with deference to the national question. In this context, Schmitt (1988: 75) early identified the value of the Sorelian myth in simultaneously galvanizing nationalism and deflating socialism: "In the mouth of an international Marxist that is remarkable praise, for it shows that the energy of nationalism is greater than the myth of class conflict. Sorel's other examples of myth also prove that when they occur in the modern period, the stronger myth is national." And in that precise sense, of offering a much-needed anti-dote to socialism, Schmitt construes, a few sentences further on, the significance of the still fresh fascist experiment (he writes in 1923):

> But wherever it comes to an open confrontation of the two myths, such as in Italy, the national myth has until today always been victorious. Italian fascism depicted its communist enemy with a horrific face, the Mongolian face of Bolshevism; this has made a stronger impact and has evoked more powerful emotions than the socialist image of the bourgeois.... In his famous speech of October 1922 in Naples before the March on Rome, Mussolini said, 'We have created a myth...Our myth is the nation, the great nation which we want to make a concrete reality for ourselves.' In the same speech he called socialism an inferior mythology (75–76).

Sorelian fascism indicates to the keen Schmitt, as it will soon do to a host of his countrymen, the way to overcome socialism: the myth of the nation. Nor will the use of anti-communist imagery, "the horrific, Mongolian face of Bolshevism," be lost upon such observers who will soon put it to good use, to eclipse the socialist attacks on "the bourgeois." Schmitt, accordingly, went out of his way to clarify that an uncompromising struggle can only "legitimately" unfold between nations, the proper enemies, whereas the Christian dictum of "love your enemies" only holds *within* one's nation, vis-à-vis the private competitor:

> The enemy is not...the private adversary whom one hates.... The enemy is solely the public enemy, because everything that has a relationship to such a collectivity of men, *particularly to a whole nation*, become public by virtue of such a relationship.... The often quoted 'Love your enemies'... reads 'diligite inimicos vestros,'...and not *diligite hostes vestros*. No mention is made of the political enemy. Never in the thousand-year struggle between Christians and Moslems did it occur to a Christian to surrender rather than defend Europe out of love toward the Saracens or Turks. The enemy in the political sense need not be hated personally, and in the *private sphere only* does it makes sense to *love one's 'enemy,'* i.e. one's adversary (Schmitt 2007: 28–29; emphases added).

If Schmitt's overt polemical target is liberalism, his entire theoretical construct is in truth devised to offset socialism. He is not a detached political scientist, interested in understanding how politics *actually* functions, but a pedagogic instructor, educating his readers about how politics *should* function, equipped with an "understanding" of "the political" as such. Where socialism, in actual political life, upholds international fraternity between nations and peoples who have done no wrong to each other, say Muslims and Christians, Schmitt insists that this concept falsifies the political and hence has no place. And where socialism points out the necessity of class struggle within the nation, to end the exploitation of the workers by the bourgeois, Schmitt emphasizes that here one is dealing not with "an enemy" properly speaking but with a "private adversary," and therefore neighbourly love would not be unbefitting. The reader, who hitherto hated the capitalist with whom he has a real grievance, and did not care about the Saracen (or the Jew, or the French, or the Bolshevik), is advised by the counselling jurist to consider reconciling himself with the capitalist and start arming himself against the Saracen, whom he does not hate in the least. Relying on Plato, Schmitt explicitly argues that the political friend-enemy distinction truly holds in the fight against an external enemy, whereas within the nation one only engages in a pseudo-political, futile and purely destructive civil war:

> In his *Republic* Plato strongly emphasizes the contrast between the public enemy and the private one, but in connection with the other anti-thesis of war and insurrection, upheaval, rebellion, civil war. Real war was for Plato a war between Hellenes and Barbarians (those who are 'by nature enemies'), whereas conflicts among Hellenes are for him discords. The thought expressed here is that a people cannot wage war against itself and a civil war is only a self-laceration and it does not signify that perhaps a new state or even a new people is being created (28–29).[21]

Thomas Mann, when he was no longer a conservative peer of Schmitt, equally drew the distinction between *external* and *internal* war, a *national* and a *social* one, but giving precedence to the *latter*. As stated by the narrator of *Doctor Faustus*: "morally considered, the people's means of breaking through to a higher form of communal life—if indeed it must involve bloodshed—should not be the external war, but the civil war" (Mann 1967: 402).

---

[21] The corresponding Greek terms which Schmitt added in parentheses, I have here omitted without indicating empty spaces, since the terms are irrelevant for our discussion and, indicated, would have interrupted the flow of the passage.

Nationalism and its Vicissitudes

At this point, an important caveat is due: my aim is to stress the
weighty liberal contribution to nationalism, indeed to the fascist variant of nationalism, but not to *reduce* nationalism, not even at the historical period with which we are dealing, to liberalism. The national,
indeed, is "a completely neutral concept, which can be filled with the
most disparate content" (Thomas Mann). And without doubt it can
accommodate a content highly resistant to capitalism. To realize this,
it suffices to think about the familiar opposition between "nationalization" and "privatization." This unruliness of nationalism, which
became eminently clear during the epoch of anti-colonialist liberation
struggles, and which continues today in the face of "globalization," is
by no means a phenomenon of the last decades. 19th century nationalism was never fully subservient to capitalism or entirely congruent with
liberal economics: in Germany, in particular, but elsewhere as well, it
often served as a rallying point for those forces that were unhappy
about industrialism but equally averse to socialism. In the writings
of such ideologues as Paul de Lagarde or Julius Langbehn, who could
scarcely be sociologically described other than "petty bourgeois," one
finds an explicit opposition to industrialism and its alleged deleteri-
ous effects, social, moral, cultural. For them—taken as spokesmen for
independent artisans, small scale producers, as well as sections of the
intelligentsia and the so-called *Bildungsbürgertum* (Lagarde, for example, was one of Germany's leading biblical scholars and orientalists
before taking on a career as a political agitator)—nationalism meant a
putative defense of these groups' endangered prerogatives against the
encroaching of big-business.

A constellation of this kind meant that, as far as liberalism was
concerned, nationalism was a tricky weapon to handle: on the one
hand, precisely because of its inherent ambiguity and potential appeal
to diverse constituencies, nationalism was highly suitable to galvanize
support behind a—de facto—capitalist-imperialist agenda and dissolve
the attractions of socialism. On the other hand, it meant harboring
and fuelling hopes and expectations which were not seamlessly harmonious with capitalism, and which might turn into a challenge in
their own right. This applies to other topics we have been discussing.
For one can indeed disseminate myths and stir up the irrational in the
hope of collecting the fruits of such policies, but the unleashed irratio-

nal is a Pandora's box burst open: the starting point may be known, but the lengths to which such policies may lead, or haul one, can hardly be gauged. Some of the more cautious bourgeois-liberal thinkers, even as they contributed to the nationalistic and irrational build up, did not fail to notice the hazards accompanying such practices. Mosca, for example, while a vital figure in the move to a markedly mythical and propagandistic politics, while pointing out the benefits of patriotism in the fight against socialism, and while advocating the need of the ruling classes to disentangle themselves from political liberalism since it has turned too democratic ("the bourgeoisie has been...the prisoner not only of its democratic principles but also of its liberal principles" Mosca 1939: 392), was nonetheless aware of the associated dangers (hardly a visionary feat, it must be said, given the fresh lesson of the First World War):

> Unfortunately, love of country, and a natural desire that one's country should make its influence more and more felt in the world, often goes hand in hand with diffidence toward other countries and sometimes with hatred of them. The overexcitation of these patriotic sentiments undoubtedly helped to create the moral and intellectual atmosphere that brought on the World War (482).

In view of such an "unfortunate" repercussion of nationalistic feelings considered in and of themselves natural (and—we may add—useful), Mosca recommended, especially after the War, a modicum of caution: to excite, yes, but not to *over*excite. This applied in other domains as well: not to abolish the representative system altogether but to drastically curtail it; not to espouse a "bureaucratic and military dictatorship" (487) but to practice elitism and strive for the rule of "a small moral and intellectual aristocracy" (493), not to eliminate freedom of expression, but to ensure that it doesn't overstep its proper boundaries (492): "Ways can surely be found to maintain freedom for scientific investigation and for honest criticism of acts of government, and at the same time to place restraints on the corruption of minds that are, and will forever remain, minds of children. That corruption has so far been freely practiced in our European countries." While proto-fascist in many regards, Mosca's final word was one of—relative—moderation, warning against the dangers of a new "Caesarism" (while even then, to be sure, insisting [488] that Italy's *greatest* danger was *not* the fascists but the Syndicalists and their plan to socialistically dominate parliament).

In Germany, equally, fascist nationalism brought with it not only a pro-capitalist consensus but also an undercurrent of dissent: the culmination of this duality was the famous mid-1934 purge of the SA's leadership and the expurgation of their and their cadres' ominous demand for a "second revolution." For in the form of the leftist—with or without quotation marks—factions of Nazism, particularly those led by the Strasser brothers, a variant of nationalism survived which was considerably less subservient to the hegemonic purposes of the military-industrial complex. In Otto Strasser, in particular, such nationalism included a desire to see Germany move towards a socialized economy as well as an explicit repudiation of imperialism. The following words, from the July 1930 proclamation of the Otto-Strasser-group explaining their reasons for breaking with the NSDAP, encapsulate the vastly different understanding of nationalism between the Hitlerite, dominant line, and the marginalized voices on the "left," by those who regard themselves as "socialists":

> We have understood and still understand National Socialism as a consciously *anti-imperialist movement*, whose nationalism is limited to the preservation and protection of the life and growth of the German nation, without any tendencies to rule over other peoples and countries.... For us the endorsement of the *struggle of the Indian people to liberate itself* from British rule and capitalist exploitation was and remains a necessity,... since it is a compelling consequence of our idea of nationalism that the right of fulfilling one's national [*völkisch*] particularity [*Eigenart*], which we claim for ourselves, is also the right of all other peoples and nations, and given that the liberal concept of the 'blessings of culture,' is alien to us (Kühnl 2000: 113).

For Hitler, nationalism rather stood for the right of the *master*-races and nations to fulfill their imperialistic designs, a right that he fully acknowledged for Britain as well, not least in India, as a few reminders will exemplify: "The Englishman is the German's superior because of his self-confidence. Self-confidence possesses only he who can command" (in Picker 2003: 79); or: "The birthplace of English self-confidence is India. 400 years ago the English had none of it. The enormous space of India compelled them to rule millions with few people.... What India was to England, the space-in-the-east [*Ostraum*] would be to us" (93).

In this comparison with the Otto-Strasser faction, it is also useful to record the fact that for Hitler the "liberal notion of the blessings of culture," the proverbial "white man's burden," was not in the least "alien." He shared this discourse with British imperialism (as well as with a host of liberals: Renan's support of the benefits of the British Empire for the Indian natives, that I mentioned above, is just an example):

> He who had shed blood, also has the right to rule. Indian freedom will not last 20 years. The English reproach themselves today for wrongly ruling the country, because the country does not show enthusiasm. But they did it right. It is wrong to expect enthusiasm. Had the English not been the rulers, there would not now be 380 million Indians. England exploited India; but English rule also handsomely benefited India (164).

It is also interesting that among those comparatively left-wing circles within National Socialism there was a marked disinclination to understand the movement in terms of fascism at all. Thus, in the same proclamation, the Otto-Stasserites distanced themselves from the "excessive worship of the fascist authoritarian state" (in Kühnl 2000: 114).[22] The Strassers, particularly the organizational skills of Gregor, have played a major role in spreading the gospel of National Socialism and building the party machine, but they also did a lot to disseminate the vagueness concerning its final goals and contents. And the core of such ambiguity indeed centrally involved defining the precise nature of both the "nationalism" and the "socialism" of "National Socialism." For Otto Strasser, the point was to subordinate nationalism to a socialist imperative, whereas for Hitler, "socialism" was a means of mobilizing support for nationalism of a capitalist and imperialist kind.[23] My argument, in summary, means not to let liberalism sop up nationalism, but, by foregrounding the long suppressed affinities and interplay between liberalism and nationalism, to counterbalance those mainstream interpretations that have been content with portraying nationalism simply as a petty-bourgeois anti-capitalism.

Germany Above All?

Concluding this discussion, I wish to draw attention to another paradox underlying fascist "ultra-nationalism." Does it in fact mean that

---

[22] See also, Strasser (1940: 112–13), where Hitler and Otto Strasser engage in a heated dispute, Hitler taking the side of fascist Italy and praising its solution of the social problem, while Strasser criticizes Italian fascism for leaving "capitalism … intact, just as you yourself propose to leave it intact." For a very useful and meticulous discussion of the variants and shades of "anti-fascism" which was current among the Nazi left-wing, see Hoepke (1968: 197–240).

[23] Cf. Strasser (1940: 9–12; 106–7; 110–114).

nationalism was *the main factor*, the ultimate motivation behind all that fascists did or think? Such an assumption implicitly credits those who have recklessly sent millions of their compatriots to their deaths, with a love of nation and people that they scarcely deserve. Take Hitler's understanding of the nation. Was the German nation Hitler's sine qua non? To be sure, exoterically, in his public utterances, meant to court public consensus and calculated to encourage the greatest sacrifices, Hitler never tired of emphasizing that Germany was the first, indeed the only priority, as when, in his *Last Testament*, he expressed his "self-evident" gratitude to the efforts of the German people and wished them the best of success in creating, after his death, the genuine *Volksgemeinschaft*, along the National Socialist line he had set forth. Privately and esoterically, however, in the ears of those persons in the know, Hitler often articulated a rather different set of priorities. In March 1945, he told Albert Speer, according to the latter's testimony in the Nuremberg Trials, that there is no need to take measures to preserve what remained of the German economy for the post-War era:

> If the war is lost, the people would be lost too. That is an inevitable fate. It is not needed to show consideration to the rudimentary necessities which the people requires for its primitive survival. It would actually be better to destroy such things ourselves, since the people have proven themselves the weaker, and the future belongs exclusively to the stronger people of the East. Those who remain after the fight are the inferior ones, since the good ones had fallen (in Domarus 1973, vol. 4: 2213–14).

The authenticity of this statement has been questioned, for example by Max Domarus, who pointed out Speer's more than probable subsequent interest in discrediting Hitler and therewith shedding a more positive light on himself, as the true patriot concerned with Germany's welfare.[24] It might also be attributed to Hitler's mood of morose pessimism and resignation, corresponding to the utterly hopeless situation during the final weeks of the war. And yet, in its gist regarding Hitler's real, if covert, attitude to the German people, this utterance is confirmed by several other ones, and Domarus himself immediately added (2214) that Hitler "on other occasions made numerous disparaging comments on the German people, particularly for the eventual-

---

[24] Domarus (1973, vol. 4: 2214) highlighted the completely atypical way in which Hitler allegedly commended the people of the East, whereas elsewhere he constantly spoke of Russian primitivism.

ity of 'failure.' Apart from that, it is doubtless that at bottom he was indifferent to the fate of the German people." Thus, always in private and surrounded by his intimate entourage or in front of his officers, Hitler made clear that his "love" of the German nation was anything but unconditional. In December 1940, when the war was still winnable, Hitler exclaimed:

> I was determined not to do things by half, but to stake everything on one card.... The question is whether these 85 million people, nationally united, could assert their claim to life, or not. If yes, then the future of Europe belongs to this people. If not, then this people will die away, will fade [*zurücksinken*], and it will no longer be worth it, to live in this people! (Domarus 1973, vol. 3: 1639)

Ultra-nationalism was thus embedded in, indeed *subservient to*, ultra Social Darwinism. In the final analysis, it was not a case of *Deutschland über alles!* but of the *Leistungsprinzip*, the principle of achievement, above all else. It did not occur to Hitler that nationalism might have an inherent significance or prerogative *independent* of ultraist capitalism, apart from the-survival-of-the-fittest matrix. It is a case of "do or die," and if you do not "do" you *deserve* to "die," individually, as well as nationally. A life apart from *doing*, at the margins of the perennial cycle of competition and war, is inconceivable:

> Nature herself, in times of great distress…steps in by restricting the population of certain countries or races; this, however, is a method that is as wise as it is ruthless. She does not restrict the procreative faculty as such, but the conservation of the propagated, by subjecting them to such severe trials and deprivations that all less strong and healthy are forced to return to the bosom of the eternally Unknown (Hitler 1941: 169).

Or:

> Nature does not know political frontiers. She first puts the living beings on this globe and watches the free game of energies. He who is strongest in courage and industry receives, as her favorite child, the right to be the master of existence.... Mankind has grown strong in eternal struggles and it will only perish through eternal peace (174–5).

Negating such Social Darwinism is "primarily the Jew," in his attempt "to play a little trick on Nature, to make the hard and inexorable struggle for life superfluous" (176). Ultra-nationalism was not the goal to which capitalism should serve as means, but, on the contrary, eschatological capitalism employed nationalism for its purposes, and drove it to its utmost limits. The nation provided the necessary platform, from which to launch a capitalistic expansion campaign. Germany was worth fighting for, but on the assumption that it was indeed nature's "favorite child." In the fascist axiological hierarchy, to the extent that Hitler is its legitimate interpreter, the nation comes only after a fetishized Nature, whose graces are conferred upon those who are successful in the business of imperialism and capitalism, those "strongest in courage and industry." Countless individuals were sacrificed, exoterically for the good of "Germany." But "Germany" too, was being—esoterically—sacrificed, put entire on the gambling table, "on one card." Hence the nonchalance with which Hitler could dismiss the German nation once it had failed the test of nature, had proven itself its unworthy child. As Hitler stated, once more, in private: "Here, too, I am ice cold: if the German people is not willing to commit itself to its self-preservation, very well: then it should vanish!" (Picker 2003: 135).[25] The notion of "nationalism" or "ultra-nationalism" as defining "the fascist minimum" is thus largely devoid of meaning, unless one is willing to acknowledge the concrete class content of such "nationalism," and the way the national "palingenesis" was itself predicated on the bedrock of imperialistic-capitalistic triumph. A prosaic complicity that is revealingly encapsulated in the following, terse formulation, by one of the leading theorists and advocates of the German national renaissance, Oswald Spengler (1933b: 335), whose insider's testimony can serve as a befitting conclusion to this chapter: "If, instead of nationalism, one were to say healthy economic egoism, the difference would not be very great."

---

[25] This cavalier dismissal of Germany's survival on the part of its *Führer* is documented in Joachim Fest's *Inside Hitler's Bunker* (2005). The author, however, sees this only in terms of Hitler's personal traits, that of a reckless "gambler turned politician" (41), etc. By contrast, Hitler's peculiarities notwithstanding, I suggest seeing this attitude as symptomatic of the general cynicism of fascism when exploiting the nation. In fact, Fest's attempt to reduce Nazism into Hitler's extravagant personality runs constantly into trouble. He claims, for example, that the "boundless force that drove him throughout his life was the maxim of the survival of the fittest. From start to finish, it alone describes what he propounded as his philosophy of life," and that all of Hitler's further "concepts," such as—"suppression, enslavement, and 'racial cleansing'"—"grew out of this Darwinist principle" (166). This is a sound theory, in my view, and Fest points to a vital pillar of fascism. And yet it contradicts his own core argument about the uniqueness of Hitler, which allegedly sets Nazism apart from both the German and the Western tradition. Hitler, we are told, was "a phenomenon unlike any other in history," since "his goals included absolutely no civilizing ideas," as opposed to ancient Rome, the Holy Roman Empire, Napoleon's France, the British Empire, and "even Stalin's bloody despotism" (165). The obvious problem with this claim, however, is that Hitler can be ascribed many things, but not the invention of social Darwinism. And if indeed, as Fest avers, all the horror resulted from "the maxim of the survival of the fittest," then the effort to isolate Hitler from the Western tradition is self-refuting.

SUB-MAN, UNDERMAN, *UNTERMENSCH*:
FASCISM AS AN INTERNATIONAL CO-PRODUCTION

Ever since the scope of the destruction it unleashed, the depths of horror it plunged the world into and the apex of brutality it reached, fascism has duly become a taboo, something to be condemned, repudiated, and disclaimed. But this has not always been the case. There was a time when fascism held a great attraction for many people, including first-rank intellectuals and highly placed politicians in countries that did not turn fascist; a time when Winston Churchill, today remembered mainly as a staunch fighter against fascism, could say that fascism "has rendered a service to the whole world.... Hereafter no great nation will be unprovided with an ultimate means of protection against the cancerous growth of Bolshevism" (Goldring 1945: 223), and described Mussolini further as "the greatest law-giver among living men" (Harbutt 1986: 30);[1] and a time when Foreign Secretary Lord Halifax and Prime Minister Neville Chamberlain—today remembered mainly as feeble, pacifistic democrats, too slight to take up Hitler's gauntlet and too blind even to perceive that it had been thrown down—could express admiration for Hitler personally, and for his National Socialism politically: Lord Halifax, regarded Nazi Germany in November 1937 as "a bulwark of the west against Bolshevism" (Leibovitz and Finkel 1998: 103), while in Chamberlain's view, as reported to the King on September 1938, Germany and England "were the two pillars of European peace and buttresses against communism" (25–26).

This large-scale appreciation and at times outright collusion—finding expressions political, economic, cultural—has now traditionally become, not so much a source of embarrassment, as of denial. The attempt is frequently to *dis*-own fascism, to make it the affair of someone else, preferably of one's political and ideological antagonists. Conservatives and liberals have recurrently laid it at the door of socialism

---

[1] Churchill's "admiration" for Mussolini, the author stresses, "continued to the brink of World War II."

and of communism and have been content with making fascism at least the dialectical twin of socialism, if not its outright manifestation. It mattered little that, when fascism was still an historical reality, it was widely regarded precisely as the universal cure against socialism and communism, "the necessary antidote to the Russian poison," again in Churchill's words, and that whole parties, conservative and liberal, had drastically thinned and dwindled in direct proportion to the degree that the fascists had been beating up *the lefties;*[2] that conservative and liberal politicians had formed all kinds of alliances with the fascists, ran with them to parliament, sat with them in coalitions, invited them to take power, while the left-wing parties, who retained their mass support almost undiminished,[3] were being outlawed, their leaders and supporters persecuted, imprisoned, driven into exile, even murdered.

The Liberal Northwest: Immune to Fascism?

Not all interpretations, of course, have gone quite that far. But even many of the more moderate readings portray fascism as something alien, and employ, as I have argued, a Brechtian *Verfremdungseffekt*, yet not in order to problematize the familiar, but to make it appear safe, habitable, reasonable. The common effort is to localize the catastrophe, so as to envelop its environs in a tranquil, civilized light. There are numerous instances of such a procedure. I take Michael Mann's book on fascism as an example, which lends this approach to history one of its more sophisticated and erudite voices and whose theoretical framework processes and incorporates the contributions of Sternhell,

---

[2] See the case of such major German parties as the centrist-liberal DVP and the right-wing DNVP, which, between them, had 22.9 percent of the national vote in 1928, before the great Nazi electoral breakthrough of 1930, only to be reduced to a combined 7.3 percent in July 1932, and making the slightest of recoveries in November, with 9.8 percent (see Gluckstein 1999: 79). A similar situation obtained in Italy in the years preceding the fascist take over (see, De Grand 1982: 34–35, 45).

[3] During the last phase of the Republic of Weimar and the meteoric rise of the Nazis, the combined electoral share of the left-wing parties, communists and socialists, suffered only marginal losses: from 40.4 percent in 1928 to 36.1 in July 1932 and 37.3 in November. In fact, in the last year of the Republic, the total left-wing share of the votes was *higher* than it had been in the two elections of 1924: 33.9 and 35.1 (see Gluckstein 1999: 79). In Italy, as well, in May 1921, amid the violence of the *squadristi*, "the combined Socialist and Communist vote…dropped only slightly from the high point of 1919," at the time that the fascist party outvoted Giolitti's Liberals, their allies of the national bloc (De Grand 1982: 34).

Griffin and the later work of Mosse, etc. Mann, though, wishes to endow this body of work with a more empirical and sociological foundation. He reinvents and schematizes the long-standing explanation, which distinguishes between countries who turned fascist and those who did not, on the basis of the existence, or lack thereof, of a solid liberal tradition and institutions. Mann draws a geo-political demarcation line between the northwest of Europe, at the heart of which is, unsurprisingly, England (and France, to a lesser extent), which had remained immune to fascism, and the center and southeast, at the heart of which are Germany and Italy, which had embraced it.[4] He writes: "Whatever crises world war and capitalism threw at the northwest, its liberal states survived" (Mann 2004: 77). "The northwest," he affirms (90), "withstood crises until Hitler's armies marched on them. Though buffeted by the Great Depression, by strike waves, and by fluctuating party alliances, it was not in serious danger from its own authoritarian right." This theory allows Mann to draw some encouraging conclusions, with regards to the soundness and workability of "northwestern" liberal-democratic institutions, their moral as well as practical advantages:

> Liberal and social democracies recognize no monopoly of virtue, no absolute truth. They are antiheroic. I have learned from writing these two books not to expect our democratic politicians to be too principled. We need their instrumentalism, their dirty deals. But fascists differed. They saw politics as unlimited activism to achieve moral absolutes (8).

From a northwestern perspective, a study of the historical experience of fascism, its horrors notwithstanding, thus ultimately produces a reassuring sensation. The unfamiliar vindicates the familiar, and the historian and his readers, if they are north-westerners as well, can take comfort in the knowledge that "we" are well served by the liberal and social democracies surrounding us. Even more than simply obviating the need for self-introspection, fascism makes the otherwise unappealing features of western democracies emerge in a new, positive light.

---

[4] This reads like a belated attempt at a generalized *Sonderweg* theory of fascism, now applied not only to the proverbial black sheep of European nations, Germany, but to *all* countries who turned fascist, fatally departing from the northwestern path. For a by now almost classic critique of the *Sonderweg* thesis in its original form, disputing the alleged exceptionality of 19th-century Germany by way of a very useful comparison with England, see Blackbourn and Eley (1984).

The opportunism, loose principles and shadowy maneuvers of their politicians are all made good, regarded as some useful antidote to the pitfalls of totalitarian politicians, by implication pedantic, unwavering and incorruptible. Mussolini and Hitler, one is almost induced to believe, never struck dirty deals, in their single-minded, fanatical effort to pursue their projects of "class transcendence." The facts evident today to so many observers and citizens that democracy in western countries glosses over social differences, neutralizes them politically while *exacerbating* them economically; that it increasingly deprives political alternatives of real substance, and that it does all this, moreover, not so much as a "compromise" but to promote the interests of social elites, is re-interpreted as an extra bonus attached to the western way of doing things. In the northwest, Mann tells us, "Conservatives resisted authoritarian rightists, but social democrats also resisted revolutionaries. Thus both were able to process and to compromise their conflicts *through democratic institutions*, which *deepened* as a result. Yet authoritarians prospered in the center, east, and south of the continent. In Austrian, German, and Spanish free elections they reached near 40 percent of the votes" (41; emphases added). This does not remain a strictly historical exposition, but expands (38) into a laudation of current, western democracy: "At the end of the millennium, all of Europe's states were formally committed to multiparty democracy...Though democracy proves hard to export to other parts of the world, it dominates the west." Coming from an historian of Mann's caliber, this last sentence is breathtakingly ingenuous, suggesting that the west over the last fifty years was trying to "export" democracy to countries not yet ripe for it (not yet liberal enough, apparently; or maybe still "too principled"). Does the record of western involvement in third world matters, indeed of the western flagships England and the USA, even remotely bear out such an implication? One might at this point unfold a long list of countries to which the west had exported dictatorships, and a list about as long of countries which saw their home-grown democracies, enjoying substantial mass support, overthrown with indispensable western connivance. But I will leave it at that. After all, if we are willing to take fascists at their word rather than at their deed, as does the historiographic school to which Mann belongs, it would certainly be uncouth to mistrust western politicians and their discourses.

But let us return to the past and ask: how justified are such reassuring conclusions, how warranted the trust in the northwestern liberal tradition and its ability to resist fascism? Mann is right, of course, to point out that England—the model northwestern country—did not turn fascist whereas Germany or Italy—presumably the prototype countries of the center and the south, respectively—did. Yet does he have a case to affirm that what made the difference was the strength of the liberal tradition-cum-institutions in the former? An answer to the question of why fascism did not attain power in England, would require a separate study. Here we can only make some suggestions, draw attention to some pertinent question marks, and warn against them being turned into ones of exclamation.

Mann, we may recall, asserted that, "Whatever crises world war and capitalism threw at the northwest, its liberal states survived." The obvious problem with this equation is that England did not face a crisis anywhere near as acute as did Germany. Mann in reality mistakes a speculation for a statement of fact. So let us speculate, too: had the English ruling classes 1) lost the war 2) had they seen their empire crumble and parts of their perceived homeland under occupation and 3) their monarchy turned into a republic as a result of a Bolshevik revolutionary wave 4) had they confronted an organized and militant working class to a far greater degree than they did and, finally, 5) had they been plunged into an economic crisis—inflation, unemployment—significantly greater than they did, would they then, in the face of all that, have been able to resist the pressure or the temptation to install in power some authoritarian, or indeed fascist, dictator? Would their strong liberal institutions and tradition have been able to weather *such* a storm? Perhaps, and it would certainly be unwise to dismiss the importance of national traditions; but this remains a conjecture. We might equally speculate whether *Germany* would have succumbed to a Hitler in the absence of all the factors numbered. And we may here register the fact that a politician as quintessentially English as Churchill did not only emphasize the universal applicability of fascism as an emergency solution but, as late as September 1937, argued that, "one may dislike Hitler's system yet admire his patriotic achievement. If our country were defeated, I hope we should find a champion as indomitable to restore our courage and lead us back to our place among the nations" (James 1978: 526). Be that as it may, we are clearly not entitled to affirm that England and Germany faced the same challenge and responded differently on account of their different geo-political traditions. Here we ought to pause, not take a leap of faith asserting the wholesomeness of liberal institutions. It is impossible to assess how weighty they actually were, and irresponsible to ascribe to them a decisive importance.

There are other problems with Mann's neat geo-political scheme, such as the assertion that "parliamentary sovereignty was routinized across the northwest and so resilient.... The northwest withstood crises until Hitler's armies marched on them." Yet what about such countries in south and central Europe like, for example, Spain and Czechoslovakia? There, no less than in the northwest, there was no internal implosion of democracy but a military defeat before the armies of Hitler (in the former indirectly, in the latter directly so). This complicates the geographical aspect of the theory; but there is a second complication, more profound, affecting its very political pillar. For the defeat of both Spain and Czechoslovakia would have been unthinkable without the passivity of the liberal northwest, particularly England, who had the power to stop fascist aggression but chose not to; and not out of weakness and reluctance to join the fight. The political leaders of England, as the historians Clement Leibovitz and Alvin Finkel cogently argued in an important study, positively *desired* for Czechoslovakia to give way, so that Germany might gain its corridor to the east, and be able to attack the hated USSR. Neville Henderson, the British ambassador to Nazi Berlin from 1937 to 1939, expressed this point of view in unmistakable terms:

> To put it bluntly,...the German is certainly more civilized than the Slav, and in the end, if properly handled, also less potentially dangerous to British interests—One might even go so far as to assert that it is not even just to endeavour to prevent Germany from completing her unity or from being prepared for war against the Slavs provide her preparations are such as to reassure the British Empire that they are not simultaneously designed against it (in Leibovitz and Finkel 1998: 103).

Similarly, the English government much preferred to see authoritarianism triumph in Spain rather than the democratic republicans, since the latter happened to be socialistic. "The triumph of fascism in Spain," write Leibovitz and Finkel (188), "did not trouble Chamberlain—unsurprisingly, since he supported Franco over Spain's democratic forces, like most of the British elite." Reading Mann, one gets the soothing impression that the leaders of liberal democracies, whatever their petty faults, were ultimately upright defenders of democracy. He never undertakes an examination of the stance of the leaders of England or France, and is content with *presupposing* their democratic commitment. Leibovitz and Finkel, who by contrast undertake a close reading of all the relevant foreign policy documents, demolish such widespread and complacent assumptions. They show in detail that the British political elite was generally contemptuous of democracy. Neville

Chamberlain, for one, is cited (155) describing the British electorate as "an immense mass of very ignorant voters of both sexes whose intelligence is low and who have no power of weighing evidence."

Guided by such conceptions, the British elite, with Chamberlain at its head, proceeded to connive with Hitler behind the back of the ignorant populace, reaching a series of semi-formal and then formal agreements whose main goal was not to avoid war as officially proclaimed—the fateful remilitarization of Germany, both before and after the accession of the Nazis to power, was sanctioned, if not outright encouraged, by England—but to see Nazi Germany chastise the less civilized Slavs, as Henderson "bluntly" put it. This casts a serious doubt on Mann's sanguine statement (2004: 90) that, in the northwest, "the rise of fascism was not... viewed as the dawn of a brave new age but as a distant distasteful threat to civilization." On what is this based? If this holds true for large sections of the British and French masses who, incapable or not of weighing evidence, viewed Mussolini and Hitler with extreme dislike, is there any indication that the ruling elite in both countries, particularly England, in general shared such aversion? We have seen how, in the eyes of both Foreign Secretary Halifax and Prime Minister Chamberlain, fascism, indeed of the Nazi variety, signified an indispensable ally and guardian of the west. Nor should it be imagined that such politicians were merely the representatives of a tiny group of leaders which happened to take hold of the helm of the British Empire at the most inopportune historical moment. In truth, they ought more properly to be regarded as the tip of the iceberg. Fascism was esteemed by most of the British ruling class, an appreciation which, for many, included its utmost example: Nazism.[5] The European demarcation line separating the liberal-democratic northwest and the authoritarian-fascist center, south and east was hence much more blurry than Mann would have us believe.

Perhaps, after all, we are not so well served by the less than principled "instrumentalism" of our politicians and by the "dirty deals" they are prone to strike behind our backs. It might have helped if such politicians would have been more committed to principles, for example "democracy." Facing fascism, English democracy was in truth finally vindicated not by the plots and cynical opportunism of the politicians, but by the pressures exerted by public opinion, by those whom Chamberlain and Co. held in contempt, who were not willing to

---

[5] Cf. Leibovitz and Finkel 1998: 224.

tolerate further compromises with fascist aggression on the part of their leaders. The lesson to be gleaned from fascism is thus not in favor of elitist intrigues, but of popular initiative and pressure.[6]

British Interwar Fascism beyond Mosley

Commonly, the abortive experience of Oswald Mosley's BUF provides historians with seemingly hard evidence that fascism was, in Britain, a foreign political breed, bound to come to nothing. But this is to take cognition only of explicit, nominal fascism. For Stanley G. Payne (1996: 304), for example, the British Union of Fascists was "a contradiction in terms, a sort of political oxymoron," given that, at most, it might have united "a variety of totally insignificant grouplets using the name fascist…each pettier and more irrelevant than the others." Quite so; but what about British political groups *not* "using the name fascist"? One more time we come up against an issue that has been at the centre of this book ever since the Introduction, namely the difference between political rhetoric and reality, ideology and practice, between *names* and *substances*. The problematic of fascism in England, I take it, cannot be reduced to the BUF and adjacent "grouplets." And while historians overwhelmingly tend to look at British fascism strictly through the prism of expressly fascist groups, contemporary observers, among them some of the most incisive, approached affairs with a political outlook more subtle as well as more profound, less concerned with epithets and more with fundamental social and economic interests. Churchill's idea that Mussolini's new political experiment had provided "the ultimate means of protection" for every "great nation" was a commonplace rather than an oddity. We may consult a figure as different from the future Prime Minister as the novelist Evelyn Waugh who, in 1936, commended the ostensible civilizing effects of the Italian occupation of Abyssinia. Similarly, writing in 1938, and without both-

---

[6] The indispensable role of anti-fascist public opinion in ultimately drawing their "democratic" leaders to war against Hitler contrary to their inclinations and schemes, was repeatedly and forcefully underscored by Carroll Quigley (1981). He wrote, for example (261), that "The fear of Hitler's using war was based not so much on a dislike of force (neither Lothian nor Halifax was a pacifist in that sense) but on the realization that if Hitler made war against Austria, Czechoslovakia, or Poland, public opinion in France and England might force their governments to declare war in spite of their desire to yield these areas to Germany. This, of course, is what finally happened."

ering to refer to Mosley, he made it quite clear that fascism in Britain is by no means an impossibility, and if it remained unlikely at the time of writing this was decidedly *not* on account of any immanent incompatibility with the English character. Quite the contrary, the English disposition, or more specifically the disposition of the *English middle class*, was eminently suitable for embracing fascism, according to Waugh. It was only that the middle class had not been forced to go to such lengths by strictly external circumstances, namely because the Marxist challenge had not been strong enough:

> [Fascism] is a growth of certain peculiar soils; principally it needs two things—a frightened middle class who see themselves in danger of extinction in a proletarian state, and some indignant patriots who believe that their country, through internal dissension, is becoming bullied by the rest of the world. In England we had something like a Fascist movement in 1926, when the middle classes broke the General Strike. We have a middle class that is uniquely apt for strenuous physical adventures, amenable to discipline, bursting with *esprit de corps*, and a great fund of patriotism.... It is quite certain that England would become Fascist before it became communist; it is quite unlikely to become either...(Waugh, as quoted in Patey 2001: 147).

Elsewhere (146), Waugh clarified that what holds true for the English middle class in general also applies in his own, personal case: "If I were a Spaniard I should be fighting for General Franco. As an Englishman, I am not in the predicament of choosing between two evils. I am not a Fascist nor shall I become one unless it were the only alternative to Marxism. It is mischievous to suggest that such a choice is imminent." For Douglas Lane Patey, Waugh's biographer, statements such as these show that Waugh's conservatism never "veered to Fascism" (142). I see them as calling for a very different interpretation. To my mind, they rather show how Waugh, by his own admission, and by extension the English bourgeoisie, was a *potential* fascist; what distinguished him as an Englishman from the *actual* fascists in other countries was not any substantial ideological disagreement but a matter of expediency: in other countries, one was forced to make a choice, pressed to the corner by the proletariat of one respective country, in a way that Waugh and his middle-class compatriots were not. Or rather they had been so threatened in 1926, but were able to subdue the forces of "communism," with a kind of provisional, rough-and-ready fascism, suitable to meet the emergency of the General Strike. Fascism, of course, is "evil," something which it is so much pleasanter and more convenient to do

without. But it is clearly preferable to general strikes. It is unappealing
in the sense that a bitter medicine is: you don't take it, unless you
have to, unless the workers' start to get unruly in earnest. There is
thus no distinctly English, principled argument against such evil, one
that pushes it beyond the pale, say the liberal commitment to the rule
of law or to democracy (far from it: Waugh unswervingly admits that
he is "no more impressed by the 'legality' of the Valencia government
than are English Communists by the legality of the Crown, Lords and
Commons"); it is simply the fact that such evil, under the political
and social circumstances presently prevailing in England, is not yet a
necessary evil. One wonders: how many Spaniards, Italians and
Germans would have become "fascists," would have rallied to Franco,
Mussolini and Hitler, were they not convinced that such was the only,
last-ditch response to Marxism, in both its revolutionary and reformist
incarnations?

British interwar fascism is therefore not to be reduced to the BUF.
In fact, even Mosley's failure does not seamlessly or necessarily attest
to the alleged inadaptability of the foreign implant of fascism to British
soil. It would be interesting to draw an analogy between the weakness of official fascism in Britain to that of official liberalism in Italy
and Germany, but one that will reverse the usual terms of the debate:
European fascists, the reader will recall, often complained of the fact
that "liberalism," in their country, was taken literally, understood truly
to mean the limitless rule of the masses, whereas, in countries such as
England, democratic liberalism was actually a camouflaged version of
elite rule. By the same token, it is possible that Mosley's movement
failed to gain ground since it understood *European fascism* all too literally, as truly implying some Third Road between the classes, a genuine attempt to transcend class strife. Something like this was suggested
by a major contemporary, the Fabian Socialist Beatrice Webb, who
prophesized that Mosley's "New Party will never get born alive; it will
be a political abortion." But her entirely correct prediction was based
not on the immanent unsuitability of fascism to England as much it
highlighted the fact that Mosley's plan failed to align itself clearly with
one of the major social forces, either with the workers' movement or
with capitalism, thus falling "dead in a No Man's Land between those
who wish to keep and those who wish to change the existing order."
As a result of such social vagueness, she added, there was nothing in
Mosley's programme "that will *grip* any section of the population—

the curious assortment of reforms...have no emotional appeal—they excite neither love nor hate" (in Cole 1956: 267–8). If these comments are anything to go by, then nominal fascism went flat in England not because it was too crass and aggressive to be incorporated into the local political landscape, but because it was not full-blooded enough to make itself appealing, not socially partisan enough to be relevant to any given constituency. It appears as if, contrary to mainstream historians, what turned fascism attractive was not its promise for social transcendence, not its bid to water down either socialism or capitalism, but rather the prospect of a clear-cut resolution, only outwardly disguising itself as "neutral" and "unbiased." Yet those truly neutral in a modern, class society, it seems, scarcely form a large enough constituency on which to build a successful party.

Crypto-Fascism

In view of these long suppressed historical realities, it is in truth tempting to argue that there is a sense in which England, the hub of the liberal-democratic west, short of becoming fascist, *did* succumb to fascism, only that we were never notified of the fact. This ties into the problematic of what Gaetano Salvemini, that astute and lucid observer with the remarkable capacity of sieving through countless details of political and social life and rescuing the important from the trivial, called "crypto-fascism." As early as 1927, Salvemini classified three different forces set against democracy:

> Democratic institutions are attacked not only from the left by the communists, but also from the right by the crypto-fascists, who despair of destroying them and look to appropriate their most delicate organs in order to pervert them, and by the fascists who attack them openly in the hope of establishing a dictatorship of the capitalist class (Salvemini and Shaw 1997: 145).

Though he did not give a concrete example of what he had in mind, it is clear that under "crypto-fascism" Salvemini would have included those politicians leading Britain vis-à-vis the open fascism of Italy and Germany. In *Prelude to World War II*, Salvemini wrote that during his study of international politics, his "opinion not only of the intelligence but also of the moral integrity of the men who governed England in those years (as distinct from the British people) underwent a series of disastrous shocks" (Salvemini 1954: 9). And he specified:

> [U]nder parliamentary, no less than under dictatorial governments, decisions, especially on matters of foreign policy, are taken, not by the peoples themselves, but by small cliques of 'experts' who often deceive their peoples: see what happened In England In 1935.... From the end of 1924 to the autumn of 1935 all British Foreign Ministers worked more or less hand in glove with Mussolini.... Mussolini is not the only villain in this book. The present writer... [does not] feel any respect, any admiration, any enthusiasm for Sir Austen Chamberlain, Sir John Simon, Sir Samuel Hoare, Stanley Baldwin, or Neville Chamberlain (8).

In another book, Salvemini (1973: 57) cited approvingly the views of the many who in 1938 "complained that England's foreign policy was determined by a small circle of pro-German magnates," and referred to the "convincing evidence" that "the M.P.s of the Tory party belong to a network of capitalist interests which have nothing to do with the masses of the British people." Clearly then, in Salvemini's view, the British elite was vigorously practising a brand of "crypto-fascism," taking possession of "the most delicate organs of democratic institutions in order to pervert them."

And the exiled Italian was not alone in detecting an important, if concealed, parallel between the praxis of British democracy and that of Italian fascism. Writing in 1930, G. K. Chesterton reached a remarkably similar conclusion, though from a position far less hostile to Mussolini:

> Mussolini does openly what enlightened, liberal and democratic governments do secretly. This is not the same as saying that Mussolini necessarily does right. Far from it; quite otherwise; heaven forbid. What enlightened, liberal and democratic governments do is generally wrong. What Mussolini does is, in my opinion, sometimes wrong...But the point to grasp is that he does and defends what they do and do not defend. They conceal; they effect the same thing, because they think it convenient; but they do not defend it, because they think it indefensible. He is acting with his own principles of Fascism; they are acting against their principles of Freedom (Chesterton 1990: 429).[7]

---

[7] Chesterton has been accused of sympathy for fascism, particularly in *The Resurrection of Rome*. And certainly, naïveté and wishful-thinking characterize his approach to the fascist regime, a myopia which in turn was grounded in his distinctly lower middle-class ideology. Such illusions, however, did not turn him into a foreign supporter of fascism: unlike Churchill, who assured Mussolini that, had he been an Italian, he would have fought alongside him unreservedly in the "struggle against the bestial appetites and passions of Leninism" (Goldring 1945: 223), or the fellow writer, Waugh, who made it public that, had he been a Spaniard, he would have fought for General Franco, Chesterton clarified that, had he been an Italian, he would have sup-

In all but designation, this, too, is an account of "crypto fascism," a concept which could be usefully juxtaposed with the liberal tradition of esoteric politics, discussed in Chapter 6, from Bagehot to the Straussians of this day and age, and which aims to lead king Demos by the nose, while feigning to do its wishes. It is thus appropriate that careful secrecy and covert deals played a vital role in the politics of the British elite when dealing with the fascist regimes, a fact amply documented in the pages of such rare, truly critical historians, who dare to probe beneath the surface of probity.[8] The point is not that negotiations were confidentially conducted, which is justifiable as part of an effort to reach diplomatic agreements. For what was kept hidden was not this or that detail, or even initiative, but rather the very substance of the deals themselves, the very goals that the politicians pursued, and for good reason, since these often enough formed the very opposite of what was openly proclaimed in order to soothe the public. Thus, exoterically, Chamberlain was reprimanding Germany, in the knowledge that the British public was fed up with Hitler's expansionism, while esoterically sending the *Führer* assurances *not* to take such public utterances seriously (Leibovitz and Finkel 1998: 150–1). The ultimate example of such doublespeak was the very notion of appeasement, the lofty façade of the effort to maintain the European peace, under whose cover the British politicians were briskly facilitating the next war between Germany and the USSR (and of course ultimately the war which Britain itself would be compelled to fight, though this was against their intentions). "War," as famously proclaimed in *1984*,

---

ported Don Sturzo's Popular Party, undeterred, indeed *encouraged*, by the criticism that this party was "too democratic" and amounted even to "Bolshevism dressed in white instead of red;...Communism masquerading as Catholicism." These claims, Chesterton emphasized (1990: 410), he had actually heard "with a deep feeling of pride."

Indeed, Chesterton's argument as a whole did not so much justify fascism as it deconstructed the pretence of English democracy, and denounced the way it had been silently handed over to a furtive, fraudulent, moneyed elite. The problem he identified with liberal democracy was not "Liberty, or even Liberalism," but rather the way that "Liberals [are] not even true to Liberalism, let alone Liberty.... Ours has not been an age of popular self-government; but of very unpopular secret government" (426–7). Its weaknesses notwithstanding, Chesterton's polemics is neither pro-fascist nor anti-democratic; on the contrary: its ultimate butt is English crypto-tyranny, subverting popular rule. "By every instinct of my being," he affirmed, "I should prefer English liberty to Latin discipline. But there is the Latin discipline; and where is the English liberty? Not, I deeply regret to explain, anywhere in England" (433).

[8] Such as Leibovitz and Finkel (1998), who themselves follow in the wake of the likes of Salvemini (1954), Quigley (1981) and Schuman (1942).

"is peace." Yet Orwell's critical gaze, it appears, did not have to stray far from home to discover the abuses of "totalitarianism." And there were other contemporaries who were alarmed by the patent analogies between the modus operandi of the British government and that of the European dictators. Among those dismayed by Chamberlain's cynical strategies of spreading mass panic was the celebrated historian R. G. Collingwood, who wrote in 1938:

> To me, therefore, the betrayal of Czechoslovakia was only a third case of the same policy by which the 'National' government had betrayed Abyssinia and Spain; and I was less interested in the fact itself than in the methods by which it was accomplished; the carefully engineered war-scare in the country at large, officially launched by the simultaneous issue of gas-masks and the prime minister's emotional broadcast, two days before his flight to Munich, and the carefully staged hysterical scene in parliament on the following night. These things were in the established traditions of Fascist dictatorial methods; except that whereas the Italian and German dictators sway mobs by appeal to the thirst for glory and national aggrandizement, the English prime minister did it by playing on sheer stark terror (in Leibovitz and Finkel 1998: 157).

To be sure, to the extent that such collective hoodwinking is successful, one can indeed dispense with the need for some of the more drastic and violent measures to which open fascism has regular recourse. By its very nature crypto-fascism is a milder, low-key fascism which might make it appear an appealing alternative. This is part of the pragmatic solution to the "problem" of mass democracy, which, given its historical antecedents, might be described as "the English model." Its essence consists of accepting democratic rule precisely to the extent that it is *not democratic*.

Michael Oakeshott, the ingenious English conservative—in fact pre-neo-liberal, inasmuch as he opposed the welfare state and espoused small government, individual initiative and unrestrained market forces—provides a good case in point. For example, writing in 1955, he disagreed with Walter Lippmann's pessimistic analysis of the crisis of liberal democracy, which the then famous American journalist understood in terms of the irrational, "Jacobine" tendency of the modern masses to exaggerate democratic demands at the expense of mandatory liberal limitations, notably the right of property. This, in Lippmann's view, was the key factor that has led to the collapse of liberal-democratic regimes and to the rise of authoritarian ones. Oakeshott, however, sensed here a "misplaced gloom." His confidence in the prospect of liberal-democracy was much greater; yet he completely partook in Lippmann's unflattering diagnosis of the masses. It was only that he *feared* them much less than his American counterpart. Implicitly falling back on the English political tradition, which he on many other occasions explicitly extolled, Oakeshott was confident that elites in liberal countries will continue to be intelligent and responsible enough not to incite the masses. For, quite à la Mosca and Pareto, he dismissed the notion that political initiatives ever come from below; not *really*, that is. What the masses clamour for in the final account is nothing other than what their leaders have instructed them to want:

> It is safe to say that we, 'the people,' never ask for what we have not been prompted to desire; we corrupt policy, not by our own shortsighted demands, but by our responsiveness to what is suggested and promised to us. Our voice is loud, but our utterance is the repetition of simple lessons well learned (Oakeshott 1993: 114–15).

Given that the masses as an independent actor, indeed the people, are completely *ruled out*, both literally and metaphorically, construed as mere clay in the hands of the potter, it is only a question of what *the leaders* will do, for good and bad. Oakeshott thus supported the rule of the people under the assumption that such a rule is an impossibility; that what we actually have under political liberalism is not a democracy, but—to use the neologism suggested by Robert Dahl—a *polyarchy*, an interplay of ruling elites. A keen appreciation of the advantages of such a polyarchic, stolid, "English" model, it would seem, underlines Michael Mann's position. He therefore expresses wonderment at the failure of the fascists to notice, and subsequently copy and employ, the same tested, liberal and "democratic" methods of the northwest:

> But a question still arises. Why should upper and middle classes increase the level of repression, abolish parliaments and civil liberties, and mobilize mass parties—still less call in dangerous fascists—if *tried and tested milder forms were available at lower cost and risk?* In fact the best solution to class struggle was visible in the northwest. Its unions, socialist parties, and strikes were larger than in most of the center, east, and south but were implicated in class compromise, *posing little threat to capitalist property relations.... The center, east, and south's neglect of all this experience appears puzzling* (Mann 2004: 61; emphases added).

Mann provides the sanguine definition of the liberal model, underlining the "class compromise" it entails; but one can grasp the same phenomenon in a less positive light: precisely as a sophisticated way to *defuse* democratic potential, to *dilute* the people's sovereignty and, in extremis, to avail oneself of crypto-fascism, with all the dangerous pitfalls on this path. Nor is it altogether just to reproach the center, east and south for "neglecting" to consider the pluses of this model. As we have seen, many fascists in both Germany and Italy envied the western-liberal ability to create a democracy "in appearance," as Mosca put it, a democracy where the proverbial, terrifying, many-headed hydra of the people is gratifyingly transformed, to paraphrase Oakeshott, into a well-trained, if gargantuan, parrot. We have seen how it was not uncommon for continental, "open" fascists and their fellow travelers— such as Moeller, Jung, or Rocco—to expressly ground their politics on the inability to develop a democratic model of the English or French type. In Italy, it was notably the resonant failure of this "best solution," according to Mann, embodied in Giolitti. Fascists in general had to face a democracy declining a nominal status and threatening to become real and substantial. And indeed, what happens if the masses are not so sensible (or insensible) as to "compromise" their interests? What if—pace Oakeshott—they refuse to repeat their "simple lessons"? And what if—pace Mann—they are determined to use democracy not to underpin but to *question* "capitalist property relations"? Is fascism, then, an understandable, viable, legitimate option?[9] For all Mann's negation of the class analysis of fascism, we are irreducibly back at the liberal cul-de-sac, which sees the bourgeoisie confronted with the masses, the economic domain against the political, capitalism vs. democracy. We are back again at the doorstep of the Lockes, the Burkes, the Donosos, the Mills, the Paretos, and the Spenglers, defending the sanctity of private property against the encroachment of "the mob."

Certain nuances and novel emphases notwithstanding, Mann's argument echoes the long-standing notion of fascist countries succumbing to the weakness of their liberalism, in diverse interpretations stressing their national idiosyncrasies, particularly the *Sonderweg* construal/s of the German case. But upon closer examination, and if for the sake of simplicity and clarity we continue to take as our points of comparison the cases of England—on the part of the liberal west—and Germany,

---

[9] Reading Mann, it is at times difficult to avoid the impression that this, indeed, is his opinion. As when he states (57) that "If we place ourselves in the shoes of the Spanish latifundistas, threatened by anarcho-syndicalist and socialist land occupations, bombings, and ostensibly 'revolutionary' uprisings, we might also reach for the gun."

on the part of the illiberal center, some doubts about the soundness
of this scheme begin to creep in. Was the fate of interwar liberalism
in both countries in reality so radically different? If by "liberalism" we
mean liberal parties, then certain parallels suggest themselves. German
political liberalism, admittedly, was hardly strong, and in general had
to play second fiddle to conservative and right-wing forces. But how
strong was *English liberalism*? Was it not on the defensive too? In
the interwar period, the liberals of both countries generally garnered
weak crops at elections, increasingly ceasing to play a major political function. The German DNVP—successor of the pre-War National
Liberals—was arguably as important in German politics as was the
liberal party in England, if not more so. Nor was this condition of
relative political marginality simply a question of liberalism being
assailed by its irascible, leftist and rightist critics, the celebrated "values" and "ideals" of liberalism losing ground. In fact, liberalism was
falling victim to its own, immanent, long-term contradictions: the
intrinsic tension between economic and political liberalism, between
bourgeois capitalism and mass democracy. The values, in other words,
were inconsistent in the first place, and in distilled form, they *did*
survive: political liberalism going leftwards, the economic, bourgeois
values, rightwards. Political liberalism, for one, was absorbed by the
social democrats to the point that they arguably became more politically liberal than the liberals. The historian Albert Lindemann, himself
no socialist, asserted: "[B]y the early twentieth century the socialists
proved to be more consistent and unshakable defenders than the liberals themselves of many values that have been vaguely termed liberal (free and reasoned discourse, toleration, defense of civil liberties,
international harmony)" (Lindemann 1997: 162).[10] The conservatives,
on the other hand, appropriated large chunks of the economic legacy
of classical liberalism—not necessarily with regards to doctrinaire *laissez faire*, which was widely considered unfeasible under the modern
economic terms dictated by so-called "monopoly capitalism," but with
regards to defending the interests of the upper- and middle-classes
against the working masses—thus becoming more liberally observant
than the liberals themselves, a point Paul Adelman (1995: 32) clearly
made, with regards to the situation of English liberalism in the years
immediately following World War I: "Too often the Liberal 'old gang'

---

[10] See also 169.

merely echoed in a more muted form the harsh *economic orthodoxies of the Conservative party*" (italics added). Perhaps the symbolic moment in the passing of the economically liberal torch from Liberal to Tory hands was the so-called "Geddes Axe" of 1921, when the Tories were able to push through a policy of drastic cuts in public expenditure *against* the Liberals.[11] And, in a highly symptomatic historical turn of events, the revival of classical economic liberalism was famously undertaken, after World War II, by *the Tories*.

In both England and Germany during the interwar period, liberalism, for good or bad, survived, even if liberal parties "declined." It survived in split form, schizophrenic, which corresponded to the inner conflict of liberalism: the English bourgeoisie went to the Tories, the masses to Labour, these becoming the two great parties, the Liberals dragging considerably behind; while in Germany, confronted by the forces of the left which, combined, remained fairly constant (SPD and KPD) the bourgeois-liberal bloc (DDP, DVP, DNVP) was nearly swallowed by a more vigorous party, the NSDAP, once it had established itself as the leader of the "national" forces. In mass society reaching maturation, liberalism as an independent political force lost its social basis, fell and dashed back and forth between the two great social camps: a fact reflected also in the personal affiliation of many British liberals, who eventually parted with their former party to join either Labour— one could mention here the likes of Charles Roden Buxton, Arthur Ponsonby, Charles Trevelyan and William Wedgwood Benn—or the Conservatives: Neville Chamberlain's government during "appeasement" was staffed by important liberals, such as Walter Runciman and John Simon. And let us not forget that Chamberlain himself had liberal roots, so to speak, his father, Joseph Chamberlain, having been largely responsible for the original split of the Liberal party that led to the formation of the Liberal Unionist Party, working closely with the conservatives. In short, what needs to be grasped, against the familiar story of the regrettable demise of liberalism amid political extremism, is that that liberalism was in truth *less liberal* than its opponents: less politically liberal than the left, and less economically liberal than the right. Donoso Cortés' prediction, from a century earlier, had *almost* been vindicated. Let us recall his words:

---

[11] Cf. McDonald (1989).

The liberal school, enemy at the same time of darkness and of light, has chosen for itself a God-knows-what uncertain twilight zone between the illuminated regions and the murky ones...Placed in this nameless region it embarked on the enterprise of governing without the people and without God, an extravagant and impossible enterprise: its days are numbered, for on one side of the horizon God is emerging, and on the other side the people. No one can say where it would be on the tremendous day of battle, when the field would be covered by the Catholic phalanxes and those of socialism (Donoso 1851: 206).

What Donoso did not foresee, or rather did not conceptualize, was the fact that, come the last battle, liberalism would in truth not so much disappear or vacillate but rather fight *on both sides*, with socialism and with the fascist phalanxes, with the democratic people and with the capitalist God (or is it the Antichrist?). As indeed attested to by the case of Donoso himself, a former liberal turned a zealous fighter on behalf of the conservative cause.

An International Co-production

In view of this objective split of liberalism, it is not surprising that fascism—quasi, embryo, crypto, or whatever other qualification one might add—did find a receptive ground in England, where English politics were undergoing a considerable, if in a sense subterranean, process of, let us say, accommodation to fascism. I have pointed out the way esoteric fascism permeated the political circles in England, infecting its very core.[12] A political process which, in turn, fed on

---

[12] Unlike Mann, Hitler's celebrated biographer Ian Kershaw (2004) does not simply ignore the attraction of Nazism in the eyes of numerous, high-placed British contemporaries. Far from it, he actually dedicated an entire book, tellingly entitled *Making Friends with Hitler*, to explore precisely such attraction, which he did mainly via the personal case of Lord Londonderry, one of the most vocal and persistent among those who had sought to "appease" Hitler. Kershaw's book is highly informative, particularly the first chapter, which provides an overview of widespread contemporary British "Illusions and Delusions about Hitler." And yet he too prefers to resort to quasi-dramaturgic strategies of estrangement in order gently to defuse the truly critical potential of his inquiries. This he does, firstly, by depicting such support precisely as prompted by *illusions*, confusions, "uncertainty and miscalculation" (27) rather than by a significant measure of political and ideological *conformity* with Hitlerism. Thus he underscores (25) the fact that "Hitler was a puzzle," and that those who tended to treat him benignly, for example the members of Ramsay Macdonald's cabinet, "were nothing if not well-intentioned, and in some respects even idealistic. But, nevertheless, almost all were in some degree baffled by Hitler" (27). At that level of apologetic

cultural and ideological developments. Contrary to the notion of the
immunity of the English temperament—stereotypically reserved, practical, moderate, understated—to such continental extravagances as fascism, the British intelligentsia at the beginning of the 20th century
was awash with continental influences, above all that of Nietzsche,
who exercised an enormous impact on the ideological and cultural
climate. Such influences, whose political and social effect was overwhelmingly to boost elitism and opposition to democracy and perceived "massification,"[13] were documented by the literary critic John
Carey in his iconoclastic book on *The Intellectuals and the Masses.*
These belligerently elitist currents of thought and feeling, so prevalent

---

suggestion, *decisions* are presented as *indecision*, activities as *vacillations*, in a way
which is of course generally characteristic of the "appeasement" historiographic narrative, which wants to convince us that what was wrong with the British political elite
was not so much what they did, but what they *failed* to do; not so much what they
believed in and envisioned as right and moral, but what they *wouldn't* believe and
couldn't see.

But accompanying such *attenuating* strategy is typically one of *estrangement*,
namely of making the deeds and decisions of the "appeasers" appear bizarre, improbable and atypical. I quote the following example not because the author here does
anything extraordinary—in fact I repeat my conviction that Kershaw's attempt to
draw attention to the activities of such people as Lord Londonderry is in and of
itself commendable—but, on the contrary, because it is so symptomatic and illustra-
tive of mainstream devices of rhetorical defusing. Thus, Kershaw argues that "The
Londonderry letters...provide insight into the reasons, *so alien to us today* in full
awareness of what Hitler would eventually inflict upon the world, why so many in Great
Britain at the time—and in well-informed and well-connected sections of society—
were attracted to Nazi Germany" (xx; italics added). Thus, even as the historian *exposes*,
he *conceals*; even as the complicity of British elites is documented, we are not meant
to take the support for an antidemocratic, anti-socialistic, ruthless dictator for what it
really is: namely, a normal and normative feature of British foreign policy; instead, it
is construed as an aberration, a strange echo returning from times not only past but
superseded: "In a way, too, as the social world inhabited by the Londonderrys, and
the values that underpinned it, have vanished, his rise to political prominence then
his slide into disrepute have claim to be seen as an elegy on the decline and fall of
the British aristocracy" (xxi). But has this social world and its underlying values truly
"vanished"? Post-War Britain, at any rate, regularly continued to work closely with,
support, equip and even help bring to power a number of notoriously corrupt and
dictatorial regimes, in countries such as Iran, Chile and Indonesia, if a few examples
are needed. But such a *continuity* between past and present is precisely what most historiographic accounts are meant to conceal, or at least are mindful not to uncover. For
truly radical, if less elegiac narratives, one would have to turn to such exceptionally
plucky historians as Mark Curtis (2003; 2004), who, working somewhat on the margins of mainstream historiography, has systematically unveiled "Britain's Real Role in
the World" as well the values—not altogether new ones—which underpin it.

[13] We might of course give this formulation a materialistic twist and, reversing
cause and effect, say that structural elitism and opposition to democracy have allowed
such theories as Nietzsche's to become so popular.

among the British upper- and middle classes, even led Carey, in the book's final pages, to stress the affinities between such ideology and the worldview of none other than Hitler:

> In the introduction to his edition of Hitler's *Table Talk*, Hugh Trevor-Roper maintained that Hitler's ideas on culture were 'trivial, half-baked and disgusting.' This seems questionable. At least, there are marked similarities between the cultural ideals promulgated in the Führer's writings and conversation and those of the intellectuals we have been looking at (Carey 1992: 198).[14]

These "similarities" are such as to warrant, in Carey's view, the following conclusion (208): "The tragedy of *Mein Kampf* is that it was not, in many respects, a deviant book but one firmly rooted in European intellectual orthodoxy." More recently, Dan Stone has questioned the accepted notion that English culture and fascism were dichotomous. Challenging "the view...which dismisses British fascism as a pale imitation of its continental counterparts," Stone argues that

> there was a well-developed indigenous tradition of ways of thinking which, while they cannot be called 'fascist'—not before 1918 at any rate—can certainly be seen as 'proto-fascist.'...I am proposing...that we reassess the intellectual provenance of proto-fascist ideas in Britain, suggesting that they may be found to quite a large degree in the Nietzsche and eugenics movements, movements that represented the 'extremes of Englishness' (Stone 2002: 2).

Fixing their gaze above all on cultural matters, Carey and Stone assume that British proto-fascism remained politically barren. Carey, for one, imagines that the elitist trends he discusses were simply manifestations of unsettled intellectualism, and shows little interest in pursuing their concrete social and political ramifications. Stone, for his part, accepts the conventional notion that political fascism was a total failure in Britain. He correspondingly suggests (4) that "British fascism failed not because it was an imitative movement, but because mainstream conservatism did not need to co-opt its ideas in order to remain in power." This is a valid point concerning the marginality of open fascism in Britain. But as we have seen, with the aid of political historians, British "mainstream conservatism" was *itself*, to a degree, *co-opted*

---

[14] Among the many intellectuals here alluded to are George Gissing, W. B. Yeats, D. H. Lawrence, H. G. Wells, Wyndham Lewis, and Rayner Heppenstall.

by fascism. This was possible because fascist currents were in reality not so unrelated to the British mainstream as one might imagine.

In the international—perhaps better said *western*—co-production that was fascism, Britain's main contributions, apart from the imperialist model itself which so inspired fascists, were indeed Social Darwinism and eugenics. These ingredients were to prove of such importance to the fascist project in general and the National Socialist one in particular, so as to complicate any attempt at employing a reverse *Verfremdungseffekt*. Mann, however, is undeterred. Insisting on the non-fascist nature of the northwest, he re-circulates the widespread belief that British eugenics was fundamentally different than its Germanic version, in that the former concerned predominantly class, not race: "Though Social Darwinism encouraged eugenicism everywhere, the northwest saw the reproduction of the lower classes rather than of 'lower races' as the main problem" (Mann 2004: 82). Stone, however, in a study largely dedicated to a re-examination of British eugenics and racism, challenges precisely such apodictic affirmations. He argues that "although class concerns were a major factor behind the ideas and enquiries of the British eugenicists, no less important was a concern with race. British eugenics cannot so simply be separated from an ostensibly 'harder' continental school, since race-thinking, so often overlooked by the historians, was integral to the worldview of the British eugenicists" (Stone 2002: 95). Stone maintains that the origins of the distinction—in his view a mythical one—between British and German eugenics, are to be traced back to the attempt of the British eugenicists to establish retroactively a crucial difference between themselves and their German counterparts.[15] And yet he cannot find any evidence for such a self-serving distinction in the times preceding the war, when the reputation of eugenics was not yet shattered by the revelations of Nazi atrocities. He insists (99), on the contrary, that back then, "even among the most moderate figures among British eugenicists, racial and class considerations blurred into one another." Such questioning of the relative uprightness of "northwestern" eugenics (assuming, that is, that class eugenics is somehow less pernicious than racial ones), is complemented, for example, by Stefan Kühl's excellent

---

[15] "The claims served two vital purposes if eugenics was to enjoy a postwar role: to establish a large gap between Nazi racism … and British eugenics … and to acknowledge, thereby overcoming, the class bias of pre-war British eugenicists" (Stone 2002: 99).

book (1994), which amply documented the many ideological affinities and manifold concrete collaboration which existed between Nazi eugenicists and American ones. And he too, had to show this expressly in defiance of post-War notions that American eugenics was somehow "different" and less insidious than the Nazi variety.

One must indeed question the very attempt to chart a genealogy for racial prejudice as distinct from that of class. Was not Gobineau himself, the originator of modern racism, adamant on the *racial* difference allegedly existing between the French *classes*, the working masses being descendants of the Gallic Celts, the bourgeoisie and particularly the aristocracy being the heirs of the Franks?[16] Similarly, in his incomparable denunciation of eugenics, indeed of the *British* variant with which he was familiar, Chesterton pointed out "the strange new disposition to regard the poor as a *race*" (Chesterton 1922: 142). While not identical, racial and class prejudice were thus from the beginning woven together, and subsequently fed upon each other in diverse and complex ways, which can hardly be sorted out with recourse to the supposed geo-ideological line separating north and west from center, east and south. And surely it is vacuous to assume that the western heritage, once Germany is excluded, was relatively free from racial bias? Clearly racism deeply informed the ideology and the practice of western imperialism, to the point of occasionally justifying, even, genocide? I have above already cited Karl Pearson, a leading British eugenicist and Galton's disciple, to that effect; let us listen now to a voice that was certainly not particularly shrill within the British political landscape of the time nor, it may be assumed, especially prone to echo continental, fascist notions, namely that of Churchill:

> I do not agree that the dog in a manger has the final right to the manger, even though he may have lain there for a very long time. I do not admit that right. I do not admit, for instance, that a great wrong has been done to the Red Indians of America, or the black people of Australia. I do not admit that a wrong has been done to these people by the fact that a stronger race, a higher grade race, a more worldly-wise race, to put it that way, has come in and taken their place (quoted in Anderson 2001: 9).

---

[16] Georg Lukács' account (1962: 579–91) of the distinctly class origins of modern racism and of Gobineau's foundational role remains highly instructive.

True, this was said in support of Zionism, underscoring the right of the perceived stronger race, i.e., the Jewish one, vis-à-vis the canine Arabs. So this position could scarcely be squared with the Holocaust. And yet, adopting Churchill's view, expressed in 1937, can one still argue that "any great wrong" has been done to the Slavs a few years later, when the Nazis invaded Eastern Europe? Surely, from a strictly moral point of view, and leaving aside the question of whether or not the interests of the British Empire happened to be compromised with such an attack, the Slavs can find just as little cause to complain as the Red Indians, or the black people of Australia, or the Palestinian Arabs? Perhaps the wrong done to them must even be judged *lesser*, in that they, unlike the Indians or Aborigines, provided the mass army for the barbaric menace of Bolshevism, which Churchill so keenly perceived and denounced? Perhaps, finally, evacuating them from their long-occupied manger should even be considered a virtuous act, a service to civilization? And if Churchill himself failed to follow his own racial logic on that point, or was swayed by special interests, it appears that others in the British ruling elite, such as Neville Henderson, Lord Halifax or Neville Chamberlain, were more consistent.

Racism, if anything, was even more accentuated in the eugenic teachings coming from that other bastion of the northwest, from across the Atlantic. Addressing eugenics in the USA, too, it would be a vain effort to try to separate the bias of race from that of class. In a bestselling polemics against the "democratic theories of government," the American eugenicist Madison Grant retorted:

> Those engaged in social uplift and in revolutionary movements are therefore usually very intolerant of the limitations imposed by heredity. Discussion of these limitations is also most offensive to the advocates of the obliteration, under the guise of internationalism, of all existing distinctions based on nationality, language, race, religion and class. Those individuals who have neither country, nor flag, nor language, nor class,...very naturally decry and sneer at the value of these attributes of the higher types (Grant 1936: xx).

Elevated race *and* class are as a matter of course "the attributes" of the "higher types." Far from posing two incommensurable problems, this is a discourse in which race and class are interchangeable, which allows one to switch seamlessly from one to the other, as the following sample of Grant's rhetoric nicely illustrates:

> To admit the unchangeable differentiation of race in its modern scientific meaning is to admit inevitably the existence of superiority in one race and of inferiority in another. Such an admission we can hardly expect

from those of inferior races. These inferior races and classes are prompt
to recognize in such an admission the very real danger to themselves of
being relegated again to their former obscurity and subordinate position
in society. The favorite defense of these inferior classes is an unqualified denial of the existence of fixed inherited qualities, either physical or
spiritual, which cannot be obliterated or greatly modified by a change of
environment (xxvii–xxix).

In the space of three short sentences, Grant starts with "inferior races,"
moves on to "inferior races and classes" and ends up with "inferior
classes." He does not feel that any explanation is due for this flexible use of terminology, nor does he seem to expect his reader to be
too particular on that point. For Grant, as for his implied readers, the
social question is clearly a racial question, and the racial struggle is a
social struggle:

> The resurgence of *inferior races and classes* throughout not merely
> Europe but the world, is evident in every despatch from Egypt, Ireland,
> Poland, Rumania, India and Mexico. It is called nationalism, patriotism,
> freedom and other high-sounding names, but it is everywhere the phe-
> nomenon of the long suppressed, conquered *servile classes* rising against
> *the master race* (xxxi; emphases added).

Similarly, another American eugenicist, S. K. Humphrey (1917: 79),
regarded as "inevitable that *class lines* shall harden as a protection
against the growing numbers of the underbred, just as in all previous
cultures. However remote a cataclysm may be, our present *racial trend*
is toward social chaos or a dictatorship" (italics added). And Grant's
protégé, Lothrop Stoddard (1924: 89), who considered "the negroes"
one of the "existing savage and barbaric races of a demonstrably low
average level of intelligence," was equally convinced that "as civilization progresses, *social status* tends to coincide more and more closely
with *racial value*;…the upper social classes containing an ever larger
proportion of persons of superior natural endowments while the lower
social classes contain a growing proportion of inferiors" (77; emphases added). It is senseless, on such terms, to regard the "problem" of
the lower races as separate from that of the lower classes. Yet Grant,
Humphrey and Stoddard are all north-westerners.

The central European Nazis, for their part, highly valued such theories. Hitler himself, in private correspondence with Grant, thanked
him for writing *The Passing of the Great Race* and said that "this book
was his bible" (Kühl 1994: 85). Nor were the Germans irritated by the
conflation of race and class, regarding it as some western departure
from eugenics' proper concern, the lower races. While by necessity

engaging in a form of "horizontal racialism," purporting to elevate the German people in its entirety to a position of racial superiority,[17] the Nazi "race experts" at the same time hardly doubted the inextricability of race and class. The highly representative figure of Hans F. K. Günther, for example, admired Grant and Stoddard, saw them as state-of-the-art racial thinkers and often referred to them in his own works. And he was thoroughly of one mind with them with regards to class as a racial attribute. Stoddard (1924: 120) complained against the "crushing burden of taxation throughout Europe, which hits especially the increase of the upper and middle classes," and demanded (243–4) that "habitual paupers should be prevented from having children," otherwise becoming a "harmful and unfair" yoke on the "thrifty and capable members of society who pay the taxes." And his German counterpart could not agree more; specifically citing Grant, he articulated the same middle-class social-cum-racial sensibility:

> The deeply penetrating de-nordization of the World War was followed in all Western peoples, even those who had not taken part in the War, by the de-nordization through the ever-increasing burden of taxation, which imposes a further restriction on the number of children precisely on those classes richest in Nordic blood. Nordic blood—as Grant put it—is now being effectively taxed away throughout the West. The economical tearing apart of the middle class hits precisely the Nordic stream of the population which rises through this class, keeping down its birth-rate (Günther 1929: 314).

Against this literally blood-sucking taxation on the Nordic bourgeoisie, this ever escalating assault by welfare institutions, there is only one adequate response, and this was attempted in only one country, the United States of America: "The strong increase in inferior hereditary qualities caused by the 19th century ought to have been met by a correspondingly active interest among the nations in the problems of eugenics, an interest which in turn should have led to the legal measures which have today been adopted by the United States" (305). For a prominent German eugenicist as Günther, soon to play an important part in The Third Reich, it is the northwest—how strange!—that leads the way in matters pertaining to race and to class, and Germany, if she knows what is good for her, ought to follow suit.

---

[17] Again with reference to Domenico Losurdo's proposed distinction, mentioned in Chapter 2, between "vertical racialism" and "horizontal racialism."

To Stoddard (1924: 23), the Nazis further owed the coining of the term under-man, which was Germanized into the *Untermensch*: "I have coined a term which seems to describe collectively all those kinds of persons whom I have just discussed. This term is *The Under-Man*—the man who measures *under* the standards of capacity and adaptability imposed by the social order in which he lives. And this term I shall henceforth employ." As Domenico Losurdo showed (2004: 886–7), Alfred Rosenberg, the important Nazi ideologue, recognized his debt to the admired Stoddard, while the American, in turn, was clearly inspired by the Nietzschean jargon and the notion of the superman, coming, of course, from Germany, where he had also studied for a year and a half.[18] To this may be added the interesting fact that, a year before Stoddard coined the term under-man, the British author, Austin Freeman, in his 1921 book *Social Decay and Regeneration*, wrote in nearly interchangeable terms on the "menace" of what he chose to dub "the sub-man":

> Now the importance of the sub-man in the economy of Society is not generally appreciated.... And the reason for this I take to be a failure to realize his numerical strength. The abnormal unfit...numerically,...are probably not more than a fiftieth of the population, and their increase, as an entire class, is not extremely rapid; whereas the normal unfit—the class of men who are conspicuously below the average of the race—are probably nearer a fifth of the population, if not more, and are the most prolific class in the whole community (Freeman 1921: 248).

---

[18] Those who would reflexively argue at this point that this was a mere distortion of Nietzsche's intentions, which were "of course," infinitely superior and would have nothing to do with the base purposes of a Stoddard—to say nothing of a Rosenberg (a passionate admirer of Nietzsche, by the way)—may wish to ponder the fact that Stoddard specifically distanced himself from the Nietzschean project on account of its *extremity*, advocating a closed caste system, rather than an open, meritocratic society: "The eugenic ideal is thus seen to be *an ever-perfecting super race*. Not the 'superman' of Nietzsche—that brilliant yet baleful vision of a master caste, blooming like a gorgeous but parasitic orchid on a rotting trunk of servile degradation; but a super *race*, cleansing itself throughout by the elimination of its defects, and raising itself throughout by the cultivation of its qualities" (Stoddard 1924: 262). "We must absolutely banish the notion that Neo-Aristocracy will perpetuate that cardinal vice of traditional aristocracy—*caste*. *Classes* there probably will be; but these classes...will be extremely fluid as regards the individuals who compose them. No true superior, wherever born, will be denied admission to the highest class; no person, whenever born, can stay in a class unless he measures up to specifications" (267).

Freeman, too, was responding to the Nietzscheanism so widespread among the British intelligentsia.[19] Under-man, Sub-man, *untermensch.* This is but one concrete illustration of how fundamentally fascist ideas and projects, even at their most insidious, were conceived through a convoluted, direct and indirect, international, actually inter-western, dialogue. Fascism, an open one at any rate, did not take hold of the reigns of power in the northwest, but without the major contribution—ideological, economic, political—of north-western politicians, industrialists, scientists, thinkers, and artists, it would have been unthinkable elsewhere. Let us therefore beware of over-"alienating" fascism, or over-localizing it. The real *Sonderweg*, it appears, is not a German, or an Italian, or a Spanish, or an Austrian way, but the way of the west.

---

[19] Cf. Stone 2002: 85, 113–14.

REFERENCES

Adelman, Paul. 1995. *The Decline of the Liberal Party 1910–1931*. Harlow: Longman Group.

Adler, Franklin Hugh. 1995. *Italian Industrialists from Liberalism to Fascism. The Political Development of the Industrial Bourgeoisie, 1906–1934*. Cambridge: Cambridge University Press.

Anderson, Perry. 2001. "Scurrying Towards Bethlehem." *New Left Review* 10: 5–30.

Anonymous. 1912–1913. "The Ethics of Empire." *The Round Table. A Quarterly Review of the Politics of the British Empire* 3: 484–501.

Arendt, Hannah. 1960 [1951]. *The Origins of Totalitarianism*. New York: Meridian.

——. 1993 [1954]. "Truth and Politics," in Hannah Arendt, *Between Past and Present*, Harmondsworth: Penguin, pp. 227–264.

Aron, Raymond. 1965. *Démocratie et totalitarisme*. Paris: Gallimard.

Baeumler, Alfred. 1937. *Studien zur deutschen Geistesgeschichte*. Berlin: Junker und Dünnhaupt Verlag.

Bagehot, Walter. 1891a. "Letters on the French Coup D'etat," in *The Works of Walter Bagehot*. Volume II, Hartford, pp. 371–447.

——. 1891b. "The English Constitution," in *The Works of Walter Bagehot. Volume IV*, Hartford, pp. 1–425.

Balakrishnan, Gopal. 2002. *The Enemy: An Intellectual Portrait of Carl Schmitt*. London, New York: Verso.

Bambach, Charles. 2003. *Heidegger's Roots. Nietzsche, National Socialism, and the Greeks*. Ithaca and London: Cornell University Press.

Bellamy, Richard. 2002. "Social and Political Thought, 1890–1945," in Adrian Lyttelton, ed., *Liberal and Fascist Italy*, Oxford: Oxford University Press, pp. 233–248.

Bielefeldt, Heiner. 1998. "Carl Schmitt's Critique of Liberalism. Systematic Reconstruction and Countercriticism," in David Dyzenhaus, ed., *Law as Politics: Carl Schmitt's Critique of Liberalism*, Durham, North Carolina: Duke University Press, pp. 23–36.

Blackbourn, David and Geoff Eley. 1984. *The Peculiarities of German History. Bourgeois Society and Politics in Nineteenth-Century Germany*. Oxford: Oxford University Press.

Bobbio, Norberto. 2005. *Liberalism and Democracy*. London, New York: Verso.

Boesche, Roger. 2006. *Tocqueville's Road Map. Methodology, Liberalism, Revolution, and Despotism*. Lanham: Lexington.

Böhm, Franz. 1937. "Ewiger Cartesianismus?" *Volk im Werden* 11: 555–562.

Boyd, Kelly, ed. 1999. *Encyclopedia of Historians and Historical Writing*. London: Taylor & Francis.

Buchheim, Christoph and Jonas Scherner. 2006. "The Role of Private Property in the Nazi Economy: The Case of Industry." *The Journal of Economic History*. Cambridge University Press 66, 2: 390–416.

Buckmiller, Michael. 1985. "Sorel et le 'conservatisme révolutionnaire' en Allemagne." *Cahiers Georges Sorel* 3, 1: 51–75.

Burke, Edmund. 1826. *The Works of the Right Honourable Edmund Burke*. London.

Bylund, Per. "Anarchism, Capitalism, and Anarcho-Capitalism." <http://anarchism.net/anarchism_anarchismcapitalismandanarchocapitalism.htm>.

Calic, Edouard. 1968. *Ohne Maske. Hitler-Breiting Geheimgespräche 1931*. Frankfurt am Main: Societäts-Verlag.

Carey, John. 1992. *The Intellectuals and the Masses*. London: Faber and Faber.

Carlyle, Thomas. 1867. *Shooting Niagara: And After?* London: Chapman and Hall.

——. 1869a. "Chartism," in Thomas Carlyle, *Critical and Miscellaneous Essays*, volume 4, Chicago: The American Bookmart, pp. 36–117.

——. 1869b. "Occasional Discourse on the Nigger Question," in Thomas Carlyle, *Critical and Miscellaneous Essays*, volume 4, Chicago: The American Bookmart, pp. 293–326.

Charzat, Michel. 1983. "Georges Sorel et le fascisme. Éléments d'explication d'une légende tenace." *Cahiers Georges Sorel* 1: 37–51.

Chesterton, G. K. 1922. *Eugenics and Other Evils*. London, New York: Cassell and Company.

——. 1990. "The Resurrection of Rome," in G. K. Chesterton, *Collected Works. Vol. XXI*, San Francisco: Ignatius Press, pp. 265–466.

Cohen, G. A. 1995. *Self-Ownership, Freedom and Equality*. Cambridge: Cambridge University Press.

Cole, Margaret, ed. 1956. *Beatrice Webb's Diaries. 1924–1932*. London, New York, Toronto: Longman, Green and Co.

Constant, Benjamin. 1988. *Political Writings*. Cambridge: Cambridge University Press.

Croce, Benedetto. 1933a. *History of Europe in the Nineteenth Century*. New York: Harcourt, Brace & Company.

——. 1933b. "The State as Friend and as Enemy," in Benedetto Croce, *My Philosophy. And Other Essays on the Moral and Political Problems of Our Time*, London: Allen & Unwin, 1951, pp. 55–63.

——. 1943. "Liberalism and Democracy," in Benedetto Croce, *My Philosophy. And Other Essays on the Moral and Political Problems of Our Time*, London: Allen & Unwin, 1951, pp. 93–96.

——. 1951. "Political Truth and Popular Myths," in Benedetto Croce, *My Philosophy. And Other Essays on the Moral and Political Problems of Our Time*, London: Allen & Unwin, pp. 88–92.

Curtis, Mark. 2003. *Web of Deceit. Britain's Real Role in the World*. London: Vintage.

——. 2004. *Unpeople. Britain's Secret Human Rights Abuses*. London: Vintage.

Dahl, Robert A. 2003. *How Democratic is the American Constitution?* New Haven, London: Yale University Press.

De Cecco, Marcello. 2002. "The Economy from Liberalism to Fascism," in Adrian Lyttelton, ed., *Liberal and Fascist Italy*, Oxford: Oxford University Press, pp. 62–82.

De Grand, Alexander. 1982. *Italian Fascism. Its Origins and Development*. Lincoln & London: University of Nebraska Press.

De Grazzia, Victoria and Sergio Luzzatto, eds. 2005. *Dizionario del fascismo*. 2 vols. Turin: Einaudi.

DeGrood, David H. 1978. *Dialectics and Revolution*. Amsterdam: B. R. Grüner.

Domarus, Max. 1973. *Hitler: Reden und Proklamationen, 1932–1945*. 4 volumes. Wiesbaden: R. Löwit.

Donoso Cortés, Juan. 1851. *Ensayo sobre el catolicismo, el liberalismo y el socialismo, considerados en sus principios fundamentales*. Barcelona.

Drury, Shadia B. 1999. *Leo Strauss and the American Right*. New York: St. Martin's Press.

Duggan, Christopher. 1994. *A Concise History of Italy*. Cambridge: Cambridge University Press.

Dwinger, Edwin Erich. 1935. *Die letzten Reiter*. Jena: Eugen Diederichs Verlag.

Eatwell, Roger. 1996. "On Defining the 'Fascist Minimum,': The Centrality of Ideology." *Journal of Political Ideologies*, 1/3: 303–319.

Eley, Geoff. 1986. *From Unification to Nazism. Reinterpreting the German Past*. Boston: Allen & Unwin.

Engels, Friedrich. 1895. *Introduction to Karl Marx's The Class Struggles in France 1848 to 1850*. <http://www.marxists.org/archive/marx/works/1895/03/06.htm>.

——. 1990 [1893]. "Kann Europa abrüsten?" in *Marx Engels Werke* vol. 22, Berlin: Dietz Verlag, pp. 371–399.

Engels, Friedrich and Karl Marx. 2005. *The Communist Manifesto.* Chicago: Haymarket.

Evans, Michael. 1975. *Karl Marx.* Bloomington: Indiana University Press.

Faye, Emmanuel. 2005. *Heidegger. L'introduction du nazisme dans la philosophie. Autour des séminaires inédits de 1933–1935.* Paris: Albin Michel.

Fest, Joachim. 2005. *Inside Hitler's Bunker. The Last Days of the Third Reich.* London: Macmillan.

Finer, Herman. 1935. *Mussolini's Italy.* New York: Henry Holt.

Fischer, Kurt Rudolf. 2002. "A Godfather too: Nazism as a Nietzschean 'experiment,'" in Jacob Golomb and Robert S. Wistrich, eds., *Nietzsche, Godfather of Fascism? On the Uses and Abuses of a Philosophy,* Princeton, New Jersey: Princeton University Press, pp. 291–300.

Foster, R. F. 2005. *Yeats—A Life. II. The Arch-Poet.* Oxford: Oxford University Press.

Fox Bourne, H. R. 1876. *The Life of John Locke.* Vol. 2. London: Henry S. King.

Freeman, R. Austin. 1921. *Social Decay and Regeneration.* London: Constable.

Friedrich, Carl and Zbigniew Brzezinski. 1956. *Totalitarian Dictatorship and Autocracy.* Cambridge: Harvard University Press.

Furet, François and Ernst Nolte. 2004. *Fascism & Communism.* Lincoln and London: University of Nebraska Press.

Gentile, Giovanni. 2007. *Origins and Doctrine of Fascism. With Selections from Other Works.* New Brunswick: Transaction Publishers.

Gluckstein, Donny. 1999. *The Nazis, Capitalism and the Working Class.* London: Bookmarks.

Goldring, Douglas. 1945. *The Nineteen Twenties: A General Survey and Some Personal Memories.* London: Nicholson & Watson.

Goodrick-Clarke, Nicholas. 2001. *Black Sun: Aryan Cults, Esoteric Nazism and the Politics of Identity.* New York: New York University Press.

Gramsci, Antonio. 2000. "Some Theoretical and Practical Aspects of 'Economism.'" <http://www2.cddc.vt.edu/marxists/archive/gramsci/editions/spn/modern_prince/ch07.htm>.

——. 2007. *Quaderni del carcere.* 4 vols. Turin: Einaudi.

Grant, Madison. 1936. *The Passing of the Great Race. Or the Racial Basis of European History.* New York: Charles Scribner's Sons.

Griffin, Roger. 1993. *The Nature of Fascism.* London, New York: Routledge.

——, ed. 1998. *International Fascism: Theories, Causes, and the New Consensus.* London: Arnold.

Gumplowicz, Ludwig. 1899. *The Outlines of Sociology.* Philadelphia: American Academy of Political and Social Science.

Günther, Hans F. K. 1929. *Rassenkunde Europas. Mit besonderer Berücksichtigung der Rassengeschichte der Hauptvölker indogermanischer Sprache.* Munich: J. F. Lehmanns Verlag.

Hamilton, Alastair. 1971. *The Appeal of Fascism: A Study of Intellectuals and Fascism. 1919–1945.* New York: Macmillan.

Hamilton, Richard. 1982. *Who Voted for Hitler?* Princeton, New Jersey: Princeton University Press.

Hammond, J. L. 1900. "Colonial and Foreign Policy," in F. W. Hirst, ed., *Liberalism and the Empire,* London: R. Brimely Johnson, pp. 158–210.

Harbutt, Fraser J. 1986. *The Iron Curtain. Churchill, America, and the Origins of the Cold War.* Oxford: Oxford University Press.

Hardt, Michael and Antonio Negri. 2004. *Multitude. War and Democracy in the Age of Empire.* New York: Penguin.

Harvey, David. 2005. *A Brief History of Neoliberalism*. Oxford: Oxford University Press.

Hay, Douglas and Nicholas Rogers. 1997. *Shuttles and Swords. Eighteenth-Century English Society*. Oxford: Oxford University Press.

Hayek, F. A. 1981. Interview in *El Mercurio* [A Chilean Daily]. <http://www.fahayek .org/index.php?option=com_content&task=view&id=121>.

——. 1988. *The Fatal Conceit. The Errors of Socialism*. Chicago: The University of Chicago Press.

——. 2007. *The Road to Serfdom: Text and Documents—The Definitive Edition*. Chicago: Chicago University Press.

Heidegger, Martin. 1967. *Sein und Zeit*. Tübingen: Max Niemeyer Verlag.

——. 1998. *Gesamtausgabe. Band 38. Logik als die Frage nach dem Wesen der Sprache*. Frankfurt am Main: Vittorio Klostermann.

Hill, Christopher. 1972. *The World Turned Upside Down: Radical Ideas During the English Revolution*. London: Maurice Temple Smith.

——. 2006 [1961]. *The Century of Revolution. 1603-1714*. London and New York: Routledge.

Hirst, Paul. 1987. "Carl Schmitt's Decisionism." *Telos* 72: 15–26.

Hitler, Adolf. 1941. *Mein Kampf*. New York: Reynal & Hitchcock.

Hobbes, Thomas. 1990. *Behemoth*. Chicago, London: Chicago University Press.

Hobhouse, L. T. 1919. *Liberalism*. London: Williams & Norgate.

Hoepke, Klaus-Peter. 1968. *Die deutsche Rechte und der italienische Faschismus*. Düsseldorf: Droste Verlag.

Hofstadter, Richard. 1960. *Social Darwinism in American Thought*. Boston: The Beacon Press.

Holstun, James. 2000. *Ehud's Dagger. Class Struggle in the English Revolution*. London, New York: Verso.

Horváth, Ödön von. 2001. *Ein Kind unserer Zeit*. Frankfurt am Main: Suhrkamp.

Humphrey, Seth King. 1917. *Mankind; Racial Values and the Racial Prospect*. New York: Charles Scribner's Sons.

James, Robert Rhodes. 1978. *The British Revolution: British Politics. 1880-1939*. London: Methuen.

Jaspers, Karl. 1999. *Die geistige Situation der Zeit*. Berlin: Walter de Gruyter.

Jaurès, Jean. 2008 [1901]. "Grève générale & révolution," in Miguel Chueca, ed., *Déposséder les possédants. La grève générale aux 'temps heroïqués' du syndiclisme révolutionnaire (1895-1906)*, Marseille: Agone, pp. 111–128.

Jennings, Jeremy. 1999. "Introduction," in Georges Sorel, *Reflections on Violence*, Cambridge: Cambridge University Press, pp. vii–xxi.

Julliard, Jacques. 1984. "Sur un fascisme imaginaire: à propos d'un livre de Zeev Sternhell." *Annales* 39. 4: 849–861.

Jung, Edgar J. 1933. *Sinndeutung der deutschen Revolution*. Oldenburg: Gerhard Stalling.

Kershaw, Ian. 2004. *Making Friends with Hitler. Lord Londonderry, the Nazis, and the Road to World War II*. Harmondsworth: Penguin.

Kühl, Stefan. 1994. *The Nazi Connection. Eugenics, American Racism, and German National-Socialism*. Oxford: Oxford University Press.

Kühnl, Reinhard. 1999. *Liberalismus als Form bürgerlicher Herrshcaft–Von der Befreiung des Menschen zur Freiheit des Marktes*. Heilbronn: Distel Verlag.

——. 2000. *Der deutsche Faschismus in Quellen und Dokumenten*. Cologne: Papy-Rossa.

Lagarde, Paul de. 1994. *Deutsche Schriften*. Berlin: Verlag der Freunde.

Landa, Ishay. 2007. *The Overman in the Marketplace: Nietzschean Heroism in Popular Culture*. Lanham: Lexington.

——. 2008a. "Eyes Wide Shut: Liberalismus, Faschismus und die diskursiven Grenzen der 'Open Society'" *Marburger Forum, Beiträge zur geistigen Situation der Gegenwart*, 9, 2. < http://www.philosophia-online.de/mafo/heft2008-2/Lan_Eye.htm >.

———. 2008b. "Heideggers entwendeter Brief: Die liberale Volksgemeinschaft," in Bernhard H. F. Taureck, ed., *Politische Unschuld? In Sachen Martin Heidegger*, München: W. Fink Verlag, pp. 97–127.

Langewiesche, Dieter. 1995. *Liberalismus in Deutschland*. Frankfurt am Main: Suhrkamp.

Laslett, Peter. 1988. "Introduction," in John Locke, *Two Treatises of Government*, Peter Laslett, ed., Cambridge: Cambridge University Press, 1772, pp. 3–122.

Le Bon, Gustave. 1905. *Psychologie des foules*. 9th edition. Paris: Félix Alcan.

———. 1960. *The Crowd*. New York: The Viking Press.

Le Cour Grandmaison, Olivier. 2002. *Haine(s). Philosophie et politique*. Paris: Presses Universitaires de France.

———. 2005. *Coloniser. Exterminer. Sur la guerre et L'Etat colonial*. Paris: Fayard.

Leibovitz, Clement. 1993. *The Chamberlain-Hitler Deal*. Edmonton: Les Éditions Duval.

Leibovitz, Clement and Alvin Finkel. 1998. *In Our Time. The Chamberlain-Hitler Collusion*. New York: Monthly Review Press.

Lenin, Vladimir. 1920. *Left-Wing Communism: an Infantile Disorder*. <http://www.marxists.org/archive/lenin/works/1920/lwc>.

Lindemann, Albert S. 1997. *Esau's Tears–Modern Anti-Semitism and the Rise of the Jews*. Cambridge: Cambridge University Press.

Linebaugh, Peter. 2006. *The London Hanged. Crime and civil Society in the Eighteenth Century*. London, New York: Verso.

Livingston, Arthur. 1935. "Biographical Note" in Vilfredo Pareto, *The Mind and Society: A Treatise on General Sociology*, vol. I, New York: Harcourt, Brace, pp. xv–xviii.

Locke, John. 1824. *The Reasonableness of Christianity: As Delivered in the Scriptures*. London.

———. 1988. *Two Treatises of Government*. Cambridge: Cambridge University Press.

Losurdo, Domenico. 1994. *La Seconda Repubblica. Liberismo, federalismo, postfascismo*. Turin: Bollati Boringhieri.

———. 2004. *Nietzsche, il ribelle aristocratico. Biografia intelletuale e bilancio critico*. Turin: Bollati Boringhieri.

———. 2005. *Controstoria del liberalismo*. Rome and Bari: Editori Laterza.

Lukács, Georg. 1950. *Thomas Mann*. Berlin: Aufbau Verlag.

———. 1962. *Die Zerstörung der Vernunft*. Berlin-Spandau: Luchterhand.

Lukacs, John. 1998. *The Hitler of History*. New York: Vintage.

———. 2005. *Democracy and Populism: Fear and Hatred*. New Haven: Yale University Press.

Macpherson, C. B. 1964. *The Political Theory of Possessive Individualism. Hobbes to Locke*. Oxford: Oxford University Press.

Maine, Henry S. 1909 [1885]. *Popular Government*. London: John Murray.

Malthus, T. R. 1992. *An Essay on the Principle of Population*. Cambridge: Cambridge University Press.

Mann, Michael. 2004. *Fascists*. Cambridge: Cambridge University Press.

Mann, Thomas. 1967. *Doktor Faustus*. Frankfurt am Main: S. Fischer.

———. 1974. *Betrachtungen eines Unpolitischen*. Frankfurt am Main: S. Fischer.

———. 1981.*Von Deutscher Republik*. Frankfurt am Main: S. Fischer.

Marx, Karl. 1848. "On the Question of Free Trade." <http://www.marxists.org/archive/marx/works/1848/01/09ft.htm>.

———. 1963. *The Eighteenth Brumaire of Louis Bonaparte*. New York: International Publishers.

———. 1990. *Capital. Volume 1*. Harmondsworth: Penguin.

———. 1991. *Capital. Volume 3*. Harmondsworth: Penguin.

McCormick, John P. 1997. *Carl Schmitt's Critique of Liberalism: Against Politics as Technology*. Cambridge: Cambridge University Press.

McDonald, Andrew. 1989. "The Geddes Committee and the Formulation of Public Expenditure Policy, 1921–1922." *The Historical Journal* 32, 3: 643–674.

Mehta, Uday Singh. 1999. *Liberalism and Empire. A Study in Nineteenth-Century British Liberal Thought.* Chicago, London: The University of Chicago Press.

Meier, Heinrich. 1995. *Carl Schmitt and Leo Strauss: The Hidden Dialogue.* Chicago: The University of Chicago Press.

Mill, John Stuart. 1862. *Considerations on Representative Government.* New York: Harper & Brothers.

——. 1905. *On Liberty.* London: The Walter Scott Publishing.

Mészáros, István. 2006. "A Key Problem of Method: Dualism and Dichotomies in Philosophy and Social Theory in Capital's Epoch." *Critique. Journal of Socialist Theory* 34: 27–77.

Mises, Ludwig. 1951. *Socialism. An Economic and Sociological Analysis.* New Haven: Yale University Press.

——. 2002. *Liberalism in the Classical Tradition.* San Francisco, California: Cobden Press.

Moeller van den Bruck, Arthur. 1934. *Germany's Third Empire.* London: Allen & Unwin.

——. 2006. *Das Dritte Reich.* Toppenstedt: Uwe Berg-Verlag.

Mommsen, Hans. 2004. *Aufstieg und Untergang der Republik von Weimar.* Ulm: Ullstein.

Mosca, Gaetano. 1939. *The Ruling Class.* New York: McGraw-Hill.

Mosse, George. 1987. *Masses and Man. Nationalist and Fascist Perceptions of Reality.* Detroit: Wayne State University press.

Mosse, George L. 1989. "Fascism and the French Revolution." *Journal of Contemporary History* 24: 5–26.

——. 1996. "Fascist Aesthetics and Society: Some Considerations." *Journal of Contemporary History* 31: 245–252.

Mouffe, Chantal, ed. 1999a. *The Challenge of Carl Schmitt* [editorial introduction], London, New York: Verso.

——. 1999b. "Carl Schmitt and the Paradox of Liberal Democracy," in Chantal Mouffe, ed., *The Challenge of Carl Schmitt*, London, New York: Verso, pp. 38–53.

Neocleous, Mark. 1997. *Fascism. Concepts in Social Thought.* Minneapolis: University of Minnesota Press.

Neumann, Boaz. 2002. *The Nazi Weltanschauung: Space, Body, Language.* [Hebrew] Haifa: Haifa University Press.

Newsinger, John. 2002. "Elgin in China." *New Left Review* 15: 119–140.

Nietzsche, Friedrich. 1968. *The Will to Power.* New York: Vintage.

——. 1988. *Sämtliche Werk: Kritische Studienausgabe in 15 Einzelbänden.* Giorgio Colli and Mazzino Montinari, eds. Berlin, New York: Walter de Gruyter.

——. 1990. *Twilight of the Idols and The Anti-Christ.* Harmondsworth: Penguin.

——. 1992. *Ecce Homo.* Harmondsworth: Penguin.

——. 1997. *Daybreak.* Cambridge: Cambridge University Press.

Nolte, Ernst 1984 [1963]. *Der Faschismus in seiner Epoche.* Munich: Piper.

Oakeshott, Michael. 1993. *Religion, Politics and the Moral Life.* New Haven, London: Yale University Press.

Oliphant, Laurence. 1860. *Narrative of the Earl of Elgin's Missions to China and Japan in the Years 1857, '58, '59.* New York: Harper and Brothers Publishers.

Pareto, Vilfredo. 1935. *The Mind and Society: A Treatise on General Sociology,* New York: Harcourt, Brace.

——. 1966. *Sociological Writings.* New York: Frederick A. Praeger.

——. 1974. *Scritti politici, vol. II, Reazione, libertá, fascismo (1896–1923).* Turin: Unione tipografico-editrice torinese.

Patey, Douglas Lane. 2001. *The Life of Evelyn Waugh.* Oxford, Cambridge: Blackwell.

Paxton, Robert O. 2004. *The Anatomy of Fascism.* London: Penguin.

Payne, Stanley G. 1996. *A History of Fascism. 1914–45.* London, New York: Routledge.

Pearlman, Estelle. 2004. "The Representation of Jews on Edwardian Postcards," in Brian Cheyette and Nadia Valman, eds., *The Image of the Jew in European Liberal Culture, 1789-1914*, London, Portland: Vallentine Mitchell, pp. 217-242.

Pearson, Karl. 1905. *National Life from the Standpoint of Science.* 2nd edition. London: Adam and Charles Black.

Petzold, Joachim. 1978. *Konservative Theoretiker des deutschen Faschismus.* Berlin: VEB.

Piccone, Paul and G. L. Ulmen. 1987. "Introduction to Carl Schmitt." *Telos* 72: 3-14.

Picker, Henry. 2003. *Hitlers Tischgespräche im Führehauptquartier.* Munich: Propyläen.

Pirandello, Luigi. 1993. *Il fu Mattia Pascal.* Torino: Einaudi.

Pitts, Jennifer. 2005. *A Turn to Empire. The Rise of Imperial Liberalism in Britain and France.* Princeton, New Jersey: Princeton University Press.

Powers, Charles H. 1984. "Introduction: The Life and Times of Vilfredo Pareto," in Vilfredo Pareto, *The Transformation of Democracy,* New Jersey: Transaction Publishers, pp. 1-24.

Preparata, Guido G. 2005. *Conjuring Hitler. How Britain and America made the Third Reich.* London: Pluto Press.

Primor, Adar. 2002. "Le Pen ultimate." *Haaretz* [Israeli daily]. 18/04/2002. <http://news.haaretz.co.il/hasen/pages/ShArt.jhtml?itemNo=153419>.

Proudhon, Pierre Joseph. 1994. *What is Property?* Cambridge: Cambridge University Press.

——. 2007a. *General Idea of the Revolution in the Nineteenth Century.* New York: Cosimo.

——. 2007b. *The Philosophy of Misery.* New York: Cosimo.

Quigley, Carroll. 1981. *The Anglo-American Establishment. From Rhodes to Cliveden.* San Pedro, California: GSG & Associates.

Renan, Ernest. 1875. *La réforme intellectuelle et morale.* Paris: Michel Lévy.

Renton, Dave. 1999. *Fascism: Theory and Practice.* London: Pluto Press.

Riley, Dylan. 2004. "Enigmas of Fascism." *New Left Review* 30: 134-147.

Rizi, Fabio Fernando. 2003. *Benedetto Croce and Italian Fascism.* Toronto: University of Toronto Press.

Rocca, Massimo. 2004. "Un neo-liberalismo?" in Renzo De Felice, ed., *Autobiografia del fascismo. Antologia di testi fascisti 1919-1945*, Torino: Einaudi, pp. 86-91.

Rocco, Alfredo. 1931. "The Transformation of the State," in Tomaso Sillani, ed., *What is Fascism and Why?* New York: Macmillan, pp. 15-29.

——. 2004. "La dottrina politica del Fascismo," in Renzo De Felice, ed., *Autobiografia del fascismo. Antologia di testi fascisti 1919-1945*, Torino: Einaudi, pp. 230-247.

Röpke, Wilhelm. 1946. *Civitas Humana.* Zürich: Erlenbach.

Rumpler, Helmut. 2005. *Eine Chance für Mitteleuropa, Bürgerliche Emanzipation und Staatsverfal in der Habsburgermonarhie. Österreichische Geschichte 1804-1914.* Vienna: Ueberreiter.

Salem-Wiseman, Jonathan. 2003. "Heidegger's Dasein and the Liberal Conception of the Self." *Political Theory* 31, 4: 533-557.

Salvemini, Gaetano. 1954. *Prelude to World War II.* New York: Doubleday & Company.

——. 1969. *Under the Axe of Fascism.* New York: Howard Fertig.

——. 1973. *The Origins of Fascism in Italy.* New York: Harper & Row.

Salvemini, Gaetano and George Bernard Shaw. 1997. *Polemica sul fascismo.* Rome: Ideazione Editrice.

Sand, Shlomo. 1993. "Georges Sorel entre utopie et politique." *Mil neuf cent* 11, 1: 87-93.

Sauer, Wolfgang. 1967. "National Socialism: Totalitarianism or Fascism?" *The American Historical Review* 73, 2: 404-424.

Schivelbusch, Wolfgang. 2006. *Three New Deals: Reflections on Roosevelt's America, Mussolini's Italy, and Hitler's Germany, 1933-1939.* New York: Metropolitan Books.

Schapiro, J. Salwyn. 1949. *Liberalism and the Challenge of Fascism. Social Forces in England and France (1815-1870).* New York, Toronto, London: McGraw Hill.

Schmitt, Carl. 1950. *Donoso Cortés in gesamteuropäischer Interpretation. Vier Aufsätze.* Cologne: Greven Verlag.

——. 1985. *Die geistesgeschichtliche Lage des heutigen Parlamentarismus.* Berlin: Duncker & Humblot.

——. 1988. *The Crisis of Parliamentary Democracy.* Cambridge, Massachusetts, London: The MIT Press.

——. 1994. *Positionen und Begriffe im Kampf mit Weimar-Genf-Versailles, 1923–1939.* Berlin: Duncker & Humblot.

——. 2002. *Der Begriff des Politischen. Text von 1932 mit einem Vorwort und drei Corollarien.* Berlin: Duncker & Humblot.

——. 2006. *Die Diktatur. Von den Anfängen des modernen Souveränitätsgedankens bis zum proletarischen Klassenkampf.* Berlin: Duncker & Humblot.

——. 2007. *The Concept of the Political.* Chicago: The University of Chicago Press.

Schoenbaum, David. 1966. *Hitler's Social Revolution: Class and Status in Nazi Germany, 1933–1939.* New York: Garden City.

Schuman, Frederick L. 1942. *Europe on the Eve: the Crises of Diplomacy 1933–1939.* New York: A. A. Knopf.

Sheehan, James J. 1978. *German Liberalism in the Nineteenth Century.* Chicago: The University of Chicago Press.

Sinclair, Upton. 1951. "Letter to Norman Thomas." <http://www.spartacus.schoolnet.co.uk/USAsocialismP.htm>.

Sloterdijk, Peter. 2000. *Die Verachtung der Massen—Versuch über Kulturkämpfe in der modernen Gesellschaft.* Frankfurt am Main: Suhrkamp.

Smith, Adam. 1789. *An Inquiry into the Nature and Causes of the Wealth of Nations.* Volume I. Philadelphia: Thomas Dobson.

Sorel, Georges. 1903. *Introduction à l'économie moderne.* 2nd ed. Paris: Librairie G. Jacques.

——. 1911. *Les illusions du progress.* 2nd ed. Paris: Marcel Rivière.

——. 1972. *Reflections on Violence.* New York, London: Collier.

Spencer, Herbert. 1851. *Social Statics.* London: John Chapman.

Spengler, Oswald. 1928. *The Decline of the West. Perspectives of World history.* Volume II. London: Allen & Unwin.

——. 1933a. *Politische Schriften. Volksausgabe.* Munich: C. H. Beck.

——. 1933b. "Das heutige Verhältnis zwischen Weltwirtschaft und Weltpolitik," in Oswald Spengler, *Politische Schriften. Volksausgabe,* Munich: C. H. Beck, pp. 311–338.

——. 1933c. "Das Verhältnis von Wirtschaft und Steuerpolitik seit 1750," in Oswald Spengler, *Politische Schriften. Volksausgabe,* Munich: C. H. Beck, pp. 297–310.

——. 1933d. "Preussentum und Sozialismus," in Oswald Spengler, *Politische Schriften. Volksausgabe,* Munich: C. H. Beck, pp. 1–105.

——. 1980. *Jahre der Entscheidung.* Munich: C. H. Beck.

Stackelberg, Roderick. 2002. "Critique as Apologetics: Nolte's Interpretation of Nietzsche," in Jacob Golomb, Robert S. Wistrich, eds., *Nietzsche, Godfather of Fascism? On the Uses and Abuses of a Philosophy,* Princeton, New Jersey: Princeton University Press, pp. 301–320.

Steingart, Gabor, and others. 2005. *Der Fall Deutschland. Abstieg eines Superstars.* Munich: Piper.

Stern, Fritz. 1961. *The Politics of Cultural Despair: A Study in the Rise of the Germanic Ideology.* Berkeley, Los Angeles, London: University of California Press.

Sternhell, Zeev. 1986. *Neither Right nor Left. Fascist Ideology in France.* Princeton, New Jersey: Princeton University Press.

——. 1988a. "Introduction", in Zeev Sternhell, ed., *The Fascist Thought and Its Variations. Collection of Texts in Political and Social Thought,* [Hebrew], Tel Aviv: Sifriat Poalim, pp. 9–45.

——. 1988b. *Ni droite ni gauche: L'Idéologie fasciste en France* [Hebrew translation]. Tel Aviv: Am Oved.

——, Mario Sznajder and Maia Asheri. 1994. *The Birth of Fascist Ideology*. Princeton, NJ: Princeton University Press.

Stirner, Max. 1995. *The Ego and Its Own*. Cambridge: Cambridge University Press.

Stoddard, Lothrop. 1924. *The Revolt against Civilization. The Menace of the Under Man*. New York: Charles Scribner's Sons.

Stone, Dan. 2002. *Breeding Superman. Nietzsche, Race and Eugenics in Edwardian and Interwar Britain*. Liverpool: Liverpool University Press.

Stone, Lawrence. 2002 [1972]. *The Causes of the English Revolution, 1529–1642*. London, New York: Routledge.

Strasser, Otto. 1940. *Hitler and I*. Boston: Houghton and Mifflin.

Strauss, Leo. 1952. *Persecution and the Art of Writing*. Chicago and London: The University of Chicago Press.

——. 1953. *Natural Right and History*. Chicago and London: The University of Chicago Press.

——. 1968. *Liberalism Ancient and Modern*. Chicago and London: The University of Chicago Press.

——. 1978. *The City and Man*. Chicago and London: The University of Chicago Press.

——. 1988. *What is Political Philosophy?* Chicago and London: The University of Chicago Press.

Struve, Walter. 1973. *Elites against Democracy. Leadership Ideals in Bourgeois Political Thought in Germany, 1890–1933*. New Jersey: Princeton.

Sullivan, Eileen P. 1983. "Liberalism and Imperialism: J. S. Mill's Defense of the British Empire." *Journal of the History of Ideas* 44, 4: 599–617.

Talmon, Jacob L. 1952. *The Origins of Totalitarian Democracy*. London: Secker & Warburg.

Tocqueville, Alexis de. 1866. "De la classe moyenne et du peuple," in Alexis de Tocqueville, *Oeuvres complètes*, vol. 9, Paris: Michel Lévy, pp. 514–519.

——. 1899. *Democracy in America*. Vol. 1. New York: The Colonial Press.

——. 1997. *Recollections. The French Revolution of 1848*. New Brunswick, London: Transaction Publishers.

Tong, Q. S. 2006. "The Aesthetic of Imperial Ruins: The Elgins and John Bowring." *boundary 2*, 33: 123–150.

Townshend, Jules. 2000. *C. B. Macpherson and the Problem of Liberal Democracy*. Edinburgh: Edinburgh University Press.

Treitschke, Heinrich von. 1916. *Politics*. Volume I. New York: Macmillan.

Tully, James. 1991. "Locke," in J. H. Burns, ed., *The Cambridge History of Political Thought 1450–1700*, Cambridge: Cambridge University Press, pp. 616–652.

Turner, Henry Ashby. 1987. *German Big Business and the Rise of Hitler*. New York, Oxford: Oxford University Press.

Ure, Andrew. 1835. *The Philosophy of Manufactures: or, An Exposition of the Scientific, Moral, and Commercial Economy of the Factory System, of Great Britain*. London: Charles Knight.

Verhey, Jeffrey. 2000. *Der "Geist von 1914" und die Erfindung der Volksgemeinschaft*. Hamburg: Hamburger Edition.

Vincent, John. 1966. *The Formation of the British Liberal Party*. New York: Charles Scribner's Sons.

Vocelka, Karl. 2004. *Geschichte Österreichs. Kultur-Gesellschaft-Politik*. Munich: Heyne.

Voegelin, Eric. 1974. "Liberalism and Its History." *The Review of Politics* 36, 4: 504–520.

Wadl, Wilhelm. 1987. *Liberalismus und soziale Frage in Österreich. Deutschliberale Reaktionen und Einflüsse auf die frühe österreichische Arbeiterbewegung (1867–1879)*. Vienna: Verlag der Österreichischen Akademie der Wissenschaften.

Weber, Eugen. 1964. *Varieties of Fascism*. Princeton, New Jersey: D. Van Nostrand.

Weiss, John. 1967. *The Fascist Tradition. Radical Right-Wing Extremism in Modern Europe.* New York: Harper & Row.

Williams, Raymond. 1983. *Keywords. A Vocabulary of Culture and Society.* Oxford: Oxford University Press.

Winkler, Heinrich August. 2002. *Der lange weg nach Westen.* Vol. 1. Munich: C. H. Beck.

Wolfe, Alan. 2004. "A Fascist Philosopher Helps Us Understand Contemporary Politics." *Chronicle of Higher Education* <http://chronicle.com/free/v50/i30/30b01601.htm>.

Wolin, Richard. 2003. "Arbeit Macht Frei: Heidegger as Philosopher of the German Way," in Richard Wolin, *Heidegger's Children*, Princeton, New Jersey: Princeton University Press, pp. 173–202.

——. 2006. "The Disoriented Left: A Critique of Left Schmittianism," in Richard Wolin, *The Frankfurt School Revisited*, New York, London: Routledge, pp. 243–252.

Zöberlein, Hans. 1940. *Der Befehl des Gewissens.* Munich: Zentralverlag der NSDAP, Franz Eher Nachfolger.

Zweig, Stefan. 1947. *The World of Yesterday.* London: Cassell and Company.

——. 1990. "Die Monotonisierung der Welt," in Stefan Zweig, *Zeiten und Schicksale*, Frankfurt am Main: S. Fischer, pp. 30–39.

Zweiniger, Arthur. 1933. *Spengler im Dritten Reich. Eine Antwort auf Oswald Spenglers "Jahre der Entscheidung."* Oldenburg: Gerhard Stalling.

INDEX

CPSIA information can be obtained
at www.ICGtesting.com
Printed in the USA
LVOW12s1200120917
548409LV00002B/21/P